THIRD-PARTY AND SELF-CREATED TRUSTS

A Modern Look

Rebecca C. Morgan,
Robert B. Fleming,
and Bryn Poland

ABA
AMERICAN BAR ASSOCIATION
Real Property, Trust and
Estate Law Section

Cover design by Andrew Alcala

Printed in the United States of America.

27 26 25 24 23 5 4 3 2 1

ISBN 978-1-63905-269-1
e-ISBN 978-1-63905-270-7

A catalog record for this book is available from the Library of Congress.

TABLE OF CONTENTS

APPENDICES

All appendices can be downloaded
at https://ambar.org/TPSCT

ACKNOWLEDGMENTS

We owe a terrific debt to the late Clifton B. Kruse, who was a huge leader in the national elder law movement. Clif was the consummate gentleman in manner, dress, and professionalism. In fact, he was a leading figure and guiding resource in the development of the National Academy of Elder Law Attorneys' "Aspirational Standards for the Practice of Elder Law and Special Needs Law," first adopted in 2005, shortly before Clif's death.

In 1995 Clif authored the first edition of *Third-Party and Self-Created Trusts*, published by the American Bar Association (ABA). It was a groundbreaking and comprehensive review of the law governing special needs trusts (and much more). It was must-reading for elder law practitioners, and established Clif as not only a gentleman but also a scholar. We are honored and humbled to work within his legacy—but it has taken three of us to revise and update his work.

I also have a personal story that perfectly illustrates that Clif was both gentleman and scholar.

At a National Academy of Elder Law Attorneys meeting in Boston in the late 1990s, I gave a presentation at the end of the day. Clif was in my audience, and very supportive. But I started the session somewhat under the weather, and by the end of my presentation I was both feverish and chilled. I thanked Clif for his support and started back to my room.

Clif was not hearing of it. He took my briefcase and papers and walked me to the elevator and then took me to my room. He helped me in, drew a hot bath, saw to it that I had aspirin, and stayed until I was in the tub. He promised to check back on me. Then he left for an after-session award program, for which he would be about a half hour late.

The award program was to honor him for his service and scholarship. I will never forget his insistence on helping me through what of course turned out to be a few hours of mild discomfort, at the cost of his own recognition and accolades. I heard later from participants that he had made vague excuses for being late, and never explained his acts of charity and humanity.

—Robert Fleming

ABOUT THE AUTHORS

Rebecca C. Morgan

Rebecca C. Morgan is the Boston Asset Management Chair in Elder Law. Professor Morgan teaches a variety of elder law courses in the J.D. and LL.M. programs and is the Director of the M.J. in Health Care Compliance. She is the successor co-author of *Matthew Bender's Tax, Estate, and Financial Planning for the Elderly* and its companion forms book (Lexis), co-author of *Representing the Elderly in Florida* (Lexis), *The Fundamentals of Special Needs Trusts* (Lexis), *Ethics in an Elder Law Practice* (ABA), *Planning for Disability* (Bloomberg BNA Portfolio), *Elder Law in Context and Bankruptcy in Context* (Aspen), as well as *Mastering Interviewing and Counseling* (Carolina Academic Press). Professor Morgan has authored a number of articles on a variety of elder law issues and has spoken a number of times on subjects of elder law. She is the co-editor of the Elder Law Prof Blog.

Professor Morgan received the Theresa Award from the Theresa Alexandra Russo Foundation in 2008. She was the 2009 recipient of the Treat Award from the National College of Probate Judges. In 2018 Professor Morgan received the Ben C. Willard alumni award for humanitarian achievements from Stetson University College of Law. She was inducted into Stetson Law's Hall of Fame in 2018. In 2021, Professor Morgan received a lifetime achievement award from the Elder Law Section of the Florida Bar and received the inaugural lifetime achievement award from the Association of American Law Schools Section on Aging and the Law in January 2023.

Robert B. Fleming

Robert B. Fleming is a partner in the Tucson elder law firm of Fleming & Curti, P.L.C., with a practice limited to trust (and special needs trust) administration, guardianship, conservatorship, estate planning, and probate. Mr. Fleming was the original author of *The Elder Law Answer Book*, and co-author (with the late Professor Kenney Hegland) of *New Times, New Challenges: Law and Advice for Savvy Seniors and Their Families*. He is certified as an Estate and Trust specialist by the State Bar of Arizona, and as a Certified Elder Law Attorney (CELA) by the National Elder Law Foundation. Mr. Fleming is a founding member of the Special Needs Alliance (https://www.specialneeds alliance.org/). He has lived in (and is passionate about) downtown Tucson, Arizona (a UNESCO International City of Gastronomy), for more than four decades.

Bryn Poland

Ms. Poland is partner at the law firm Mayo & Poland, PLLC, in Baytown, Texas. She focuses her practice on special needs trust planning and administration, Medicaid planning, and qualified settlement funds. Born and raised a Kansas girl, Ms. Poland was inspired to become an elder law attorney when she watched her family struggle with care options for her great-grandmother, Lulu Sleeper, who lived to the age of 109. Ms. Poland is a member of, and has served in various leadership roles for, the Houston Bar Association, the Texas Chapter of the National Academy of Elder Law Attorneys, and the Special Needs Alliance. When Ms. Poland is not helping clients, she loves taking family adventures with her husband and their twin daughters and young son.

CHAPTER 1

Introduction of Planning for Special Needs with Trusts[1]

I. Demographics

America is aging. In fact, the aging of the American population is expected to continue for decades.[2] Over the next few decades, the share of the U.S. population over age 65 is expected to approximately double.[3]

One particular aging cohort, the baby boomers (those folks born between 1946 and 1964), have been turning 65 at a rate of approximately 10,000 per day, which will continue until 2030, when the last of the boomers turns 65.[4] The magic does not stop just when a boomer reaches 65. Instead, with increased life expectancy, elders are expected to live into their 80s, or even beyond.[5] Not only that, by 2034, for the first occurrence in the United States, the number of elders in the country will outnumber those under 18.[6] This imbalance in the cohort numbers has long-term implications, especially for caregivers.

1. There is a difference of opinion as to what is the appropriate term to describe this type of planning. Some prefer to refer to these types of trusts as disability trusts, and the beneficiaries as people with disabilities. Others refer to these types of trusts as special needs trusts and the beneficiaries as individuals with special needs. It seems to us that the current popular parlance is the use of the phrase "special needs," so we use that phrase in this book.

2. *See* Wan He et al., U.S. Census Bureau, An Aging World: 2015 (2016).

3. For an interesting graphic illustration, see the "Population Pyramid" animation at U.S. Census Bureau, *International Database (IDB)*, https://www.census.gov/data-tools/demo/idb/#/country?YR_ANIM=2060&FIPS_SINGLE=US (last updated Sept. 2020), and the accompanying data source cited therein.

4. *See* U.S. Census Bureau, *By 2030 All Baby Boomers Will Be Age 65 or Older*, https://www.census.gov/library/stories/2019/12/by-2030-all-baby-boomers-will-be-age-65-or-older.html (last revised Feb. 25, 2022).

5. *Id.* The recent reduction in life expectancy experienced because of the COVID-19 pandemic notwithstanding, the aging of the population will likely proceed apace, because deaths from COVID among the elderly have been experienced at approximately the same as "all-cause" deaths. *See* Joshua R. Goldstein & Ronald D. Lee, *Demographic Perspectives on the Mortality of COVID-19 and Other Epidemics*, 117 PNAS 22035 (2020).

6. Goldstein & Lee, *supra* note 5.

Of course, it is not just older Americans who can benefit from the use of trusts in planning. It is important to also consider the number of Americans with disabilities. About 25 percent of Americans have a disability,[7] and about 40 percent of those 65 and older have a disability.[8] Consider the breakdown by functional ability:

- 13.7 percent of people with a disability have a mobility disability with serious difficulty walking or climbing stairs.
- 10.8 percent of people with a disability have a cognition disability with serious difficulty concentrating, remembering, or making decisions.
- 6.8 percent of people with a disability have an independent living disability with difficulty doing errands alone.
- 5.9 percent of people with a disability are deaf or have serious difficulty hearing.
- 4.6 percent of people with a disability have a vision disability with blindness or serious difficulty seeing even when wearing glasses.
- 3.6 percent of people with a disability have a self-care disability with difficulty dressing or bathing.[9]

The type and degree of disability varies from person to person. "A disability is any condition of the body or mind (impairment) that makes it more difficult for the person with the condition to do certain activities (activity limitation) and interact with the world around them (participation restrictions)."[10] To understand the breadth of potential disability, consider the impact a disability may have on a person's ability to see, move, recall, hear, reason, think, learn, communicate (verbally or otherwise), and maintain social relationships, as well as the person's mental health.[11]

The World Health Organization explains three elements of disability:

1. **Impairment** in a person's body structure or function, or mental functioning; examples of impairments include loss of a limb, loss of vision or memory loss.
2. **Activity limitation**, such as difficulty seeing, hearing, walking, or problem solving.

---

7. Ctrs. for Disease Control & Prevention, *Disability Impacts All of Us*, https://www.cdc.gov/ncbddd/disabilityandhealth/infographic-disability-impacts-all.html (last reviewed Oct. 28, 2022).
8. *Id.*
9. *Id.*
10. Ctrs. for Disease Control & Prevention, *Disability and Health Overview*, https://www.cdc.gov/ncbddd/disabilityandhealth/disability.html (last reviewed Sept. 16, 2020).
11. *Id.*

3. **Participation restrictions** in normal daily activities, such as working, engaging in social and recreational activities, and obtaining health care and preventive services.[12]

A person can become disabled at any point in time from birth to before death.[13]

A. The Costs of Long-Term Care

According to the annual Cost of Care Survey by Genworth,[14] 70 percent of individuals will need long-term care[15] at some point during their lives.[16] The cost of long-term care varies based on the type and amount of needed care as well as the geographic location of the person needing care.[17] Like most every other product or service, expect the cost of long-term care to rise with the passage of time.[18]

B. Why Plan to Become Eligible for Public Benefits?

It is estimated that 13 percent of the U.S. population has a disability, making it the largest minority population and the only one that anyone can become

---

12. *Id.* (citations omitted).

13. *Id.* The Centers for Disease Control and Prevention identifies these various types:

- Related to conditions that are present at birth and may affect functions later in life, including cognition (memory, learning, and understanding), mobility (moving around in the environment), vision, hearing, behavior, and other areas. These conditions may be:
  - Disorders in single *genes* (e.g., Duchenne muscular dystrophy)
  - Disorders of *chromosomes* (e.g., Down syndrome)
- The result of the mother's exposure during pregnancy to infections (e.g., rubella) or substances (e.g., alcohol or cigarettes)
- Associated with developmental conditions that become apparent during childhood (e.g., autism spectrum disorder and attention-deficit/hyperactivity disorder (ADHD))
- Related to an injury (e.g., traumatic brain injury or spinal cord injury)
- Associated with a long-standing condition (e.g., diabetes), which can cause a disability such as vision loss, nerve damage, or limb loss
- Progressive (e.g., muscular dystrophy), static (e.g., limb loss), or intermittent (e.g., some forms of multiple sclerosis)

14. Genworth, *Cost of Care Survey*, https://www.genworth.com/aging-and-you/finances/cost-of-care.html (last visited Nov. 25, 2022).

15. Long-term care is defined as

> the care [one] may need if [one is] unable to perform daily activities [alone]. That means things like eating, bathing, dressing, transferring and using the bathroom. The goal of long-term care is to help [one] maintain [one's] lifestyle as [one ages]. Medicare, Medicare supplement insurance, and health insurance [one] may have at work usually won't pay for long term care.

Id.

16. *Id.*

17. *Id.*

18. *See, e.g.*, Genworth, Genworth Cost of Care Survey: Summary and Methodology (2022), https://pro.genworth.com/riiproweb/productinfo/pdf/131168.pdf.

a member of at any time.[19] It is likely that most of the population will move between disability and ability over their lifetimes: whether through illness, injury, or merely the aging process.[20] Without a social policy in the United States on providing for long-term care, folks are left to cobble together their own plans for paying for disability or long-term care should the need arise. Some folks may purchase long-term care insurance. Others hope that their savings will be enough to get them through. Still others may plan to rely on family to provide the necessary care to survive. Others spend all their savings to pay for their care, and, having outlived their savings, then apply for public benefits.

For those who plan, planning for eligibility for means-tested public benefits is one aspect of planning to pay for disability. High-net-worth individuals should be able to pay for any type of care they need, for as long as they need, without any reliance on means-tested public benefits. Those in the middle class, however, will find it likely that they have not saved enough to pay for care for any significant length of time. Those who can create a special needs trust (SNT) for themselves will find that their trustee may authorize certain expenditures that will improve their quality of life, without jeopardizing their continuing eligibility for public benefits.

Parents should also consider planning for their child with disabilities. In many instances, parents are primary or sole caregivers, but at some point, the parent may no longer be able to fulfill that role. If the adult child with a disability is unable to manage his or her finances, then the parent's estate plan needs to include a plan for doing so. Some clients may want to disinherit their child with disabilities, or give the child's share to siblings, with precatory language hoping the siblings will do the right thing. Both approaches are fraught, and the better course of action is to create a third-party SNT with the child with disabilities as the beneficiary.

II. History of Trust Planning

A. Early Trust Practice (No Holds Barred)

Prior to 1985, individuals were sheltering a large amount of assets in irrevocable trusts. By adopting 42 U.S.C. § 1396a(k) in that year, Congress substantially reduced the options for planning with trusts of any kind. The new

19. A. Houtenville et al., Univ. of N.H. Inst. on Disability, Annual Report on People with Disabilities in America: 2021 (2021).

20. As stated by Professor Emily Rapp Black, "Everyone will have a disability if they live long enough. You're either a decade or a random disease or an accident away from having one," *quoted in* Farnoosh Torabi, *How Ableism Contributes to the Wealth Gap in America and What We Can All Do about It*, NextAdvisor (July 7, 2021), https://time.com/nextadvisor/in-the-news/how-ableism-contributes-to-the-wealth-gap/.

provision established the concept of a "Medicaid qualifying trust" (MQT), which, paradoxically, would *dis*qualify the trust establisher from eligibility for Medicaid, as later described in *Ramey v. Rizzuto*:[21]

> Medicaid eligibility is determined by a needs-based analysis and coverage is denied if the applicant exceeds a ceiling in countable assets. Generally, funds in irrevocable trusts are not countable assets. The exception to that general rule was codified in the Social Security Act prior to the Act's amendment in 1993. Before its repeal in 1993, the exception provision at issue here read
>
>> For purposes of this subsection, a "Medicaid qualifying trust" is a trust or similar legal devise, established (other than by will) by an individual (or an individual's spouse) under which the individual may be the beneficiary of all or part of the payments from the trust and the distribution of such payments is determined by one or more trustees who are permitted to exercise any discretion with respect to the distribution to the individual.
>
> 42 U.S.C. § 1396a(k)(2)
>
> Subsection (3) provided
>
>> [t]his subsection shall apply without regard to—(A) whether or not the Medicaid qualifying trust is irrevocable or is established for purposes other than to enable a grantor to qualify for medical assistance under this title; or (b) whether or not the discretion described in paragraph (2) is actually exercised.
>
> 42 U.S.C. § 1396a(k)(3).
>
> Thus, prior to the amendment in 1993, an irrevocable trust established by an individual or her spouse was considered a Medicaid qualifying trust if the trustee could exercise any discretion to make payments from trust principal or income to the beneficiary.
>
> On August 10, 1993, Congress again amended the provision relating to irrevocable MQTs (though it had been renumbered in the intervening years to become part of 42 U.S.C. § 1396p(d)(3)) to provide:
>
>> (I) if there are any circumstances under which payment from the trust could be made to or for the benefit of the individual, the portion of the corpus from which, or the income on the corpus from which, payment to the individual could be made shall be considered resources available to the individual, and payments from that portion of the corpus or income—

21. 72 F. Supp. 2d 1202 (D. Colo. 1999).

> (I) to or for the benefit of the individual, shall be considered income of the individual, and
>
> (II) for any other purpose, shall be considered a transfer of assets by the individual subject to subsection (c); and
>
> (ii) any portion of the trust from which, or any income on the corpus from which, no payment could under any circumstances be made to the individual shall be considered, as of the date of establishment of the trust (or, if later, the date on which payment to the individual was foreclosed) to be assets disposed by the individual for purposes of subsection (c), and the value of the trust shall be determined for purposes of such subsection by including the amount of any payments made from such portion of the trust after such date.
>
> § 42 U.S.C. § 1396p(d)(3)(B).[22]

B. MQT

MQTs were in use prior to Congress adopting the Omnibus Budget Reconciliation Act of 1993 (OBRA '93) (discussed in the following section).[23] OBRA '93 deleted MQTs from the Social Security Act.[24] An MQT is defined as

> a trust or similar legal device established (other than by a will) by an individual (or spouse) under which the individual may be the beneficiary of all or part of the payments from the trust. The amount from the MQT deemed available to the individual is the maximum amount of payments that may be permitted under the terms of the trust to be distributed to the individual by the trustee.[25]

22. *Id.* at 1209–10 (citations omitted).

23. *See, e.g.*, Hegadorn v. Dep't of Hum. Servs. Dir., 931 N.W.2d 571, 579 (Mich. 2019) (explaining that "[t]he Consolidated Omnibus Budget Reconciliation Act of 1985, Pub. L 99-272; 100 Stat. 82, formally codified at 42 U.S.C. 1396a(k), instructed states to treat as countable assets the maximum amount of a trust's principal a trustee could pay to a Medicaid applicant if the trustee were to exercise his or her discretionary authority, whether or not that discretion was actually exercised").

24. *See* Soc. Sec. Admin., *Program Operations Manual System (POMS): SI 01730.048 Medicaid Trusts*, https://secure.ssa.gov/poms.NSF/lnx/0501730048 (last revised Nov. 15, 2001).

25. *See id.* Effective August 11, 1993, section 1902(k) of the Social Security Act was replaced by provisions recognizing Medicaid trusts. *Id.* The amendments to 42 U.S.C. § 1396a list: "Subsec. (k). Pub. L. 103-66, § 13611(d)(1)(C), struck out subsec. (k)," which related to treatment of potential payments for Medicaid qualifying trusts. U.S. House of Representatives Off. of the L. Revision Counsel—U.S. Code, *42 USC 1396a: State Plans for Medical Assistance*, https://uscode.house.gov/view.xhtml?req=(title:42%20section:1396a%20edition:prelim)%20OR%20(granuleid:USC-prelim-title42-section1396a)&f=treesort&edition=prelim&num=0&jumpTo=true#amendment-note (last visited Nov. 25, 2022).

Because there are still trusts created pre-OBRA '93, it is important to remember how those trusts are treated. Per the Social Security Program Operations Manual System (POMS):

> Prior to October 1, 1993, existence of an MQT could result in Medicaid ineligibility by the State agency counting resources from the trust as described in SI 01730.048B.1. . . . This rule still applies to trusts established before August 11, 1993. Waiver of this rule is possible when there has been a State determination of "undue hardship."[26]

A brief history of MQTs was offered in the Tenth Circuit case of *Ramey v. Reinertson*,[27] which noted:

> In an effort to maximize their income that would not tally as an "available" asset, many applicants for Medicaid and SSI [Supplemental Security Income] tried to "shelter," or shield, their assets. One common instrument for sheltering was an irrevocable trust. Not surprisingly, Congress responded to the use of this technique with condemnation. For example, in 1986, Congress reiterated its intent that Medicaid was designed to provide basic medical care for those without sufficient income or resources to provide for themselves and thus passed 42 U.S.C. § 1396a(k).
>
> Section 1396a(k) was known as the MQT statute, "MQT" being an acronym for Medicaid qualifying trust. The statute defined MQT as
>
>> a trust, or similar legal devise, established (other than by will) by an individual (or an individual's spouse) under which the individual may be the beneficiary of all or part of the payments from the trust and the distribution of such payments is determined by one or more trustees who are permitted to exercise any discretion with respect to the distribution to the individual.
>
> 42 U.S.C. § 1396a(k)(2).
>
> With the passage of § 1396a(k), MQTs were no longer a permissible means to shelter assets for purposes of Medicaid eligibility. Section 1396a(k) clarified that the amount "available" to an applicant for purposes of determining Medicaid eligibility *included*
>
>> the maximum amount of payments that may be permitted under the terms of the trust to be distributed to the grantor, assuming the full exercise of discretion by the trustee or trustees for the distribution of the maximum amount to the grantor.
>
> *Id.* § 1396a(k)(1).

---

26. *See* Soc. Sec. Admin., *supra* note 24.
27. 268 F.3d 955 (10th Cir. 2001).

In the years that followed, Congress remained true to its conviction that MQTs were an impermissible means of sheltering assets for purposes of Medicaid eligibility. In fact, in 1993, § 1396a(k) was repealed by Congress and replaced by another statute even less forgiving of such trusts. *See* 42 U.S.C. § 1396p(d) (1993). This statute added stringent criteria regarding the treatment of MQTs such as the inclusion of the corpus and proceeds of various irrevocable trusts as countable resources. *See* H.R. Rep. No. 103-111, at 207–08 (1993), U.S. Code Cong. & Admin. News 1993, 378, 534–35.[28]

C. OBRA '93

In 1993, Congress continued tightening up transfers for Medicaid eligibility with the passage of OBRA '93.[29] As already noted, MQTs were repealed as part of the new law and more specific criteria were established regarding the use of trusts.

1. Why OBRA '93?

As explained in the Third Circuit opinion *Lewis v. Alexander*:[30]

> Congress has created a comprehensive system of asset-counting rules for determining who qualifies for Medicaid. Under Medicaid's original asset-counting rules, individuals could put large sums of money in trust, thereby vesting legal title to those assets in the trust and reducing (on paper) the amount of assets owned by the individual.
>
> A trust is a legal instrument in which assets are held in the name of the trust and managed by a trustee for the benefit of a beneficiary. *Black's Law Dictionary* 1546 (8th ed. 2004) (definition of "trust"). This structure means

28. *Id.* at 958–59. The court ruled that the provision, although removed by OBRA '93, still applied to those trusts created before August 11, 1993, stating:

> We believe it is clear that, when Congress amended the Medicaid qualifications in 1993 to provide even more restrictive requirements on MQTs (i.e., the repeal of § 1396a(k) and the enactment of § 1396p(d)), it did not at the same time intend to abandon *all* eligibility requirements for trusts created before August 10, 1993, and once again allow persons to "divert scarce Federal and State resources." *Id.* In other words, the 1993 amendments did not remove trusts dated before August 10, 1993 from the ambit § 1396a(k). *See Cook v. Department of Soc. Servs.*, 225 Mich. App. 318, 570 N.W.2d 684, 686–87 (1997).

Id. at 961. As far as the MQTs, section 1396a(k), known as the MQT statute, forbade the use of MQTs as a mechanism for sheltering assets for Medicaid eligibility purposes. *See* 42 U.S.C. § 1396a(k)(1). The MQT statute clarified that the amount "available" to a potential applicant included "the maximum amount of payments that may be permitted under the terms of the trust to be distributed to the grantor." *Id.*

29. Omnibus Budget Reconciliation Act of 1993, Pub. L. No. 103-66, tit. XIII § 13611(d)(1)(c), 107 Stat. 312. *See also* Off. of Inspector Gen., U.S. Dep't of Health & Hum. Servs., The Use of Trusts by Medicaid and Supplemental Security Income Recipients Receiving Third Party Liability Settlements and Awards 12–13 (1994), https://oig.hhs.gov/oas/reports/region9/99300033.pdf.

30. 685 F.3d 325 (3d Cir. 2012).

that the beneficiary does not actually own the assets of the trust, but instead has an equitable right to derive benefits from them. (The benefits vary according to the terms of the trust.). . .

But this same bifurcated ownership structure has been used to manufacture eligibility for government welfare programs like Medicaid. As with many government programs, eligibility for Medicaid is partially dependent on the claimant's income and assets. Wealthy individuals are expected to exhaust their own resources before turning to the public for assistance. But trusts can enable these same individuals to technically "own" nothing at all, even though they may have access to substantial wealth. Such claimants may then qualify for Medicaid. . . . Individuals have gained access to taxpayer-funded healthcare while retaining the benefit of their wealth and the ability to pass that wealth to their heirs.

Congress understandably viewed this as an abuse and began addressing the problem with statutory standards enacted in 1986. *See* Consolidated Omnibus Budget Reconciliation Act of 1985, Pub. L. No. 99-272, § 9506(a), 100 Stat. 82 (Apr. 7, 1986). These standards were repealed and replaced in 1993 by the current trust-counting rules. *See* Omnibus Budget Reconciliation Act of 1993, Pub. L. No. 103-66, Title XIII § 13611(d)(1)(c), 107 Stat. 312 (Aug. 10, 1993) (OBRA 1993). . . .

In the 1993 OBRA amendments, Congress established a general rule that trusts would be counted as assets for the purpose of determining Medicaid eligibility. But Congress also excepted from that rule three types of trusts meeting certain specific requirements. Taken together, these are generally called "special needs trusts" or "supplemental needs trusts." "A supplemental needs trust is a discretionary trust established for the benefit of a person with a severe and chronic or persistent disability and is intended to provide for expenses that assistance programs such as Medicaid do not cover." These expenses—books, television, Internet, travel, and even such necessities as clothing and toiletries—would rarely be considered extravagant.[31]

There were several significant changes to the Medicaid statute contained in OBRA '93. Specifically, as to trusts for people with special needs, section 13611 added what is now 42 U.S.C. § 1396p(d)(4)(A)–(C) exempting three disparate kinds of trusts from the counting rules regarding trust assets for Medicaid eligibility:

(4) This subsection shall not apply to any of the following trusts:

(A) A trust containing the assets of an individual under age 65 who is disabled (as defined in section 1614(a)(3)) and which is established for

31. *Id.* at 332–33 (citations omitted).

the benefit of such individual by an individual,[32] parent, grandparent, legal guardian of the individual, or a court if the State will receive all amounts remaining in the trust upon the death of such individual up to an amount equal to the total medical assistance paid on behalf of the individual under a State plan under this title.

(B) A trust established in a State for the benefit of an individual if—

(i) the trust is composed only of pension, Social Security, and other income to the individual (and accumulated income in the trust),

(ii) the State will receive all amounts remaining in the trust upon the death of such individual up to an amount equal to the total medical assistance paid on behalf of the individual under a State plan under this title, and

(iii) the State makes medical assistance available to individuals described in section 1902(a)(10)(A)(ii)(V), but does not make such assistance available to individuals for nursing facility services under section 1902(a)(10)(C).

(C) A trust containing the assets of an individual who is disabled (as defined in section 1614(a)(3)) that meets the following conditions:

(i) The trust is established and managed by a nonprofit association.

(ii) A separate account is maintained for each beneficiary of the trust, but, for purposes of investment and management of funds, the trust pools these accounts.

(iii) Accounts in the trust are established solely for the benefit of individuals who are disabled (as defined in section 1614(a)(3)) by the parent, grandparent, or legal guardian of such individuals, by such individuals, or by a court.

(iv) To the extent that amounts remaining in the beneficiary's account upon the death of the beneficiary are not retained by the trust, the trust pays to the State from such remaining amounts in the account an amount equal to the total amount of medical assistance paid on behalf of the beneficiary under the State plan under this title.

---

32. The Fairness in Medicaid Supplemental Needs Trusts (known colloquially as the Special Needs Trusts Fairness Act) amended (d)(4)(A) to include the beneficiary to the list of those who can establish the trust. 21st Century Cures Act § 5007, Pub. L. No. 114-255, 130 Stat. 1033 (2016).

D. Medicaid Trusts

As explained in the POMS:

> Medicaid trusts consist of any type of trust established by an individual on or after August 11, 1993 made up in whole or in part of **assets (resources and/or income)** of the individual and which are created by a means other than by will. A trust is considered established by an individual if established by the individual, the individual's spouse, or a person, including a court, or administrative body with legal authority to act for the individual or spouse or who acts at the direction or request of the individual or spouse.
>
> A Medicaid trust can be either a revocable or irrevocable trust or a legal instrument or device similar to a trust. There are certain specific exceptions to this provision.[33]

III. Distinctions between Self-Settled and Third-Party Trusts

The self-settled trusts under 42 U.S.C. § 1396p(d)(4)(A) and (C) are two types of SNTs (or disability trusts) authorized in the Medicaid statute.[34] The (d)(4)(A) trust is frequently called the self-settled SNT or the first-party SNT. The (d)(4)(C) trusts are called pooled SNTs. They are similar in that the money used to establish the (d)(4)(A) and (C) trusts is that of the beneficiary. They are different in that, oversimplified, the (d)(4)(A) is the beneficiary's individual trust. With the (d)(4)(C), the beneficiary has a trust, but the assets are pooled for the purpose of investments, overhead, and so on. They are similar in that they can be established by the same list of individuals. They are different in that the (d)(4)(A) trust must contain a Medicaid payback provision, while the (d)(4)(C) may, but is not required, to contain a Medicaid payback provision in the joinder agreement. They are the same in that each type of trust has a beneficiary and a trustee. They are different in that the (d)(4)(C) must be managed by a nonprofit.

Compare these two trusts to a third-party trust where the money for the trust is that of a third party, rather than the beneficiary. They are the same in that they all have beneficiaries and trustees. They are different given the source of funds and the third-party trust is not required to have a payback provision. They are the same in that they will all have language that indicates the

---

33. Soc. Sec. Admin., *supra* note 24.

34. (d)(4)(B) covers qualified income trusts. Because our focus is on individuals with disabilities, we are not doing an in-depth discussion of the use of trusts in Medicaid or long-term care planning. Medicaid programs vary state to state, making general commentary on the subject in this context outside of the scope of this book. The law there is well settled and there are a number of fine resources available on Medicaid and the use of trusts for long-term care planning.

distributions are discretionary with the trustee and intended to "supplement but not supplant" Medicaid and any other means-tested public benefits program for which the individual is or may be eligible. They are different in that the (d)(4)(A) and (C) language specifically requires the beneficiary have a disability and there is no specific statute governing the third-party trust with that requirement[35]—however, if the beneficiary is on means-tested public benefits, having a disability may be a prerequisite for receiving those benefits. They are also different in that the (d)(4)(A) statute has a specific age limit (available for a beneficiary under 65) while third-party trusts do not have an age limit. Although the (d)(4)(C) statute does not contain an age limit, some states impose one.[36] The over-65 limit for the (d)(4)(C) trust has been successfully challenged in some courts.[37]

A. When Can a Self-Settled Trust Actually Be a Third-Party Trust?

Because 42 U.S.C. § 1396p(c)(2)(B) exempts transfers by a Medicaid applicant to "a trust . . . established solely for the benefit of an individual under 65 years of age who is disabled," the opportunity for a hybrid type of trust is created. Such a trust is often referred to as a "sole benefit" trust by reference to the "solely for the benefit of" language of the statute.

A "sole benefit" trust might be useful for a potential Medicaid applicant who happens to have a spouse, child, or other family member (though family connection is not required) who has a disability. If the settlor transfers assets to the "sole benefit" trust, the settlor may thereafter qualify for Medicaid eligibility without experiencing a period of ineligibility. Of course, from the perspective of the trust beneficiary with disabilities, the transfer should not be disqualifying, because the trust appears (to that beneficiary) as a third-party trust, which would not have to qualify as under 42 U.S.C. § 1396p(d)(4)(A).

Though not required by the statute, states usually impose a requirement of "actuarial soundness" on "sole benefit" trusts. The logic of this requirement was widely adopted from the language of Health Care Financing Administration (HCFA) Transmittal 64,[38] an attempt to provide guidance to state Medicaid plan administrators. In that transmittal, the agency suggested that a trust could be determined to be "for the sole benefit of" an individual with disabilities only if it could not benefit any other person "at any time in the future."[39] Thus, a remainder beneficiary would destroy the "sole benefit" eligibility.

---

35. Some states do have such requirements. *See, e.g.*, MINN. STAT. § 501C.1205 subdiv. 2 (2015).

36. Special Needs All., *Two Different Types of Special Needs Trusts*, https://www.specialneedsalliance.org/the-voice/two-different-types-of-special-needs-trusts/ (last visited Nov. 25, 2022).

37. *See, e.g.*, Pfoser v. Harpstead, 953 N.W.2d 507 (Minn. 2021).

38. HCFA STATE MEDICAID MANUAL 3258.1 (1994) (*see* Appendix O).

39. *Id.* § 6 at 5.

Transmittal 64's solution? The trust must include a payback provision, akin to the requirement of 42 U.S.C. § 1396p(d)(4)(A), to become effective upon the death of the disabled beneficiary.

1. What about a Trust Established for the Spouse by the Other Spouse?

Notice that 42 U.S.C. § 1396p(d)(4)(A) and (C) does not list "spouse" as one of the individuals who can create a statutory SNT for the beneficiary. However, 42 U.S.C. § 1396p(d)(2)(A) does address the availability of a trust created by one spouse for another.[40] Although

> [t]hird party SNTs are used most frequently by parents or grandparents who want to provide for a child or grandchild with a disability while maintaining that child's eligibility for public benefits . . . [the third-party] trust . . . is also commonly used by a potential Medicaid recipient's spouse, who wants to leave some or all of the estate in trust for the benefit of the potential Medicaid recipient.[41]

Here is a common example: if one spouse is receiving Medicaid, as typically would be the case of an institutional spouse, the community spouse who is not receiving Medicaid can establish an SNT for the institutionalized spouse by creating a third-party testamentary trust.

IV. Examples of Various Public Benefits Programs[42]

- **Supplemental Security Income (SSI).** This is the "cash assistance program funded and administered by the Federal Government. The program is authorized by Title XVI (Supplemental Security Income for the Aged, Blind, and Disabled) of the Social Security Act. . . . Beginning in January 1974, SSI replaced the Federal/State matching grant program of adult assistance to the aged, blind, and disabled. Under SSI, there is no minimum age limit for establishing eligibility based on blindness or disability."[43]

---

40. 42 U.S.C. § 1396p(d)(2)(A) ("For purposes of this subsection, an individual shall be considered to have established a trust if assets of the individual were used to form all or part of the corpus of the trust and if any of the following individuals established such trust other than by will:

(i) The individual.

(ii) The individual's spouse.

(iii) A person, including a court or administrative body, with legal authority to act in place of or on behalf of the individual or the individual's spouse.

(iv) A person, including any court or administrative body, acting at the direction or upon the request of the individual or the individual's spouse.").

41. Bradley J. Frigon & W. Eric Kuhn, *Which SNT, When, and Why?*, 5 NAELA J. 1, 6 (2009).

42. Note that Chapter 3 discusses many public benefits programs in detail.

43. Soc. Sec. Admin., Social Security Handbook § 2100, https://www.ssa.gov/OP_Home/handbook/handbook.21/handbook-2100.html (last revised Nov. 3, 2003).

- **The POMS.** It is important to be familiar with the POMS, which "is a primary source of information used by Social Security employees to process claims for Social Security benefits."[44] The public version of POMS is identical to the version used by Social Security employees except that it does not include internal data entry and sensitive content instructions.
- **Medicaid.** Medicaid is a joint federal-state program that covers health care for eligible individuals (eligibility based upon status as well as income and assets). State participation in Medicaid is voluntary and all 50 states participate in Medicaid. States file a plan with the Centers for Medicare and Medicaid Services (CMS) that must be approved, providing, among other things, eligibility, optional eligibility, benefits, liens, and recoveries. The law is found in 42 U.S.C. § 1396 *et seq.*, accompanying regulations 20 C.F.R. Part 416), as well as through publications, memorandums, and other instructive publications through CMS and the individual state Medicaid agency.[45]
- **Veterans Affairs (VA) benefits.** The VA offers a variety of programs and services for eligible veterans, ranging from cash benefits, to health care, to spousal and/or dependent benefits, and burial benefits.[46]
- **Housing programs.** The U.S. Department of Housing and Urban Development (HUD) offers housing assistance programs for eligible individuals, often based upon age, family status, disability, and income/resource levels.[47]
- **Supplemental Nutrition Assistance Program** (formerly known as "Food Stamps"). "The Supplemental Nutrition Assistance Program (SNAP) provides help for low-income households to buy the food needed for good health."
- **Social Security Disability.** To be considered disabled, according to the Social Security Administration, an individual "must not be able to engage in any substantial gainful activity (SGA) because of a medically determinable physical or mental impairment(s) that is either:
  - Expected to result in death.
  - Has lasted or is expected to last for a continuous period of at least 12 months."[48]

---

44. Soc. Sec. Admin., *POMS Home*, https://secure.ssa.gov/apps10/poms.nsf/Home?readform (last visited Nov. 25, 2022).

45. *See*, *e.g.*, CMS, https:/www.medicaid.gov/ (last visited Nov. 25, 2022); *see also* CMS, *Regulations & Guidance*, https://www.cms.gov/regulations-and-guidance/regulations-and-guidance (last visited Nov. 25, 2022).

46. *See*, *e.g.*, VA, https://www.va.gov/ (last visited Nov. 25, 2022) (search the VA Benefits and Health Care tab).

47. *See*, *e.g.*, HUD, https://www.hud.gov/ (last visited Nov. 25, 2022).

48. Soc. Sec. Admin., *How Do We Define Disability?*, https://www.ssa.gov/redbook/eng/definedisability.htm?tl=0 (last visited Nov. 25, 2022).

V. SNT Requirements Summary[49]

This table may help distinguish the types of trusts frequently involved in eligibility determinations:

Trust	Statute	Established By	Funded By	Payback	Age Limit
(d)(4)(A) Disability trust	42 U.S.C. § 1396p(d)(4)(A) (2000)	Individual* Parent Grandparent Legal guardian Court	Individual with disability	Yes	Yes, funding must be completed by 65
Third-party SNT	No statute (excluded by introductory language of 42 U.S.C. § 1396p(d)(4)(A) and (C))	Third parties (not individual with disability)	Third parties (not individual with disability)	No	No
(d)(4)(C) Pooled trust	42 U.S.C. § 1396p(d)(4)(C) (2000)	Parent Grandparent Legal guardian Court Individual	Individual with disability	Depends on joinder agreement	No, but possible penalty period if funded at age 65 or older

* Individual was added to the list of those who can establish the first-party SNT. The Fairness in Medicaid Supplemental Needs Trusts (known colloquially as the Special Needs Trusts Fairness Act) amended (d)(4)(A) to include the beneficiary to the list of those who can establish the trust. 21st Century Cures Act § 5007, Pub. L. No. 114-255, 130 Stat. 1033 (2016).

VI. Vocabulary

The vocabulary around disability can be fraught, even for well-meaning people. Different constituencies within the disability community debate the politics of naming and identification. "People-first" language asserts that language recognizes the humanity of an individual first and that we consider an impairment a modification or special need. Others prefer the term "disabled people" as a claim to—and pride in—an identity. We can agree that many terms from the past are derogatory and are not appropriate or polite. President Obama, in 2010, signed Rosa's Law, which replaced references to "mental retardation" with "intellectual disability" in all federal statutes.

49. With some modification, based on Frigon & Kuhn, *supra* note 41, at 2. The authors remind the readers to check case law in their jurisdictions to determine their jurisdiction's position on the over-65 issue.

The authors acknowledge this debate around language and its importance. For consistency in this book, we use people-first language and we use the term "special needs trust." We understand that as language evolves there may be better or preferred terms.

CHAPTER 2

Ethical Issues and Fiduciary Representation[1]

I. Introduction

There are at least five typical scenarios to consider in drafting special needs trusts (SNTs) as part of planning for the clients who are elders or who have a disability. Is the attorney:

1. Only the drafter of the documents?
2. Representing the trustee or other fiduciary?
3. Hired by, and representing, the beneficiary?
4. Expected to draft the documents and represent one of the parties?
5. Drafting the documents and serving as a fiduciary once the drafting is finalized?

Whichever scenario applies, there will typically be ethical issues that an attorney may face in these discrete roles. Sometimes those issues will result from multiple roles—or at least multiple expectations—affecting the representation.

II. Who Is the Client?

The first step in any representation is to always, always determine who the attorney represents and make it clear to all concerned. In the creation of an SNT, the answer to the question may not be quite clear initially.

For example, with a first-party SNT, when only hired to draft the documents, the attorney may be hired by the personal injury attorney,

1. This chapter assumes the reader has a working knowledge of the applicable state Rules of Professional Conduct, and of the attorney's ethical duties.

court-appointed guardian ad litem, or another to draft the SNT. In such instances, does the drafting attorney have any duty to the SNT beneficiary or another, such as the parents when the beneficiary is a minor? Is the SNT court-created and the drafting attorney's fees will be approved by the court? Who is signing the drafting attorney's engagement agreement?[2] In other cases, the client might be the beneficiary whose money will be used to establish the trust. In other instances, the client may be the parents, guardian, or grandparents[3] who act for the beneficiary. Although a court can "establish" the first-party SNT,[4] the attorney will not represent the court. Instead, the attorney may represent those who petitioned the court for approval of the SNT, who hired the attorney for the creation of the SNT, or who was appointed by the court to create the SNT. Keep in mind that with the first-party SNT, the settlor may not be the client, but instead the individual who has provided the money to fund the SNT.[5] Even if everyone understands that the client is the person who will sign the trust, or the person or entity that will fund it, the attorney's obligation to the beneficiary will often be both clearer and more complicated.[6] Although the attorney's duty to the nonclient beneficiary is going to be state specific, guidance may be taken from the Life Passages PSNT Best Practices Guidelines[7] for pooled trust administrators regarding when and how to best communicate with beneficiaries.[8]

When the attorney is hired to draft a third-party trust, it may be easier to identify the client. There is no scenario as in the first-party SNT where the beneficiary's money is used to fund the trust. The beneficiary is not the client.

The creation of the client-attorney relationship is critical for the imposition of duties on the attorney. The Restatement (Third) of the Law Governing

2. Who signs the engagement agreement is one factor to be considered when identifying who is the client. *See generally* Model Rules of Pro. Conduct scope [17] (Am. Bar Ass'n 1983).

3. 42 U.S.C. § 1396p(d)(4)(a).

4. *Id.*

5. *In re* Hertsberg Inter Vivos Tr., 578 N.W.2d 289, 291–92, 292 (Mich. 1998) (mother created trust and funded trust pursuant to court order for benefit of daughter; court held the money was that of the daughter) ("settlor is the one who provides consideration for a trust").

6. See, for example, Model Rules of Professional Conduct Rule 1.14 comment 2, which states: "The fact that a client suffers a disability does not diminish the lawyer's obligation to treat the client with attention and respect. Even if the person has a legal representative, the lawyer should as far as possible accord the represented person the status of client, particularly in maintaining communication." See also comment 4, which states:

> If a legal representative has already been appointed for the client, the lawyer should ordinarily look to the representative for decisions on behalf of the client. In matters involving a minor, whether the lawyer should look to the parents as natural guardians may depend on the type of proceeding or matter in which the lawyer is representing the minor.

7. Stetson L., Life Passages PSNT Best Practices Guidelines (2020), https://www.stetson.edu/law/academics/elder/home/media/Best_Practices_Guidelines_Final_42022.pdf.

8. *Id.* at 13.

Lawyers section 14, Formation of a Client-Lawyer Relationship, explains how a client-attorney relationship is typically created:

> A relationship of client and lawyer arises when:
>
> (1) a person manifests to a lawyer the person's intent that the lawyer provide legal services for the person; and either
>
> (a) the lawyer manifests to the person consent to do so; or
>
> (b) the lawyer fails to manifest lack of consent to do so, and the lawyer knows or reasonably should know that the person reasonably relies on the lawyer to provide the services; or
>
> (2) a tribunal with power to do so appoints the lawyer to provide the services.[9]

A. First-Party Trusts: Is the Question, "Who Is the Client?" More Complicated?

It is possible that the attorney is hired by another just to draft the trust. The attorney first must determine who the attorney represents. Typically, the attorney represents the individual who will sign the documents, such as a will, revocable or irrevocable inter vivos trust, testamentary trust, and so on.[10] In situations of third-party SNTs, the client is not the beneficiary.

The money is that of the beneficiary, but who does the attorney represent? Remember as noted earlier, 42 U.S.C. § 1396p(d)(4)(a) provides that the trust

---

9. Restatement (Third) of the Law Governing Lawyers § 14 (Am. L. Inst. 2000).

10. *See, e.g.*, S.D. State Bar Ethics Op. 2007-3 (A niece, agent under power of attorney, demanded client's estate planning documents, claiming status as "co-client" who stands in client's shoes. Committee determined "who is the client" is question answered by substantive law and circumstances may be relevant, and decision may be question of fact, communications, and circumstances.). *See also* Pa. Bar Ass'n Comm. on Legal Ethics Op. 2004-7 (2004), 2004 WL 5333296 (attorney represented a guardian in capacity as guardian; discusses duties to nonclient beneficiaries, quoting with approval American College of Trust and Estate Counsel (ACTEC) Commentaries to Model Rules 1.2 and 1.6); Ky. Bar Ass'n Ethics Op. KBA E-401 (amended 2019), which states:

> This Committee adopts the ACTEC Commentaries because the Commentaries properly set forth a lawyer's ethical obligations. Further, this Committee agrees with ABA Formal Opinion 94-380, and adopts the majority view; that is, that a lawyer who represents a fiduciary does not also represent the beneficiaries. We reject the view that a lawyer who represents a fiduciary also owes fiduciary obligations to the beneficiaries that in some circumstances will override obligations otherwise owed by the lawyer to the fiduciary, such as the obligation of confidentiality. We also reject the view that when a lawyer represents a fiduciary in a trust or estate matter, the client is not the fiduciary, but is the trust estate. We adopt the following comments made in the ABA's Formal Opinion. . . .
>
> Further, "[t]he fact that a fiduciary has obligations to the beneficiaries of the trust or estate does not in itself either expand or limit the lawyer's obligations to the fiduciary under the Rules of Professional Conduct, nor impose on the lawyer obligations toward the beneficiaries that the lawyer would not have toward other third parties."

may be established by the beneficiary, the beneficiary's parents, grandparents, guardian, or the court. So, it is possible the attorney is hired by another—not the beneficiary—to draft the trust that will benefit the beneficiary, and the beneficiary is not the client, even though it is the beneficiary's money that is used to fund the trust. The party hiring the attorney to draft the trust for the beneficiary has, in some way, a relationship to the beneficiary and is acting in that capacity to the beneficiary.[11] The client may be an official or unofficial representative of the beneficiary; an unofficial representative by virtue of the relationship to the beneficiary, such as the parent or grandparent, or official, such as the agent under a durable power of attorney[12] or a court-appointed guardian.

There will be occasion where the beneficiary hires the attorney and thus is the client. Although as a result of the Special Needs Trust Fairness Act[13] the individual can establish the trust for his or her own benefit, it may be more common that someone else is establishing the first-party trust for the individual. However, when the beneficiary is the client, consider whether the client is an adult[14] and has capacity both to hire the attorney and to create the trust. In those situations, the attorney's ethical duties are much clearer. The beneficiary is the client and although the client will have been determined to be disabled by the Social Security Administration (SSA),[15] that determination does not mean the client lacks capacity to hire the attorney.[16] The client may have a physical disability and have the needed capacity to hire the attorney as well as the capacity to create the SNT.[17] This analysis would hold true if the agent under

---

See also Ala. Ethics Op. 2010-03, Representation of an Estate and Client Identity (2010), https://www.alabar.org/assets/2019/02/2010-03-1.pdf (when attorney hired by personal representative for the estate, attorney's only client is the personal representative); Legal Ethics Comm. Ind. State Bar Ass'n Op. 2 (2001).

11. For example, the individual contacting the attorney may be the parent or grandparent. *See* 42 U.S.C. § 1396p(d)(4)(a).

12. *See, e.g.*, Draper v. Colvin, 779 F.3d 556 (8th Cir. 2015) (discussing whether the parents, also agents under a power of attorney, could establish the SNT for the beneficiary). The *Draper* case was decided prior to the amendment to 42 U.S.C. § 1396p(d)(4)(a), which added the provision to allow the beneficiary to establish his or her own SNT.

13. 42 U.S.C. § 1396p(d)(4)(a) provides:

> A trust containing the assets of an individual under age 65 who is disabled (as defined in section 1382c(a)(3) of this title) and which is established for the benefit of such individual by the individual, a parent, grandparent, legal guardian of the individual, or a court if the State will receive all amounts remaining in the trust upon the death of such individual up to an amount equal to the total medical assistance paid on behalf of the individual under a State plan under this subchapter.

14. An SNT can be established for a minor, so if the beneficiary is a minor, an authorized representative of the beneficiary would have to hire the attorney and direct the attorney to draft the SNT.

15. 42 U.S.C. § 1382c(a)(3)(c).

16. *See also* Model Rules of Pro. Conduct r. 1.14 cmt. 6 (Am. Bar Ass'n 1983).

17. *See, e.g.*, *id.* r. 1.14.

a durable power of attorney hires the attorney to create the SNT on behalf of the beneficiary.

In some instances, the beneficiary is an unemancipated minor. In this case, the client would either be a parent, since the parent is typically the natural guardian of the minor,[18] the grandparent (likely through some grant of authority), or the court-appointed guardian because the beneficiary has a legal incapacity of age. Consider whether the attorney will have any duty to the beneficiary.[19]

In this area of practice, it is possible that the beneficiary is an adult with a disability that results in the beneficiary lacking legal capacity. In this case, the beneficiary would not be the client, and the client would either be a parent, grandparent, or the court-appointed guardian or guardian ad litem, and the money will still be that of the beneficiary. Even though the parents have the authority under 42 U.S.C. § 1396p(d)(4)(A), the parents may not have legal authority beyond creating the SNT. The more traditional view of client representation would be that the client is the parent or the court-appointed guardian. When the court orders the creation of the SNT, the court is not assuming the role of client, but instead is either appointing a representative such as a guardian or guardian ad litem to hire the attorney to create the trust or directing the petitioner's attorney to submit an order to the court for the court's signature directing the creation of the SNT. In the first scenario, the fiduciary will be the client and, in the latter, the attorney for the petitioner (if the court order directs the petitioner's attorney to hire the drafting attorney), or the petitioner, depending on the exact language of the order.

B. Third-Party SNTs: Is the Question, "Who Is the Client?" Easier to Answer?

Here, the situation is much clearer. The client hires the attorney to create the trust and the client provides the assets to fund the trust. The SNT can either be inter vivos or testamentary. The client is not the beneficiary, but a third party, the settlor of the trust for the benefit of another. The client is not creating and funding the trust in a representative capacity to the beneficiary. The client signs the documents. Although the client may be related to the beneficiary,

18. *See, e.g.*, Unif. Tr. Code § 303(6) (Unif. L. Comm'n 2022).

19. Think of this in terms of whether an attorney who drafts any trust has any duties to beneficiaries of the trust. *See* Model Rules of Pro. Conduct r. 1.14 cmt. 4 (Am. Bar Ass'n 1983) ("In matters involving a minor, whether the lawyer should look to the parents as natural guardians may depend on the type of proceeding or matter in which the lawyer is representing the minor.").

for example the grandparent, sibling, or parent of the individual with special needs, there is nothing in trust law[20] that requires such a family relationship.

III. When an Attorney Represents the Trustee: The Ethical Issues

In many instances the attorney may be hired by the trustee to be the drafter only, or to be the drafter and represent the trustee—or is it the trust? With the question of fiduciary representation, there is a split amongst the jurisdictions as to whom the attorney represents.[21] In fiduciary representation, the question of who is the client is not easily answered. There are three prevailing views of the answer to the question.[22] The first, the majority view, is that the client is the fiduciary, with the position that the trust or estate is a thing, not a client.[23] The second view is that the attorney represents the entity.[24] The third

20. *See, e.g.*, Unif. Tr. Code § 103(15) (Unif. L. Comm'n 2022) (defining "settlor" as "a person, including a testator, who creates, or contributes property to, a trust").

21. *See, e.g.*, Kennedy Lee, *Representing the Fiduciary: To Whom Does the Attorney Owe Duties?*, 37 ACTEC L.J. 469 (2011) (discussing the three most common approaches: traditional, joint-client, and entity.)

22. *See, e.g.*, Ala. Ethics Op. 2010-03, *supra* note 10. J. Anthony McLain, *Representation of an Estate and Client Identity*, 72 Ala. Law. 149, 151 (2011) explains:

> There are three theories regarding the identity of the client when a lawyer handles an estate. The American Bar Association, in Formal Opinion 94-380, recognized that the majority view is that the lawyer represents only the personal representative or fiduciary of the estate and not the beneficiaries of the estate, either jointly or individually. In reaching a similar conclusion, a number of other state bars have relied, in part, on state law that indicated that an estate is not a separate legal entity. In Ethics Opinion No. 91-2, the Alaska State Bar noted that an estate is "for probate purposes a collection of assets rather than an organization, and is not an entity involved in the probate proceedings." In Formal Opinion 1989-4, the Delaware State Bar also concluded that under state law, the term "estate" only referred to the actual property of the decedent and did not have an independent legal existence. As such, the Delaware State Bar concluded that the estate could not be a "client" under their rules of professional conduct (citations omitted).

23. *See, e.g.*, *In re* Est. of Gory, 570 So. 2d 1381, 1383 (Fla. Dist. Ct. App. 1980). "In Florida, the personal representative is the client rather than the estate or the beneficiaries." *Id.* at 1383 (citing Rules Regulating the Florida Bar r. 4-1.7 (comment)). The comment specifically states that "[i]n estate administration the identity of the client may be unclear under the law of some jurisdictions. In Florida, the personal representative is the client rather than the estate or the beneficiaries. The lawyer should make clear the relationship to the parties involved." *See also* Roberts v. Fearey, 986 P.2d 690 (Or. Ct. App. 1999) (attorney for trustee represents trustee, citing to Or. State Bar Ethics Op. 1991-119). *See also* Huie v. DeShazo, 922 S.W.2d 920 (Tex. 1996) (trustee who hires attorney is the client, citing to Tex. R. Civ. Evid. 503(a)(1)).

24. McLain, *supra* note 22, at 152 explains:

> The second approach to client identity in estate representation holds that the client is the estate itself. This view is identical to the entity theory of representation most commonly employed under Rule 1.13, *Ala. R. Prof. C.*, when representing businesses and corporations. Under this approach, the lawyer represents the "estate" as a freestanding legal entity. The lawyer does not have a lawyer-client relationship with either the fiduciary or beneficiaries of the estate. One argument in favor of this position is that estates and trusts are treated as separate legal entities for taxation purposes and,

view, espoused by Geoffrey C. Hazard, Jr. and W. William Hodes, is the joint-representation model.[25]

The attorney may find himself or herself in this situation when either (1) hired by the settlor to create the SNT and then hired by the trustee to represent the trustee or (2) when the attorney, although not hired to draft the trust, was hired by the trustee after the trust was established.

Beyond determining who is the client, the attorney will be faced with issues surrounding conflicts of interest[26] and confidentiality.[27] Further consideration must be given to the question of whether the attorney owes any duties to the beneficiary of the SNT.[28]

The American Bar Association (ABA) issued a seminal ethics opinion in 1994 (under the older version of the Model Rules), ABA Formal Ethics Opinion 94-380, Counseling a Fiduciary:

> When the fiduciary is the lawyer's client, all of the Model Rules prescribing a lawyer's duties to a client apply. The scope of the lawyer's representation is defined by and limited by Model Rule 1.2. The lawyer must diligently

---

therefore, an estate or trust is a recognizable legal entity. Under this approach, the fiduciary of the estate is merely an agent of the entity (citations omitted).

25. *Id.* at 152–53 explains:

The third view holds that the lawyer jointly represents the fiduciary and beneficiaries of the estate. This view of estate representation has been most prominently advocated by Geoffrey C. Hazard, Jr. and W. William Hodes in *The Law of Lawyering*, § 57.3, 4. 3rd Edition (2005), in which the authors argue the following:

> Where the lawyer's client is a fiduciary, however, there is a third party in the picture (namely the beneficiary) who does not stand at arm's length from the client; as a consequence, the lawyer also cannot stand at arm's length from the beneficiary. Clients with such responsibilities include trustees, partners, vis-à-vis other partners, spouses, corporate directors and officers vis-à-vis their corporations, and many others, including parents. In the situations posited, because the lawyer is hired to represent the fiduciary and because the fiduciary is legally required to serve the beneficiary, the lawyer must be deemed employed to further that service as well.
>
> It is only a small additional semantic step, and not a large analytic one, to say that in such situations the fiduciary is not the only client, but merely the "primary" client. [Footnote omitted] In this view, the beneficiary is the "derivative" client. The beneficiary, strictly speaking a non-client, may be entitled to the loyalty of the lawyer almost as if he were a client. [Footnote omitted]
>
> A number of consequences follow from adopting the derivative client approach to representation of a fiduciary. First, the lawyer's obligation to avoid participating in a client's fraud . . . is engaged by a more sensitive trigger. The fiduciary is subject to a high standard of fair dealing as regards the beneficiary, but may face temptation to engage in improper overreaching. The lawyer therefore faces a correspondingly greater risk of being implicated in the fiduciary's misconduct, and also has a greater duty to ensure that the purpose of the representation is not subverted.

26. Lee, *supra* note 21, at 470.

27. *See* Model Rules of Pro. Conduct r. 1.6 (Am. Bar Ass'n 1983).

28. Lee, *supra* note 21, at 470–71. *See also In re* Est. of Fogleman, 3 P.3d 1172, 1177 (Ariz. Ct. App. 2000) (in discussing whether the beneficiaries of an estate were the "clients" of the personal representative, the court noted that the "personal representative owes a beneficiary the lesser duty of fairness, rather than the duty of undivided loyalty, demonstrates that the beneficiary is not the . . . client").

> represent the fiduciary, see Model Rule 1.3, preserve in confidence communications between the lawyer and the fiduciary, see Model Rule 1.6, and be truthful in statements to others, see Model Rule 4.1(a). The fact that the fiduciary client has obligations toward the beneficiaries does not impose parallel obligations on the lawyer, or otherwise expand or supersede the lawyer's responsibilities under the Model Rules of Professional Conduct.
>
> A lawyer's duty of confidentiality to a client is not lessened by the fact that the client is a fiduciary. Although the Model Rules prohibit the lawyer from actively participating in criminal or fraudulent activity or active concealment of a client's wrongdoing, they do not authorize the lawyer to breach confidences to prevent such wrongdoing.
>
> ***
>
> The Model Rules provide important guidelines for defining a lawyer's duties to a client. These guidelines contain no exceptions when the client owes duties, fiduciary or otherwise, to third parties. So long as a fiduciary is the lawyer's only client in the matter, that client is entitled to the same protections under the Model Rules as any nonfiduciary client, including, most importantly, the duty of confidentiality set forth in Model Rule 1.6.[29]

The scope of representation under Rule 1.2 becomes critical to the analysis regarding whom the attorney represents, for example, as noted in the American College of Trust and Estate Counsel (ACTEC) Commentaries on the Model Rules of Professional Conduct:

> The scope of the representation of a fiduciary is an important factor in determining the nature and extent of the duties owed to the beneficiaries of the fiduciary estate. For example, a lawyer who is retained by a fiduciary individually may owe few, if any, duties to the beneficiaries of the fiduciary estate other than duties the lawyer owes to other third parties generally. Thus, a lawyer who is retained by a fiduciary to advise the fiduciary regarding the fiduciary's defense to an action brought against the fiduciary by a beneficiary may have no duties to the beneficiaries beyond those owed to other adverse parties or nonclients. . . . The relationship of the lawyer for a fiduciary to a beneficiary of the fiduciary estate and the content of the lawyer's communications regarding the fiduciary estate may be affected if the beneficiary is represented by another lawyer in connection with the fiduciary estate. In particular in such a case, unless the beneficiary and the beneficiary's lawyer consent to direct communications, the lawyer for the fiduciary should communicate with the lawyer for the beneficiary regarding matters concerning the fiduciary estate rather than communicating directly with the beneficiary.

---

29. ABA Comm. on Ethics & Pro. Resp., Formal Op. 94-380, Counseling a Fiduciary (1994) (citations omitted).

> See MRPC [Model Rules of Professional Conduct] 4.2 (Communications with Persons Represented by Counsel). . . . [E]ven though a separately represented beneficiary and the fiduciary are adverse with respect to a particular matter, the fiduciary and a lawyer who represents the fiduciary generally continue to be bound by duties to the beneficiary.[30]

According to the ACTEC Commentaries on Rule 1.2:

> As a general rule, the lawyer for the fiduciary should consider informing the beneficiaries that the lawyer has been retained by the fiduciary regarding the fiduciary estate and that the fiduciary is the lawyer's client; that while the fiduciary and the lawyer will, from time to time, provide information to the beneficiaries regarding the fiduciary estate, the lawyer does not represent them; and that the beneficiaries may wish to retain independent counsel to represent their interests. As indicated in MRPC 2.3 (Evaluation for Use by Third Persons), the lawyer may, at the request of a client, evaluate a matter affecting a client for the use of others.[31]

Comment f to the Restatement (Third) of the Law Governing Lawyers section 14 offers this caution:

> In trusts and estates practice a lawyer may have to clarify with those involved whether a trust, a trustee, its beneficiaries or groupings of some or all of them are clients and similarly whether the client is an executor, an estate, or its beneficiaries. In the absence of clarification the inference to be drawn may depend on the circumstances and on the law of the jurisdiction. Similar issues may arise when a lawyer represents other fiduciaries with respect to their fiduciary responsibilities, for example a pension-fund trustee or another lawyer.[32]

The Delaware State Bar Association Committee on Professional Ethics in Opinion 1989-4[33] concluded that an attorney who represents "an estate" actually represents the personal representative:[34]

> [W]e are of the view an "estate" has no legal existence, but instead describes the property and debts of a decedent. Given that conclusion, we do not believe an estate can be a "client" as that term is used under Rule 1.7, and

30. ACTEC, Commentaries on the Model Rules of Professional Conduct 40 (5th ed. 2016), https://www.actec.org/assets/1/6/ACTEC_Commentaries_5th_rev_06_29.pdf?hssc=1.

31. *Id.* at 37.

32. Restatement (Third) of the Law Governing Lawyers § 14 cmt. f (Am. L. Inst. 2000).

33. Del. State Bar Ass'n Comm. on Pro. Ethics Op'n 1989-4 (1989), https://media1.dsba.org/public/media/ethics/pdfs/1989-4.pdf (discussing attorney's representation of personal representative in that capacity and in the person's individual capacity).

34. *Id.*

> the commonly used phrase "attorney for the estate" incorrectly describes the relationship existing between a lawyer and the executor. An attorney does not serve as an attorney for the estate; rather he or she serves as an attorney for the executor or other personal representative in that person's dealings concerning the estate of the decedent.[35]

The Alabama Bar General Counsel issued an ethics opinion on fiduciary representation in 2011.[36] Two questions were discussed, the first considering who the attorney represents in an estate administration:[37]

> Generally, the lawyer represents the individual who hired him to assist in the administration or probate of the estate. If that person has only one role and is not a fiduciary, the lawyer represents only that person, unless the client and lawyer agree otherwise. If the person is the personal representative, the lawyer represents the personal representative individually, unless the personal representative and lawyer agree otherwise. The lawyer must be careful not to give the impression, either by affirmative action or omission, that he also represents the beneficiaries of the estate. As a result, if the client is the personal representative only, the lawyer must advise the heirs and devisees ("beneficiaries") and other interested parties in the estate known to the lawyer that the lawyer's only client is the personal representative in order to avoid violating Rule 4.3. A lawyer must comply with certain duties upon undertaking representation of a fiduciary or risk violating certain rules of professional conduct. If the lawyer failed to give such notice, it could be found that he has undertaken to represent both the fiduciary and the beneficiaries of the estate.[38]

Prior to the issuance of the formal opinion, the opinion references earlier informal opinions on the topic:

> The Disciplinary Commission is also aware that the Office of General Counsel has given recent informal opinions concerning this issue. In their informal opinions, the Office of General Counsel has opined that the client is the estate. The lawyer represents the estate by acting for and through the fiduciary of the estate for the ultimate benefit of the beneficiaries of the estate. Because the lawyer is retained by the personal representative to represent the estate and because the personal representative is legally required to serve the beneficiaries, the lawyer also has an obligation to the beneficiaries. This relationship has been characterized as one where the fiduciary is not the only

35. *Id.*
36. McLain, *supra* note 22.
37. *Id.*
38. *Id.* (citations omitted).

client, but merely the "primary client," while the beneficiary is the "derivative client." In some situations where there is a sole beneficiary of the estate, that beneficiary (ostensibly a non-client) may be entitled to the loyalty of the lawyer to much the same extent as the fiduciary.[39]

IV. When the Attorney Is the Trustee (or Other Fiduciary)

Occasionally an attorney or law firm may act as trustee, or in some other fiduciary capacity. The practice is permissible, but fraught with potential dangers. The fiduciary/attorney should pay particular attention to the following:

1. The possibility of conflicts of interest, particularly in moving from attorney/counselor/advocate to fiduciary. In any case in which an attorney prepares documents for a client naming the attorney, his or her firm or others in a business relationship as fiduciary, the attorney should pay particular attention to the requirements of full disclosure to the client.[40] With some variation in the language of Model Rule 1.4 as adopted by various states, and as a good practice in any event, the drafting attorney should usually spell out the terms under which the attorney (or his or her firm or associated business) would act, what costs would be associated with that fiduciary action, and what effect the fiduciary role would have on the continued attorney-client relationship.
2. The costs for preparation of documents naming the attorney as fiduciary. While there is no requirement that the attorney charge less for preparation of such documents, there may be an expectation that "reasonableness" of the attorney's fee might be affected by the prospect of future compensation for fiduciary services.[41]
3. The potential for future conflicts of interest arising from the change in roles.[42] What, for example, would the attorney's role be if the client sought to remove him or her as fiduciary at a time when the attorney believed the client was incapacitated, or subject to undue influence—perhaps even the exact problem that led to the client initially naming the attorney as fiduciary?[43] And what are the ethical concerns inherent

39. *Id.* at 151.
40. Model Rules of Pro. Conduct r. 1.4(b) (Am. Bar Ass'n 1983).
41. *Id.* r. 1.5(a); *see also* Colo. Formal Op. 02-426 (2002).
42. Model Rules of Pro. Conduct r. 1.7 (Am. Bar Ass'n 1983).
43. For an illustration of how easy it is for the lawyer's competing roles to raise problems, consider *In re Disciplinary Proceeding against Eugster*, 209 P.3d 435 (Wash. 2009).

in an attorney/trustee having to initiate proceedings (which might not be judicial proceedings) to determine capacity of the lawyer's former client or otherwise handle the fiduciary responsibility?[44]

4. The need for the attorney to have appropriate staff, training, and mechanisms to effectively act as fiduciary.[45]

Of course, there are other fiduciary roles that an attorney might fulfill, including trust protector or trust advisory committee member. While the possibilities for conflict might be lowered in such roles (as compared to the role as trustee), the same considerations should be kept in mind.

V. Does the Attorney for the Trustee Have Any Duty or Liability to the Trust Beneficiary?

The answer is some instances is yes. But that answer is qualified by "it depends." The Restatement (Third) of Law Governing Lawyers section 51, Duty of Care to Certain Non-Clients, provides:

> For purposes of liability under § 48, a lawyer owes a duty to use care within the meaning of § 52 in each of the following circumstances:
>
> (1) . . .
>
> (2) to a nonclient when and to the extent that:
>
> (a) the lawyer or (with the lawyer's acquiescence) the lawyer's client invites the nonclient to rely on the lawyer's opinion or provision of other legal services, and the nonclient so relies; and
>
> (b) the nonclient is not, under applicable tort law, too remote from the lawyer to be entitled to protection;
>
> (3) to a nonclient when and to the extent that:
>
> (a) the lawyer knows that a client intends as one of the primary objectives of the representation that the lawyer's services benefit the nonclient;

44. *See* Model Rules of Pro. Conduct r. 1.14 (Am. Bar Ass'n 1983) (and especially comment 5 to that rule). And consider for a moment whether the same logic might apply to, say, an administrative proceeding initiated by an attorney to remove the attorney's former client's ability to drive a vehicle—as just one illustrative example.

45. *Id.* r. 1.1.

(b) such a duty would not significantly impair the lawyer's performance of obligations to the client; and

(c) the absence of such a duty would make enforcement of those obligations to the client unlikely; and

(4) to a nonclient when and to the extent that:

(a) the lawyer's client is a trustee, guardian, executor, or fiduciary acting primarily to perform similar functions for the nonclient;

(b) the lawyer knows that appropriate action by the lawyer is necessary with respect to a matter within the scope of the representation to prevent or rectify the breach of a fiduciary duty owed by the client to the nonclient, where (i) the breach is a crime or fraud or (ii) the lawyer has assisted or is assisting the breach;

(c) the nonclient is not reasonably able to protect its rights; and

(d) such a duty would not significantly impair the performance of the lawyer's obligations to the client.[46]

The attorney may have "special obligations" to a beneficiary when the client is the fiduciary.[47] With the erosion of privity,[48] even though the beneficiary is not the client, the attorney for the trustee may have a duty to the beneficiary.[49] For example, in *Spinner v. Nutt*,[50] the court was concerned with whether the attorneys for the trustees owed the "duty of care" to the beneficiaries who were not clients.[51] The court considered several theories of liability

46. Restatement (Third) of the Law Governing Lawyers § 51 (Am. L. Inst. 2000). The comments to this Restatement explain the differences between (3) and (4) as follows:

> Subsections (3) and (4), although related in their justifications, differ in application. In situations falling under Subsection (3), the client need not owe any preexisting duty to the intended beneficiary. The scope of the intended benefit depends on the client's intent and the lawyer's undertaking. On the other hand, the duty under Subsection (4) typically arises when a lawyer helps a client-fiduciary to carry out a duty of the fiduciary to a beneficiary recognized and defined by trust or other law.

47. Model Rules of Pro. Conduct r. 1.2 cmt. 11 (Am. Bar Ass'n 1983).

48. Restatement (Third) of the Law Governing Lawyers § 51 cmt. h (Am. L. Inst. 2000) ("A lawyer representing a client in the client's capacity as a fiduciary (as opposed to the client's personal capacity) may in some circumstances be liable to a beneficiary for a failure to use care to protect the beneficiary. The duty should be recognized only when the requirements of Subsection (4) are met and when action by the lawyer would not violate applicable professional rules (see § 54(1)). The duty arises from the fact that a fiduciary has obligations to the beneficiary that go beyond fair dealing at arm's length. . . . The duty recognized by Subsection (4) is limited to lawyers representing only a limited category of the persons described as fiduciaries—trustees, executors, guardians, and other fiduciaries acting primarily to fulfill similar functions.").

49. *See, e.g.*, Est. of Treadwell v. Wright, 61 P.3d 1214 (Wash. Ct. App. 2003) (in guardianship case, discussing test to determine whether attorney has duty to nonclient).

50. 631 N.E.2d 542 (Mass. 1994).

51. *Id.* at 544.

and concluded that the attorneys had no duty to the beneficiaries; the duty was only to the client trustee.[52]

In the California case of *Goldberg v. Frye*,[53] the court held that the attorney for the personal representative of the estate represents the personal representative, not the estate.[54] Although the actions of the attorney and the attorney's services may benefit the beneficiaries of the estate, the attorney does not represent the beneficiaries.[55] The court identified six factors that must be found to impose a duty.[56] "The very purpose of the fiduciary is to serve the interests of the estate, not to promote the objectives of one group of legatees over the interests of conflicting claimants."[57] In explaining the rationale for determining the client is the fiduciary, the court observed:

> It would be very dangerous to conclude that the attorney, through performance of his service to the administrator and by way of communication to estate beneficiaries, subjects himself to claims of negligence from the beneficiaries. The beneficiaries are entitled to even-handed and fair administration by the fiduciary. They are not owed a duty directly by the fiduciary's attorney.[58]

The engagement agreement plays an important role in structuring the client-attorney relationship. Under Rule 1.2, Scope of Representation, the attorney delineates the parameters of the representation. An ambiguous or insufficient description of the scope of representation in the engagement agreement can lead subsequently to issues regarding whom the attorney represents and the services the attorney is to perform. For example, in *Svaldi v.*

---

52. *Id.* at 547. The court considered when a duty to a beneficiary of a trust might be imposed and noted the potential of creating conflicting loyalties if the attorney owed a duty to the trustee and to the beneficiaries, which would impinge on the attorney's ability to effectively represent the trustee. *Id.* at 544–45. As well, it would be counter to the Massachusetts ethics rule, referencing Supreme Judicial Court Rule 3.07, Cannon 4, DR 4-101. *Id.* at 545. The court also considered and rejected the application of the third-party beneficiary theory of recovery. *Id.* at 546. *See also* Roberts v. Fearey, 986 P.2d 690, 691 (Or. Ct. App. 1999) (attorney did not have a duty to beneficiaries).

53. 217 Cal. App. 3d 1258 (Cal. Ct. App. 1990).

54. *Id.* at 1267.

55. *Id.* (opinion discusses duty and liability in cases where there is no privity).

56. *Id.* at 1268. The six factors are:

> [The] extent to which transaction was intended to affect the plaintiff; (2) the foreseeability of harm to the plaintiff; (3) the degree of certainty that the plaintiff suffered injury; (4) the closeness of the connection between the defendant's conduct and the injury; (5) the policy of preventing future harm; and (6) whether recognition of liability under the circumstances would impose an undue burden on the profession.

(citations omitted).

57. *Id.* at 1269 (citations omitted).

58. *Id.* (citations omitted).

Holmes,[59] the attorney drafting the power of attorney included two safeguard clauses that required an initial inventory and annual accountings.[60] In a malpractice suit against the attorney, the court considered whether the inclusion of these paragraphs created a duty that the attorney owed to the client to provide oversight of the actions of the agents.[61] The court concluded that the inclusion of the safeguard clauses "expanded the scope of [the attorney's] representation of [the client] beyond the mere drafting of the legal documents" and the attorney had undertaken "a responsibility to make [the inventory and accounting] work."[62] Although the attorney had an expanded representation of the client, the attorney did not have the duty to supervise the agents.[63]

The ACTEC Commentaries address this issue as follows:

> *Representation of Client in Fiduciary, Not Individual, Capacity.* If a lawyer is retained to represent a fiduciary generally with respect to an estate, the lawyer's services are in furtherance of the fulfillment of the client's fiduciary responsibilities and not the client's individual goals. The ultimate objective of the engagement is to assist the client in properly administering the fiduciary estate for the benefit of the beneficiaries. Confirmation of the fiduciary capacity in which the client is engaging the lawyer is appropriate because of the priority of the client's duties to the beneficiaries. The nature of the relationship is also suggested by the fact that the fiduciary and the lawyer for the fiduciary are both compensated from the fiduciary estate. Under some circumstances it is acceptable for the lawyer also to represent one or more of the beneficiaries of the fiduciary estate, subject to the fiduciary client's overriding fiduciary obligations. See ACTEC Commentary on MRPC 1.7 (Conflict of Interest: Current Clients) and Example 1.7-2.
>
> *General and Individual Representation Distinguished.* A lawyer represents the fiduciary generally (i.e., in a representative capacity) when the lawyer is retained to advise the fiduciary regarding the administration of the fiduciary estate or matters affecting the estate. On the other hand, a lawyer represents a fiduciary individually when the lawyer is retained for the limited purpose of advancing the interests of the fiduciary and not necessarily the interests of the fiduciary estate or the persons beneficially interested in the estate. For example, a lawyer represents a fiduciary individually when the lawyer, who may or may not have previously represented the fiduciary generally with

59. 986 N.E.2d 442, 447 (Ohio Ct. App. 2012) (discussing the duty of the lawyer to the client comes from the scope of the representation) (citations omitted).

60. *Id.* at 445.

61. *Id.* at 447–48.

62. *Id.* at 448 (attorney had duty to contact agents regarding requirement of inventory and accounting).

63. *Id.* at 449.

> respect to the fiduciary estate, is retained to negotiate with the beneficiaries regarding the compensation of the fiduciary or to defend the fiduciary against charges or threatened charges of maladministration of the fiduciary estate. A lawyer who represents a fiduciary generally may normally also undertake to represent the fiduciary individually. If the lawyer has previously represented the fiduciary generally and is now representing the fiduciary individually, the lawyer should advise the beneficiaries of this fact.[64]

As far as the attorney's duties to beneficiaries, if any, according to the ACTEC Commentaries, the scope and nature of the attorney's duties to beneficiaries are not static and in fact

> may vary according to the circumstances, including the nature and extent of the representation and the terms of any understanding or agreement among the parties (the lawyer, the fiduciary, and the beneficiaries). The lawyer for the fiduciary owes some duties to the beneficiaries of the fiduciary estate although he or she does not represent them.[65]

The Commentaries describe these duties owed as limiting the actions of the attorney; thus, the attorney may not "[take] advantage of [the attorney's] position to the disadvantage of the fiduciary estate or the beneficiaries."[66] Additionally there may be some situations where the attorney has to affirmatively act to safeguard the beneficiaries' interests.[67]

VI. Ability to Share Information with Nonclient Beneficiary

The ACTEC Commentaries caution that "the [attorney's] communications with the beneficiaries should not be made in a manner that might lead the beneficiaries to believe that the lawyer represents the beneficiaries in the matter except to the extent the lawyer actually does represent one or more of them."[68]

Consider the use of the engagement agreement to make clear who is represented and who is not.[69] Provide a copy to both the trustee and the

64. ACTEC, *supra* note 30, at 39.
65. *Id.*
66. *Id.*
67. *Id.*
68. *Id.* at 40.
69. *See, e.g.*, Lee, *supra* note 21, at 488–89. *See also* RESTATEMENT (THIRD) OF THE LAW GOVERNING LAWYERS § 14 cmt. f (AM. L. INST. 2000) (regarding inadvertent representation: "[u]nder Subsection (1)(b), a lawyer's failure to clarify whom the lawyer represents in circumstances calling for such a result might lead a lawyer to have entered into client-lawyer representations not intended by the lawyer. Hence, the lawyer must clarify whom the lawyer intends to represent when the lawyer knows or reasonably should know

beneficiary,[70] or if the trustee prefers that the attorney not provide the engagement agreement to the beneficiary, then the attorney could write a letter to the beneficiary noting that the attorney has been hired by the trustee and represents the trustee, not the beneficiary, and including a copy of the trust agreement for the beneficiary's file, if the beneficiary does not already have one.

Train staff on how to respond if a beneficiary contacts the office either requesting action or complaining about a trustee. A desire to be helpful might create an obligation, or even liability. Although it is hard to say no, make sure staff know how to handle these scenarios.

What obligation does the attorney have to notify beneficiaries of the bad acts of the trustee? ACTEC Commentaries suggest the need in some jurisdictions to notify the beneficiaries of the trustee's bad acts.[71] The Commentaries direct the attorney to consult Rules 1.6 and 1.8(b) in determining whether to make the disclosures.[72] But what about jurisdictions where disclosure is not allowed? The Commentaries suggest adding a provision to the engagement agreement that allows the attorney to make the disclosures.[73] Even in jurisdictions that permit disclosure, this provision in the engagement agreement has advantages. It cautions the trustee to realize that there are ramifications to the trustee's bad acts. Further, it adds weight to achieving the "intentions of the creator of the fiduciary estate to benefit the beneficiaries."[74]

---

that, contrary to the lawyer's own intention, a person, individually, or agents of an entity, on behalf of the entity, reasonably rely on the lawyer to provide legal services to that person or entity." (citations omitted)).

70. Lee, *supra* note 21, at 488–89. *See also* Ala. Ethics Op. 2010-03, *supra* note 10 (discussing the three theories); McLain, *supra* note 22, at 154–55 explains: "Upon commencement of representation, the lawyer should clarify with the personal representative the role of the lawyer, the scope of representation and the personal representative's responsibilities toward the lawyer, the court, the beneficiaries and other interested third parties." McLain also states:

> First and foremost, upon being hired by a personal representative to assist in the administration of an estate or trust, the lawyer should explain to the beneficiaries or other interested parties that the lawyer's sole client in the matter is the Personal Representative, individually. A lawyer who fails to do so could be in violation of Rule 4.3, *Ala. R. Prof. C.* . . .

Id. at 155.

71. ACTEC, *supra* note 30, at 38. The commentary offers: "In some jurisdictions a lawyer who represents a fiduciary generally with respect to the fiduciary estate may disclose to a court or to the beneficiaries acts or omissions by the fiduciary that might constitute a breach of fiduciary duty."

72. *Id.*

73. *Id.* ("lawyer engaged by a fiduciary may condition the representation upon the fiduciary's agreement that the creation of a lawyer-client relationship between them will not preclude the lawyer from disclosing to the beneficiaries of the fiduciary estate or to an appropriate court any actions of the fiduciary that might constitute a breach of fiduciary duty").

74. *Id.*

A. What about Privileged Information? Is That Protected from Disclosure?

Some, but not all, jurisdictions have recognized a fiduciary exception to attorney-client privilege.[75] This exception prevents "a fiduciary, such as a trustee of a trust, . . . from asserting the attorney-client privilege against beneficiaries on matters of trust administration."[76] The exception is recognized on two grounds, that the trustee is not the sole client, but instead is serving as a "proxy for the beneficiary," and that the trustee has a "duty to disclose all information related to trust management to the beneficiary."[77] The second ground has been viewed as "an instance of the attorney-client privilege giving way in the face of a competing legal principle, . . . the duty to disclose."[78] In *Murphy v. Gorman*,[79] a case of first impression in New Mexico, the question[80] of the fiduciary exception and attorney-client privilege was discussed in the context of a revocable trust.[81] The federal court noted that the trustee retained the attorney to represent himself, not himself *and* the beneficiary, concerning the dispute between the beneficiary and the trustee over the trust terms and trust administration.[82]

Canarelli v. Eighth Judicial District Court of Nevada[83] also considered whether Nevada would recognize the fiduciary exception to attorney-client privilege.[84] The Nevada Supreme Court noted that the Nevada legislature had previously adopted five exceptions to the attorney-client privilege but did not adopt the fiduciary exception.[85] The Nevada Supreme Court as a result specifically decided to not approve the fiduciary exception.[86] In discussing various arguments raised, the court recognized that a beneficiary typically can review the records and "books" of the trust, but if a beneficiary could see the

75. *See, e.g.*, Murphy v. Gorman, 271 F.R.D. 296, 305–09, 314–15 (D.N.M. 2010) (discussing, among other things the fiduciary exception). *See also* Huie v. DeShazo, 922 S.W.2d 920, 925 (Tex. 1996) (rejecting the "fiduciary exception" because it is not in the evidence code) ("trustee must fully disclose material facts regarding the administration of the trust, the attorney-client privilege protects confidential communications between the trustee and . . . attorney under Rule 503").

76. *Murphy*, 271 F.R.D. at 305–06 (citations omitted).

77. *Id.* at 306 (citations omitted).

78. *Id.* (citations omitted)

79. 271 F.R.D. 296.

80. *Id.*

81. *Id.* at 300–02, 308.

82. *Id.* at 317, 318.

83. 464 P.3d 114 (Nev. 2020).

84. *Id.* at 117. Two sets of documents were under consideration. The first were the prior trustee's notes from a conversation with the attorney and the second, the same trustee's notes from a meeting with the attorney, other trustees, opponents, and an appraiser.

85. *Id.*

86. *Id.*

attorney and trustee communications for situations where the trustee is in an adverse position with the beneficiary, it would cause the trustee to be reluctant to obtain legal advice[87] and attorneys may be hesitant to give "transparent advice."[88]

The Restatement (Third) of the Law Governing Lawyers section 84 provides an exception:

> In a proceeding in which a trustee of an express trust or similar fiduciary is charged with breach of fiduciary duties by a beneficiary, a communication otherwise within § 68 is nonetheless not privileged if the communication:
>
> (a) is relevant to the claimed breach; and
>
> (b) was between the trustee and a lawyer (or other privileged person within the meaning of § 70) who was retained to advise the trustee concerning the administration of the trust.[89]

In *Barnett Banks Trust Co. v. Compson*,[90] the trustee sued the brokerage firm and the widow of the settlor. The attorney for the trustee inquired whether privilege protects the documents. Although beneficiaries have to be kept reasonably informed by a trustee under Florida law, the court held that the "statute does not require disclosure of privileged materials concerning a pending lawsuit in which an individual, who happens to be a beneficiary, seeks to deplete, rather than return, trust assts."[91] The court determined that the widow, who counterclaimed, and, as such, "does not stand to benefit from the trustee's actions" in the litigation, as a result "is not the real client of the trustee's attorneys. The real client of the law firms is the trustee . . . [and the court found] that the attorney-client privilege, belonging to the trustee as client,

87. *Id.* at 122. The court was discussing the application of the common interest exception.
88. *Id.*
89. Restatement (Third) of the Law Governing Lawyers section 84 comment b explains:

Rationale. In litigation between a trustee of an express trust and beneficiaries of the trust charging breach of the trustee's fiduciary duties, the trustee cannot invoke the attorney-client privilege to prevent the beneficiaries from introducing evidence of the trustee's communications with a lawyer retained to advise the trustee in carrying out the trustee's fiduciary duties. The exception applies in suits brought directly by a beneficiary or by a representative of the beneficiary. It does not apply to communications between the trustee and a lawyer specifically retained by the trustee to represent, not the trust or the trustee with respect to executing trust duties, but the trustee in the trustee's personal capacity, such as to assist the trustee in a dispute with a beneficiary or to assert a right against the beneficiary.

The exception does not require the beneficiary to show good cause (compare § 85 [fiduciary within organization]). Nonetheless, the tribunal might enter a protective order to safeguard the interests of other beneficiaries or the trust against unnecessary disclosure.

90. 629 So. 2d 849 (Fla. Dist. Ct. App. 1993).
91. *Id.* at 851 (citations omitted).

prohibits disclosure of communications . . . absent any waiver."[92] Even though the law firm and the trustee had shared information with "aligned beneficiaries," that was not waiver of privilege since their "interests coincide with the trustees. The 'common interest' or 'joint defense' exception applies among the entities sharing common interests and their attorneys."[93]

VII. Always an Attorney Must Be Competent

Regardless of which of the five scenarios face the attorney, the attorney must always be competent. Model Rule 1.1 requires that the attorney be competent to handle the legal matter; "[a] lawyer shall provide competent representation to a client. Competent representation requires the legal knowledge, skill, thoroughness and preparation reasonably necessary for the representation." Comment [1] to Rule 1.1 is particularly applicable in the context of SNT practice. The comment provides:

> In determining whether a lawyer employs the requisite knowledge and skill in a particular matter, relevant factors include the relative complexity and specialized nature of the matter, the lawyer's general experience, the lawyer's training and experience in the field in question, the preparation and study the lawyer is able to give the matter and whether it is feasible to refer the matter to, or associate or consult with, a lawyer of established competence in the field in question. In many instances, the required proficiency is that of a general practitioner. *Expertise in a particular field of law may be required in some circumstances.*[94]

We point this out because of the complexity of the practice of special needs planning. In drafting the trust, the attorney must be cognizant of the trust law in the jurisdiction (both in drafting, funding, and even choice of law), as well as public benefits laws and regulations (federal and state), the Social Security Program Operations Manual System (POMS),[95] any applicable SSA regional pronouncements, and more. In our view, SNT practice is not for the faint of heart or the novice practitioner.

---

92. *Id.*

93. *Id.* For an excellent discussion on fiduciary representation, see Renée C. Lovelace, *Representing Fiduciaries: Guidance from NAELA's Aspirational Standards*, NAELA J. (Special Edition) 119 (2018).

94. Model Rules of Pro. Conduct r. 1.1 cmt. 1 (Am. Bar Ass'n 1983) (emphasis added).

95. The POMS is available at https://secure.ssa.gov/apps10/poms.nsf/Home?readform (last visited Nov. 25, 2022). As SSA describes them, the purpose of the POMS is to be the "primary source of information used by Social Security employees to process claims for Social Security benefits. The public version of POMS is identical to the version used by Social Security employees except that it does not include internal data entry and sensitive content instructions." *Id.*

Illustrative of this is *Redies v. Attorneys Liability Protection Society (ALPS)*,[96] a first-party SNT case. The beneficiary, injured in a bicycle accident, had a permanent conservator and a guardian.[97] The conservator sought advice from an attorney about the beneficiary's property in light of the beneficiary's mounting bills.[98] The attorney hired by the conservator had suggested selling off the beneficiary's assets, rather than recommending an SNT.[99] As the attorney for the beneficiary noted in a demand letter:

> Lawyers in particular, are obligated to know about the laws which are relevant to their client's case. . . . To diligently represent Ms. Redies, . . . [the attorney] had a duty to do sufficient research to learn about the Montana Self Sufficiency Trust statutes . . . [and the] failure to do so [resulted in] Redies' estate [being] quickly depleted [with her] now [living] in poverty.[100]

VIII. Conclusion

Fiduciary representation, just like a special needs planning practice, is not for the faint of heart. The takeaways from this chapter might be summarized as follows:

1. Review your state's rules of professional conduct and ethics opinions.
2. Download and read carefully the ACTEC Commentaries and the National Academy of Elder Law Attorneys (NAELA) Aspirational Standards.
3. Determine the scope of your practice—what are you willing to do?
4. Consider whether you are competent to handle the matter.
5. Determine whom you represent.
6. Make it clear to everyone whom you represent.
7. Be sure to use an engagement agreement that identifies whom you represent and the scope of representation. Take care to not alter the scope of representation accidentally.
8. In cases where you represent the trustee, include a proviso in the engagement agreement that if the trustee breaches the duty to beneficiaries, you will advise the beneficiaries, the court, and withdraw if the trustee does not remedy the breach within (x days).

---

96. 150 P.3d 930 (Mont. 2007).
97. *Id.* at 932.
98. *Id.* at 933.
99. *Id.*
100. *Id.* at 934. The suit was eventually settled. *Id.* at 935. The rest of the opinion is devoted to the beneficiary's claim against the ALPS. *Id.* at 935 *et seq.*

9. In cases where you represent the trustee, communicate with beneficiaries that you represent the trustee, not them, and what that means.
10. Document, document, document.
11. Train your staff so they do not inadvertently cause problems when trying to be helpful.

CHAPTER 3

Public Benefits

I. Introduction

This chapter is an overview of the largest public benefits programs for individuals with disabilities. Although many of the laws establishing these programs are federal laws, some programs have state-specific requirements. Therefore, it is important for every practitioner to review the state-specific regulations and rules in addition to the information covered here.

II. Various Programs

A. Supplemental Security Income

Supplemental Security Income (SSI) is a federal program that provides a monthly cash benefit to help people with disabilities who have little or no income and who need assistance meeting their basic needs for food and shelter.[1] To be eligible for the monthly cash benefit, a beneficiary must have limited income and limited assets. The monthly stipend can be reduced if a beneficiary receives income from sources other than SSI.

Often, the money is less important than the other major benefit of SSI: a beneficiary who receives SSI is also eligible for Medicaid. Even if, after all reductions are applied, a beneficiary only receives $1 in SSI, he or she is eligible for all Medicaid benefits. To a person without private health insurance and with ongoing medical expenses, the access to Medicaid is often more important than the SSI monthly cash benefit.

1. Soc. Sec. Admin. (SSA), *What Is Supplemental Security Income?*, https://www.ssa.gov/ssi/ (last visited Nov. 28, 2022). The SSI sources of law are the federal statute: Social Security Act § 1611 *et seq.*, 42 U.S.C. § 1382 *et seq.*; the federal regulations: 20 C.F.R. pt. 416 (2021); and the federal agency policies and procedures: SSA's Program Operations Manual System (POMS), https://secure.ssa.gov/apps10/ (last visited Nov. 28, 2022).

SSI is administered by the Social Security Administration (SSA) and is often confused with Social Security Disability Insurance (SSDI or SSD) and other benefits because some of those programs also have disability criteria. The major distinction between SSI and SSDI is that SSI is a needs-based program while SSDI is an insurance program that most workers access through paycheck withholdings in the event a disability renders them unable to work. Eligibility for SSDI requires completion of a certain work history (qualifying quarters) and a determination of disability. Financial need is not a factor for SSDI eligibility.

A person who has a disability and the requisite work history, but a small SSDI benefit, may be eligible for both programs and could receive SSI in addition to SSDI.

Most Social Security benefits are paid for by workers through the Social Security taxes. In contrast, SSI is paid for by general funds in the U.S. Treasury.[2] The program rules are published in the Social Security Handbook and it includes the provisions of the Social Security Act, regulations issued under the act, and precedential case decisions (rulings).[3]

1. Eligibility

To qualify for SSI, a beneficiary must be a citizen of the United States, must be determined to be disabled, blind, or at least 65 years old, and must meet the financial limits on both income and assets.[4]

a. "Categorical" Requirements: Aged, Blind, or Disabled

i. Disabled

The SSA defines disability for adults as "unable to engage in any substantial gainful activity because of a medically determinable physical or mental impairment that is either expected to result in death or that has lasted or can be expected to last for a continuous period of at least 12 months."[5] In 2021, an adult who is not blind and is earning more than $1,310 per month is able to

2. SSA, Social Security Handbook § 2105, http://www.ssa.gov/OP_Home/handbook/handbook.21/handbook-2105.html (last visited Nov. 28, 2022).

3. SSA, Social Security Handbook preface, https://www.ssa.gov/OP_Home/handbook/handbook-preface.html (last visited Nov. 28, 2022). More information can be found at https://www.benefits.gov/ (last visited Nov. 28, 2022).

4. *See* SSA, *Supplemental Security Income (SSI) Eligibility Requirements,* https://www.ssa.gov/ssi/text-eligibility-ussi.htm (last visited Nov. 28, 2022).

5. 42 U.S.C. § 1382c(a)(3)(A); 20 C.F.R. § 416.905 (2021); *see* SSA, *supra* note 4.

perform "substantial gainful activity," and thus does not meet the definition of "disabled."[6]

A child under age 18 is disabled if he or she has "a medically determinable physical or mental impairment or combination of impairments that causes marked and severe functional limitations, and that can be expected to cause death or that has lasted or can be expected to last for a continuous period of not less than 12 months."[7]

"Marked and severe functional limitations" caused by impairments can be if the impairment meets, medically equals, or functionally equals the severity of a set of criteria for an impairment in the "Listing of Impairments."[8] A person's "impairment(s) is medically equivalent to a listed impairment . . . if it is at least equal in severity and duration to the criteria of any listed impairment."[9]

ii. Aged

A person age 65 or older who meets the other income and citizenship requirements is eligible for SSI. A person eligible for both SSI and SSDI can be dually eligible. While SSDI provides Medicare and an income subsidy, SSI provides Medicaid plus an income subsidy. While Medicare provides short-term hospital and out-patient benefits, only Medicaid provides certain benefits like long-term support services.

iii. Blindness

To meet the definition of "blind," a person does not need to have total blindness. The requirement is for central vision acuity of 20/200 or less in the better eye with the use of correcting lenses or a visual field limitation in the better eye, such that the widest diameter of the visual field subtends an angle no

6. *See* SSA, Fact Sheet: 2021 Social Security Changes, https://www.ssa.gov/news/press/factsheets/colafacts2021.pdf. This standard is more difficult to meet when compared to the standards of most disability insurance policies. For example, the SSA will not provide benefits if:

- The person is partially but not totally disabled
- The person is unable to do his or her previous job (e.g., teaching or driving a truck) but is qualified for a much lower-paying job
- There is no work available locally but there is work available somewhere else in the United States

7. 20 C.F.R. § 416.906 (2021); *see* SSA, *Child Disability Starter Kit—Fact Sheet*, https://www.ssa.gov/disability/disability_starter_kits_child_factsheet.htm (last visited Nov. 28, 2022).

8. 20 C.F.R. pt. 404, subpt. P, app. 1 (2021), https://www.ssa.gov/OP_Home/cfr20/404/404-app-p01.htm (last visited Nov. 28, 2022).

9. *Id.* § 416.926(a). Section 416.926(a) explains further: "By 'functionally equal the listings,' we mean that your impairment(s) must be of listing-level severity; *i.e.*, it must result in 'marked' limitations in two domains of functioning or an 'extreme' limitation in one domain, as explained in this section."

greater than 20 degrees.[10] In 2023, a blind person earning more than $2,260 per month is presumptively able to perform "substantial gainful activity" and does not meet the definition of "disabled."[11]

b. Residency

To qualify for SSI, a person must be a resident of one of the 50 states of the United States, the District of Columbia, or the Northern Mariana Islands. Puerto Rico residents are excluded from eligibility.[12] Absence from the United States for 30 consecutive days disqualifies the client for SSI benefits and the beneficiary cannot regain qualification until he or she has again resided in the United States for at least 30 days.[13]

i. Citizen or Entitled Alien

Only U.S. citizens—by birth or naturalization—are eligible for public benefits. Non-citizens are ineligible for federal public benefits, with the exception of certain "qualified aliens."[14]

A "qualified alien" is a non-citizen who is any of the following:

- A permanent resident alien
- An asylee
- A refugee
- An alien paroled into the United States for at least a year
- An alien whose deportation is withheld under 8 U.S.C. § 1253
- A person granted conditional entry under 8 U.S.C. § 1153(a)(7)
- A Cuban or Haitian entrant[15]

A "qualified alien" may be eligible for SSI, if he or she meets any of the following requirements:

- Entered the United States before August 22, 1996 (an alien entering the United States on or after that date is ineligible unless he or she falls into one of the categories below)[16]
- For the first seven years after the non-citizen was granted one of the following statuses:

10. *See* SSA, *Supplemental Security Income (SSI) Eligibility Requirements—What Is "Blindness" for an Adult or Child?*, http://www.ssa.gov/ssi/text-eligibility-ussi.htm#blind (last visited Nov. 28, 2022).

11. *See* SSA, *Fact Sheet: 2023 Social Security Changes*, https://www.ssa.gov/news/press/factsheets/colafacts2023.pdf.

12. *See* 20 C.F.R. §§ 416.202, 416.1603 (2021). Part 416 of the C.F.R. can be accessed through the SSA's website at https://www.ssa.gov/OP_Home/cfr20/416/416-0000.htm (last visited Nov. 28, 2022).

13. *See* 20 C.F.R. § 416.1327 (2021).

14. 8 U.S.C. § 1611(a).

15. *Id.* § 1641(b).

16. *Id.* § 1612(a)(2)(E).

- An asylee
- A refugee
- Alien whose deportation has been withheld
- Certain Cuban or Haitian entrants
- Certain Amerasian immigrants[17]
- Certain Native Americans[18]
- Non-citizen children of a battered parent[19]
- Active duty troops, their spouses, their un-remarried surviving spouses, unmarried dependent children, and honorably discharged veterans meeting the minimum service requirement (generally, 24 months active duty)[20]
- A permanent resident who has worked 40 qualifying quarters and earned Social Security coverage, or who can be credited with such quarters due to the work of a parent or spouse under certain specified rules[21]

c. Income

SSI is a needs-based program: recipients are only eligible if they have limited income and limited resources. The SSA has separated the eligibility determination into two limitations. The first is income, or the value of everything a person receives during a given period of time (calendar month).[22]

The SSA publishes the thresholds every year. For 2021, an unmarried person had to have less than $841 per month of countable income to qualify for SSI. A married couple's countable income totals had to be less than $1,261 per month for either spouse to be eligible. The first $20 of income is not counted and, therefore, these numbers were sometimes expressed as $861 and $1,281, respectively. These numbers change annually.

17. *Id.* § 1612(a)(2)(A).
18. *Id.* § 1612(a)(2)(G).
19. *Id.* § 1612(c).
20. *Id.* § 1612(a)(2)(C).
21. *Id.* § 1612(a)(2)(B). The general rule prohibiting aliens from receiving public benefits does have a few important exceptions:

- Legal immigrants residing in the United States who were receiving SSI as of August 22, 1996, continue to be eligible.
- Immigrants who were legally in the United States on August 22, 1996, retain their potential SSI eligibility (i.e., they are not subject to the "qualified alien" rules summarized at the beginning of this subsection, which in effect apply only to persons who were not legally in the United States on August 22, 1996). (*See* 8 U.S.C. § 1612(a)(2)(E), (F).)

Aliens receiving SSI only because of the August 22, 1996, exceptions are not eligible for the Supplemental Nutrition Assistance Program (SNAP). (*See* 8 U.S.C. § 1612(a)(1), (a)(2)(E), (a)(2)(F).) However, all aliens receiving SSI are eligible for Medicaid. (*See* 8 U.S.C. § 1612(b)(2)(F).)

22. The income rules for SSI eligibility are located in 20 C.F.R. Part 416, Subpart K.

Some states have a state-sponsored "SSI supplement" that gives SSI beneficiaries more than the federally mandated maximum. The SSA definition of "income" is different than the Internal Revenue Service definition of "income" for income tax rules. Where a cash gift is excluded from the definition of "income" for tax purposes, gifts *are* income for SSI purposes. The SSI rules and exclusions distinguish between "earned" income and "unearned" income. All income reduces a beneficiary's monthly SSI benefit and changes in income and corresponding reductions must be carefully reviewed and calculated. As previously mentioned, if after all reductions are implemented, a person is still eligible to receive at least $1 of SSI benefits, he or she will continue to be eligible to receive *all* Medicaid benefits.

i. Direct Income

Any money a beneficiary receives directly will be considered income—either earned or unearned—and will reduce the SSI benefits on a dollar-for-dollar basis after exclusions. If a beneficiary receives direct income high enough to reduce his or her SSI benefits to nothing, then both the beneficiary's SSI *and* Medicaid benefits will be jeopardized because the Medicaid benefits depend on SSI eligibility.

Additionally, if a beneficiary receives anything that is equivalent to cash (e.g., a winning lottery ticket, bus ticket, or postage stamps), it will be counted as direct income.[23]

(a). Earned Income

Earned income includes the gross wages of employees and net earnings from self-employment.[24] The first $65 of earned income is excluded from countable income, as is one-half of the remaining earned income each month. The first $30 of infrequent or irregular income is excluded for the SSI income calculation. Additionally, there are certain work expenses for beneficiaries who are blind or disabled that can be excluded from the income calculation. The general $20/month income exclusion can be applied to earned income to the extent it has not been applied to unearned income.[25]

(b). Unearned Income

"Unearned" income is all income that does not meet the definition of "earned" income as described earlier. Unearned income includes annuity payments, dividends, prizes and gifts, and inheritances, among other payments. There are several exclusions for unearned income. Some exclusions include:

23. 20 C.F.R. § 416.1121 (2021).
24. 42 U.S.C. § 1382a(a)(1); 20 C.F.R. § 416.1110 (2021).
25. 42 U.S.C. § 1382a(b); 20 C.F.R. §§ 416.1102, 416.1112 (2021).

- Certain federal assistance payments (including Supplemental Nutrition Assistance Program (SNAP))
- Up to $60 of irregular or infrequent unearned income
- One-third of child support payments

ii. Not Income

Some receipts of a beneficiary are "not income" because they are not cash, nor are they food or shelter. Examples of benefits that are "not income" include payments made by a third party or trust for certain kinds of medical care and social services. Also, bills paid by someone other than the beneficiary are not income. However, if the beneficiary receives any asset because of payment from some other source, the value he or she receives is counted under the "in-kind" income rules discussed in the following subsection.

iii. In-Kind Support and Maintenance

When a beneficiary receives food or shelter that is furnished or paid for by any source other than his or her own money, SSA defines that as "in-kind support and maintenance" (ISM).

It is safe to provide the beneficiary with any asset other than food or shelter because the value of any other non-cash item (other than food or shelter) is *not* counted as income if the item will become an exempt asset when it is retained into the following month.

As a result, a beneficiary can receive any exempt asset (such as books, furniture, or recreational equipment) without an impact to his or her income. For example, if a beneficiary receives a television as a gift, it will not be counted as income because the definition of ISM only includes the receipt of food and shelter.

The beneficiary's receipt, or right to receive, food or shelter as ISM will reduce his or her SSI benefits because SSI benefits are specifically intended to pay for a person's food and shelter and if that person receives those goods or services from another source, then less SSI income is needed to provide for the basics needs. As a result, if any source other than SSI or the beneficiary's own resources are used to pay rent, grocery bills, or meals (e.g., a restaurant meal), the beneficiary receives ISM and SSI is reduced.

There are fine distinctions between allowable in-kind income and countable ISM. For example, a trustee may pay for some entertainment expenses but not others (e.g., a movie pass but not a restaurant meal, because that is food).

If a beneficiary receives ISM, his or her SSI benefits will be reduced, but not on a dollar-for-dollar basis as with cash. Instead, the formula Social Security uses to reduce the SSI benefits for ISM depends on two further factors: the household and living arrangement of the SSI recipient.

(a). Presumed Maximum Value Rule

If the beneficiary lives in his or her *own household*, or lives in someone else's household but does not receive *both food and shelter* from that household, then the presumed maximum value (PMV) rule applies. In general, under the PMV rule, the value of the ISM is the *lesser* of

a. its actual value; or
b. its "presumed" value of one-third of the federal benefit portion (in 2023: one-third of $841 was $280.33).[26]

Note there is a balancing of the ISM under this rule, and the reduction is the *lesser* of the actual amount or the "presumed value."

For example, if someone directly pays the beneficiary's rent, his or her SSI benefits will only be reduced by one-third, even if the rent payment was $800. One dramatic result of this rule is that someone could buy a house for the beneficiary and the beneficiary only would lose one-third of his or her monthly SSI benefits in the month the house is given to the beneficiary because the "presumed value" (one-third of SSI check) is less than the actual value of the house. The reduction would occur only in the one month the beneficiary receives the house. It would be considered ISM for "shelter" in the month of receipt. And in the following month, the home would be an exempt asset (discussed further in subsection d.i).

Ownership of a home by the beneficiary, however, may cause some greater problems. For example, ISM would arise in each month someone other than the beneficiary pays the mortgage payments, property taxes, insurance required by the mortgage lender, or utilities (garbage, water, gas, and electricity). Interestingly, *no* ISM exists if someone other than the beneficiary pays for the beneficiary's phone, cable television, or voluntary home insurance—these are not considered "shelter" by Social Security.

On the other hand, if the *actual* value of the ISM is below one-third (e.g., beneficiary receives only one restaurant meal), then the SSI reduction can be adjusted from one-third to reflect the actual value of the ISM the beneficiary actually received. One-third is only a "presumed" value.

(b). One-Third Reduction Rule

The PMV rule does not apply if the beneficiary lives in someone else's household and receives *both food and shelter* from that household. Instead, the one-third reduction rule applies and the federal benefit portion of the beneficiary's

26. 20 C.F.R. § 416.1140(a)–(b) (2021); POMS SI 00835.300.A–.C.

SSI benefits is reduced by a flat one-third of the federal benefit rate ($280.33 in 2023).[27]

The exception to the one-third reduction rule is when the beneficiary lives in the household of someone whose income may be "deemed" to the beneficiary. ISM is not counted in this instance because that person's income is already "deemed" to the beneficiary. For example, the SSI income calculation of a minor applicant who is living in the household of a parent includes certain income belonging to the parent and therefore the parent's provision of food and shelter does not further reduce the child's SSI payment.

iv. Deeming of Income

For SSI eligibility, the income of certain relatives of a beneficiary is "deemed" the client's income.[28] Income is deemed to the SSI recipient from:

- An ineligible spouse living in the same household
- An ineligible parent, or parent's spouse, living in the same household with a client under age 18
- A non-citizen client's sponsor (i.e., someone who signed an affidavit of support for the alien's admission to the United States) (certain limitations and exceptions apply)

v. Child Support

Cash child support given to the child or to another on the child's behalf counts as income for the month in which it was received. If the child is (1) unmarried, (2) under age 22, and (3) a student, only two-thirds of the actual amount counts as income.[29] Otherwise, child support is counted dollar for dollar.

d. Resources

The third eligibility criteria for SSI is that a beneficiary must be under the resource limit. The SSA defines "resources" to include "cash, other liquid assets, and any real or personal property that an individual (or spouse, if any) owns and could convert to cash or spouse owns and can convert to cash." An unmarried SSI beneficiary cannot have more than $2,000 in resources. A married couple when one or both spouses are SSI recipients cannot have more than $3,000 in resources.[30]

27. 20 C.F.R. § 416.1131 (2021); POMS SI 00835.200.A.1.
28. POMS SI 01320.001. For specific rules, see 20 C.F.R. §§ 416.1160–.1169 (2021).
29. 42 U.S.C. § 1382a(a)(2)(E), (b)(1), (b)(9).
30. 20 C.F.R. § 416.1205 (2021). While income limits for SSI have adjusted annually, the resource limits for SSI have not changed since 1989.

i. Exceptions

Not every item owned by an SSI beneficiary is a countable resource. Some of the most valuable assets that an SSI beneficiary may own could be exempt while determining SSI resource eligibility. For instance, the following assets are not included in the resource calculation for SSI eligibility:

- The entire value of the beneficiary's primary residence, without limit, including all contiguous acreage.[31]
- "Household goods" and "personal effects" are not resources.[32] Personal effects are items ordinarily worn or carried by the beneficiary or having an "intimate relation to" the beneficiary. Jewelry, including wedding and engagement rings, personal care items, prosthetic devices, and educational or recreational items such as books or musical instruments are considered personal effects. Items acquired or held "for their value or as an investment" are not personal effects and will be included in the resource calculation. Examples of items that might not be "personal effects" include "[g]ems, jewelry that is not worn or held for family significance, or collectibles."[33]
- One vehicle used for transportation of the beneficiary or a member of the beneficiary's household.[34]

ii. Deeming of Resources

In certain cases, resources of other household members are "deemed" the beneficiary's just as income can be deemed. For example:

- All resources of the SSI beneficiary's spouse when the spouse is living in the same household as the beneficiary[35]
- Resources of the beneficiary's parent(s) in excess of $2,000, or parent and the parent's spouse together in excess of $3,000, if the beneficiary is under age 18 and living in the same household with a parent
- Certain resources of an alien's sponsor[36]

31. *Id.* § 416.1212.
32. *Id.* § 416.1216.
33. *Id.*; 70 Fed. Reg. 6,340, 6,342 (Feb. 7, 2005).
34. 20 C.F.R. § 416.1218 (2021); 70 Fed. Reg. 6,340, 6,343 (Feb. 7, 2005).
35. 20 C.F.R. § 416.1202(a) (2021).
36. *Id.* § 416.1204.

2. Benefits

a. Cash Benefits

An SSI beneficiary with no other income receives the monthly "federal benefit rate" ($841 for a single individual or $1,261 for a married couple with both spouses eligible in 2023).[37] Countable income, as explained earlier, reduces the amount of SSI cash benefit dollar for dollar.

b. Medicaid Eligibility

SSI beneficiaries are automatically eligible for the comprehensive medical benefits of the Medicaid program.[38] These benefits are often more important than the monthly cash benefit.

3. Transfer Rules

A beneficiary may be subject to a period of ineligibility for transferring certain assets or resources prior to applying for SSI because the SSA imposes a transfer penalty on such transactions. The transfer penalty penalizes transfers of assets or resources—subject to certain exceptions—made during a "look-back period." The look-back period is calculated starting at the application date or the date of transfer (whichever is later) and "looking back" a certain number of months. For SSI, the look-back period is 36 months prior to application.

When a beneficiary applies for SSI, the beneficiary must disclose the existence of any uncompensated transfers made within the look-back period.[39] If the transfers were made prior to the look-back period, there is no penalty, regardless of how much was transferred, and the beneficiary does not need to disclose transfers made outside of the look-back period. If transfers were made during the look-back period, those transfers may be subject to a "transfer penalty." The penalty starts on the date of transfer and the duration of ineligibility is determined by dividing the total uncompensated value of the transferred resources by the maximum monthly SSI benefit effective on the date of application.[40]

---

37. *See* SSA, *supra* note 6.

38. *See* SSA, *Supplemental Security Income (SSI) Overview*, https://www.ssa.gov/ssi/text-over-ussi.htm (last visited Nov. 28, 2022).

39. 42 U.S.C. § 1382b(c)(1)(A); Foster Care Independence Act of 1999, Pub. L. No. 106-169, § 206, 113 Stat. 1822; *see also* 20 C.F.R. § 416.1240 (2021).

40. For example, if an application is filed in the year 2021, a transfer of $2,000 on June 14, 2021, will result in a penalty period of $2,000 ÷ $794 = 2.51, which is rounded down to two months. Ineligibility will begin the first date of a calendar month and end on the last day of the second calendar month.

The maximum penalty period for SSI is 36 months from the date of the transfer.

Among transfers that are not penalized are the following:

- Transfers to a child who is blind or has a disability or to a trust (including an "under-65 special needs trust" (SNT) under 42 U.S.C. § 1396p(d)(4) or to an Achieving a Better Life Experience (ABLE) Act account),[41] established solely for the benefit of the transferor's child who is blind or has a disability
- Transfers to a trust established solely for the transferor if he or she is under age 65 and has a disability and the trust is created under 42 U.S.C. § 1396p(d)(4)(a), (c) (self-settled under-65 SNTs and pooled trusts)
- Transfers proven by the individual to have been transferred exclusively for a purpose other than to qualify for SSI
- Social Security may also waive denial of eligibility for a transfer on a finding that it would cause an "undue hardship" under criteria established by the agency[42]

4. Application

To receive SSI benefits, a beneficiary must file an application. A beneficiary is not entitled to cash benefits until the application is filed and all eligibility criteria are met. However, a beneficiary may be entitled to Medicaid retroactively for the month of application and three prior months if all other requirements for eligibility have been met for that time period.

B. SSDI

A person who has paid into the Social Security system through federal withholdings and who is unable to work due to a disability may be eligible for SSDI. Eligible beneficiaries receive a monthly cash benefit and Medicare health care coverage.

---

41. According to Shari Nichols, attorney at Texas Health and Human Services Commission, citing 42 U.S.C. § 1369p(c)(2)(B)(III), transfers to an ABLE Account to a disabled child will not result in a penalty period to the donor, whereas transfers to an ABLE account to a non-disabled individual will result in a transfer penalty to the donor. For a complete discussion on ABLE accounts, see Stephen W. Dale's ABLE Act Update, presented at the 2018 Special Needs Trust Conference in February 2018, which is available at https://utcle.org/ecourses/OC7096 (last visited Nov. 28, 2022).

42. 42 U.S.C. § 1382b(c)(1)(C)(iv).

1. Work History

Eligibility for SSI depends on a beneficiary's work history: whether the beneficiary paid Social Security taxes on sufficient income during certain time periods. If a beneficiary's work history includes employment under the Social Security system for at least ten years and if the beneficiary has had such employment for at least 20 of the 40 preceding calendar quarters, he or she will meet the work history requirement. Beneficiaries who have a disability that begins prior to age 31 are eligible with less work experience.[43]

2. Disability

A beneficiary must be unable to engage in substantial gainful activity due to a medically determinable physical or mental impairment that can be expected to (or has lasted for) a continuous period of at least 12 months.[44] A beneficiary is not entitled to benefits for the first five months from the date of the disability onset.

3. Benefits

As an SSDI recipient, a beneficiary is entitled to a monthly payment that is determined based on contributions to the Social Security system. A beneficiary can obtain an estimate of SSDI benefits by signing Form SSA-7004-SM-OP1 or creating an account online with the SSA.[45]

Eligibility for SSDI is unlike SSI in that the amount of monthly cash benefit a beneficiary is entitled to receive does not depend on the amount of income a beneficiary receives from other sources. There is no asset limit for SSDI, either. Even the wealthiest beneficiaries can qualify if they meet the disability and contribution requirements.

The beneficiary does not receive a monthly cash benefit for the first five months of disability but can receive a lump-sum payment for up to 12 months before the date of application filing.[46]

A beneficiary also receives Medicare benefits once eligible for SSDI. The Medicare benefits, however, do not start until 24 months after a beneficiary is entitled to receive monthly SSDI cash payments. This Medicare waiting period does not apply for beneficiaries with end-stage renal disease. Beneficiaries with

---

43. SSA, Disability Benefits (2022), https://www.ssa.gov/pubs/EN-05-10029.pdf.

44. 42 U.S.C. § 423(d)(1)(A). See Section II.A.1 for a definition of "substantial gainful activity."

45. This form is available at https://www.ssa.gov/forms/ssa-7004.pdf. A beneficiary can create an account at https://www.ssa.gov/myaccount/ (last visited Nov. 28, 2022).

46. 20 C.F.R. § 404.621 (2021).

end-stage renal disease are eligible for Medicare Part A after three months from the beginning of dialysis and persons with amyotrophic lateral sclerosis (ALS) are eligible for Medicare immediately.[47]

a. Medicaid Benefits

The term "Medicaid" generally applies to all benefits provided under title XIX of the Social Security Act, codified at 42 U.S.C. § 1396 *et seq*. Medicaid includes a host of programs, some of which are state specific. Traditional Medicaid benefits are available to all SSI beneficiaries. Other Medicaid programs may also be available to beneficiaries of Children and Pregnant Women Medicaid, Medicaid Buy-In, Medicaid Buy-In for Children, and beneficiaries of Medicaid Long Term Care who are not eligible for Medicare.

i. Eligibility

Most Medicaid beneficiaries access Medicaid through eligibility for another program that includes Medicaid as a benefit, for instance:

- SSI
- Temporary Assistance for Needy Families (TANF)
- Children's Medicaid
- Pregnant Women's Medicaid

It is also provided to beneficiaries of Nursing Home Medicaid in addition to paying for nursing home care and related services when Medicare does not cover their acute-care needs.

Low-income Medicare beneficiaries who meet certain income and resource limits may be eligible for Medicare Savings Programs—sometimes referred to as the Qualified Medicare Beneficiary (QMB) and related programs—which pay for Medicare premiums, deductibles, and co-pays. Medicare beneficiaries who are eligible for the Medicare Savings Programs and for other Medicaid programs are often referred to as dually eligible. Eligibility for the QMB program or the Specified Low-Income Medicare Beneficiary (SLMB) program does not, however, automatically confer eligibility for the full range of regular Medicaid benefits.

Beneficiaries of home or community care programs for the aged and disabled may not be eligible for all the benefits of regular Medicaid but can receive some important medical benefits, which vary depending on each particular program.

47. 42 U.S.C. § 1395c; 42 C.F.R. § 406.13(c), (e)(2) (2021); 42 U.S.C. § 426(h); POMS DI 11036.001.

Medicaid is a comprehensive medical assistance program that covers health care costs. Medicaid does not require payment of premiums, deductibles, and co-payments in the same way that Medicare does.

The federal government sets some requirements in federal Medicaid legislation and rules; each state, however, administers the programs and sets its own laws and regulations. For instance, Texas legislation generally requires that the Texas Medicaid program provide the minimum necessary to obtain federal matching funds, with some flexibility for providing additional benefits if available funding permits. Other states have expanded Medicaid and offer additional benefits or extended eligibility.

Generally, Medicaid is a payer of last resort. A provider must, therefore, bill private insurance, Medicare, and other parties before billing Medicaid.

b. Medicare

i. Eligibility

U.S. citizens become eligible for Medicare at age 65. There is not an income or asset limit for Medicare, so even the country's most wealthy can receive Medicare benefits. All beneficiaries who are eligible for Social Security retirement benefits or for railroad retirement benefits become eligible for Medicare at age 65, regardless of whether they begin receiving the monthly payments before, at, or after age 65. Medicare also provides benefits to dependents and survivors of an insured worker.

(a). Work Requirements

To be automatically eligible, an individual must work a certain number of quarters in "covered employment." For most, this is usually 40 quarters (ten years) of covered employment. Those who are not automatically eligible may enroll by paying additional premiums.

(b). Eligibility in Connection with Social Security and Railroad Retirement Disability Benefits

An SSDI, Retirement, Survivors, and Disability Insurance (RSDI), or Railroad Retirement Disability (RRDB) beneficiary is eligible for Medicare after 24 months of entitlement to benefits under those programs. However, persons with end-stage renal disease can qualify for Medicare after a three-month waiting period, and persons with ALS are eligible immediately at the date of onset of disability.

ii. Benefits

Medicare is divided into Part A (hospital benefits) and Part B (physicians, tests, medical equipment, etc.). It is important to know whether a particular service is covered under Part A or Part B because some beneficiaries only receive benefits under one part.

Medicare Part C (also called a "Medicare Advantage" plan) is an alternative to traditional coverage under Part A and Part B with various combinations of managed care and private-pay service delivery. Medicare Advantage plans provide care via health maintenance organizations (HMOs) or through preferred provider organizations (PPOs). In 2021, 42 percent of Medicare recipients were enrolled in a Medicare Advantage plan, according to the Kaiser Family Foundation (KFF).[48]

Medicare Part D offers all Medicare beneficiaries a variety of prescription drug plans with monthly premiums, a yearly deductible, and co-pays that all vary, depending on the plan.

iii. Medicare Part A

Part A covers inpatient hospital services, post-hospital extended care services, home health services, and hospice services. A Medicare beneficiary is eligible to receive hospital coverage for 90 days per spell of illness, plus a lifetime reserve of 60 days of hospital care. Beneficiaries eligible for Medicare in connection with Social Security or railroad retirement benefits pay nothing for Medicare Part A. Ineligible individuals may purchase Part A by paying monthly premiums.[49]

Medicare beneficiaries must pay an annual deductible for Medicare Part A inpatient hospital services ($1,600 in 2023). The beneficiary must also pay co-payments of $389 per day for the 61st through 90th day of hospitalization for each benefit period, and $778 per "lifetime reserve day."

Medicare Part A coverage includes up to 100 days in a skilled nursing facility when the beneficiary:

- Requires and receives "skilled care" (not "custodial" or "intermediary") "as a practical matter," in an inpatient facility on a daily basis
- Has been admitted to the skilled nursing facility immediately after a hospital stay of at least three consecutive days, not counting the day of discharge
- Was admitted to the nursing facility within 30 days after discharge from the hospital unless it was medically inappropriate

48. Meredith Freed et al., *Medicare Advantage in 2022: Enrollment Update and Key Trends*, KFF (Aug. 25, 2022), https://www.kff.org/medicare/issue-brief/medicare-advantage-in-2021-enrollment-update-and-key-trends/.

49. The Part A premium in 2021 was $471 per month. One of the Medicare Savings Programs (QMB, SLMB, Qualified Individual-1 (QI-1), and Qualified Disabled and Working Individuals (QDWI)) may pay the Medicare Part A and Part B premiums for those who meet the income and resource requirements.

During the 100 days of nursing facility coverage under Part A, Medicare pays the full cost for the first 20 days of skilled care. The beneficiary pays a co-pay for days 21 through 100 ($194.50 per day in 2023). If a beneficiary has a Medicare Supplement Insurance policy (also called Medigap), the co-payment is usually covered by Medicare Supplement Insurance.

Medicare Part A covers 100 visits during a home health spell of illness. For those with Part A and Part B, after an individual exhausts 100 visits of Part A, Part B finances the balance of the home health spell of illness. To qualify for Medicare home health services, the individual must be:

- Confined to a home
- Under care of a doctor
- Receiving services under a plan of care established and periodically reviewed by a physician with services provided by or through a Medicare-certified home health agency
- In need of one of the following: intermittent skilled nursing care, physical therapy, speech-language pathology services, or occupational therapy

Hospice services are provided to beneficiaries with a terminal illness who request comfort measures instead of pursuing treatment. Medicare Part A hospice coverage includes services for supportive and palliative assistance for terminally ill beneficiaries. To receive Medicare hospice care, a beneficiary must:

- Have a certification of life expectancy of six months or less if not treated
- Elect to receive hospice services and waive Medicare services that related to treatment of the terminal condition

The beneficiary is entitled to two 90-day periods of hospice care and an unlimited number of subsequent periods of 60 days. Each 60-day renewal is contingent on the required recertification of terminal illness at the start of each benefit period. The election for hospice care may be revoked at any time.

iv. Medicare Part B

Medicare Part B includes physicians' services, medical equipment, ambulance services, outpatient physical and speech therapy, and certain preventative services.

All beneficiaries eligible for Medicare Part A are also eligible for Medicare Part B. Unlike Medicare Part A, which is free, however, Medicare Part B has requirements for premiums, co-pays, and deductibles. The Part B premium for 2023 started at $164.90 and increased for beneficiaries with annual income of more than $97,000 (individual return) or $194,000 (joint return). Premium payments are based on the two years before the year in question.[50] This premium may be paid by the QMB/SLMB/Qualified Individual-1 (QI-1) programs for eligible beneficiaries.

If a beneficiary is over the age of 65 and still working, he or she may be covered by a group insurance policy. The beneficiary is receiving Part A and needs to decide whether to also take Part B (requires payment of a premium). The issue may also arise when a retired person has health insurance through a spouse who is still working.

It is possible that the retired spouse of a currently working person may be covered by a group health plan (GHP) through the working spouse's company. The GHP coverage may be free or cost less than Part B premiums. A beneficiary then must decide if he or she should take Part B and pay monthly premiums even when the beneficiary has coverage under a GHP. The monthly cost of the benefit is not the only reason that potential beneficiaries might be concerned about this question. If a beneficiary does not sign up for Part B when first eligible, he or she may have to pay a late enrollment penalty.[51] That penalty comes as increased premiums for as long as the beneficiary is enrolled in Part B. The monthly premium for Part B may go up 10 percent for each full 12-month period that a beneficiary could have had Part B but did not sign up for it.[52] If a person does not enroll at initial enrollment, he or she may also have to wait until the general enrollment period (from January 1 to March 31) to enroll in Part B, and coverage starts July 1 of that year.[53]

Spouses and workers over age 65 who are covered by a GHP are protected from the increase in Part B premiums based on failure to enroll in Part B during their initial enrollment period because they are allowed a special enrollment period (SEP).[54] The SEP allows a beneficiary to enroll any time during an eight-month period that begins when he or she leaves the GHP.

There may be a more important reason for a retired spouse or currently working individual over age 65 to enroll in Part B other than to save the monthly premium. If the GHP has fewer than 20 employees, then the GHP is secondary to Medicare.[55] In cases where the employer has fewer than 20

50. For 2023 premium calculations, the Centers for Medicare and Medicaid Services (CMS) used 2021 income (the tax return filed in 2022).

51. 42 C.F.R. § 408.22 (2021).

52. *Id.*

53. Example: A client's initial enrollment period ended September 30, 2009. She waited to sign up for Part B until the general enrollment period in March 2012. Her Part B premium penalty is 20 percent. (While she waited a total of 30 months to sign up, this included only two full 12-month periods.) She will have to pay this penalty for as long as she has Part B.

54. 42 C.F.R. § 407.20(b) (2021).

55. *Id.* § 411.100.

employees the beneficiary should contact the human resources department of his or her employer and determine if Medicare has primary responsibility for coverage. If Medicare is primary, then the beneficiary should sign up for Part B. If the GHP has more than 19 employees, then it is likely that the best decision is to delay enrollment for Part B.

An additional reason to sign up for Part B upon turning age 65: federal law grants a "guarantee issue" period for Medicare Supplement Insurance policy coverage for six months upon a beneficiary reaching age 65.[56] Delay in seeking Medigap coverage after that time could subject a beneficiary to exclusion for preexisting conditions.

Part B preventative care includes a one-time initial wellness physical exam, called the "Welcome to Medicare" preventative visit to new enrollees within 12 months of Medicare Part B enrollment and can also include screening blood tests for early detection of cardiovascular diseases and diabetes screening for beneficiaries at risk.

The Part B deductible for the 2023 calendar year was $226. Beneficiaries eligible for the QMB program, SLMB program, or QI-1 program will have their premiums and deductible paid through those programs.

After the deductible is met, Part B requires a co-payment of 20 percent of the Medicare-approved amount. This co-payment can also be paid by the QMB program for eligible beneficiaries. A provider who "accepts assignment" can bill no more than 20 percent of the Medicare-approved charge, plus the $226 annual deductible. A provider who does not accept assignment can also bill for an additional amount, not to exceed 15 percent of the approved charge.

Medicare Supplement Insurance and HMOs pay varying amounts of the Medicare co-payments and deductibles; and HMOs sometimes provide non-covered items, such as limited prescription medications.

v. Medicare Part D

Medicare Part D is an optional program for Medicare beneficiaries, but there is a late enrollment penalty for those who choose not to enroll when first eligible when beneficiaries do not otherwise have prescription drug coverage as good as or better than Part D.

A person enrolling after his or her first enrollment period will not be subject to the late enrollment penalty if the person has prescription drug coverage through the U.S. Department of Veterans Affairs, TRICARE, Federal Employees Health Benefits Program, Railroad Retirement Board, Program of All-Inclusive Care for the Elderly (PACE), or Indian Health Service. If enrolled in a Medicare HMO or other Medicare Advantage plan with

56. 42 U.S.C. § 1395ss(s).

prescription drug coverage, enrolling in Part D or other separate drug plan may disenroll the recipient from their Medicare Advantage plan and return them to Original Medicare.

Most people who enroll in a Medicare Part D plan will pay a premium of approximately $25 to $50 per month and will have co-payments and deductibles, in addition to the monthly premiums. However, Part D Extra Help aids recipients with low income by covering the premiums and reducing the deductibles and co-pays.

The program requires an income below 150 percent of the federal poverty income limits, calculated using the number of people in the beneficiary's household. Any Medicare beneficiary enrolled in Medicaid, the QMB program, the SLMB program, or the QI-1 program qualifies for Part D Extra Help.

Enrollment is only available during the annual enrollment period with coverage starting January 1.

vi. Application

An individual should be automatically enrolled in Medicare if the individual:

- Is already receiving Social Security or railroad retirement benefits at age 65
- Has received SSDI or RSDI benefits for 24 months
- Is applying initially for Social Security or railroad retirement benefits at age 65

If a Medicare card does not arrive after the abovementioned events, or if the person becomes eligible in other situations (e.g., a retiree not applying for Social Security retirement until after age 65), an application for Medicare should be filed at the local Social Security office. If the application is not filed within certain time periods, a beneficiary may lose eligibly or incur enrollment penalties.

vii. Medicare Supplement Insurance Policies

The costs associated with Medicare deductibles and co-payments, commonly referred to as "gaps," can cause financial havoc for beneficiaries on a fixed income. If the beneficiary has Medigap coverage, then he or she is assured that no matter how expensive the medical treatment, the cost of that treatment will not lead to financial ruin. For example, Part B generally pays 80 percent of the Medicare approved rate for covered services, and the beneficiary is responsible for the remaining 20 percent.[57] Cost of care can be very expensive, and the 20

57. Fact Sheet, CMS, 2022 Medicare Parts A & B Premiums and Deductibles/2022 Medicare Part D Income-Related Monthly Adjustment (Nov. 12, 2021), https://www.cms.gov/newsroom/fact-sheets/2022-medicare-parts-b-premiums-and-deductibles2022-medicare-part-d-income-related-monthly-adjustment.

percent co-payment may be many thousands of dollars. A Medigap policy can provide 100 percent coverage of this co-payment such that the beneficiary has zero out-of-pocket costs. In most instances, if a beneficiary has Original Medicare (fee-for-service Medicare) and a Medigap policy and seeks treatment from a physician who accepts Medicare assignment, then the beneficiary will never have any out-of-pocket costs for any service covered by Medicare.

A Medigap or Medicare supplemental policy is health insurance sold by private insurance companies to fill the "gaps" in Original Medicare plan coverage (fee-for-service). A Medigap policy meets the statutory definition of a "Medicare supplemental policy" contained in section 1882(g)(1) of title XVIII of the Social Security Act and the definition contained in the National Association of Insurance Commissioners (NAIC) Model Regulation that is incorporated by reference to the statute. If a beneficiary has a Medigap policy, then if Medicare pays toward a covered service, the Medigap policy will pay its share of covered health care costs. Generally, Medigap will only pay for a service if that service is covered by Medicare. However, some Medigap policies also cover certain benefits Original Medicare does not cover (like emergency foreign travel expenses). Medigap policies do not include limited benefit coverage available to Medicare beneficiaries such as "specified disease" or "hospital indemnity" coverage. Also, the definition of a "Medigap policy" explicitly excludes a policy or plan offered by an employer to employees or former employees, as well as that offered by a labor organization to members or former members.

To buy a Medigap policy, the beneficiary must have Medicare Part A and Part B. In addition to the Part B premium, the beneficiary will have to pay a premium to the Medigap insurance company. For as long as the premium is paid, the Medigap policy is guaranteed renewable. This means it is automatically renewed each year.

Insurance companies can only sell standardized Medigap policies. Medigap policies must follow federal and state laws. The front of a Medigap policy must clearly identify it as "Medicare Supplement Insurance." Each standardized Medigap policy must offer the same basic benefits, no matter which insurance company sells it.

It is important to compare Medigap policies because costs can vary. The standardized Medigap policies that insurance companies offer must provide the same benefits. Generally, the only difference between Medigap policies sold by different insurance companies is the cost. Different insurance companies may charge different premiums for the same exact policy.

Medigap insurance companies are generally allowed to use medical underwriting to decide whether to accept a beneficiary's application and how much to charge for the coverage. However, during the beneficiary's Medigap open enrollment period (OEP), a beneficiary can buy any Medigap policy the company sells—even if he or she has health problems—for the same price as people with no preexisting health problems. Every beneficiary has a guaranteed right to purchase a Medigap policy during his or her six-month Medigap OEP. If a beneficiary is 65 or older, this period automatically starts the first month the beneficiary is enrolled in Medicare Part B. If a beneficiary has delayed enrollment in Part B because he or she had other credible coverage such as a GHP, then the beneficiary still has the right to purchase a Medigap policy once he or she enrolls in Part B. If a beneficiary purchases a Medigap policy after his or her OEP, the Medigap insurance company can refuse to cover out-of-pocket costs for these preexisting health problems for up to six months. This is called a "pre-existing condition waiting period." After six months, the Medigap policy will cover the preexisting condition.

Once a decision is made to purchase a Medigap policy, it can be a daunting task to select the best policy for a beneficiary's situation. In most cases, Medigap insurance companies can sell only a "standardized" Medigap policy. All Medigap policies must have specific benefits, so the policies can be easily compared. Insurance companies that sell Medigap policies do not have to offer every Medigap plan. However, they must offer Plan A if they offer any Medigap policy. If they offer any plan in addition to Plan A, they must also offer Plan C. Each insurance company decides which Medigap plan it wants to sell, although state laws might affect which ones are offered. The Medigap policies can be confusing because policy categories are titled with letters starting with "A" and go through "N," but there are some letters missing because those policies are no longer sold. There were several plans sold in the past that are no longer available. Plans E, F, H, I, and J are no longer sold, but some beneficiaries who had these plans in the past may still have them.

III. Childhood Disability Benefits: Transitioning from SSI to SSDI

The term "childhood disability benefits" (CDB) refers to public benefits available to a child who is suffering from a disability that began prior to reaching age 22.[58] This discussion of CDB will be confined to four programs: SSI, Medicaid, SSDI, and Medicare.

A common CDB situation occurs when a parent retires, becomes disabled, or passes away when that parent has a child who has suffered a disability since

58. 42 U.S.C. § 402(d) (1935).

birth and has previously been determined eligible for SSI benefits. The child receives a notice from SSA that he or she is entitled to benefits based on the deceased (or retired or disabled) parent's Social Security earnings record. The increased benefit may be higher than the SSI income limit and, if higher, the child will receive a notice that his or her SSI benefits are being terminated. This notice may cause the child's caregivers to panic. The caregiver usually understands that Medicaid benefits are piggybacked on the SSI eligibility of the child, and loss of SSI means loss of Medicaid benefits.[59] The child may be receiving expensive medical treatment and it may be cost prohibitive to obtain private health insurance. The loss of Medicaid may be devastating to the child's well-being.

Many times, the adult child or the caregiver may be unaware that the child may be entitled to continue to receive Medicaid benefits even though the child is now receiving SSDI on the earnings record of his or her parent. The child may also be unaware that after a 24-month waiting period, the adult child will be eligible for Medicare benefits. The child can be dually eligible for both programs and be able to receive any medical treatment he or she was previously receiving, including prescription medications.

Any advocate who is advising the parents of a child applying for, or already receiving, SSI should counsel the parents about CDB benefits to prevent such panic when the notice of CDB benefits arrives. In fact, qualifying for CDB benefits should be part of any planning for any child with disabilities.

A. Description of Programs

The CDB "benefit" is a monthly payment based on the earnings record of someone other than the beneficiary. It is a monthly check or a direct deposit in most cases. The amount of the payment is based on a wage earner's primary insurance amount (PIA).[60] The child is entitled to one-half of the individual's PIA if the wage earner is living and three-fourths of the PIA if the wage earner is deceased.[61] A worker has his or her PIA and also has a family maximum benefit amount (FMBA). If the worker's regular benefit equals his or her FMBA, then even though an adult child may meet the criteria for entitlement to CDB, the child may not receive any cash benefit until the death of his or her parent. In other words, the CDB benefits must be payable from the FMBA and if there is no amount of FMBA available because of the amount

59. SSA, *Understanding Supplemental Security Income SSI and Other Government Programs—2022 Edition*, https://www.ssa.gov/ssi/text-other-ussi.htm (last visited Nov. 28, 2022).

60. 20 C.F.R. § 404.353 (2021).

61. *Id.*

the parent receives, then the adult child will not receive any benefit.[62] Once the worker has passed away, that will free up the FMBA so that the adult disabled child will then receive benefits. However, as discussed in Section III.D, the adult child will also be eligible for Medicare after a 24-month waiting period.[63]

B. Eligibility Requirements

The eligibility requirements for CDB appear to be very simple. But, much like any of the federal benefit programs, the basic requirements can each be the subject of thousands of pages of interpretations and regulations in the SSA's Program Operations Manual System (POMS) and the *Code of Federal Regulations*. One issue, such as who qualifies as a "dependent" on another person's earnings record, can require examining many factors and take many hours of research and investigation to determine the correct result.

The eligibility requirements are found in the Social Security Handbook[64] and in the POMS.[65] A child is entitled to Child's Insurance benefits on the Social Security record of a parent if the following conditions are met:

- An application for Child's Insurance benefits is filed
- The child is (or was) dependent upon the parent (see sections 333–337)
- The child is not married
- The child meets any of the following conditions
    - Is under age 18
    - Is age 18–19 and a full-time elementary or secondary school student
    - Is age 18 or older and under a disability (which must have begun before age 22) (see section 517)
- The parent meets any of the following conditions:
    - Is entitled to disability insurance benefits
    - Is entitled to retirement insurance benefits
    - Died and was either fully or currently insured at the time of death[66]

C. Proving Disability

In many cases, proving an adult child suffers from a disability that began before age 22 can be difficult. At the time a "child" becomes eligible for CDB benefits, he or she may be middle-aged because the child becomes eligible

62. *Id.* § 229.48.
63. 42 C.F.R. § 406.5 (2021).
64. SSA, Social Security Handbook § 323.
65. POMS DI 10115.001.
66. SSA, *supra* note 64.

based on the death, disability, or retirement of a parent. Depending on the disability, the proof of the beginning of a period of disability may require utilizing records that are decades old. In such a case, it is imperative that a Social Security expert be consulted. The SSA rules state that a person reaches his or her birthday the day before the *actual* birthday.[67] Therefore, you must prove disability no later than two days prior to a child's 22nd birthday.[68] However, if the adult child was already receiving SSI as a result of a disability, then the switch to CDB is virtually automatic. The SSA adopts the prior disability determination.[69] SSA workers are instructed to inquire if the applicant has any children with disabilities who might qualify as a dependent on the applicant's earnings record when an adult files an application for disability or retirement benefits.[70] SSA workers are instructed to make the same type of inquiry when an application for a Lump Sum Death Payment benefit is made, but SSA officials admit that there may be adult children who are not identified during this process.[71]

There is no waiting period in CDB claims.[72] CDB benefits may be paid retroactively for no more than six months, however.[73] The Texas Medicaid Eligibility Handbook at section F-2150 states that SSI and RSDI retroactive lump-sum payments are excluded from countable resources for nine months after the month of receipt.[74] The exclusion applies only to the lump-sum payments.

The first eligibility requirement set forth in the POMS is that the child must be a child of and a dependent of the worker/parent. The term "child" includes the worker's natural (i.e., biological) child, or any other child who would have the right under applicable state law to inherit intestate personal property from the worker as a child.[75] The state law that applies to the case is the law applied by the courts of the state where the worker was domiciled at the time of entitlement to benefits. If the worker was not domiciled in any state, applicable state law is the law that the courts of the District of Columbia would apply. The child can be the stepchild of the worker or a legally

---

67. POMS DI 25501.061.
68. *Id.*
69. *Id.* DI 25501.330.
70. *Id.* GN 00204.022.
71. Thomas E. Bush, Social Security Disability Practice 1–28 (2d ed. 2007).
72. POMS RS 00203.010 and DI 10115.001.
73. *Id.* DI 10115.001.
74. Tex. Health & Hum. Servs. Comm'n, Medicaid for the Elderly and People with Disabilities Handbook § F-2150 (2012), https://www.hhs.texas.gov/handbooks/medicaid-elderly-people-disabilities-handbook/f-2100-resource-exclusions-limited (last visited Nov. 28, 2022).
75. POMS GN 00306.

adopted child or any child of an invalid ceremonial marriage due to certain circumstances such as a failure to complete a prior divorce.[76] The child can be the natural child of the worker if the worker has acknowledged in writing that the child is his or her child or the parent has been decreed by a court to be the parent of the child.[77] Proof of parenthood can also be shown by other acceptable evidence, such as if a person was living with the child or contributing to the child's support when the child's application is filed (in life cases), or when the worker died (in survivor cases).[78] If the stepparent becomes divorced from the natural parent of the child, then the child's benefits will cease.[79] The child can be eligible on the earnings record of a grandparent or stepgrandparent, in some cases.[80] Ultimately, the child must be a dependent of the worker.[81] In most of the situations set forth earlier, a child will be presumed to be dependent on the worker.

D. Medicare

Once a child is eligible for CDB on a parent's earnings record, the child will, in turn, be eligible for Medicare after a 24-month waiting period.[82] Medicare coverage for a CDB beneficiary is the same, in all respects, as Medicare coverage for aged individuals (i.e., the rules on benefit periods, deductible and coinsurance amounts, etc., are the same for both disabled and aged individuals). In most cases, Medicare entitlement begins after an individual has been entitled (or deemed entitled) to CDB benefits for 24 months (i.e., Medicare begins with the first day of the person's 25th month of CDB entitlement).

There is an exception under section 115 of the Medicare, Medicaid, and SCHIP Benefits Improvement and Protection Act of 2000 that waives the 24-month waiting period for beneficiaries whose primary or secondary diagnosis is chronic renal disease and who need a kidney transplant or maintenance dialysis, or ALS.[83] If a beneficiary is diagnosed with ALS after the initial disability onset date and is within the 24-month Medicare waiting period, he or she is entitled to Medicare effective with the ALS onset month.

---

76. SSA, *supra* note 64, § 328.
77. POMS GN 00306.010.
78. *Id.*
79. SSA, *supra* note 64, § 331.
80. *Id.* § 325.
81. *Id.* § 333.
82. POMS RS 00203.001 D.
83. *See* 42 C.F.R. § 406.13 (1983).

For example, Beneficiary is entitled to CDB beginning May 2002. In September 2003, while still in the 24-month Medicare waiting period, she is diagnosed with ALS. She is entitled to Medicare effective September 2003.

Because CDB entitlement can begin no earlier than age 18, Medicare entitlement based on CDB entitlement can never begin before the month the beneficiary attains age 20 (or age 18 if the individual's disability is ALS). This is true even though the individual may have been disabled and entitled to Child's Insurance benefits for many months prior to age 18. For example, Beneficiary, who was born May 7, 1973, became disabled at age five. In September 1984, when her father died, she became entitled to minor child's benefits on her father's record. The 24-month Medicare qualifying period begins with May 1991, the month Beneficiary attained age 18, and she is entitled to Medicare beginning May 1993, the month she attains age 20.

To protect against the unknown costs of the co-payments and deductibles under Medicare, many Medicare recipients purchase Medigap or supplemental insurance to pay these costs. In Texas, people under age 65 who receive Medicare because of their entitlement to SSDI benefits have a six-month OEP beginning the day they enroll in Medicare Part B. This open enrollment right entitles the beneficiary to purchase only Medicare supplement Plan A with a preexisting condition limitation of no more than six months.

E. Medicaid

As set forth earlier, the loss of Medicaid benefits for a disabled child upon reaching age 18 and receiving CDB can be a traumatic event in the life of a child and also for the child's caregivers. This trauma could be avoided if information about CDB eligibility was imparted to the child or his or her caregivers when the child was originally applying for SSI benefits and the child's original Medicaid eligibility was granted. Many times, however, these two events may be separated by long periods of time. Even if this information were given to the child and family members, it may not be something that the caregivers will remember after the passage of many years. It is vital that any advocate counseling parents of disabled children make sure that parents are made aware that the child need not lose Medicaid eligibility. If the adult disabled child receives CDB and loses eligibility for SSI, he or she can continue eligibility for Medicaid.[84] The program that allows the child to continue eligibility is called Disabled Adult Children (DAC) in the Texas Medicaid for the Elderly and

84. Tex. Health & Hum. Servs. Comm'n, *supra* note 74, § A-2310.

People with Disabilities Handbook.[85] The handbook describes the program as applying to persons denied SSI after July 1, 1987, and who meet SSI eligibility criteria. When such an individual qualifies for DAC benefits, the additional income is excluded from countable income.[86] These individuals are persons denied SSI benefits because of an increase in, or receipt of, disabled children's benefits. These persons may continue to be eligible for Medicaid if they

- are at least 18;
- become disabled before they are 22;
- are denied SSI benefits because of entitlement to or an increase in RSDI disabled children's benefits received on or after July 1, 1987, and any subsequent increase; and
- meet current SSI criteria, excluding the children's benefit specified above.[87]

When the individual is denied SSI as a result of CDB, SSA sends an electronic notification to the state Medicaid agency. The notification generates a Form H1296, which is mailed to the denied SSI recipient and it informs him or her of the possibility of maintaining Medicaid benefits. The applicant should contact the nearest Medicaid office and ask for an application for DAC. For example, the Texas form is an H1200-EZ, Application for Assistance—Aged and Disabled.[88]

Application for this program will allow the adult disabled child to continue Medicaid benefits just as they existed prior to eligibility for CDB. Once he or she receives Medicare eligibility, the child will then be dually eligible for both programs.

F. Tips and Tricks

The special income exclusion for payments from CDB does not include any other forms of income that are normally countable for SSI/Medicaid purposes. In some cases, an adult disabled child may be entitled to receive benefits from insurance or a pension from private sources as the result of the death of a parent. These sources of income will be treated just as income is treated for any SSI/Medicaid applicant. If the income were to be such that the person would not be eligible for SSI/Medicaid benefits as a result of this additional

85. *Id.*
86. *Id.*
87. *Id.*
88. This form is available at https://hhs.texas.gov/laws-regulations/forms/1000-1999/form-h1200-application-assistance-your-texas-benefits (last visited Nov. 28, 2022).

income, then the CDB program will not save the person's eligibility.[89] In such a case, the opportunity to direct the income to an SNT should be examined. If the income can be irrevocably assigned to the trust, then it may be excluded and prevent the additional income from disqualifying the applicant.

The notice of eligibility for CDB may be a surprise to many beneficiaries and their caregivers. The later notice of the loss of the SSI-linked Medicaid may trigger all kinds of anxiety and fear in the beneficiary and his or her family. Prior knowledge that this is just a transition from one type of benefit to another that may provide increased income and access to Medicare would prevent any such trauma. It is incumbent upon all advocates for adult disabled children to make sure that families are aware that such a transition will take place and that it is not a reason for concern or worry. Further, if there are other sources of income that may result in disqualification from SSI-linked Medicaid it will give families and beneficiaries opportunity to plan for the increased income such that it will not cause a loss of benefits as well.

IV. Federal Housing Programs under the U.S. Department of Housing and Urban Development

The three largest federally subsidized housing programs are the Public Housing Program; the Housing Choice Voucher Program (formerly called Section 8); and the Multifamily Housing Program (formerly called project-based Section 8). These programs are administered through the Department of Housing and Urban Development (HUD).[90]

A. Description of Programs

Public housing authorities (PHAs) are public agencies that own, operate, and manage public housing programs across the country.[91] PHAs can be run and funded through state, county, or municipal programs, as enabled through state legislation.[92] HUD contracts with PHAs for administration of the public housing projects and supplies capital and operating funds for the local agencies. There are more than 3,300 PHAs in the United States and a significant majority of them own and operate public housing.[93] The PHAs have a manual

89. *Id.*

90. *See* 24 C.F.R. (2021).

91. *See* Tex. Loc. Gov't Code ch. 392 (1987), *available at* https://statutes.capitol.texas.gov/Docs/LG/htm/LG.392.htm.

92. *Id.*

93. HUD, *HUD's Public Housing Program*, https://www.hud.gov/topics/rental_assistance/phprog (last visited Nov. 28, 2022).

similar to the POMS manual for the administration of their programs. The Public Housing Occupancy Guidebook was published in 2003 and addresses the program's rules and procedures.[94]

In the Multifamily Housing Program, HUD contracts directly with various types of for-profit and nonprofit organizations to provide housing specific to the organization's housing developments. HUD provides direct oversight and hires contractors to oversee the administration. Families rent units in projects and the subsidized rents stay with the unit and are not transferable. Two such project-based housing programs are Supportive Housing for Persons with Disabilities and Supportive Housing for the Elderly.[95] The manual for multifamily housing programs is called the HUD Handbook 4350.3.[96]

PHAs also manage the Housing Choice Voucher Program. HUD contracts with PHAs to administer the vouchers. Whereas public housing is project-based—meaning the subsidy stays with the rental unit or project—the Housing Choice Voucher Program is tenant-based. A family who qualifies for the program finds an apartment or home to rent with a landlord willing to accept the housing voucher. PHAs pay the rent subsidy to the landlord and the family pays the difference between the actual rent charged and the amount of the subsidy.[97] Because the voucher stays with the family, this program is the largest and most popular housing program. There are a number of specialized voucher programs, such as Vouchers for People with Disabilities and Veterans Affairs Supportive Housing vouchers.[98] The Housing Choice Voucher Program Guidebook is the manual used by PHAs to administer the program.[99]

B. Eligibility Rules

Housing vouchers are designed to meet the needs of low-income families. Under HUD rules, a "family" is defined as one or more person constituting a household.[100] A family consists of one or more persons who share a residence and whose income and resources are available to meet the family's needs.[101] This definition includes those related by blood, marriage, or the operation

94. HUD, Public Housing Occupancy Guidebook (2003), https://www.hud.gov/sites/documents/DOC_10760.PDF.

95. *See* 42 U.S.C. § 8013 (1991); 24 C.F.R. pt. 891 (2022).

96. HUD, HUD Handbook 4350.3: Occupancy Requirements of Subsidized Multifamily Housing Programs, https://www.hud.gov/sites/documents/DOC_35639.PDF.

97. 24 C.F.R. § 982, subpt. J (2021).

98. 28 U.S.C. § 2003(b).

99. HUD, Housing Choice Voucher Program Guidebook (2001), http://www.lb7.uscourts.gov/documents/15c6523.pdf.

100. 24 C.F.R. § 5.403 (2021).

101. HUD, *supra* note 94, at 2.2.

of law, but it is also purposefully broad so that it can include, for example, two unrelated parents "who want to share housing because they work differing shifts and can save money on childcare costs by sharing an apartment."[102] PHAs must target 75 percent of their vouchers to households with incomes below 30 percent of the area median income.[103]

The basis for federal housing policy is that low-income families should be allowed safe housing for no more than 30 percent of the household income. The family should contribute up to 30 percent of its income to housing and the balance of a modestly priced rental unit cost will be paid through a HUD subsidy.

Each year, HUD releases a survey of "fair market rents" that is then used by PHAs to create the PHA payment standard for its rental units, adjusted for number of bedrooms.[104] The PHA payment standard is a fixed dollar amount of rent against which both the tenant's maximum rent and the subsidy maximum amount are determined.[105] The HUD report is a survey of fair market rents for modestly priced rental units in the applicable market area. With certain exceptions, neither the rent subsidy furnished by HUD nor the total tenant payment (TTP) can exceed the PHA payment standard for the market area. For example, in 2023, the payment standard for a one-bedroom rental in Houston, Texas, was $2,118.[106] The PHA could set the payment standard anywhere between $1,906.20 (90 percent of the HUD fair market rent) to $2,329.80 (110 percent of the HUD fair market rent).[107] Once the PHA standard is set, the PHA calculates a family's income using the methods described in subsection 2 below to determine eligibility for the program and also to calculate the TTP.

1. Resources

Strictly speaking, HUD does not consider the value of an applicant family's resources when determining eligibility. However, if the family has net family assets greater than $5,000, annual income includes the greater of the actual income derived from all net family assets or the percentage of the value of all family assets based on the current passbook savings rate.[108] HUD determines

---

102. *Id.*

103. HUD, *supra* note 99, ch. 5 (https://www.hud.gov/sites/documents/DOC_35615.PDF).

104. 42 U.S.C. § 1437f. The 2023 and earlier fair market rents are available at https://www.huduser.gov/portal/datasets/fmr.html (last visited Nov. 28, 2022).

105. 24 C.F.R. § 982.503 (2021).

106. Hous. Hous. Auth., Payment Standards Amounts 2023 (2023), https://housingforhouston.com/wp-content/uploads/2022/10/2022-23-Payment-Standards.pdf.

107. *Id.*

108. 24 C.F.R. § 5.609(b)(3) (2021).

the passbook savings rate and that rate is currently set at .06 percent for all programs.[109] The actual income from all net family assets will be compared to .06 percent of all net family assets to determine which amount to use. For example, if an applicant owns unimproved land valued at $50,000, the PHA will deem annual income to the owner of $30 (passbook savings rate of .06 percent). If the land is rented for more than the passbook savings rate, the PHA will include the actual earning on the resource as income to the applicant.

Similarly, if an applicant gives away a nonexempt resource, HUD requires a PHA to deem income on the gifted asset at the passbook rate of interest for a period of two years from the month of transfer.[110]

2. Income

Income is relevant in two different aspects of eligibility for public housing programs. The first is consideration for eligibility for the program and the second is the calculation of monthly rent. For initial eligibility, the programs determine the members in the family unit and then determine the family's annual income including income from the family's net assets.[111]

Determining income eligibility is done at least annually. PHA rules vary about the need to report changed circumstances within the one-year eligibility period. While a family's eligibility is based on its gross annual income, the family's share of the rent is based on its adjusted income—gross income less certain deductions.[112]

Annual income includes the following:

- **Earnings**. This includes gross wages, net earnings from self-employment, and the first $480 of the earnings of a full-time student age 18 or older who is not the head of the household or his or her spouse.
- **Periodic payments**. These payments include Social Security, unemployment benefits, pensions, annuities, alimony, child support, military pay, and regular gifts or household contributions. Gifts include regular payments made on the household's behalf for rent and/or utilities.
- **Income generated by resources**. This form of income includes interest and dividend payments, as well as net earnings from real or personal property. This includes deemed income from assets using the method described earlier.[113]

---

109. HUD Notice 2016-1 (Jan. 19, 2016), https://www.hud.gov/sites/documents/16-01HSGN.PDF.
110. HUD, *supra* note 94, at 10.1.
111. 24 C.F.R. § 5.609 (2021).
112. *Id.* § 5.611 (2021).
113. HUD, *supra* note 94, at 10.1.

Annual income does not include the following: wages of children under age 18; foster care payments; payments to cover past or future medical expenses; student financial aid; payments for participation in state or local job training programs; back payments from Social Security and SSI; adoption assistance; income of a live-in aide; inheritances; insurance payments; temporary nonrecurring or sporadic income (including gifts); and earnings above $480 per year for full-time students age 18 or older.[114] There may be other payments that are not considered income under these rules.

While a family's eligibility for HUD programs is based on annual income, the family's payment toward the rent—the TTP—is based on "adjusted income."[115] Adjusted income is the family's income less the following mandatory deductions:

- **Dependent allowance**. This is $480 per year for each dependent. A dependent is a family member under age 18, or who is either disabled or a full-time student.
- **Allowance for elderly/disabled family**. This is $400 per year if the head of household, his or her spouse, or the sole family member is elderly (age 62 or older) or disabled.
- **Child care**. There is a deduction for reasonable and non-reimbursable child care expenses that are necessary for a family member to work or to attend school.
- **Disability assistance expenses**. These include attendant care expenses and/or the cost of any auxiliary apparatus for a family member with a disability if such expenses are required to enable any family member to work. The amount of the deduction is the amount by which such expenses exceed 3 percent of the family's gross annual income but cannot exceed the wages of the family member who is enabled to work by reason of such expenses.
- **Medical expenses**. If the head of the household, his or her spouse, or sole household member is elderly (age 62 or older) or disabled, non-reimbursable medical expenses anticipated by the entire household over the next 12 months are deducted to the extent they exceed 3 percent of the family's gross annual income. A family can deduct expenses for doctor services, hospital charges, prescriptions, transportation to medical care, dental work, durable medical equipment, eyeglasses and hearing aids, and attendant care.

114. 24 C.F.R. § 5.628 (2000).
115. *Id.*

- **Disability assistance expenses and medical expenses.** If a family has both disability assistance expenses and medical expenses, the threshold of 3 percent of the family's annual income must only be applied once. Therefore, if a family has disability expenses that exceed 3 percent of annual income and also has medical expenses, the family can deduct the amount by which disability expenses exceed 3 percent of annual income plus *all* medical expenses.[116]

Once a PHA determines a family's adjusted income, it must then compute the TTP. The TTP is the highest of the following amounts:

> (1) 30% of adjusted monthly income;
>
> (2) 10% of gross monthly income;
>
> (3) If the family is receiving payments for welfare assistance from a public agency and a part of those payments, adjusted in accordance with the family's actual housing costs, is specifically designated by such agency to meet the family's housing costs, the portion of those payments which is so designated; or
>
> (4) the minimum rent,[117] [which is between $25 and $50 as determined by the PHA.[118]]

After determining a family's eligibility for a HUD program and the TTP, a PHA then awards the family a voucher based on the PHA standard payment amount. The eligible family has the ability to search the open market for suitable housing with a monthly rent within the standard payment amount. The family pays its share (TTP) to the landlord, and the PHA issues the remaining balance to the landlord.

C. Tips and Tricks

1. Income Considerations for SNTs

When attempting to qualify for HUD programs when someone in the family is the beneficiary of an SNT, there are several important considerations. First, family income includes the income of all family members, including minors.[119] While there is an exclusion for earned income for minors, it is important to

116. HUD, *supra* note 94, at 10.2.
117. *Id.* at 10.4.
118. 24 C.F.R. § 5.630 (2022).
119. HUD, *supra* note 94, at 10.1.

note that if an SNT is being established to hold settlement proceeds belonging to a minor, the settlement may impact the entire family's eligibility for federally subsidized housing and the family's monthly rent.

Next, "income" is defined as money or other amount paid to or on behalf of a family member.[120] Does "on behalf of" include payments from a trustee of an SNT to a vendor for the benefit of the SNT beneficiary? The rule implies the answer is "maybe." A further investigation into the program manuals for the housing programs is appropriate. Income also includes amounts that are anticipated to be received from any source outside the family for the next 12 months.[121] Under this provision, trust distributions that are temporary, nonrecurring, and unscheduled would not likely be considered, but any scheduled periodic trust distributions that can be predicted might be.

A revocable trust or the right of any family member to withdraw money from the trust may also open up the trust to consideration. The law references trusts in the definition of "net family assets."[122] The value of a nonrevocable trust that is under the control of any family member will not be considered an asset "so long as the fund continues to be held in trust. Any income distributed from the trust fund shall be counted when determining annual income."[123] Additionally, net family assets include the value of any family assets disposed of by a family member for less than fair market value, "including a disposition in trust," during the two years preceding the date of application or reexamination.[124] This section does exclude foreclosures, bankruptcy sales, or dispositions as part of a separation or divorce settlement when the family member received "important consideration not measurable in dollar terms."[125]

2. Housing Program Manuals and SNTs

All three of the housing program manuals expand on the definitions of "income," but they differ in their discussions about SNTs. Of the three manuals, only HUD Handbook 4350.3 specifically addresses SNTs. The discussion is very simple and focuses on third-party trusts. It addresses a family member's ability to access the funds in the trust. If no one in the family has access to the income, then the trust is not considered when calculating net family assets.[126]

120. *Id.*
121. *Id.*
122. 24 C.F.R. § 5.630 (2022). HUD, *supra* note 94.
123. HUD, *supra* note 94, at 10.1.
124. *Id.*
125. *Id.*
126. *Id.*

If income or principal is provided regularly, however, then those payments are considered income.[127]

The Public Housing Occupancy Guidebook is the reference tool for PHA staff to calculate TTPs.[128] Its discussion is limited only to the circumstance in which a family transfers assets to an irrevocable trust not under the control of any family member. Under this circumstance, the value of the trust is not included in the net family assets when the transfer was made more than two years prior to the family's application.[129] If a family transfers within two years of its application, the PHA must consider the fair market value of the trust at the HUD imputed interest rate of 2 percent as part of the income calculation.[130]

The Housing Choice Voucher Program Guidebook is the manual for the Housing Choice Voucher Program.[131] It establishes the income limits by family size for each PHA service area. Chapter 5 of the Voucher Guidebook defines "income" as "all amounts that are not specifically excluded by regulation."[132] It further states that "PHAs must count as income any regular contributions and gifts (monetary or not) from persons outside the family. This may include rent and utility payments paid on behalf of the family and other cash or non-cash contributions provided on a regular basis."[133] The Guidebook's only reference to trusts comes in the discussion of asset inclusions and exclusions. Assets include "the cash value of trusts that may be withdrawn by the family."[134]

3. Implications for Trusts

SNTs, both first-party and third-party, provide that the trust assets are not accessible to the trust beneficiary. If the trustee of an SNT is a family member or someone living in the same household as the beneficiary, it might cause the trust to be considered a net family asset. If the goal is to qualify a trust beneficiary for HUD programs, the best practice is to name a trustee who does not share a household with the beneficiary. When drafting, it may also be important to limit a beneficiary's ability to name a new trustee in favor of a family member or household member.

---

127. *Id.*
128. HUD, *supra* note 94.
129. *Id.*
130. HUD, *supra* note 94, at 10.1.
131. HUD, *supra* note 94.
132. *Id.*
133. *Id.*
134. *Id.*

A trustee should consider making some distribution guidelines if attempting to qualify a beneficiary for HUD programs. Among the recommended guidelines, a trustee should make every effort to keep distributions irregular, nonrecurring, and unpredictable. Rather than paying every bill monthly, would it be possible to prepay a certain expense all at one time, varying the payments from month to month and year to year? Review the handbooks to issue vendor payments for medical expenses or child care payments so that these payments do not impact net family income. While navigating the inconsistent HUD rules can be tricky, it is possible to provide an additional benefit to a trust beneficiary through one of these valuable programs.

CHAPTER 4

First-Party Special Needs Trusts

I. Introduction

The first-party special needs trust (SNT) goes by many names. It may be called a first-party SNT, a d(4)(A) or (d)(4)(C) trust, a self-settled trust, a Medicaid payback trust, or a disability trust.[1] As mentioned in Chapter 1, the self-settled trusts under 42 U.S.C. § 1396p(d)(4)(A) and (C) are two types of SNTs (or disability trusts) authorized in the Medicaid statute.[2] The (d)(4)(A) trust is frequently called the self-settled SNT although some state statutes may use the term "supplemental needs trusts." With the continuing movement away from ableist language,[3] practitioners are referring to these types of trust as

1. Some early commentators even used "Zebley" trust. After the 1990 U.S. Supreme Court holding in *Sullivan v. Zebley*, 493 U.S. 521 (1990), a large number of Supplemental Security Income applicants were awarded back benefits, which created the perverse result that delayed eligibility could trigger an excess of resources, creating a new basis for continued ineligibility for a means-tested benefit. The 1993 adoption of 42 U.S.C. § 1396p(d)(4)(A) was partly seen as a recognition of the growing body of trusts established to deal with the *Zebley* problem. *See* Sterling L. Ross, *Sheltering* Zebley *Retroactive SSI Benefits in Trust*, 25 Clearinghouse Rev. 1335 (1991–1992).

2. 42 U.S.C. § 1396p(d)(4)(B) covers qualified income trusts.

3. The vocabulary around disability can be fraught, even for well-meaning people. Different constituencies within the disability community debate the politics of naming and identification. "People-first" language asserts that language recognizes the humanity of an individual first and that we consider an impairment a modification or special need. Others prefer the term "disabled people" as a claim to—and pride in—an identity. We can agree that many terms from the past are derogatory and are not appropriate or polite. In 2010, President Obama signed Rosa's Law, which replaced references to "mental retardation" with "intellectual disability" in federal statutes.

The authors acknowledge this debate around language and its importance. For consistency, we use people-first language and we use the term "special needs trust." We understand that as language evolves there may be better or preferred terms. We also encourage practitioners to remove even "approved" language when it is not necessary to understanding. So, for instance, the name of a given trust might be the "John Doe Trust" or the "John Doe Irrevocable Trust" rather than the "John Doe Special Needs Trust" or the "John Doe Disability Trust."

"disability trusts," rather than "special needs trusts." As noted in Chapter 1, the (d)(4)(C) trusts are called pooled SNTs.[4]

What is a first-party SNT? It is an inter vivos, discretionary, irrevocable trust established with the beneficiary's assets to be used for the sole benefit of the beneficiary who is under age 65 at the time of trust creation and it includes Medicaid payback provisions. According to the Special Needs Alliance:[5]

> A **first-party SNT**, also referred to as a "self-settled" or "(d)(4)(A) trust," is funded with assets or income that belong to an individual with a disability . . . and who is the beneficiary of the trust. In order for the assets of this type of trust not to count for Medicaid or SSI [Supplemental Security Income] purposes, federal law requires that the beneficiary must be under the age of 65 when the trust is created and funded; the trust must be irrevocable and provide that Medicaid will be reimbursed upon the beneficiary's death or upon termination of the trust, whichever occurs first; and the trust must be administered for the sole benefit of the beneficiary. Typically the funding comes from a personal injury settlement or inheritance the beneficiary receives directly.[6]

First-party trusts are often used when an SSI beneficiary recovers money in a lawsuit or when he or she receives money or property as an unrestricted inheritance. If these funds are not placed into an SNT, the beneficiary will become ineligible to receive SSI and Medicaid. Because the medical expenses for people with disabilities can be quite high, the money or property may be used quickly for those costs without the opportunity for the beneficiary to improve his or her quality of life in any meaningful way.

II. The Statutes and More

42 U.S.C. § 1396p(d)(4) provides that the SSI transfer rules "shall not apply to any of the following trusts":

> **(A)** A trust containing the assets of an individual under age 65 who is disabled (as defined in [42 U.S.C. § 1382c(a)(3)]) and which is established for the benefit of such individual by the individual, a parent, grandparent, legal guardian of the individual, or a court if the State will receive all amounts

4. Because pooled SNTs, or (d)(4)(C)s, are not typically drafted by an attorney, there will be no detailed discussion in this book of pooled trusts.

5. Special Needs All., *About the Special Needs Alliance*, https://www.specialneedsalliance.org/about-special-needs-alliance/ (last visited Nov. 28, 2022).

6. *Your Special Needs Trust ("SNT") Defined*, 7 Voice (Special Needs All.), Jan. 2013, https://www.specialneedsalliance.org/the-voice/your-special-needs-trust-snt-defined-2/.

remaining in the trust upon the death of such individual up to an amount equal to the total medical assistance paid on behalf of the individual under a State plan under this subchapter.

. . .

(C) A trust containing the assets of an individual who is disabled (as defined in [42 U.S.C. § 1382c(a)(3)]) that meets the following conditions:

(i) The trust is established and managed by a nonprofit association.

(ii) A separate account is maintained for each beneficiary of the trust, but, for purposes of investment and management of funds, the trust pools these accounts.

(iii) Accounts in the trust are established solely for the benefit of individuals who are disabled [42 U.S.C. § 1382c(a)(3)] by the parent, grandparent, or legal guardian of such individuals, by such individuals, or by a court.

(iv) To the extent that amounts remaining in the beneficiary's account upon the death of the beneficiary are not retained by the trust, the trust pays to the State from such remaining amounts in the account an amount equal to the total amount of medical assistance paid on behalf of the beneficiary under the State plan under this subchapter.

42 U.S.C. § 1396p(c)(2)(B)(iii)–(iv) addresses the requirement of sole benefit:

(2) An individual shall not be ineligible for medical assistance by reason of paragraph (1) to the extent that—. . . [assets]—

(iii) were transferred to, or to a trust (including a trust described in subsection (d)(4)) established solely for the benefit of, the individual's child described in subparagraph (A)(ii)(II). . . .

(iv) were transferred to a trust (including a trust described in subsection (d)(4)) established solely for the benefit of an individual under 65 years of age who is disabled. . . .

Disability is defined in 42 U.S.C. § 1382c(a)(3) as follows:

(A) Except as provided in subparagraph (C), an individual shall be considered to be disabled for purposes of this subchapter if [the individual] is unable to engage in any substantial gainful activity by reason of any medically determinable physical or mental impairment which can be expected to result in death or which has lasted or can be expected to last for a continuous period of not less than twelve months.

(B) For purposes of subparagraph (A), an individual shall be determined to be under a disability only if [the individual's] physical or mental impairment or impairments are of such severity that [the individual] is not only unable to do [the individual's] previous work but cannot, considering [the individual's] age, education, and work experience, engage in any other kind of substantial gainful work which exists in the national economy, regardless of whether such work exists in the immediate area in which [the individual] lives, or whether a specific job vacancy exists for [the individual], or whether [the individual] would be hired if [the individual] applied for work. For purposes of the preceding sentence (with respect to any individual), "work which exists in the national economy" means work which exists in significant numbers either in the region where such individual lives or in several regions of the country.

(C)

(i) An individual under the age of 18 shall be considered disabled for the purposes of this subchapter if that individual has a medically determinable physical or mental impairment, which results in marked and severe functional limitations, and which can be expected to result in death or which has lasted or can be expected to last for a continuous period of not less than 12 months.

(ii) Notwithstanding clause (i), no individual under the age of 18 who engages in substantial gainful activity (determined in accordance with regulations prescribed pursuant to subparagraph (E)) may be considered to be disabled.

(D) For purposes of this paragraph, a physical or mental impairment is an impairment that results from anatomical, physiological, or psychological abnormalities which are demonstrable by medically acceptable clinical and laboratory diagnostic techniques.

. . .

(F) Notwithstanding the provisions of subparagraphs (A) through (E), an individual shall also be considered to be disabled for purposes of this subchapter if [the individual] is permanently and totally disabled as defined under a State plan approved under subchapter XIV or XVI as in effect for October 1972 and received aid under such plan (on the basis of disability) for December 1973 (and for at least one month prior to July 1973), so long as [the individual] is continuously disabled as so defined.[7]

7. Minor edits were made to the statute to make it gender neutral.

III. The Program Operations Manual System

The Social Security Administration's (SSA's) Program Operations Manual System (POMS)[8] is critical for the approval of SNTs and a beneficiary's public benefits eligibility. Although the POMS is designed for SSA employees in making determinations,[9] courts give deference[10] to the POMS, so it is important that practitioners read and be able to apply the POMS. The POMS sections regarding trusts were revised in 2000, so this chapter will focus on trusts established on or after January 1, 2000.[11]

IV. The State's Medicaid Program

Every state participates in Medicaid, and has filed a state plan that will have been approved by the Health Care Financing Administration when the state joined the Medicaid program. Waivers of the state plan are approved by the Centers for Medicare and Medicaid Services (CMS). Because there are variations with each state's Medicaid program, it suffices here to say that in creating a first-party SNT, the drafting attorney must be conversant with the state Medicaid program and laws of the jurisdiction where the beneficiary resides.

V. The State's Trust Code

Review the applicable state's trust code to determine the requirements for creating a trust, trustee powers and duties, modification, administration, termination, and more.

---

8. SSA, *Program Operations Manual System (POMS)—Table of Contents*, https://secure.ssa.gov/apps10/poms.nsf/partlist!OpenView (last visited Nov. 28, 2022).

9. *See* SSA, *POMS Home*, https://secure.ssa.gov/apps10/poms.nsf/Home?readform (last visited Nov. 28, 2022):

> This section of the SSA Program Policy Information Site contains the public version of the Program Operations Manual System (POMS). The POMS is a primary source of information used by Social Security employees to process claims for Social Security benefits. The public version of POMS is identical to the version used by Social Security employees except that it does not include internal data entry and sensitive content instructions.
>
> Please note that this document is intended for SSA employees. It contains technical terms and instructions that will be unfamiliar to you. If you have difficulty understanding these materials, please click on this link to the Social Security Handbook, which is written in plain language for use by the public.

10. *See, e.g.*, Ala. Medicaid Agency v. Hardy, 202 So. 3d 690 (Ala. Civ. App. 2016) (discussing use of the POMS). A discussion of the courts' deference to administrative agencies is beyond the scope of this book.

11. *See* POMS SI 01120.201, Trusts Established with the Assets of an Individual on or after 01/01/00, https://secure.ssa.gov/apps10/poms.nsf/lnx/0501120201 (last visited Nov. 28, 2022).

VI. Commentary

Note that for a first-party SNT under 42 U.S.C. § 1396p(d)(4)(A), the assets in the trust are that of the beneficiary (referred to in the statute as "individual") who is disabled under the abovementioned definition of "disability," and the trust meets the statutory age limit (established before the individual is 65). The trust must be for the benefit of the beneficiary and can be established by the beneficiary[12] or the parent or grandparent of the beneficiary, the legal guardian of the beneficiary if one has been appointed, or a court. The agent under a valid durable power of attorney from the beneficiary/principal can establish the SNT for the beneficiary.[13]

When a parent or grandparent establishes a first-party trust, they may provide a nominal contribution (sometimes evidenced by currency physically attached to, and photocopied as part of, the trust instrument). That nominal contribution may be essential to the creation of the trust so that the beneficiary can later fund the trust with his or her own money.[14]

When the court is "establishing" the SNT, be sure that the appropriate language is used to make clear that the court did so.[15] Note that if someone

12. Prior to the Special Needs Trust Fairness Act of 2016, an individual could not establish his or her own trust. *See* 21st Century Cures Act, Pub. L. No. 114-255, § 5007 (Fairness in Medicaid Supplemental Needs Trusts), 130 Stat. 1033 (2016) (amending 42 U.S.C. § 1396p(d)(4)(A) by adding "individual"). The Special Needs Trust Fairness Act went into effect before this book was published and the authors will not discuss any issues that arose regarding the establishment of the SNT before that amendment to the statute.

13. *See* POMS SI 01120.203.C.2.a: "Power of attorney: We consider a trust established under power of attorney (POA) for the disabled individual to be established through the actions of the disabled individual because the POA establishes an agency relationship." This applies to SNTs established on or after December 13, 2016. Prior to that date, using a POA to establish the SNT would not create an SNT because at that time the statute did not authorize the individual to establish his or her own first-party SNT. *See, e.g.*, Draper v. Colvin, 779 F.3d 556 (8th Cir. 2015).

14. POMS SI 01120.203.B.7.

15. POMS SI 01120.203.B.8 addresses the SNT established by the court prior to December 13, 2016 (which was the effective date of the 21st Century Cures Act, which amended 42 U.S.C. § 1396p(d)(4)(A) to allow the beneficiary (referred to in the statute as "individual") to create the first-party SNT) as follows:

> In the case of a trust established through the actions of a court, the creation of the trust must be required by a court order for the exception in section 1917(d)(4)(A) of the Act to apply. The special needs trust exception can be met when a court approves a petition and establishes a trust by court order, as long as the creation of the trust has not been completed before the order is issued by the court. Court approval of an already created special needs trust is not sufficient for the trust to qualify for the exception. The court must specifically either establish the trust or order the establishment of the trust. An individual is permitted to petition a court for the present establishment of a trust or may use an agent to do so. The court order establishes the trust, not the individual's petition. Petitioning a court to establish a trust is not establishment by an individual.

The POMS provides examples distinguishing between court-ordered, court-established, and court-approved trusts. *See id.* SI 01120.203.B.8.a–.d.

These POMS provisions apply to SNTs established on or after December 13, 2016. *See id.* SI 01120.203.C.4: "Additional requirements for a trust established on or after December 13, 2016:

other than the beneficiary establishes the SNT, that means that the beneficiary provides the funds and the other establishes the SNT.

This trust requires "payback" language, meaning that the trust contains language that "the State will receive all amounts remaining in the trust upon the death of such individual up to an amount equal to the total medical assistance paid on behalf of the individual under a State plan."[16] The POMS, in a note, explains what is *not* sufficient payback language.[17]

The POMS elaborates on the payback requirement:

> State Medicaid reimbursement requirement
>
> To qualify for the special needs trust exception, the trust must contain specific language that provides that, upon the death of the individual, the State(s) will receive all amounts remaining in the trust, up to an amount equal to the total amount of medical assistance paid on behalf of the individual under the State Medicaid plan(s). The State(s) must be listed as the first payee(s) and have priority over payment of other debts and administrative expenses, except as listed in SI 01120.203.E in this section.
>
> The trust must provide payback for any State(s) that may have provided medical assistance under the State Medicaid plan(s) and not be limited to any particular State(s). Medicaid payback also cannot be limited to any particular period of time; for example, payback cannot be limited to the period after establishment of the trust. If the trust does not have sufficient funds upon the beneficiary's death to reimburse in full each State that provided medical assistance, the trust may reimburse the States on a pro-rata or proportional basis.[18]

> Except as noted in SI 01120.203C.1. through SI 01120.203C.3. in this section, the requirements for an exempt special needs trust remain the same as those for a trust established prior to December 13, 2016. . . ."

16. 42 U.S.C. § 1396p(d)(4)(A). The payback is for the dollar amount of Medicaid benefits that the individual has received. *See also* POMS SI 01120.203.B.10. The POMS notes that is it insufficient to say something such as "this is a payback trust." Instead, there has to be an explained payback provision. *See* POMS SI 01120.203.B.10 (for SNTs created before December 13, 2016, which was the effective date of the 21st Century Cures Act, which amended 42 U.S.C. § 1396p(d)(4)(A) to allow the beneficiary (referred to in the statute as "individual") to create the first-party SNT). It may also be prudent to include that if a beneficiary receives Medicaid benefits from multiple states, that each agency is entitled to its pro rata share upon termination of the trust.

These POMS provisions apply to SNTs established on or after December 13, 2016. *See id.* SI 01120.203.C.4: "Additional requirements for a trust established on or after December 13, 2016: Except as noted in SI 01120.203C.1. through SI 01120.203C.3. in this section, the requirements for an exempt special needs trust remain the same as those for a trust established prior to December 13, 2016. . . ."

17. The note to POMS SI 01120.203.B.10 states:

> Merely labeling the trust as a Medicaid payback trust, an OBRA [Omnibus Budget Reconciliation Act] 1993 payback trust, a trust established in accordance with 42 U.S.C. § 1396p, or a (MQT [Medicaid qualifying trust]) is not sufficient to meet the requirements for this exception. The trust must contain specific payback language whose effect is consistent with the requirements described above. An oral trust cannot meet this requirement..

18. POMS SI 01120.203.B.10.

In considering the creation of the SNT, the drafter needs to consider how long the beneficiary has received Medicaid benefits because Medicaid statutes for Medicaid Long Term Care for beneficiaries in skilled nursing facilities generally limit the amount of payback to receipt of long-term care services for an individual aged 55 and over. However, the beneficiary of a first-party SNT will be required to pay back all Medicaid benefits received since birth.[19]

VII. The Trust Is Irrevocable

The trust has to be irrevocable, otherwise the assets are considered available to the Medicaid applicant.[20] *Black's Law Dictionary*'s definition of an "irrevocable trust" is pretty straightforward: "**irrevocable trust** [is] [a] trust that cannot be terminated by the settlor once it is created."[21]As noted in the POMS, if the beneficiary is also the grantor and can revoke the trust, the assets are available to the beneficiary, thus rendering the beneficiary ineligible for means-tested public benefits.[22] The SSA looks at the language of the trust and the actions that the trustee may take:

> In determining whether an irrevocable trust established with the assets of an individual is a resource, we must consider how the trust can make payments. If the trustee can make any payments to or for the benefit of the individual or individual's spouse, the portion of the trust from which the trustee can make payments and that is attributable to the individual is a resource. However, certain exceptions may apply. . .[23]

---

19. Commentary from the Regional Trust Review Team lead for the SSA in Region Six is that the payback language should be broad enough to encompass Medicaid charges that may not be received by the agency until after the death of the beneficiary. Trusts from Region Six have been considered a resource when the payback provision was as follows: "any assets remaining in the Trust upon the death of the Beneficiary shall first be used to reimburse the 'State' or an agency acting on its behalf, for the total amount of medical assistance paid on behalf of the Beneficiary *at any time during the lifetime* of [the beneficiary]." Amanda Flood, SSA Regional Trust Leads Presentation Regarding SSI Trusts at the University of Texas 16th Annual Changes and Trends Affecting Special Needs Trusts (Feb. 2020).

20. *See* 42 U.S.C. § 1396p(d)(3)(A)–(B), especially (B)(ii), which provides:

> [A]ny portion of the trust from which, or any income on the corpus from which, no payment could under any circumstances be made to the individual shall be considered, as of the date of establishment of the trust (or, if later, the date on which payment to the individual was foreclosed) to be assets disposed by the individual for purposes of subsection (c). . . .

21. *Irrevocable Trust*, BLACK'S LAW DICTIONARY (11th ed. 2019).

22. *See* POMS SI 01120.200.B.11, Revoke:

> The grantor of a trust may have the power or authority to **revoke** (reclaim or take back) the assets deposited in the trust. If the individual at issue (an applicant, recipient, or deemor) is the grantor of the trust, the trust is usually a resource to that individual if he or she can revoke the trust and reclaim the trust assets. For the definition of a deemor, see SI 01310.127.

23. *See id.* SI 01120.201.D.2, https://secure.ssa.gov/apps10/poms.nsf/lnx/0501120201 (last visited Nov. 28, 2022).

VIII. Sole Benefit

What does "sole benefit" mean? According to the abovementioned definition of SNT from the Special Needs Alliance, the trust must be administered for the sole benefit of the beneficiary. This means the trustee makes distributions for the benefit *only* of the beneficiary. If a trust allows disbursements that benefit others, the trust will be a countable resource. Although that seems to be a straightforward statement, the reality is that it can get complicated.[24]

The POMS addresses sole benefit in SI 01120.201, Trusts Established with the Assets of an Individual on or after 01/01/00,[25] specifically section F, Policy on Trusts and/or Payments for the Benefit of, on Behalf of, or for the Sole Benefit of an Individual. The POMS gives plain meaning to the words "sole benefit" by instructing SSA employees to "[c]onsider a trust established for the sole benefit of an individual if the trust benefits no one but that individual, whether at the time the trust is established or at any time for the remainder of the individual's life."[26] However, it is not really that simple. For example, the POMS provides:

> Consider a trust established **for the benefit** of the individual, and consider payments to be **on behalf of,** or **to** or **for the benefit of** the individual, if the trustee makes payments of any sort from the corpus or income of the trust to another person or entity such that the *individual derives some benefit from the payment.*[27]

The POMS provides illustrations by way of explanation: "such payments could be for the purchase of food or shelter or household goods and personal items that count as income. The payments could also be for services for medical or personal attendant care that the individual may need, which do not count as income."[28] What if the trustee purchases a car or a house for the beneficiary, but others drive or ride in the car or live in the house? The POMS notes in circumstances when

> the trustee uses funds from a trust that is a resource to purchase durable items, such as a car or a house, the deed or title must show **the individual (or the trust) as the owner of the item** in the percentage that the funds represent

24. *See* Hobbs v. Zenderman, 579 F.3d 1171 (10th Cir. 2009); Lewis v. Alexander, 685 F.3d 325 (3d Cir. 2012).
25. *See* POMS SI 01120.201.D.2, https://secure.ssa.gov/apps10/poms.nsf/lnx/0501120201 (last visited Nov. 28, 2022).
26. *Id.* SI 01120.201.F.1.
27. *Id.* SI 01120.201.F.2 (emphasis added).
28. *Id.*

the value of the item. Failure to do so may constitute evidence of a transfer of resources.[29]

When the trustee pays another for goods or services for the beneficiary, the POMS focuses on whether those goods or those services are mainly for the beneficiary's benefit.[30] Interestingly, the third party can be a family member.[31] When a trustee purchases goods that require a title, the title should be issued in the name of the trustee or the name of the beneficiary unless prohibited by law.[32]

When the beneficiary needs the services or presence of another, the POMS recognizes that the cost of such companion, along with incidental expenses, may be for the beneficiary's sole benefit.[33] The same may be true for the third party's travel expenses to accompany the beneficiary, if the third party's presence is necessitated due to the beneficiary's age, disability, or medical status.[34] Trustee administrative expenses or a third party's visit to a beneficiary to ensure the beneficiary's well-being also do not violate the sole benefit rule.[35]

IX. Source of Funds

The funds used could come from a variety of sources. Frequently the funds are pursuant to a settlement, which may require a court order to approve it, especially if the beneficiary is a minor. If the beneficiary has a guardian, the guardian may need to get the approval of the probate court to accept the settlement and to establish the SNT. Consider whether the state's trust code allows for the

29. *Id.*

30. *Id.* SI 01120.201.F.3. Any purchased goods that have title or registration must be in the name of the trustee or the beneficiary absent state law to the contrary.

31. *Id.* SI 01120.201.F.3.a. An example from the POMS states:

> You should not read this so strictly as to prevent any collateral benefit to anyone else. For example, if the trust buys a house for the beneficiary to live in, that does not mean that no one else can live there, or if the trust purchases a television, that no one else can watch it. On the other hand, it would violate the sole benefit rule if the trust purchased a car for the beneficiary's grandson to take her to her doctor's appointments twice a month, but he was also driving it to work every day.

Id.

32. For example, a minor cannot own a house or car. Under such circumstances, a vehicle may be titled in the name of a third party (parent, perhaps) and the trust's interest can be protected by the trustee securing a lien against the vehicle. *Id.*

33. *Id.*

34. *Id.* SI 01120.201.F.3.b: "Absent evidence to the contrary, accept a statement from the trustee that the service or assistance provided is necessary to permit the trust beneficiary to travel." Physician statements of medical necessity and evidence of a companion's medical training or certification is not required.

35. *Id.* SI 01120.201.F.3.c and 4.

trust to be established with a small amount of money. For example, the POMS recognizes a "seed" trust:

> If the legally competent, disabled adult does not establish the trust, a parent or grandparent may establish a "seed" trust using a nominal amount of his or her own money or, if state law allows, an empty or dry trust. After the seed trust is established, the legally competent, disabled adult may transfer his or her own assets into the trust, or another individual with legal authority (such as a power of attorney[36]) may transfer the individual's assets into the trust. . . .[37]

Where there is no litigation and no settlement, then most any asset owned by the beneficiary can be used to fund the SNT.[38] For example, the SNT could be funded by transferring the title of a house owned solely by the beneficiary to the SNT. An inheritance the beneficiary is receiving could be used. Life insurance proceeds where the beneficiary is a beneficiary of the insurance can be used. The same is true for other assets on which the beneficiary is named as the beneficiary of the asset, such as a pension plan or annuity.[39]

Even child support (when the beneficiary is a minor) or spousal support payable to the beneficiary can be used to fund the SNT. If these payments are pursuant to a marital settlement agreement or a judgment of dissolution or support, then a court order directing the payments be made to the SNT may be necessary.[40]

---

36. But note that the agent may be unable to act if the principal has become incompetent if, for example, the state has adopted § 402 of the Uniform Trust Code (UTC) without amendment. That UTC section requires that "the settlor has capacity to create a trust" without suggesting the possibility that someone might create the trust on behalf of the settlor.

37. *See* POMS SI 01120.203.C.2.b (for SNTs established on or after December 13, 2016).

38. *See, e.g.*, *id.* SI 01120.201.B.8:

> A **trust** is considered to have been **established with the assets of an individual** if any assets of the individual (or spouse), regardless of how little, were transferred into the trust other than by a will.
>
> **NOTE**: The grantor named in the trust document who provided the assets funding the trust and the individual whose actions established the trust may not be the same. The trust may name the individual (for example, a parent or legal guardian) who physically took action to establish the trust rather than the individual who provided the trust assets. This distinction is important, especially in developing Medicaid trust exceptions in SI 01120.203. . . .

39. *See, e.g.*, Saccone v. Bd. of Trs. of the Police & Firemen's Ret. Sys., 98 A.3d 1158, 1168 (N.J. 2014) (discussing father's request to change beneficiary for survivor's benefits of his retirement plan from son to first-party SNT for the son and noting that "[c]reating an SNT and making it the vehicle for, or beneficiary of, [son's] survivors' benefits is the only way to protect [son's] financial interest and further the Legislature's avowed public policies in favor of both SNTs and survivors' benefits").

40. For child support or other legally assignable payments to be made to a trustee for SSI purposes, the assignment must be *irrevocable*. Therefore, child support or alimony payments should be assigned to the SNT by a court order. POMS SI 01120.201.J.1.d.

In one surprising development, the Internal Revenue Service (in a private letter ruling, applicable only to the case at issue) approved transferring an inherited individual retirement account (IRA) to an SNT[41] without triggering income taxation of the IRA contents. That private letter ruling, not citable as authority in other cases, is probably not sufficient authority to extend the concept to an owned (as opposed to inherited) IRA or qualified plan.

The type of asset and the way it is titled will affect how the funds are transferred to the SNT. This is a matter of state law.

When engaged in preplanning with a beneficiary or family member, establishment of a third-party SNT to receive inheritances or life insurance policies and the like can avoid the need for a beneficiary to create a first-party trust requiring a payback.

X. Distribution Standard

Although the law is silent as to the distribution standard in an SNT, these trusts must not give a beneficiary any right to demand payments from the trust. Be sure that the distribution standard is discretionary and an SNT standard, rather than an ascertainable standard. Typical discretionary standard language is "sole and absolute discretion." A special needs standard builds on this and incorporates the purpose of the SNT, directing that the trustee shall not make any distribution that would reduce the beneficiary's public benefits or render the beneficiary ineligible unless the trustee determines that it is in the beneficiary's best interests to do so.

Cash payments to the beneficiary from an SNT, as well as payments to a third party for the trust beneficiary's support, are income under the SSI eligibility rules. Disbursements from the SNT for goods and services that are *not* for the beneficiary's support—such as educational expenses, travel, internet bills, and experimental medical treatments—are not income. A distribution of a "non-cash item would become a totally or partially excluded non-liquid resource if retained into the month after the month of receipt."[42]

The SSA categorizes any distribution made to or for the beneficiary as some form of income, subject to their income rules. Then, if the income becomes an asset itself, the asset will be subject to separate resource rules. SSI rules will treat distributions made from the trust as either (1) direct "income" to the beneficiary; (2) "[n]ot income"; or (3) "[i]n-kind support and maintenance." If the distribution becomes an asset, SSI rules will treat it as either a

41. I.R.S. Priv. Ltr. Rul. 2006-20025 (2006).
42. POMS SI 01120.2011.1.c.

"countable resource" or an "excluded resource." Each of these categories is explained in detail in Chapter 3. Classifying the disbursements from the trust as "income" or as a "resource" will usually make a big difference to the beneficiary's eligibility and benefit levels, so it is important to have knowledge about these rules.

XI. What Are "Special Needs"?

The POMS offers a definition of "special needs trust" that gives ideas of what are special needs:

> A **special needs trust**, also known as a **supplemental needs trust**, may be set up to provide for a disabled individual's extra and supplemental needs other than food, shelter, and health care expenses that may be covered by public assistance benefits that the trust beneficiary may be eligible to receive under various programs.[43]

See Appendix A for sample language.

XII. Some Specific Trust Provisions

There are number of specific provisions the drafter of a self-settled SNT should consider including. Some of those categories, and some possible language (which cries loudly for editing for specific state laws and fact patterns) might include:

- **Spendthrift provision**. "Trustee is not to recognize any transfer, mortgage, pledge, hypothecation, assignment, or order of a beneficiary that anticipates the payment of any part of the income or principal. The income and principal of the trust estate shall not be subject to attachment, garnishment, creditor's bill, or execution to satisfy any debt, obligation, or tort of any beneficiary, nor shall any part of the trust estate pass to a trustee or receiver in any bankruptcy or insolvency proceeding initiated by or against any beneficiary."
- **Material purpose[44] provision**. "The principal purpose and intention of settlors in establishing and funding this trust is to provide a system for fiscal management, administration and disbursement, advocacy, care,

43. *See id.* SI 01120.200.B.12.

44. The significance of a "material purpose" is primarily a development of the Uniform Probate Code's emphasis on maintaining a "material purpose" when considering trust modification or termination. *Cf.* Unif. Tr. Code §§ 111, 411 & 706 (Unif. L. Comm'n 2000). A thoughtful drafter might include an express

and emotional guidance for the beneficiary. In following the terms of the trust and exercising discretion, trustees should first consider the well-being and care of the beneficiary. It is further the intent of settlors to supplement any benefits received by the beneficiary (or for which he or she might be eligible, should be eligible, or would be eligible but for the government benefits program's interpretation of the terms and effect of this trust) through or from various governmental assistance programs, and not to supplant any such benefits. While all actions of trustees shall be in their sole and absolute discretion, trustees should be mindful that the purpose of the trust is to permit and encourage the beneficiary to live as independently, productively, happily, and comfortably as possible, consistent with reasonable protection of his or her health and welfare."

- **Mechanism for amendment or modification**. Though practices and circumstances differ, the drafter should consider expressly authorizing the trustee to make at least those amendments necessary to maintain continued eligibility for public benefits, or to appoint a trust protector with similar authority. Also to consider: giving the trustee the power to change situs and/or governing law, or to modify any references to specific states if the beneficiary should relocate. At the same time, the trust should include specific language precluding the beneficiary from exercising any such powers, directly or through others such as agents under a power of attorney or by a court-appointed guardian.
- **Grantor trust provision**. Some practitioners insist on including a specific power in the beneficiary to exchange property of equal value,[45] or to give the beneficiary a power of appointment over trust property (after, of course, repayment of the amount due to the state Medicaid agency or agencies).[46] But no such language is necessary, and it should probably not be included; every self-settled discretionary trust naming the settlor as beneficiary will be a grantor trust[47] without magical language (which likely will confuse and alarm public benefits eligibility workers without changing or enhancing the general rule).

---

statement of the importance of supplementing but not supplanting public benefits, and/or the significance of maintaining the most autonomy and self-determination possible, for example.

45. Internal Revenue Code § 675(4)(C) causes a trust to be treated as a grantor trust if it includes "a power to reacquire the trust corpus by substituting other property of an equivalent value."

46. *See* I.R.C. § 674(A). While inclusion of such a power might be salutary for other reasons, it is not necessary as a means of qualifying the trust as a grantor trust.

47. See *id.* § 673(a) and the treatment of trustee discretion in § 673(c).

XIII. Submitting the SNT to the SSA for Approval

When an applicant for SSI signs an application, he or she indicates that the information on the application is true and correct. A beneficiary must report any changes that may affect SSI benefits no later than ten days after the end of the month in which the change occurred. A beneficiary can report changes to the SSA in any number of ways, including by phone or mail.[48] If reporting by mail, it is advisable to retain a copy of the reporting letter and to send the original by certified mail, return receipt requested to the SSA.

Most SSA representatives in the local offices rarely have an opportunity to review SNTs and may even be unfamiliar with the POMS sections on trusts. Therefore, all new applications for SSI benefits involving trusts, and all submissions of trusts for existing SSI recipients, are sent to the SSA's Regional Trust Reviewer Team (RTRT) for approval or denial.[49] The RTRT was established within the SSA to improve the speed, consistency, and correctness of SSI decisions involving trusts. The RTRT relies on the POMS to validate or invalidate trusts using a step-action format.[50]

Following the step-action format from the POMS in a letter will eliminate delay and provide the RTRT with the necessary information to approve an SNT. Appendix E includes a sample reporting letter that follows the step-actions listed in the POMS and Appendix G includes the step-actions listed in the POMS.

In the event that a beneficiary is found "ineligible due to excess resources and those resources include a trust," the beneficiary will receive a manual notice.[51] The notice is required to explain each reason the trust is not an excluded resource and must cite the offending sections of the trust and the applicable POMS sections.[52]

XIV. Who Should Be the Trustee?

Many of the same considerations go into choosing the trustee for the third-party SNT. Here, perhaps more importantly, is the trustee's familiarity with disbursements and the rules regarding public benefits eligibility.[53] There are

48. Changes can be reported by calling the SSA's toll-free number, 1-800-772-1213, and following the prompts. Changes can also be reported by mail. 20 C.F.R. § 416.712 (2022).

49. POMS SI 01120.202.B.

50. *Id.* SI 01120.203.B for trusts drafted before December 13, 2016, and *id.* SI 01120.203.C for trusts drafted after December 13, 2016.

51. *Id.* SI 01120.204.A.

52. *Id.* SI 01120.202.A.1.g.

53. *See, e.g.*, *id.* SI 01120.201.I.

pros and cons to family members serving as the trustee. For example, the family member likely knows the beneficiary's preferences, wants, and desires, but may not understand that the money in the trust is not the "family's money" and may not understand the limitations on the use of the trust assets. The family member may have little experience in managing even small amounts of money. On the other hand, although a professional trustee is likely well versed in the laws and regulations, the professional trustee will not know the beneficiary's wants, and so on, and does not have the same stake in the beneficiary's well-being, and will charge more to serve.

A trustee of an SNT has all the traditional trustee duties, plus a primary duty to supplement, not supplant, means-tested government benefits. Instead of clear instructions about distributions, the special needs trustee has complete discretion to make—or not make—distributions for the beneficiary's special needs.

There is always an inclination to appoint family members as trustees of SNTs. Many trusts fail because of ill-equipped trustees, no matter how well intentioned. While appointing a family member may be convenient and may be top-of-mind for clients and beneficiaries, private professional trustees often outperform family members in the same role. In addition, the need for attorney advisement and the risk of a benefits battle is greatly reduced when a trust is directed by an experienced professional trustee. See Appendix K for a sample letter for clients choosing a trustee.

Even experienced SNT trustees refer to the POMS and other materials in administering SNTs. See Appendix J for a sample letter to provide trustees of SNTs.[54]

XV. Case Law

There are a significant number of cases involving SNTs, some before the adoption of 42 U.S.C. § 1396p(d)(4)(A) with the Omnibus Budget Reconciliation Act of 1993 (OBRA '93) and even more since its adoption. One of the interesting things about SNTs is the number of issues that arise: whether the trust was validly drafted, whether the trust was validly drafted as a first-party SNT, issues involving Medicaid such as transfers of assets and liens, issues involving

54. Another great resource for SNT trustees is the "Administering a Special Needs Trust: A Handbook for Trustees" publication from the Special Needs Alliance. The most current version of the handbook can be downloaded in PDF format from https://www.specialneedsalliance.org/wp-content/uploads/2022/01/2022-SNA-Handbook.pdf. *See also* Appendix L.

trust administration, family law issues such as spousal and child support, guardianship administration, and issues specifically involving the provisions of 42 U.S.C. § 1396p(d)(4)(A). The remaining portion of this chapter contains a representative sample of opinions that focus mainly on issues regarding the SNT.

XVI. Creation

Although there have been some cases concerning attorney discipline or malpractice for failing to recommend an SNT,[55] the focus of this section is on the creation of the SNT. For example, in *Delaney v. Pacchiana*,[56] the agent under the power of attorney had authority to petition to create an SNT since the power of attorney gave the agent authority to handle, among other things, "claims and litigation," "estate transactions," and "all other matters" on his behalf.[57] The agent petitioned the court for an order creating an SNT for Delaney, which would be funded with money he had inherited, although the personal representative had not yet disbursed the funds.[58] Delaney received Social Security Disability Insurance and Medicaid at the time of the agent's petition. A court-appointed guardian ad litem supported the creation of the SNT but among other things, claimed the agent lacked authority to petition to create the SNT.[59] The appellate court reversed and remanded the case, finding that the agency relationship was properly created and the agent had the authority to petition the court.[60]

In California, a court had to decide whether, using California's substituted judgment statute, it was appropriate to create a first-party SNT that would be funded by an inheritance.[61] The court determined that it would be appropriate:

> In our view, it is inconsistent with federal legislation to allow a special needs trust for litigation beneficiaries, but not for beneficiaries of an inheritance in these circumstances. The relevant federal and state statutes provide that upon the creation of such a special needs trust by a court, a conservatee in Kane's circumstance may continue to receive public benefits, and may use the proceeds of the special needs trust for his unique medical and therapeutic

55. *See, e.g.*, Redies v. Att'ys Liab. Prot. Soc'y, 150 P.3d 930 (Mont. 2006).
56. 94 N.Y.S.3d 591 (N.Y. App. Div. 2019).
57. *Id.* at 592.
58. *Id.*
59. *Id.*
60. *Id.* at 593.
61. Conservatorship of the Est. of Kane, 137 Cal. App. 4th 400 (Cal. Ct. App. 2006).

> needs. A proper purpose for application of the substituted judgment doctrine is the avoidance of taxes or other governmental assessments. We conclude the provisions [of the statute] are available to establish such a trust for his benefit.[62]

Not all courts have looked favorably on the creation of SNTs,[63] but the requirements of the statute are clear-cut. If there are assets that will pass to the beneficiary by operation of law, if those assets are not placed in an SNT, the receipt will negatively impact the beneficiary's eligibility for, or receipt of, public benefits.[64] The situation could be remedied if the assets were placed in a first-party SNT.[65] As the Arkansas Supreme Court pointed out in *In re Corn*,[66] first-party SNTs are not against the state's public policy and reversed the denial of the beneficiary's petition to establish an SNT, remanding "for a determination of whether the proposed D4A trust meets the requirements set forth in 42 U.S.C. § 1396p(d)(4)(A)."[67]

An SNT, just like any other trust, must be funded. When approving a settlement, can the trial court determine how much of it will be placed in the trust? In one case from New York, the trial court did just that;[68] the appellate court reversed—it was error for the trial court to limit the amount of the settlement that would be used to fund the SNT.[69] In fact, placing such a limit runs counter to the intent of the statute.[70] Nowhere in 42 U.S.C. § 1396p(d)(4)(A) is there a provision that limits the amount that can be placed into an SNT.[71]

---

62. *Id.* at 407 (citations omitted).

63. *See In re* Corn, 493 S.W.3d 311 (Ark. 2016).

64. *See id.* at 312.

65. *Id.*

66. *Id.*

67. *Id.* at 316.

68. *In re* Est. of Woolworth, 903 N.Y.S.2d 218 (N.Y. App. Div. 2010).

69. *Id.* at 221–22. *See also* Guardianship of Robbins, 107 N.E.3d 1080, 1081 (Ind. Ct. App. 2018) ("trial court allowed only $1 million of the $6.75 million to be placed in the trust.") *Id.* at 1083.

70. *Woolworth*, 903 N.Y.S.2d at 221 ("In refusing to approve the funding of the proposed SNT with a sum greater than $100,000, the Surrogate skewed the balance fashioned by the Legislature in favor of the State and to the detriment of petitioner. By placing that limitation on the funding of the SNT, the Surrogate ensured that petitioner would lose her eligibility for Medicaid, a result that is inconsistent with the public policy underlying SNTs and the Surrogate's function in approving and supervising their establishment. . . ."). *See also Robbins*, 107 N.E.3d at 1086 ("While the trial court is free to disagree as to the wisdom of the legislature's policy choices, the trial court exceeded the bounds of its authority by refusing to enforce this policy choice based on that disagreement.").

71. *Woolworth*, 903 N.Y.S.2d at 222 ("Indeed, it appears that Congress considered and rejected a limitation on the amount of money used to fund an SNT. In our view, the proposed SNT funded by petitioner's entire intestate share appropriately protects the needs and interests of both petitioner and the State, consistent with the purpose of the Medicaid SNT and the public policy underlying its creation.") (citations omitted).

XVII. Payback Requirements

The statute is clear that one of the requirements for a first-party SNT under 42 U.S.C. § 1396p(d)(4)(A) is the payback requirement. What the statute does not provide is the exact language that must be used to have a valid payback provision; the POMS, however, gives examples of *insufficient language*.[72] As a result, courts may be called upon to determine whether a specific SNT has adequate payback language.[73] Another issue that may arise is whether a payback will be required on the end of a first-party SNT that was created prior to the adoption of 42 U.S.C. § 1396p(d)(4)(A).[74] Some cases, practitioners, and even states have conflated the SNT payback provision with the over-55 estate claim available to Medicaid agencies, but it is increasingly clear that the SNT payback language is a different—and more expansive—animal.[75] Some few cases have reviewed the priority of the payback after the beneficiary's death (in the face of apparently clear language in the statute compelling repayment without reduction).[76]

In *Gonzalez v. City National Bank*,[77] after the beneficiary's death, the parents sought an order that the balance in the SNT be paid to them rather than to the state on the basis the beneficiary was under age 55 when she received Medicaid.[78] In construing the federal statutes on payback, estate recovery, and the state statutes, the appellate court affirmed the trial court's order that the balance in the trust would be used to reimburse the state.[79] The appellate court

72. POMS SI 01120.203.B.10; *id.* SI 01120.203.C.4.

73. *See, e.g.*, Cockrell *ex rel.* N.S.C. v. Comm'r of Soc. Sec., No. 2:18-cv-568, 2019 WL 1198361 (S.D. Ohio Mar. 14, 2019) (unreported).

74. *See, e.g.*, *In re* Calley, 232 So. 3d 68 (La. Ct. App. 2017) (1989 trust language that created payback-type requirement).

75. *See* Herting v. Cal. Dep't of Health Care Servs., 235 Cal. App. 4th 607 (Cal. Ct. App. 2015); Kevin Urbatsch, Herting v. California Department of Health Care Services*: The First-Party Special Needs Trust Payback Provision: Do Medicaid's Estate Recovery Statutory Exceptions Apply?*, 12 NAELA J. 57 (2016).

76. *See, e.g.*, Ala. Medicaid Agency v. Britton, 306 So. 3d 51 (Ala. Civ. App. 2020); POMS SI 01120.203.E.1–.2 (allowable and prohibited expenses before payback). See also *State v. Hammans*, 870 N.E.2d 1071 (Ind. Ct. App. 2007), allowing payment of years of personal services provided by the trustees/parents of the beneficiary before Medicaid repayment, but note that the Indiana legislature modified state law after the *Hammans* decision. Also note that some expenses—notably including legal and trustee fees—may be payable before the Medicaid repayment. *See In re* James H. Supplemental Needs Trs., 194 A.D.3d 1167 (N.Y. App. Div. 2021).

77. 36 Cal. App. 5th 734 (Cal. Ct. App. 2019).

78. *Id.* at 734–41.

79. *Id.* at 742–65.

emphasized the trade-off in 42 U.S.C. § 1396p(d)(4)(A)[80] and the CMS position on the differences between estate recovery and the payback requirement.[81]

XVIII. Administrative Matters

Because an SNT is a type of discretionary trust, the state's trust code regarding administration applies and, as a result, there may be issues regarding the trustee's actions. For example, in *In re Skinner*,[82] the North Carolina Supreme Court affirmed the removal of the trustee due to the trustee's noncompliance in accounting, self-dealing, and other breaches of fiduciary duty.[83] *In re James H. Supplemental Needs Trusts*[84] also concerned the removal of the trustee for breach of fiduciary duty.[85] Consider the court's observation regarding the rightness of the removal of the trustee: "the record shows that respondent is unsuitable to execute the SNTs given that he does not understand the SNTs or what expenses are permissible under the trust agreements, which makes it difficult for him to perform his most basic duties as trustee."[86] This should be kept in mind when selecting the trustee.

80. *Id.* at 759 ("The quid pro quo for not considering assets in a special needs trust for Medi-Cal eligibility purposes is that any assets remaining in such a trust at the death of the beneficiary must be used to reimburse the state for its Medi-Cal expenses on behalf of the beneficiary . . . Section 1396p(d)(4)(A) does not explicitly or implicitly permit a qualification that the Department be reimbursed only for services provided to a beneficiary over the age of 55. Accordingly, construing Probate Code section 3605 to require such a qualification would lead it to be in conflict with, and therefore preempted by, section 1396p(d)(4)(A).").

81. *Id.* at 761 ("[A]ccording to CMS, '[a] state's entitlement to reimbursement from trusts described in [section 1396p(d)(4)] exists independent of the estate recovery authority in [section 1396p(b)],' and '[t]he mandatory reimbursement terms in a [section 1396p(d)(4)] trust, and not the provisions of [section 1396p(b)], provide the basis for a state's reimbursement rights from such trusts.' 'The statutory language does not limit the states' right to reimbursement from [section 1396p(d)(4)] trusts to the services a Medicaid beneficiary receives, nor does it condition the right upon the age of a trust beneficiary or absence of surviving family members, or otherwise make the states' reimbursement rights subject to [section 1396p(b)]. No limitation on a state's entitlement to reimbursement from [section 1396p(d)(4)] trusts may be imposed other than what is expressly contained in the statute.'") (citing to CMS letter dated January 6, 2015).

82. 804 S.E.2d 449 (N.C. 2017).

83. *Id.* at 459–60 ("[T]he Assistant Clerk's unchallenged findings of fact establish that Mr. Skinner, while acting as the trustee under the Special Needs Trust and as the guardian of Ms. Skinner's estate, spent more than ninety percent of the monies that had been deposited in the Special Needs Trust for purposes for which he received some, if not all, of the benefit within sixty days of obtaining control of those monies. As a result, . . . 'Mr. Skinner's use of Trust assets to reimburse himself for personal expenditures was improper, constitutes self-dealing, and is a breach of his fiduciary duties both as Trustee and Guardian. . . .") (citations omitted). *Id.* at 460.

84. 101 N.Y.S.3d 477 (N.Y. 2019).

85. *Id.* at 481 ("Petitioner's application to have respondent removed as trustee is based not only on her difficulty communicating with respondent, but also on his refusal to timely pay for various expenses of James H., including eyeglasses, dental care, transportation and medical treatments.").

86. *Id.* at 482.

Compensation of the trustee may also be an issue. Section 708 of the Uniform Trust Code provides for reasonable compensation of the trustee if the trust itself is silent on the matter of compensation.[87] POMS SI 001120.203.E.3 provides that "[p]ayments of fees and administrative expenses during the life of the beneficiary are allowable as permitted by the trust document and are not affected by the State Medicaid reimbursement requirement." The amount of compensation is influenced by a number of factors, including the trustee's performance.[88]

XIX. Spousal and Child Support

Spousal and child support bring up interesting questions. First, can the support payments be payable to the SNT?[89] Yes. POMS SI 01120.200.G.1.d, Assignment of Income, provides:

> A legally assignable payment that is assigned to a trust or trustee is income for SSI purposes, to the individual entitled or eligible to receive the payment, **unless** the assignment is irrevocable. We consider assignment of payment by court orders to be irrevocable. For example, child support or alimony payments paid directly to a trust or trustee because of a court order are considered irrevocably assigned and thus not income. . . .

May a child with a disability continue to receive child support after reaching the age of 18?[90] The state's child support statute may provide for a continuing support obligation for a child with disability if certain factors can be shown.[91] It is most helpful if the support order directs that the child support be paid to the trustee of the SNT.[92]

If the beneficiary of the SNT is the one that owes the support obligation, can the trustee pay the support from the SNT? This question deserves a classic

87. *See also* Ala. Medicaid Agency v. Britton, 306 So. 3d 51 (Ala. Civ. App. 2020); POMS SI 001120.203.E.1.

88. *See In re* Perkins, No. 14CA4, 2014 WL 2565817, at *33 (Ohio Ct. App. June 4, 2014) (trustee fees reduced based upon trustee's failure to fulfill fiduciary duties).

89. Guthrie v. Guthrie, 455 S.W.3d 839, 846 (Ark. Ct. App. 2015) (child support payments to SNT trustee). *See also In re* Ruby G. Owen Tr., 418 S.W.3d 421(Ark. Ct. App. 2012).

90. *Guthrie*, 455 S.W.3d 839 (parent's child support obligation continues for 22-year-old child with disability). *See also* M.E.W. v. W.L.W., 240 A.3d 626 (Pa. Super. Ct. 2020); Wright v. Wright-White, 334 So. 3d 1255, 1260 (Ala. Ct. App. 2021).

91. *Guthrie*, 455 S.W.3d at 844 (discussing requirements of applicable statute). *See also Wright*, 334 So. 3d at 1260; Keller v. Keller, 516 S.W.3d 906 (Mo. Ct. App. 2017).

92. *See, e.g.*, Kim C. Martin, Divorce and the Special Needs Child or How to Save the Day by Knowing a Lot about a Little, Presented at the 2021 Stetson College of Law Special Needs Planning and Special Needs Trust Conference (2021).

law school answer: it depends. And it does, on state statutes, court opinions, whether the beneficiary is receiving Medicaid or SSI or both, the state Medicaid agency, the regional SSA office, and the terms of the trust. There still must be consideration given to[93] the sole benefit requirement, which may be a stumbling block for an SSA region, even though the beneficiary has a legally enforceable obligation. If the trust contains a spendthrift clause, does the state's trust code make a creditor's exception for support obligations? For example, in *Alexander v. Harris*,[94] the beneficiary of a (d)(4)(A) SNT was the father of the child. The SNT contained a spendthrift clause. The mother filed a petition and continuing writ of garnishment and pointed to Florida Statute section 736.0503, which provides an exception to the spendthrift clause protection in cases of child support.[95] The Florida appellate court could find no authority that requiring the SNT to pay the support obligation would in some way affect the beneficiary's public benefits eligibility[96] and further that "federal law gives great deference to state courts in family law proceedings."[97] The court noted that it had to weigh the equities between the parties and weigh the competing public policies;[98] the appellate court had previously found that "[w]here the two conflict, this court has held that Florida's public policy favoring enforcement of support orders takes precedence."[99] The appellate court reversed the trial court's denial of the mother's petition and directed "entry of a continuing writ of garnishment directed to discretionary disbursements from the special needs trust."[100] The language of the court order is critical. For example, court-ordered contributions to the SNT may not be viewed as child support without clear language.[101]

---

93. *See, e.g.*, Craig C. Reaves, *Child Support for an Adult Child with Disabilities*, 8 Voice (Special Needs All.), Dec. 2014, https://www.specialneedsalliance.org/the-voice/child-support-for-an-adult-child-with-disabilities/.

94. 278 So. 3d 721 (Fla. Dist. Ct. App. 2019).

95. *Id.* at 721–22.

96. *Id.* at 723.

97. *Id.*

98. *Id.* at 723–24.

99. *Id.* at 724.

100. *Id.*

101. *See, e.g.*, Kirby v. Semeyn, 531 S.W.3d 462 (Ark. Ct. App. 2017) (discussing differences between court-ordered contributions to SNT and child support).

CHAPTER 5

Third-Party Special Needs Trusts

I. Introduction

Trusts are an incredible tool for the estate planner and the client. They provide a level of flexibility not available through a will and allow the settlor to attach "strings" to a transfer of property through a trust. There are as many types of trusts as there are ideas. This chapter focuses on the third-party discretionary special needs trust (SNT).[1]

According to the Social Security Administration (SSA) Program Operations Manual System (POMS):

> A third-party trust is a trust established with the assets of someone other than the trust beneficiary (or his or her spouse). For example, a grandparent can establish a third party trust using his or her assets, with a grandchild as the trust beneficiary. Be alert for situations where a trust is allegedly

1. See Social Security Administration Program Operations Manual System (POMS) SI 01120.200.B.12, which states:

> A **special needs trust**, also known as a **supplemental needs trust**, may be set up to provide for a disabled individual's extra and supplemental needs other than food, shelter, and health care expenses that may be covered by public assistance benefits that the trust beneficiary may be eligible to receive under various programs. For more information on special needs trusts containing the assets of the individual, see SI 01120.203.

When reading this chapter, keep in mind state variations may change the appropriate approach to drafting the trust for the client. For example, in many states attorneys use a pure discretionary trust instead of an SNT because a beneficiary cannot compel a distribution from the trust and, as a result, the trust assets are not deemed to be an available resource. However, in Kansas a pure discretionary trust will cause a person to be disqualified from Medicaid. This is because Kansas Statutes section 39-709(e)(3) deems any trust that does not have a special needs distribution standard to be an available resource for Kansas Medicaid purposes. Because other states could adopt the Kansas rule, the safer course of action for the drafter is to include SNT language in the third-party SNT.

established with the assets of a third party but in reality is created with the trust beneficiary's property. In such cases, the trust is a grantor trust, not a third party trust.[2]

SSA considers a discretionary trust as

> a trust in which the trustee has full discretion as to the time, purpose, and amount of all distributions. The trustee may pay all or none of the trust as he or she considers appropriate to, or for the benefit of, the trust beneficiary. The trust beneficiary has no control over the trust.[3]

Although an SNT is often considered for the purpose of maintaining public benefits eligibility of a beneficiary, there are other compelling reasons for using a third-party SNT. For example, the third-party SNT can provide for the beneficiary with special needs and at the beneficiary's death pass on the trust res to others designated by the settlor; the third-party SNT has no Medicaid payback provision; and the third-party SNT can be named as the beneficiary on certain assets like a life insurance policy or an annuity.[4]

II. What Is a Discretionary Trust?

According to *Black's Law Dictionary*, a "discretionary trust" is "[a] trust in which the settlor has delegated nearly complete or limited discretion to the trustee to decide when and how much income or property is distributed to a beneficiary [and] . . . is perhaps the most common type of trust used in estate planning."[5] Contrast a discretionary trust with a support trust, which is a type of discretionary trust wherein

> the settlor authorizes the trustee to pay to the beneficiary as much income or principal as the trustee believes is needed for support, [especially] for "comfortable support" or "support in accordance with the beneficiary's standard of living" [and where a] beneficiary's interest cannot be voluntarily transferred, but creditors who provide necessaries can [usually] reach it; general creditors cannot.[6]

2. *Id.* SI 01120.200.B.16.
3. *Id.* SI 01120.200.B.1.
4. *See, e.g.*, *What Is a "Third-Party" Special Needs Trust and How Is It Different from Other Kinds of Trusts?*, Special Needs Answers (June 27, 2017), https://specialneedsanswers.com/what-is-a-third-party-special-needs-trust-and-how-is-it-different-from-other-kinds-of-trusts-15111.
5. *Discretionary Trust*, Black's Law Dictionary (11th ed. 2019) (Westlaw).
6. *Support Trust*, Black's Law Dictionary (11th ed. 2019) (Westlaw).

These distinctions are important for public benefits eligibility when drafting a third-party trust. As noted in *Bogert's The Law of Trusts and Trustees*:

> Settlors who create trusts for beneficiaries known to be disabled and receiving state care, however, may create what is known as supplemental needs trusts. In these trusts, the trustee has discretion to provide only those benefits to the beneficiary that are beyond those benefits that the state provides, and only those benefits that will not make the beneficiary ineligible for state aid. These trusts have so far withstood challenge by the state.
>
> Where a discretionary supplemental needs trust has been funded by the beneficiary's own assets, such as from an award in a tort settlement, the settlor-beneficiary will not be disqualified from Medicaid benefits if the trust terms provide that the state be repaid from the trust assets remaining at the settlor-beneficiary's death. These trusts are known as pay-back trusts, and must be created to comply with the provisions of the 1993 Omnibus Budget Reconciliation Act (OBRA).[7]

Further, compare a discretionary trust to a support trust, which

> is one in which a trustee is directed to pay or apply trust income or principal for the beneficiary's benefit, but only to the extent necessary to support the beneficiary, and only when the disbursements will accomplish support. The trustee must determine the beneficiary's needs for support and must make disbursements for what is necessary for that support. The trust instrument need not explicitly use the word "support."[8]

Bogert et al. discuss the differences between the discretionary trust and the support trust as pertains to public benefits eligibility:

> [T]he question often arises whether assets of a trust for the benefit of a person receiving public institutional care are available to the state or its public agency. In the case of a support trust, the result depends upon the trust terms as to whether the trust assets were intended to be the primary source of support or merely supplemental to public resources. The assets of a support trust constitute a beneficiary's "available assets" for purposes of Medicaid eligibility, because the state is providing for the beneficiary's health, maintenance and support. However, the assets of discretionary trusts that are created as supplemental needs trusts are not available assets for Medicaid purposes.

7. George G. Bogert et al., Bogert's The Law of Trusts and Trustees § 228 (June 2022 update) (citations omitted) (noting the distinction regarding treatment of a third-party trust from a first-party trust).

8. *Id.* § 229.

The trustees may exercise discretion only as to the beneficiary's needs beyond those that the state furnishes.[9]

The language used in the trust will signal whether the trust is a pure discretionary trust or a discretionary support trust. For example, language such as "'absolute', 'sole', or 'uncontrolled'" is signal for a pure discretionary trust.[10] One court explained the differences between a support trust with standards and one that was a pure support trust as follows:

> A settlor creates a pure support trust "[i]f a trustee is directed to pay or apply trust income or principal for the benefit of a named person, but only to the extent necessary to support him, *and only when the disbursements will accomplish support.*" In contrast, a settlor creates a [discretionary trust with standards] if "the stated purpose of the trust is to furnish the beneficiary with support, and the trustee is directed to pay to the beneficiary whatever amount of trust income [or principal] the trustee deems necessary for his support." Generally, if the trust is a [discretionary trust with standards], the beneficiary has a right that the trustee pay him the amount which in the exercise of reasonable discretion is needed for his support. . .; and the beneficiary can transfer this interest or his creditors may reach it, unless it is protected by a spendthrift clause.[11]

Another court makes the distinction this way:[12]

> In analyzing the terms of a testamentary trust to determine if the corpus is "available" to a beneficiary for purposes of Medicaid eligibility, courts have looked to whether the trust is a support trust or a discretionary trust. We find the following formulation by the Supreme Court of North Dakota helpful where, as here, the beneficiary is not a cotrustee:

9. *Id.* (citations omitted).

10. *See, e.g.*, UNIF. TR. CODE § 814(a) (UNIF. L. COMM'N 2010) ("Notwithstanding the breadth of discretion granted to a trustee in terms of the trust . . . the trustee shall exercise a discretionary power in good faith and in accordance with the terms and purposes of the trust and the interests of the beneficiaries.").

11. *See In re* Est. of Gist, 763 N.W.2d 561, 565 (Iowa 2009) (citing *In re* Barkema Tr., 690 N.W.2d 50, 54 (Iowa 2004)) (citations omitted). In this case:

> The trust agreement created by the joint will of the Piries gave the trustee the discretion to distribute the income of the trust to Elenore "as may be necessary to provide her with a reasonable standard of living, considering any other means of support or resources which she may have." The trust gave the trustee the discretion to invade the principal or corpus to provide her with a reasonable standard of living. The trust did not limit the principal and corpus payments to the mere support of Elenore, but allowed those payments to provide her with a reasonable standard of living. This language created a discretionary trust with standards.

Id. at 565–66 (citations omitted).

12. Pohlmann v. Neb. Dep't of Health & Hum. Servs., 710 N.W.2d 639 (Neb. 2006).

> The settlor's intent determines whether a trust is classified as a support or a discretionary trust, which in turn determines what portion of the trust is available to an applicant for the purpose of qualifying for Medicaid benefits. . . . A support trust essentially provides the trustee "shall pay or apply only so much of the income and principal or either as is necessary for the education or support of a beneficiary." . . . A support trust allows a beneficiary to compel distributions of income, principal, or both, for expenses necessary for the beneficiary's support, and an agency may consider the support trust as an available asset when evaluating eligibility for assistance. . . .
>
> Conversely, a discretionary trust grants the trustee "uncontrolled discretion over payment to the beneficiary" and may reference the "general welfare" of the beneficiary. . . . Because the beneficiary of a discretionary trust does not have the ability to compel distributions from the trust, only those distributions of income, principal, or both, actually made by the trustee may be considered by the agency as available assets when evaluating eligibility for assistance.[13]

Sometimes the trust language is unclear as to whether the trust is a support trust or a discretionary trust and, as a result, a court has to determine which the trust is. For example, in *Kryzsko v. Ramsey County Social Services*,[14] the question was whether the testamentary trust established for the beneficiary with a disability was a discretionary trust or a support trust. The North Dakota Supreme Court found that the trust had components of both types of trusts. Because the trustee did not have "unfettered discretion" and the "support language [used] qualifies the discretionary language[, i]t provides a standard by which the trustee's exercise of discretion may be judged."[15] The language used in the trust did not show any intent on the part of the testator for the trust to be an SNT; rather the trust language directed the trustee "to administer moneys 'necessary or advisable to provide for the proper care, maintenance, support, and education of'" the beneficiary.[16] "This support language provides a clear standard by which the reasonableness of the trustee's discretion may be judged."[17]

---

13. *Id.* at 645 (citing Eckes v. Richland Cnty. Soc. Servs., 621 N.W.2d 851, 855–56 (N.D. 2001)) (citations omitted).
14. 607 N.W.2d 237 (N.D. 2000).
15. *Id.* at 241–42.
16. *Id.* at 242–43.
17. *Id.* at 244.

III. Distinctions of a Third-Party SNT from the First-Party SNT

As seen in Chapter 4, a first-party SNT is authorized under the U.S. Code as a result of OBRA (see Appendix A) and found in 42 U.S.C. § 1396p(d)(4)(A) and (C). The authority for a third-party trust is basically found in the common law or a state statute. Unlike the first-party trust, there is no requirement for a payback.[18]

The most significant distinctions of a third-party SNT from a first-party SNT are twofold: (1) who is establishing the trust, and (2) whose money is used to establish the trust. With the third-party trust, the trust is not funded with the beneficiary's money. The person who establishes the trust can be anyone other than the beneficiary or the beneficiary's spouse (unless if by will).[19] Unlike the first-party trust, the money is not provided by the beneficiary. Instead, the money is from the settlor, or third party, often referred to by the acronym OPM, or "other people's money."[20]

A. Why a Third-Party SNT?

In many instances the settlor wishes to leave money or property in trust for someone (other than a charity) but does not want the trustee to make outright distributions to the beneficiaries. The settlor may include "strings" in the trust, limiting distributions for certain things (e.g., support, education, etc.) or requiring a beneficiary to reach a certain age before the trustee makes distributions.[21] Using typical support language such as a health, education, maintenance, and support (HEMS) standard will not make the trust an SNT; in

18. 42 U.S.C. § 1396p(d)(4). *See also* Richard A. Courtney, A Lawyer's Guide to Working with Special Needs Clients 231 (2019).

19. Recall that under 42 U.S.C. § 1396p(d)(4)(A) the trust can be created by the beneficiary (the person), the parents, a guardian, or the court.

20. See, for example, *Boyd v. Boyd*, No. G042907, 2010 WL 5125513 (Cal. Ct. App. Dec. 16, 2010) (unreported), where the settlor had created an inter vivos revocable trust that would be distributed on death to several beneficiaries including his mother (the beneficiary) who was receiving Medicaid. *Id.* at *1–3. One question concerned whether the successor trustee could establish—or could be required to establish—a third-party SNT for the beneficiary. *Id.* at *6. After observing that the beneficiary of a trust is ordinarily entitled to receive their share promptly and outright (absent other terms in the trust), the court ruled that the trustee's failure or refusal to work to create an SNT was not a breach of her fiduciary duty. In fact, noted the court, "regardless of whether [trustee], the court, or [beneficiary] formed a trust, such trust would utilize the assets of [beneficiary] and therefore amount to a first party trust." *Id.* at *7. *See also*, *e.g.*, Doyle v. Hood, 112 N.E.3d 1040 (Ill. App. Ct. 2018).

21. *See* Unif. Tr. Code § 103(2) (Unif. L. Comm'n 2010) ("'Ascertainable standard' means a standard elating to an individual's health, education, support, or maintenance within the meaning of Section 2041(b)(1)(A) or 2514(c)(1) of the Internal Revenue Code of 1986. . . ."). Note that this is not a "special needs" distribution standard and using such standard could cause a beneficiary to lose eligibility for means-tested public benefits, since public benefits agencies might take the position that the "ascertainable"

fact, in those instances the trust most likely will be deemed a support trust and available to the beneficiary, thus disqualifying the beneficiary from means-tested public benefits.[22] In fact, for a third-party SNT, "[d]istributions from a special needs trust must be discretionary with the trustee, and the beneficiary must have no control."[23]

Unfortunately, failing to include an SNT in estate planning documents may mean that the beneficiary will be ineligible for public benefits. For example, in *Conservatorship of the Estate of Kane*,[24] the beneficiary received an inheritance outright, and as the court noted:

> The estate planning previously undertaken for [the decedent] did not, unfortunately, include any special provisions for [the beneficiary], such as the establishment of a special needs trust for him. In particular, such a special needs trust is desirable for [the beneficiary], because if he were to receive his inheritance directly, he would be ineligible for SSI [Supplemental Security Income] and Medi-Cal benefits, and would likely deplete the inheritance relatively quickly to pay for ordinary living expenses and medical care. However, if the legacy was placed in a special needs trust, he could use the trust proceeds for his special needs, such as various types of therapy, while he is still receiving public benefits.[25]

---

standard creates a power in the beneficiary to seek enforcement—whether or not the beneficiary actually seeks such enforcement.

22. See, for example, Kristen M. Lewis, Planning for Beneficiaries with Special Needs § III(F) (2017), which outlines the following:

> F. Special Needs Trusts are not "available" or "countable" for purposes of most "means-tested" government benefits
>
> 1. Special Needs Trusts that are ***properly drafted*** **are not considered "available"** or "countable" for purposes of the beneficiary's eligibility for most "means-tested" government benefits, including Medicaid and Supplemental Security Income (discussed in Section IV, *infra*).
>
> **a**. A properly drafted Special Needs Trust (whether for a first-party or a third-party trust) will specify that the Trustee is not obligated, and cannot be compelled by the beneficiary, to use the assets of the trust to provide for the beneficiary's "support" or "maintenance." **The use of the "support" or "maintenance" distribution standards typically results in the trust assets being deemed "available" or "countable" to the beneficiary for purposes of means-tested benefits**. *See* POMS SI 01120.200.D.2.
>
> **(1)** Thus, the **classic "ascertainable standards"** for trust distributions found in most testamentary "Bypass/Credit Shelter Trusts" (*i.e.* "health, education, ***maintenance*** **and *support***") will generally render the assets of those trusts **"available" or "countable"** resources to a beneficiary seeking to maintain his eligibility for means-tested government benefits.

See also Courtney, *supra* note 18, at 231.

23. *See* Thomas D. Begley, Jr. & Andrew H. Hook, *A Dozen Common Mistakes with Special Needs Planning*, 39 Est. Plan. 44, 45 (2012) (citing POMS SI 01120.200.B.10). *See also* Courtney, *supra* note 18, at 231.

24. 137 Cal. App. 4th 400 (Cal. Ct. App. 2006).

25. *Id.* at 402–03.

As noted in the POMS, a properly drafted third-party SNT would not be considered a resource for determining the beneficiary's eligibility for means-tested public benefits:

> If an individual does not have the legal authority to revoke or terminate the trust or to direct the use of the trust assets for his or her own support and maintenance, the trust principal is not the individual's resource for SSI purposes.
>
> The revocability of a trust and the ability to direct the use of the trust principal depend on the terms of the trust agreement and on State (or Tribal) law. If a trust is irrevocable by its terms and under State law, and the trust beneficiary cannot control or direct use of the trust assets for the trust beneficiary's support and maintenance, the trust is not a resource.[26]

For a beneficiary with special needs, that beneficiary may never be able to manage property. A trust thus seems to be the ideal vehicle for providing for a beneficiary, but not as an outright gift to the beneficiary.[27] Although one may consider the use of the third-party SNT for a child, it can also be used for an adult with special needs, such as a sibling, or in some instances where a settlor-spouse creates the third-party SNT for the spouse with special needs.[28]

The more common scenario involves the use of a third-party SNT for a child with special needs, whether the child is a minor or adult. The parent-settlor may have cared for that child for the entirety of the child's life, and the parent-settlor is now faced with the question of who will care for the child once the parent-settlor is no longer able to do so or has died.[29] Some settlors may take the approach that one of the settlor's other children may take care of the sibling with special needs, but that is neither a foolproof nor wise approach.[30] Still other settlors may choose to disinherit the child with special needs, trusting that public benefits and the generosity of others will provide the child with the needed care. That, too, is neither a foolproof nor wise plan.[31]

---

26. POMS SI 01120.200.D.2, https://secure.ssa.gov/poms.nsf/lnx/0501120200 (last visited Dec. 11, 2022).

27. *See* Begley & Hook, *supra* note 23 (first common mistake is failing to plan and either creating a support trust or making a gift directly to the child with special needs; such will be treated as resources for means-tested public benefits).

28. *See, e.g.*, Stuart D. Zimring et al., Fundamentals of Special Needs Trusts § 1.05 (2018).

29. *See id.* ch. 4A.

30. Begley & Hook, *supra* note 23, at 44 ("[M]oney left to the healthy sibling is subject to the creditors of the healthy sibling, may be subject to claims in divorce proceeding, and may disqualify the healthy sibling's children from receiving financial aid for college expenses (or reduce the financial aid that is available). Furthermore, the healthy sibling may turn out to be less trustworthy than the parent believed. The healthy sibling may also undergo pressure from a spouse to 'borrow the money temporarily.'").

31. *See* Kristen M. Lewis, Planning for Persons with Disabilities: Recent Developments and Continued Challenges § II (2021).

At the outset of planning, even if it seems that the beneficiary will have sufficient wealth to be provided by the trust and thus not need to be eligible for means-tested public benefits, there is no guarantee that the beneficiary will die before the trust principal is exhausted. For a beneficiary who is eligible for public benefits, the trust can be written in such a way as to have the trust distributions "supplement rather than supplant"[32] such benefits, thus maintaining the beneficiary's eligibility for or receipt of such benefits.[33] On the other hand, there is no guarantee that public benefits programs will not change or be available in the future for the beneficiary but a conservative approach to drafting the trust to allow for future eligibility may be the better approach regardless.

So why then use a third-party SNT? There are significant advantages to using the third-party SNT. Because it allows the settlor to provide for the beneficiary without having to rely on family members to do so, it allows the settlor to pick a trusted trustee who will have the discretion to make distributions for the beneficiary and ensure that the beneficiary has as much of a quality of life as possible and it provides a level of protection for the beneficiary that would not be otherwise provided in a discretionary non-SNT third-party trust vis-à-vis distribution language.[34]

One other circumstance can give rise to a third-party SNT—albeit with a wrinkle. Transfer penalty rules allow a prospective SSI or Medicaid applicant to make gifts to a child[35] or other person under age 65[36] with a disability. But two problems arise with such transfers (in many, but not all, cases):

1. The disabled beneficiary may not be able to manage assets or income, and therefore may need any transfer to be in trust or subject to court supervision in a conservatorship or other protective proceeding.
2. The disabled beneficiary may also be receiving benefits from a means-tested program like SSI or Medicaid, and risk losing those benefits if he or she receives assets from the transferor.

---

32. *See, e.g.*, Lewis, *supra* note 22, § III(F)(1)(c) ("A properly drafted Special Needs Trust (whether for a first-party or a third-party trust) will specify the Settlor's intention that **the trust should 'supplement, not supplant' any public or private benefits** for which the beneficiary may be eligible as a consequence of his disability").

33. *See* Courtney, *supra* note 18, at 223 (noting the use of SNTs provides "protection and effective management of property and assets for the benefit of the disabled individual, and as a 'special needs' or 'supplemental needs' trust (SNT) to make such assets not countable for purposes of means-based public benefits for support of the individual.").

34. See Appendix M for different examples of language.

35. 42 U.S.C. § 1396p(c)(2)(B)(iii).

36. *Id.* § 1396p(c)(2)(B)(iv).

Accordingly, the transfer exemption statute expressly permits the approved transfers to either be directly to the disabled person *or* to a trust for that person's benefit. Though the language of 42 U.S.C. § 1396p(c)(2)(B) does not expressly require such a trust to be for the *sole* benefit of the beneficiary, that additional requirement is widely read into the statutory provision—with the result that most (if not all) Medicaid agencies require that the trust for a disabled child or under-65 beneficiary must be actuarially sound or include a payback provision like that required by 42 U.S.C. § 1396p(d)(4)(A) and (B).

Because of the interpretation limiting the language of these trusts, they are often referred to as "sole benefit" trusts. Usually (but not always) that term implies a third-party trust but with a payback provision for the disabled beneficiary. In a sense, such trusts are essentially hybrids—self-settled trusts from the perspective of the receiving beneficiary, with the requirement of a payback provision, but more like third-party trusts from the perspective of the settlor, who is transferring assets away from his or her own name in order to secure eligibility.

Analysis of Options for Leaving Assets for a Child Who Has a Disability*

Options	Fiduciary duty to manage for child	Flexibility to adapt to changes	Avoid court oversight	Protected from child's creditors	Maintains eligibility for public assistance
1. Outright to child either as:					
a. Gift to child	No	No	Yes	No	No
b. Conservatorship	Yes	No	No	No	No
2. Outright to third party with moral obligation	No	No	Yes	Yes, but not from third party's creditors	Yes
3. Disinherit child	No	No	Yes	Yes	Yes
4. Trust					
a. Support or discretionary support trust	Yes	Yes	Yes	Often	No
b. Discretionary	Yes, but total discretion	Yes	Yes	Yes	Possibly
5. Special Needs	Yes	Yes	Yes	Yes	Yes

* STUART D. ZIMRING ET AL., FUNDAMENTALS OF SPECIAL NEEDS TRUSTS tbl.4A.1 (2018).

Practitioners without the experience of drafting and using a third-party SNT may find that they have made one of several common mistakes that may be made when planning for clients who have a child with a disability.[37] For example, as mentioned earlier, some parents may decide to disinherit the child with a disability,[38] relying instead on public benefits or other means of supporting the child. Others will give the child's share to a sibling, thinking that the sibling will provide care for the sibling with a disability.[39] As well, the attorney may mistakenly use the wrong standard, such as a support standard, rather than the discretionary distribution standard.[40] The failure to include a spendthrift provision can also prove problematic.[41]

B. Who Is a Third Party?

Without being too glib, who is the third-party settlor? It is not the beneficiary, especially the person with a disability for whom the trust will be established. According to *Black's Law Dictionary*, a "third party" is "[s]omeone who is

37. *See* Begley & Hook, *supra* note 23, at 44.

38. Jacob H. Menashe, Spotlight on Select Special Needs Trust Issues: Third Party and First Party Examples, Counseling Considerations, and Possible Impacts of the ACA and the ABLE Act, TSWB19 ALI-CLE 1 (Mar. 10, 2015) (discussing risks that come with the approach when the money is left to the sibling, creating "a moral obligation").

39. Begley & Hook, *supra* note 23, at 44.

40. *Id.* at 45 (citing POMS SI 01120.200.B.10). For a further discussion regarding the difference between a support trust and a discretionary trust with standards, see *In re Estate of Gist*, 763 N.W.2d 561 (Iowa 2009):

> We explained the difference between a pure support trust and a support trust with standards as follows:
>
> > A settlor creates a pure support trust "[i]f a trustee is directed to pay or apply trust income or principal for the benefit of a named person, but only to the extent necessary to support him, *and only when the disbursements will accomplish support.*" In contrast, a settlor creates a [discretionary trust with standards] if "the stated purpose of the trust is to furnish the beneficiary with support, and the trustee is directed to pay to the beneficiary whatever amount of trust income [or principal] the trustee deems necessary for his support." Generally, if the trust is a [discretionary trust with standards],
> >
> > the beneficiary has a right that the trustee pay him the amount which in the exercise of reasonable discretion is needed for his support . . .; and the beneficiary can transfer this interest or his creditors may reach it, unless it is protected by a spendthrift clause.
>
> The trust agreement created by the joint will of the Piries gave the trustee the discretion to distribute the income of the trust to Elenore "as may be necessary to provide her with a reasonable standard of living, considering any other means of support or resources which she may have." The trust gave the trustee the discretion to invade the principal or corpus to provide her with a reasonable standard of living. The trust did not limit the principal and corpus payments to the mere support of Elenore, but allowed those payments to provide her with a reasonable standard of living. This language created a discretionary trust with standards.

Id. at 565–66 (citations omitted).

41. *See* LEWIS, *supra* note 31, § III(C)(2)(a).

not a party to a lawsuit, agreement, or other transaction but who is . . . somehow implicated in it; someone other than the principal parties."[42] The *Code of Federal Regulations* defines "third party" as "any individual, entity or program that is or may be liable to pay all or part of the expenditures for medical assistance furnished under a State plan."[43] Thus it is clear that the settlor for a third-party SNT should not be someone with a legal obligation to support the beneficiary, even without a court order, contract, or other way to impose an obligation of support.

IV. Uniform Trust Code

The Uniform Trust Code (UTC),[44] approved by the Uniform Law Commission[45] in 2000,[46] has been adopted in 32 states.[47] The UTC eliminated the distinction between a discretionary trust and a support trust[48] in section 504.[49] As a result of this change, some concerns were expressed about the impact on third-party SNTs.[50] UTC section 504 now just addresses discretionary trusts:

---

42. *Third Party*, Black's Law Dictionary (11th ed. 2019) (Westlaw).

43. 42 C.F.R. § 433.136 (2022) (Medicaid programs). 42 C.F.R. § 433.138 summarizes the information that the state Medicaid agency must gather to determine if there any legally obligated third parties or resources.

44. Unif. L. Comm'n, *Trust Code*, https://www.uniformlaws.org/committees/community-home?CommunityKey=193ff839-7955-4846-8f3c-ce74ac23938d (last visited Dec. 11, 2022).

45. Unif. L. Comm'n, https://www.uniformlaws.org/home (last visited Dec. 11, 2022).

46. It was adopted in 2000, and has been amended in 2003, 2004, and 2005. The last revision was in 2010; Unif. L. Comm'n, *supra* note 44.

47. *Id.*

48. Unif. Tr. Code § 504 & cmt. (Unif. L. Comm'n 2010) ("This section addresses the ability of a beneficiary's creditor to reach the beneficiary's discretionary trust interest, whether or not the exercise of the trustee's discretion is subject to a standard. This section, similar to the Restatement, eliminates the distinction between discretionary and support trusts, unifying the rules for all trusts fitting within either of the former categories."). *See, e.g.*, Jennifer Brannan, *Third-Party Special Needs Trust: Dead or Alive in a Uniform Trust Code World*, 16 Tex. Wesleyan L. Rev. 249, 263–64, 267–68 (2010) (noting the UTC elimination of distinction between discretionary and support trusts and discussing the arguments on whether UTC § 504 impacts the viability of SNTs).

49. Unif. Tr. Code § 504 & cmts. (Unif. L. Comm'n 2010) ("This section, similar to the Restatement, eliminates the distinction between discretionary and support trusts, unifying the rules for all trusts fitting within either of the former categories. . . . By eliminating this distinction, the rights of a creditor are the same whether the distribution standard is discretionary, subject to a standard, or both. Other than for a claim by a child, spouse or former spouse, a beneficiary's creditor may not reach the beneficiary's interest. Eliminating this distinction affects only the rights of creditors. The effect of this change is limited to the rights of creditors. It does not affect the rights of a beneficiary to compel a distribution. Whether the trustee has a duty in a given situation to make a distribution depends on factors such as the breadth of the discretion granted and whether the terms of the trust include a support or other standard.").

50. Brannan, *supra* note 48, at 263–65 (among other things, discussing the impact of no longer distinguishing between discretionary and support trusts on third-party SNTs).

> (a) In this section, "child" includes any person for whom an order or judgment for child support has been entered in this or another State.
>
> (b) Except as otherwise provided in subsection (c), whether or not a trust contains a spendthrift provision, a creditor of a beneficiary may not compel a distribution that is subject to the trustee's discretion, even if:
>
> > (1) the discretion is expressed in the form of a standard of distribution; or
> >
> > (2) the trustee has abused the discretion.
>
> (c) To the extent a trustee has not complied with a standard of distribution or has abused a discretion:
>
> > (1) a distribution may be ordered by the court to satisfy a judgment or court order against the beneficiary for support or maintenance of the beneficiary's child, spouse, or former spouse; and
> >
> > (2) the court shall direct the trustee to pay to the child, spouse, or former spouse such amount as is equitable under the circumstances but not more than the amount the trustee would have been required to distribute to or for the benefit of the beneficiary had the trustee complied with the standard or not abused the discretion.
>
> (d) This section does not limit the right of a beneficiary to maintain a judicial proceeding against a trustee for an abuse of discretion or failure to comply with a standard for distribution.
>
> (e) If the trustee's or cotrustee's discretion to make distributions for the trustee's or cotrustee's own benefit is limited by an ascertainable standard, a creditor may not reach or compel distribution of the beneficial interest except to the extent the interest would be subject to the creditor's claim were the beneficiary not acting as trustee or cotrustee.

From the comment to section 504, it appears that the intent was not to cause negative implications for SNTs by the elimination of the distinction between discretionary and support trusts. The comment explains:

> This section addresses the ability of a beneficiary's creditor to reach the beneficiary's discretionary trust interest, whether or not the exercise of the trustee's discretion is subject to a standard. This section, similar to the Restatement, eliminates the distinction between discretionary and support trusts, unifying the rules for all trusts fitting within either of the former categories. . . . By eliminating this distinction, the rights of a creditor are the same whether the distribution standard is discretionary, subject to a standard, or

> both. Other than for a claim by a child, spouse or former spouse, a beneficiary's creditor may not reach the beneficiary's interest. *Eliminating this distinction affects only the rights of creditors* (emphasis added).

The Restatement (Third) of Trusts section 50 comments (e)(4) take note of the acknowledgement of public benefits eligibility:

> If a discretionary beneficiary is or may be eligible to receive public benefits, this factor, like the availability of other resources generally, is to be taken into account by the trustee under the usual rule of construction. Thus, to the extent consistent with the terms and purposes of the trust, and allowable by applicable benefits statutes (see Reporter's Notes), the presumption is that the trustee's discretion should be exercised in a manner that will avoid either disqualifying the beneficiary for other benefits or expending trust funds for purposes for which public funds would otherwise be available.

Although not discussed in the context of the UTC eliminating the distinctions between support and discretionary trusts, the following case has some useful parallels. In *Pikula v. Department of Social Services*,[51] the plaintiff appealed the denial of her application for Medicaid, based on a testamentary trust.[52]

The trust in question, created by the plaintiff's father, included language that the trustee would continue payments until the plaintiff's death, specifically:

> [T]he [t]rustee shall pay to or spend on behalf of [the plaintiff] as much of the net income derived from this trust fund as the [t]rustee may deem advisable to provide properly for [her] maintenance and support and may incorporate any income not so distributed into the principal of the fund at the option of the [t]rustee.[53]

In a separate paragraph, the testator authorized

> the [t]rustee in his sole and absolute discretion at any time and from time to time to disburse from the principal for any of the trust estates created under this [will], even to the point of completely exhausting the same, such amount as he may deem advisable to provide adequately and properly for the support and maintenance of the current income beneficiaries thereof, any expenses incurred by reason of illness and disability. In determining the amount of principal to be so disbursed, the [t]rustee shall take into consideration any other income or property which such income beneficiary may have from any

---

51. 138 A.3d 213 (Conn. 2016).
52. *Id.*
53. *Id.*

> other source, and the [t]rustee's discretion shall be conclusive as to the advisability of any such disbursement and the same shall not be questioned by anyone. For all sums so distributed, the [t]rustee shall have full acquittance.[54]

Once the plaintiff entered into a long-term care facility, she applied for Medicaid; her application was denied because "her assets, including the trust, exceeded the relevant asset limits."[55] After exhausting her administrative remedies, the plaintiff availed herself of the court system, claiming that "under the terms of the trust, the assets of the trust are not available to her because she is not entitled to receive trust principal and the trustee has sole and absolute discretion regarding trust expenditures and his decisions cannot be challenged by anyone."[56] The plaintiff lost at the trial court level and the Connecticut Supreme Court transferred the case from the appellate court to itself.[57] The dispute centered around whether the testator intended to create an SNT or a support trust and the Connecticut Supreme Court determined "that the testator intended to create a discretionary, supplemental needs trust and, therefore, . . . the trust corpus and income [were] not considered to be available to the plaintiff for the purpose of determining eligibility for Medicaid."[58]

The court emphasized the importance of the testator's intent:

> It is well settled that in the construction of a testamentary trust, the expressed intent of the testator must control. This intent is to be determined from reading the instrument as a whole in the light of the circumstances surrounding the testator when the instrument was executed, including the condition of his estate, his relations to his family and beneficiaries and their situation and condition. Therefore, in determining whether the assets of a testamentary trust are available to a beneficiary, this court considers whether the testator intended to create a supplemental needs trust or a general support trust.[59]

After reviewing precedent, the court devised the following test:

> [Prior] cases provide a framework for considering the language of the trust in the present case. . . . [with] several factors that are useful in determining whether a particular testamentary trust is intended to be a general needs trust or a supplemental needs trust—namely, the amount and nature of the trustee's discretion with regards to trust income and principal, any limitations or guiding principles within which the trustee must operate, and the

54. *Id.* at 213–14.
55. *Id.* at 214.
56. *Id.* (citations omitted).
57. *Id.*
58. *Id.* at 214–15.
59. *Id.* at 217 (citations omitted).

factual circumstances regarding the establishment of the trust, including the amount of the trust.[60]

After closely examining the language of the trust in this case and the specific circumstances (noting that the trust res was rather small and as a result would not provide much support for the plaintiff),[61] the court determined that the trust in question is an SNT and thus not available as a resource for the plaintiff.[62]

V. Inter Vivos or Testamentary?

The third-party SNT can be set up as an inter vivos third-party SNT or a testamentary third-party SNT. One typical scenario is when a grandparent or parent of a child with special needs is creating an estate plan that includes a testamentary third-party SNT. However, the settlor can be from a broader universe, for example a sibling, other relative, or even someone unrelated to the individual with special needs. In this estate planning scenario, it would be a common practice for the settlor to create a testamentary SNT.

A third-party inter vivos SNT is still an option, depending on the intent of the settlor and the current needs of the beneficiary. When considering an inter vivos third-party SNT, consider whether the state of situs requires seed money at the time the SNT is created. If a so-called "dry" trust is not recognized under state law, or if the third party is reluctant to create a current trust, they might consider a testamentary trust, which of course would only come into existence upon the death of the testator and probate of the testator's estate. This approach obviously would require probate proceedings, and would not be available to receive gifts from the testator or others during the testator's life. It might provide additional flexibility, however, in some limited circumstances. Since a probate proceeding will be necessary to bring the trust into being, there would be one last opportunity to seek last-minute modifications in a necessary court proceeding, taking into consideration intervening changes in public benefits law and/or the needs and circumstances of the trust's beneficiary.

For those who want to respond to the plight of the individual beneficiary, it is likely that an inter vivos third-party SNT would be created through donations, such as gifts or maybe even through crowdfunding.[63] A third-party SNT

60. *Id.* at 220.

61. *Id.* at 220–22.

62. *Id.* at 222–23.

63. Crowdfunding is "the practice of obtaining needed funding (as for a new business) by soliciting contributions from a large number of people especially from the online community." *Crowdfunding*,

will need to be funded as per the law of the applicable state, just as any other trust would be funded, but remember—the money used is not that of the beneficiary. According to the U.S. Securities and Exchange Commission:

> Crowdfunding is a relatively new and evolving method of using the Internet to raise capital to support a wide range of ideas and ventures. An entity or individual raising funds through crowdfunding typically seeks small individual contributions from a large number of people. Individuals interested in the crowdfunding campaign—members of the "crowd"—may share information about the project, cause, idea or business with each other and use the information to decide whether to fund the campaign based on the collective "wisdom of the crowd."[64]

As far as crowdfunding, a crowdfunding company is typically used and there are variations amongst the companies.[65] One expert suggests the following:

> ***Creation of a Special Needs Trust***. For special needs planners, placing a service topic on your website listing "SNTs and Crowdfunding" would be educational and can serve as an entirely new aspect of special needs work.
>
> A special needs trust will protect the beneficiary's public benefits almost immediately. Some details will need to be worked out with the crowdfunding company. (1) Can the funds be deposited directly into an established third party trust, avoiding the need for Medicaid estate recovery? (2) If not, and the funds must be paid to the beneficiary, a first party SNT will be necessary and the Medicaid payback needs to be considered as a cost of benefit planning.
>
> Because there is no Medicaid payback requirement under a third party trust, any funds remaining after the death of the beneficiary must be paid to an identified beneficiary or beneficiaries. If the individual with the disability has already signed a Last Will and Testament, the process is easier. If not,

---

Merriam-Webster Online Dictionary, https://www.merriam-webster.com/dictionary/crowdfunding. *See also* Mary Alice Jackson & Kristina M. Ferguson, Crowdfunding Redux: Charitable Intent and Unintended Consequences in 2016, Presentation at the 2016 Annual National Conference on Special Needs Planning and Special Needs Trusts at Stetson University College of Law (2016) (on file with authors).

64. *See, e.g.*, 80 Fed. Reg. 71,388 (Nov. 16, 2015), 2015 WL 7076282 (discussing the regulation of securities-based crowdfunding); 17 C.F.R. pt. 227, Regulation Crowdfunding, General Rules and Regulations (2021). *See also* Jackson & Ferguson, *supra* note 63.

65. *See* Jackson & Ferguson, *supra* note 63 ("Crowdfunding websites established 'for a cause' have an entirely different purpose, and it is these websites which can provide much-needed help for persons with disabilities or potential disabilities, and which can unknowingly create serious consequences for those currently receiving public benefits. Though crowdfunding websites have been extremely successful in helping friends, family, and even strangers raise substantial funds for personal and charitable causes, these websites typically fail to educate their users on the possible adverse implications of fundraising for an individual receiving public assistance.").

the designated beneficiaries may need to be identified by state laws directing intestate heirs. This situation also applies if there are funds remaining in a first party trust after the Medicaid payback.

A third party SNT is created by someone other than the beneficiary. The beneficiary does not want to deposit his or her own funds into the trust because this results in the complications of tracing funds when and if Medicaid payback is required. The best situation in a crowdfunding campaign would be for the contributions to be paid directly to the Trustee of the third party SNT. Will the crowdfunding company be interested in dealing with these restrictions? Will they consider this planning to subject themselves to too much liability, make the creation of a first party trust necessary, and perhaps resulting in a period of time when the beneficiary applicant/recipient will lose or miss benefits?

Unfortunately, with crowdfunding campaigns, the campaign creator—not the beneficiary—has significant control over how the solicited funds will be distributed to the beneficiary. Even if there is a third party SNT established for the beneficiary, the campaign creator may be unaware that it exists and fail to make the funds payable to the trust. Thus, education and negotiation may be necessary when dealing with campaign creators.

The benefit of establishing a third party SNT is that the SSI rules are complicated and ever-changing, and by placing funds directly into a third party SNT, such funds are prohibited from being used in ways that could potentially affect the beneficiary's status for government benefits.[66] Also, a trust may better provide for a beneficiary's needs, especially if a large amount of funds are expected from a crowdfunding campaign. A third party SNT may give the trustee control over how the funds can be used, as opposed to an outside friend or family member who may have limited insight into the beneficiary's actual needs.[67]

VI. Distribution Standard

Trusts typically use one of four distribution standards.[68] Although the assets of a third-party SNT are not treated as an asset of the beneficiary for public benefits eligibility when the beneficiary has no authority over distributions,[69]

66. POMS SI 00815.400.

67. Jackson & Ferguson, *supra* note 63.

68. *See* ZIMRING ET AL., *supra* note 28, § 4A.06 (discussing support, discretionary support, special needs, and discretionary distribution standards) ("In most states . . . a purely discretionary distribution standard will also allow the beneficiary to maintain eligibility for Medicaid.").

69. 42 U.S.C. § 1328b(e)(3)(A)(B) (resource exclusions, noting a revocable trust established by the beneficiary is countable and irrevocable trust established by beneficiary is countable if payments are able to be made to/for the beneficiary); *see also* Fay Blix, *The World of Special Needs Trusts*, 50 ORANGE CNTY. LAW. 10 (2008).

two important provisions need to be included in order for a third-party trust to be considered an SNT. First, the trust must be a discretionary trust, with language that indicates the trustee has sole and absolute discretion regarding distributions.[70]

As the POMS notes:

> If an individual does not have the legal authority to revoke or terminate the trust or to direct the use of the trust assets for his or her own support and maintenance, the trust principal is not the individual's resource for SSI purposes.
>
> The revocability of a trust and the ability to direct the use of the trust principal depend on the terms of the trust agreement and on State (or Tribal) law. If a trust is irrevocable by its terms and under State law, and the trust beneficiary cannot control or direct use of the trust assets for the trust beneficiary's support and maintenance, the trust is not a resource.[71]

Next, even if the beneficiary is not currently receiving means-tested public benefits, "SNT language" should be included—that is, language that shows the settlor's intent that the trust distributions are not intended to supplant, but to supplement, any public benefits for which the beneficiary might be eligible.[72] If the attorney does not include special needs language and the trust cannot be amended, does the attorney have liability for failing to include the language? Consider the case of *Doyle v. Hood*[73] where the trustee of an SNT sued the law firm that had drafted the living trust for his father, which created the SNT.[74] The decedent hired the attorneys for estate planning, which resulted in a revocable living trust and will.[75] The provision within the revocable trust that established the SNT for the decedent's spouse had language indicating an intent to be a "supplemental needs trust."[76] In deciding on the spouse's application for Medicaid, the amount in the SNT was found to be an issue.[77]

70. *See* Appendices B and M. *See also* POMS SI 01120.200.B.1 ("A discretionary trust is a trust in which the trustee has full discretion as to the time, purpose, and amount of all distributions. The trustee may pay all or none of the trust as he or she considers appropriate to, or for the benefit of, the trust beneficiary. The trust beneficiary has no control over the trust.").

71. POMS SI 01120.200.D.2.

72. *See, e.g.*, Lewis, *supra* note 22, § III(F)(1)(c) ("A properly drafted Special Needs Trust (whether for a first-party or a third-party trust) will specify the Settlor's intention that **the trust should 'supplement, not supplant' any public or private benefits** for which the beneficiary may be eligible as a consequence of his disability.").

73. 112 N.E.3d 1040 (Ill. App. Ct. 2018).

74. *Id.* at 1043.

75. *Id.* at 1043–44.

76. *Id.* at 1044.

77. The Medicaid agency found the spouse to be over-asset and required the spouse to spend down, while the state Medicaid agency found the spouse received a transfer for less than fair market value,

The trustee sued for legal malpractice, which was dismissed with prejudice.[78] One argument made by the trustee was that there was no way for the attorneys to draft the estate planning for the decedent without also taking into consideration the spouse with special needs, thus leading to the conclusion that the attorneys were hired to draft an estate plan for the spouses.[79] The appellate court rejected this and other arguments from the trustee, and affirmed the dismissal:[80]

> Here, [the decedent] was the client. [The trustee] failed to plead an attorney-client relationship between defendants and [the spouse], failed to plead any duty to [the spouse] and breach thereof on defendants' part, and failed to plead that the primary purpose of defendants' services was to benefit [the spouse]. Defendants drafted two documents, the will and the Living Trust, both for [the decedent], and he executed both documents. [The spouse] is a beneficiary of one of the trusts created through the Living Trust. No documents were drafted for her. The Living Trust, which was revocable during [the decedent's] lifetime, states that, during his life, it "shall be administered for [his] primary benefit." It is true that [the trustee] alleged that [the decedent] retained defendants to "prepare necessary documents in connection with his and his disabled wife's . . . estate plan." However, in the portion of his complaint addressing the elements of a legal-malpractice claim, [the trustee] alleged that there was an "attorney-client relationship between the Defendants and [*the decedent*]," that defendants owed [*the decedent*] a legal duty as a result, and that the duty "to [*the decedent*]" was breached. (Emphases added.) The complaint contains no allegation that there was an attorney-client relationship between defendants and [the spouse] or that defendants breached any duty to her. Nor does it allege that the primary purpose or intent of seeking defendants' services was for [the spouse's] benefit.[81]

Finally, the trustee must understand that the trustee cannot make distributions for food or shelter, as those would render the beneficiary ineligible for SSI[82] or a distribution that would not be considered for the sole benefit of the beneficiary.[83]

---

approving the spouse's application but requiring payment of the assessed penalty from the SNT assets. *Id.* at 1044–45.

78. *Id.* at 1045.

79. *Id.* at 1050–51.

80. *Id.* at 1054.

81. *Id.* at 1052. *See also* Rajcan v. Garvey, 807 N.E.2d 725 (Ill. App. Ct. 2004).

82. *See, e.g.*, POMS SI 01120.200.E.1.b, Disbursements that result in receipt of in-kind support and maintenance, https://secure.ssa.gov/apps10/poms.nsf/lnx/0501120200 (last visited Dec. 11, 2022).

83. See Chapter 4 for a discussion of sole benefit. *See also* POMS SI 01120.201, Trusts Established with the Assets of an Individual on or after 01/01/00, specifically section F, Policy on Trusts and/or Payments for the Benefit of, on Behalf of, or for the Sole Benefit of an Individual.

Here is a dilemma though in doing so. If the beneficiary is not receiving SSI, then the trustee would not be allowed to make distributions for the beneficiary's food and shelter. Or if the beneficiary is on SSI, but the laws or circumstances change such that the beneficiary no longer is eligible, then the trustee's hands may be unnecessarily tied.[84] Might such a trust be decanted,[85] or language included to give the trustee leeway?[86] The drafter of a new, third-party SNT should consider how to provide the trustee appropriate flexibility.[87]

What about an older trust that does not contain special needs language and now the beneficiary has reached a time where the beneficiary needs public benefits? One expert offers these suggestions:

> [P]ractitioners are frequently confronted with **older irrevocable trusts** that utilize the classic "ascertainable standards" of "health, education, maintenance and support" for all beneficiaries. As noted, *supra*, in Section III.F.1.a., if a trust beneficiary is receiving means-tested government benefits, such as SSI and Medicaid, the **"support" and "maintenance"** distribution standards typically result in the trust assets being deemed **"available" or "countable"** to the beneficiary, thus jeopardizing those benefits. The distribution standards found in most "Bypass/Credit Shelter" Trusts, and many "Dynasty/Generation-Skipping" Trusts, threaten to disqualify the beneficiary with a disability from ongoing eligibility for means-tested government benefits. Options to deal with this challenge may include the following.
>
> 1. If the original trust grants the **power to amend** the trust provisions, the exercise of that power (by someone other than the beneficiary with special needs) is an unexpectedly easy solution.
>
> 2. The exercise of a **power of appointment** (by someone other than the beneficiary with special needs) in favor of a newly-created third-party Special Needs Trust can often solve the problem if the provisions allow for the appointment of trust assets to, "or for the benefit of," the beneficiary, including "in further and separate trust."

84. *See, e.g.*, 1 JAMES D. FUNNELL, JR., IRREVOCABLE TRUSTS § 28:8 (Myron Kove & James M. Kosakow eds., 4th ed. 2018 update).

85. *See, e.g.*, Chapter 6. *See also* FUNNELL, *supra* note 84, § 28:8(H).

86. *See, e.g.*, LEWIS, *supra* note 22, § III(F)(1)(b)(1) ("**In addition to the SNT language**, '[n]evertheless, the Trustee should also be given the latitude to **"opt out" of such benefits** if they are not "reasonably available" to the beneficiary (*e.g.* the expense of obtaining the benefits exceeds the value thereof), or if the benefits are insufficient or otherwise inadequate to provide fully for the beneficiary's needs.'").

87. In non-SNT trust administration, the trustee's discretion (and any recognizable standard) will usually provide the flexibility to deal with changing circumstances. Restrictions commonly included in an SNT may limit or even eliminate that flexibility, making careful drafting more important.

3. **A "decanting" encroachment** by the Trustee into a newly-created third-party Special Needs Trust is another frequently utilized solution. Although not all States currently have decanting statutes, well-respected practitioners who have thoroughly considered this topic have concluded that the "common law of every state likely confers decanting authority on trustees."

4. A **judicial modification** of the original trust which replaces the "support" and "maintenance" standards with Special Needs Trust provisions with respect to any distributions for the benefit of the beneficiary receiving means-tested government benefits is an expensive and labor-intensive option. State law typically provides specific procedures for the judicial modification of irrevocable trusts, which are designed to uphold the intent of the person who established the trust and to effectuate the purpose of the trust. It is typically necessary to craft and support the position that **had the creator of the trust known** that its original provisions for the beneficiary with the disability would disqualify him from ongoing eligibility for a significant source of funding his special needs (*i.e.* means-tested government benefits) the creator would have taken the steps needed to modify those provisions accordingly by replacing them with Special Needs Trust provisions.

5. The Trustee of an irrevocable trust that contains problematic distribution standards for a beneficiary who receives means-tested government benefits could also consider a **complete encroachment to the beneficiary** of the entire trust corpus, followed by an **immediate funding of a first-party Special Needs Trust** with that property. This approach would necessarily entail subjecting the property to a Medicaid payback; however, if the corpus is likely to be depleted entirely (or in large part) during the beneficiary's lifetime, the payback prospect is of little consequence. If the beneficiary is a minor or an incapacitated adult under relevant State law, it would be necessary to obtain court approval for the transfer of the encroached assets into the first-party Special Needs Trust. Furthermore, every effort should be made to time the encroachment to the beneficiary and the immediate funding of the first-party Special Needs Trust with the encroached trust property in the same month so that his eligibility for means-tested benefits is adversely impacted for only a single month.[88]

Is there such a thing as a special needs standard, like there is a HEMS standard? Some experts actually consider there to be three variations of a special needs standard:

88. *See, e.g.*, Lewis, *supra* note 22, § VI.D (citations omitted).

> A special needs distribution standard gives the trustee broad discretion to distribute trust income and/or principal for the "special needs" of the beneficiary. Special needs are usually defined as anything the beneficiary needs, or anything that would be useful or in any way helpful to the beneficiary, if it is not paid for or provided to the beneficiary from a public assistance benefit program or some other source. The trustee is often directed to distribute from the trust in a manner that supplements, but does not supplant, any public assistance the beneficiary is receiving. These trusts are also sometimes referred to as supplemental needs trusts, supplemental care trusts, and similar titles.

The court in *Hecker v. Stark County Social Service Board*[89] quoted the special needs language used in a trust as follows:

> (b) *Special Needs*. The Trustee shall pay to or apply to the benefit of the beneficiary, for his lifetime, such amounts from the principal or income, up to the whole thereof, as the Trustee in the Trustee's sole discretion may from time to time deem necessary or advisable for the satisfaction of the beneficiary's special needs. Any income not distributed shall be added to principal. As used in this instrument, "special needs" refers to the requisites for maintaining the beneficiary's good health, safety, and welfare when, in the sole discretion of the Trustee, such requisites are not deemed provided by any public agency, office, or department of the State of North Dakota, or of any other state, or of the United States. "Special needs" include, but are not limited to, medical and dental expenses, clothing and equipment, programs of training, education, treatment, and essential dietary needs to the extent that such needs are not provided by any government entity.
>
> - **Strict Special Needs**
>   Some special needs trusts expressly prohibit the trustee from making distributions for the beneficiary's food and shelter, or for anything that will cause a reduction or loss of public benefits. These are referred to as strict special needs trusts.
>
> - **Discretionary Special Needs**
>   Other special needs trusts give the trustee discretion to make distributions, even if doing so will reduce or cut off public assistance benefits, if the trustee determines that such distributions are in the best interests of the beneficiary. These are referred to as discretionary special needs trusts.[90]

89. 527 N.W.2d 226 (N.D. 1995).
90. ZIMRING ET AL., *supra* note 28, §4A.06[2] (citations omitted).

A discretionary distribution standard is not an uncommon standard to use in a third-party SNT. If worded so that the beneficiary cannot compel a distribution, the logic is that the trust would not be considered an available resource to the beneficiary. However, the state trust code may require something other than a discretionary distribution standard.[91]

With a discretionary distribution standard, be sure to use language that indicates that the distributions are intended to supplement, not supplant, public benefits.[92]

Bogert's The Law of Trusts and Trustees[93] provides a good explanation of discretionary trusts:

> A discretionary trust is one in which the settlor gives the trustee authority over the trust, for example, to use discretion in the timing and amount of income payments to the beneficiary. A settlor may provide that the trustee have "sole, absolute and uncontrolled" discretion whether to pay or apply trust income or principal to or for the benefit of the beneficiary. The settlor may also give less latitude to the trustee's discretion, for example, describing it as "sound discretion," or "as the trustee deems appropriate," or simply, "the trustee's discretion." If the settlor does not impose any standards or

---

91. *Id.*, stating:

> A discretionary distribution standard (sometimes referred to as "purely," "totally," or "wholly") grants the trustee absolute and total discretion concerning when and how to make a distribution from the trust. It does not impose any requirements on the trustee, and it even authorizes the trustee to not make any distributions at all.
>
> Some courts have held that the trustee must exercise its discretion in a manner that accomplishes, rather than frustrates, the purposes of the trust. As a result, it is important that the purposes of the trust and the intention of the settlor be clearly expressed in the trust instrument. Because the trustee has total discretion concerning whether or not to make any distribution from the trust, and neither the beneficiary nor any other person has the ability to force the trustee to make any distribution, the trust assets are normally not deemed to be countable resources to the beneficiary. However, at least one state has changed this result for third party-settled trusts. Kansas deems any assets held in a third party-settled trust that does not contain a special needs distribution standard to be an available resource for Kansas Medicaid eligibility (citations omitted).

Kansas Statutes section 39-709(e)(3)(B) provides:

> If a trust has discretionary language, the trust shall be considered to be an available resource to the extent, using the full extent of discretion, the trustee may make any of the income or principal available to the applicant or recipient of medical assistance. Any such discretionary trust shall be considered an available resource unless: (i) At the time of creation or amendment of the trust, the trust states a clear intent that the trust is supplemental to public assistance; and (ii) the trust: (a) Is funded from resources of a person who, at the time of such funding, owed no duty of support to the applicant or recipient of medical assistance; or (b) is funded not more than nominally from resources of a person while that person owed a duty of support to the applicant or recipient of medical assistance.

92. *See* Lewis, *supra* note 22, **§ III(F)(1)(c)**. *See also*, *e.g.*, Kan. Stat. § 39-709(e)(3)(B) (2022).

93. Bogert et al., *supra* note 7, § 228 (citations omitted).

> guides that the trustee is to consider, these trusts are sometimes called pure discretionary trusts. However, it has become more common for the settlor to limit the trustee's discretion by a standard, for example, for the trustee to exercise discretion for the support and education of the beneficiary. These are also now considered discretionary trusts. These descriptions of the trustee's discretion and the standards for application of discretion are useful to determine the beneficiary's interest in the trust; however, there is little uniformity between, or even within, jurisdictions.

Note the difference between a discretionary trust and a discretionary support trust, and imagine how the latter would be an issue for a beneficiary on public benefits:

> When a settlor creates a discretionary trust that imposes standards for the beneficiary's support or for support, maintenance, and education, these trusts are now often called discretionary support trusts. The courts have had difficulty determining how to enforce the beneficiary's interest in these trusts. Because of the support standard, the trustee's discretion is more restricted than it would be under a pure discretionary trust, but the trustee has more discretion than in a pure support trust. Trust terms for support have been interpreted to mean that the trustee is to be guided by the beneficiary's accustomed standard of living, or "station in life," and usually also includes support for the beneficiary's household. Discretionary support trusts are also treated in § 229, post.[94]

Bogert et al. note the rise in the importance of SNTs:

> With increasing demand for Medicaid benefits, and the rising costs of health care imposing financial burdens on the states, some courts are looking more critically at trust language in order to preserve public funds for those who are without recourse to any assets for their health services.
>
> Settlors who create trusts for beneficiaries known to be disabled and receiving state care, however, may create what is known as supplemental needs trusts. In these trusts, the trustee has discretion to provide only those benefits to the beneficiary that are beyond those benefits that the state provides, and only those benefits that will not make the beneficiary ineligible for state aid. These trusts have so far withstood challenge by the state.[95]

---

94. *Id.* (citations omitted).
95. *Id.* (citations omitted).

VII. Modification

Each state's Trust Code typically will contain a provision for modification of a trust. It may be possible for a court to determine that a trust is an SNT if there is some language contained in the trust that indicates the settlor's intent for it to be an SNT, when the state's Medicaid agency does not think the language is clear enough to create an SNT.[96]

The settlor needs to make some decisions about the future and the purpose of the trust. It needs to be clear that the beneficiary cannot compel distributions and that the trustee cannot make distributions for any disqualifying items.

In re Riddell[97] is a good example of the need to modify a discretionary trust into an SNT. The grandparents had created testamentary trusts, with their only child and his spouse as beneficiaries and, on their deaths, to the two grandchildren until they reach age 35. At the time in question, the grandparents have died, the parents are still living, and the two grandchildren are over age 35. One grandchild developed a significant and debilitating mental illness.[98] In seeking modification to create an SNT for this beneficiary, the trial court denied the trustee's request on the grounds

> that it did not have the power to modify the trust unless unanticipated events existed that were unknown to the trust creator that would result in defeating the trust's purpose. The trial court found that the trust's purpose was "to provide for the education, support, maintenance, and medical care of the beneficiaries" and that a modification would only "permit[ ] the family to immunize itself financially from reimbursing the State for costs of [the beneficiary's] . . . care." Relying on the Restatement (Third) of Trusts, it stated that it would not allow a modification "merely because a change would be more advantageous to the beneficiaries."[99]

---

96. *See, e.g.*, Restatement (Third) of the Law Governing Trusts § 66 (Am. L. Inst. 2003) ("(1) The court may modify an administrative or distributive provision of a trust, or direct or permit the trustee to deviate from an administrative or distributive provision, if because of circumstances not anticipated by the settlor the modification or deviation will further the purposes of the trust."). *See also* Unif. Tr. Code § 412(a), Modification or Termination Because of Unanticipated Circumstances or Inability to Administer Trust Effectively (Unif. L. Comm'n 2010) ("The court may modify the administrative or dispositive terms of a trust or terminate the trust if, because of circumstances not anticipated by the settlor, modification or termination will further the purposes of the trust. To the extent practicable, the modification must be made in accordance with the settlor's probable intention."). *See also id.* § 412 cmt. ("Among other things, equitable deviation may be used to modify administrative or dispositive terms due to the failure to anticipate economic change or the incapacity of a beneficiary."). *But see In re* Ruby G. Owen Tr., 418 S.W.3d 421 (Ark. Ct. App. 2012).

97. 157 P.3d 888 (Wash. Ct. App. 2007).

98. *Id.* at 888–90.

99. *Id.* at 890 (citations omitted).

On appeal, the appellate court examined the holding from their state supreme court[100] as well as the Restatement (Third) of Trusts section 66, that "[t]he court 'may modify an administrative or distributive provision of a trust, or direct or permit the trustee to deviate from an administrative or distributive provision, if [(1)] because of circumstances not anticipated by the settlor [(2)] the modification or deviation will further the purposes of the trust.'"[101]

In this case, the court reviewed the test for modification, noting:

> The first prong of the equitable deviation test is satisfied if circumstances have changed since the trust's creation or if the settlor was unaware of circumstances when the trust was established. Upon a finding of unanticipated circumstances, the trial court must determine if a modification would tend to advance the trust purposes; this inquiry is likely to involve a subjective process of attempting to infer the relevant purpose of a trust from the general tenor of its provisions.[102]

The court also discussed the role of the settlor's intent in determining whether to grant modification:

> The reason to modify is to give effect to the settlor's intent had the circumstances in question been anticipated. Courts will not ordinarily deviate from the provisions outlined by the trust creator but they undoubtedly have the power to do so, if it is reasonably necessary to effectuate the trust's *primary* purpose. A trust settlor may possess a myriad of intentions in settling a trust, but the trial court must concern itself with their *primary* objective.[103]

Applying this analysis to the facts of the case before it, the appellate court determined:

> There is no question that changed circumstances have intervened to frustrate the settlors' intent. [The beneficiary's] grandparents intended that she have the funds to use as she saw fit. Not only is [beneficiary] unable to manage the funds or to pass them to her son, but there is a great likelihood that the funds will be lost to the State for her medical care. It is clear that the settlors would have wanted a different result."[104]

---

100. Niemann v. Vaughn Cmty. Church, 113 P.3d 463 (Wash. 2005).

101. *Riddell*, 157 P.3d at 891–92 (citations omitted). The *Riddell* court noted that the Washington Supreme Court in *Niemann* had "adopted the Restatement (Third) of Trusts and noted that the Restatement (Third) requires a lower threshold finding than the older Restatement and gives courts broader discretion in permitting deviation of a trust." *Id.* at 892.

102. *Id.* at 892 (citations omitted).

103. *Id.* (citations omitted).

104. *Id.*

In sum, "[t]he proper focus is on the settlors' intent, the changed circumstances, and what is equitable for these beneficiaries."[105] Further:

> Special needs trusts were created in order to allow disabled persons to continue receiving governmental assistance for their medical care, while allowing extra funds for assistance the government did not provide. Given this legal backdrop, the trial court should not have considered any loss to the State in determining whether an equitable deviation is allowed. The law invites, rather than discourages, the creation of special needs trusts in just this sort of situation. The proper focus is on the settlors' intent, the changed circumstances, and what is equitable for these beneficiaries.
>
> [Grandparents] both died without creating a special needs trust but did not know of [grandchild's] mental health issues or how they might best be addressed. They clearly intended to establish a trust to provide for their grandchildren's general support, not solely for extraordinary and unanticipated medical bills.
>
> A special needs trust may be established by a third party or by the disabled person that would be benefited by the trust. . . . Here, the trust was established and funded by [grandparents] for the beneficiary [grandchild]. It is a third party special needs trust. The trust is not subject to State assistance payback and is not required to have a payback provision.[106]

For a further discussion of modification, see Chapter 6.

VIII. What the Courts Have to Say

In *Matter of the Estate of Escher*,[107] the question surrounded the decedent's intent vis-à-vis his daughter who had special needs. According to the court, his will initially left the residue to his five children, with the daughter's share placed in a trust that terminated when she reached age 30, and prior to termination she received the trust income in "quarter annual installments." A codicil changed the terms of the trust to run for her life, with income paid again in "quarter annual" installments or more frequently if convenient.[108] In addition, the codicil also contained the following language:

> In addition my said executors and trustees are authorized in the exercise of their discretion to pay out of the principal of said fund such sum or sums as may be necessary to provide for the payment of any and all expenses

105. *Id.* at 893.
106. *Id.*
107. 407 N.Y.S.2d 106 (N.Y. Surr. Ct. 1978).
108. *Id.* at 108.

> necessary for the maintenance and support of my said daughter Marie Escher by reason of any illness, accident, or other emergency, and such withdrawal shall be entirely within the discretion of my said trustees and the survivor and successor trustees, and said withdrawals and disbursements made for the benefit of my said daughter Marie Escher shall not be subject to objection in any proceeding by or on her behalf.[109]

The court found:

> The terms of the instrument must be reviewed in the light of the obvious knowledge, at the time of execution, which the testator had with reference to the disabilities of the life income beneficiary. The provisions made for the life beneficiary indicate a conclusion that she would never be self-supporting or fully capable of handling her own affairs. This conclusion leads to an apparent primary purpose on the part of the testator to provide for her basic needs on an ongoing basis. The codicil also reflects a recognition by the testator that this purpose could best be accomplished within the framework of a trust that would continue so long as the life beneficiary lived. It is noted that an interest in the estate equal to that of the life beneficiary is given to each of the testator's other issue, but their shares were bequeathed outright to them upon attaining age 21. This sustains the conclusion that the trust provision for the life beneficiary flowed from her being under an apparent disability.
>
> With absolute specificity, the instrument reflects that it was the desire of the testator that to the extent the corpus was not required to provide the life beneficiary with that which she would not otherwise receive, he wished the corpus to pass to her distributees, who would likely be his other issue, or, if they were deceased, to their descendants surviving at the time of the termination of the trust.[110]

The court takes an interesting view of eligibility for public benefits, including the use of trusts to maintain such eligibility:

> The cases presume that a person would prefer paying for the needs of those dear to him in lieu of welfare contributing thereto. Since the expression of this philosophy, public assistance has evolved from being a "gift" into a "right" which must be provided by state and local governments to all who show need, without even regard to the capacity of their respective taxpayers to generate the required revenue to pay the mounting cost of this right. The emergence of this right is evidenced by the fact that a recipient's benefits may no longer be terminated without all the safeguards of constitutional due process. Public assistance programs have expanded from classic "welfare"

109. *Id.*
110. *Id.* at 109–10.

> to prevent a party from becoming destitute into a multitude of social insurance programs designed to meet the peculiar needs of the ill, the aged, the disabled, and the handicapped. In the context of modern society, the stigma attached to receiving the benefits of these programs has largely disappeared, particularly with reference to those programs designed to meet the astronomical cost of illness or institutional care of any sort.
>
> Today, programs to pay medical and institutional care are viewed more as an insurance benefit than charity. In view of the vast costs involved, it is a benefit which logic suggests that most citizens would seek for their loved ones, should they require institutional care, in preference to rapidly expending their total assets before seeking the benefits of such programs. It is divorced from the realities of life to presume that if testator were aware of the facts as they now exist, he would desire to pay the immense cost for his daughter's care in preference to having society share this burden. To apply to these facts a conclusion that the testator would find accepting benefits to be a repugnant humiliation at becoming the object of charity is an anachronism.[111]

In finding that the trust did not render the daughter ineligible for public benefits, the court noted:

> In the absence of a governing statutory mandate, questions relative to invasion of the corpus of a trust must be controlled by a determination of the intent of the creator of the trust. The individual intent of testators must be determined based on the language of the instrument, the nature of the remaindermen and the relationships of the testator to the life beneficiary and the remaindermen, as well as any other pertinent facts indicative of intent.[112]

In its ruling, the court references the importance of the testator's intent:

> It is the conclusion of this court that the rigidity of any possible public policy requiring an invasion of trust corpus to relieve the burdens of a publicly funded program is subject to dilution, if it extends at all, in situations where the expenditure involved is the current astronomical cost of institutional care where the application of the total corpus to these charges would summarily render meaningless, a testamentary scheme, carefully designed to carry out an intent to retain some portion of a trust corpus for the ongoing needs of the life beneficiary, with a remainder for the benefit of other surviving issue. A contrary conclusion would, for almost all testators, except the most affluent, totally vitiate the viability of testamentary trusts as a device for

111. *Id.* at 110–11 (citations omitted).
112. *Id.* at 112.

bequeathing a remainder should the vicissitudes of life lead to an aged life beneficiary requiring extended institutional care. In the absence of a specific statutory mandate from the Legislature to this affect, it cannot be concluded that the present posture of the law requires so fatal a blow to the sanctity of testamentary intent with reference to the corpus of trusts in a situation where the invasion of corpus will not pragmatically, in any way, confer a tangible benefit upon the life beneficiary who has only an interest that is clearly circumscribed by the terms of the trust.[113]

113. *Id.* at 111–12.

CHAPTER 6

Modification, Reformation, Decanting, and Directed Trusts

I. Introduction

Expect the unexpected. Because circumstances can and do change after the execution of the third-party trust, the issue becomes whether the irrevocable trust can be amended, and how (and how easily). The state's trust code may contain provisions that allow for modification of a trust in certain circumstances. If a trust protector has been included, then the trust protector may have the power to make the necessary changes. In states that allow decanting, it may be possible to decant the res from the original trust into a new trust. Whether any changes are possible depends on the language of the trust and the applicable state law. Whether it makes sense may also depend on federal rules on taxes and public benefits. This chapter will examine the basics of modification, reformation, and decanting of third-party trusts and directed trusts, using primarily the Uniform Trust Code (UTC) for discussion. It is critical for practitioners to know their state trust code, since not all states have adopted the UTC, and those that have adopted it may have done so with adaptations.

II. Modification

The settlor may have included a clause that allows the trustee to make changes in the trust on the occurrence of specific circumstances. If the trust does not contain any provisions allowing modification, under the UTC, modification may be sought through various paths, including court order[1] or consent of

1. *See, e.g.*, Unif. Tr. Code § 410 (Unif. L. Comm'n 2010); specifically *id.* §§ 411–417.

some set of the parties to the trust.[2] A court may approve a petition to modify an irrevocable trust when all of the beneficiaries consent, as long as the court determines that the proposed modification would not be contrary to the trust's material purpose.[3]

One challenge: how to determine what constitutes a "material purpose" of the trust. The comment to UTC section 411 provides some direction, though it fails to directly define the term or identify elements to be considered.[4] The few instances of authority seem to adopt a "we'll know it when we see it" approach. Thus, a Montana Supreme Court case could confidently insist that, since the trust at issue had been created to help its beneficiary qualify for public benefits, it would be impossible for any future court to agree to terminate the trust and distribute its assets to that beneficiary directly.[5] The Nebraska Supreme Court has held that the mere existence of a spendthrift provision is a "material purpose" of the trust preventing a nonjudicial settlement agreement that would provide for outright distribution of trust assets to trust beneficiaries.[6]

If a beneficiary does not consent, the court may still grant the modification on a finding that the modification could have been granted if all of the beneficiaries consented and that the non-consenting beneficiary's interest will be sufficiently protected.[7] Consent of the settlor may be persuasive in establishing the lack of a material purpose to violate, and can permit modification or termination even over the objections of the trustee.[8]

---

2. *Id.* § 411. The court will still have to approve the changes under UTC § 410(b) ("(b) A proceeding to approve or disapprove a proposed modification or termination under Sections 411 through 416, or trust combination or division under Section 417, may be commenced by a trustee or beneficiary, [and a proceeding to approve or disapprove a proposed modification or termination under Section 411 may be commenced by the settlor].").

3. *Id.* § 411(b) ("A noncharitable irrevocable trust may be modified upon consent of all of the beneficiaries if the court concludes that modification is not inconsistent with a material purpose of the trust.").

4. The comment to UTC section 411 states:

> Material purposes are not readily to be inferred. A finding of such a purpose generally requires some showing of a particular concern or objective on the part of the settlor, such as concern with regard to the beneficiary's management skills, judgment, or level of maturity. Thus, a court may look for some circumstantial or other evidence indicating that the trust arrangement represented to the settlor more than a method of allocating the benefits of property among multiple beneficiaries, or a means of offering to the beneficiaries (but not imposing on them) a particular advantage. Sometimes, of course, the very nature or design of a trust suggests its protective nature or some other material purpose.

5. Est. of Scheidecker v. Mont. Dep't of Pub. Health & Hum. Servs., 490 P.3d 87 (Mont. 2021).

6. *In re* McGregor, 954 N.W.2d 612 (Neb. 2021).

7. Unif. Tr. Code § 411(e) (Unif. L. Comm'n 2010) ("If not all of the beneficiaries consent to a proposed modification or termination of the trust under subsection (a) or (b), the modification or termination may be approved by the court if the court is satisfied that: (1) if all of the beneficiaries had consented, the trust could have been modified or terminated under this section; and (2) the interests of a beneficiary who does not consent will be adequately protected.").

8. Garland v. Miller, 611 S.W.3d 275 (Ky. Ct. App. 2020). See also *Demircan v. Mikhaylov*, 306 So. 3d 142 (Fla. Dist. Ct. App. 2020), which reached the same result but in spite of the Florida version of the

Consider whether the third-party trust is inter vivos or testamentary. That may have an impact on the settlor's ability to seek modification. If testamentary, then the res may be viewed as an inheritance and thus owned by the beneficiary, which brings up the question of availability in the event that the beneficiary is on, or may need to receive, public benefits. Typically, pure discretionary third-party trusts where the beneficiary has no power over the property of the trust are considered unavailable to the beneficiary.[9] When making changes to the trust via modification, consider whether making the change in any way renders the property of the trust available to the beneficiary.[10]

PRACTICE NOTE

In drafting trusts—both special needs trusts and trusts with no special needs provisions or anticipated need for such provisions—consider authorizing future modifications as circumstances might change. Consider one or more of these approaches:

1. Allowing the trustee to modify trust terms, probably within narrowly defined circumstances
2. Establishing a "trust protector" or other directed trustee with authority to make future modifications
3. Authorizing someone—probably the trustee—to name an independent trust protector with similar powers
4. Clearly identifying the trust's "material purposes"—perhaps even with an express definition of the term as it is to be applied in future modification/termination proceedings—and spelling out the significance of a beneficiary's ability to maintain eligibility for public benefits, the trust's spendthrift provisions, the significance of any investment or disbursement restrictions, and the relative importance of income and remainder beneficiary interests

---

UTC, citing prior Florida law for the principal that "the [Florida Trust Code] sections on modifying trusts do not provide the exclusive means to do so" (citing Minassian v. Rachins, 152 So. 3d 719 (Fla. Dist. Ct. App. 2014)).

9. See, for example, Program Operations Manual System (POMS) SI 01120.200.D.2, https://secure.ssa.gov/apps10/poms.nsf/lnx/0501120200 (last visited Dec. 11, 2022), which provides:

> If an individual does not have the legal authority to revoke or terminate the trust or to direct the use of the trust assets for his or her own support and maintenance, the trust principal **is not** the individual's resource for SSI [Supplemental Security Income] purposes.
>
> The revocability of a trust and the ability to direct the use of the trust principal depend on the terms of the trust agreement and on State (or Tribal) law. If a trust is irrevocable by its terms and under State law, and the trust beneficiary cannot control or direct use of the trust assets for the trust beneficiary's support and maintenance, the trust **is not** a resource.

10. *Id.*

A. Guidance from the Program Operations Manual System

For third-party trusts in general, the Social Security Administration (SSA) Program Operations Manual System (POMS) SI 01120.200 is important. The POMS defines a "discretionary trust" as

> a trust in which the trustee has full discretion as to the time, purpose, and amount of all distributions. The trustee may pay all or none of the trust as he or she considers appropriate to, or for the benefit of, the trust beneficiary. The trust beneficiary has no control over the trust.[11]

A testamentary trust is acknowledged as one that is created pursuant to the will and is not operational until the testator's death.[12] A third-party inter vivos trust may have testamentary aspects, but note:

> A trust into which property is transferred under the terms of a will, and during the life (inter vivos) of the testator, is not a testamentary trust for the purposes of this section because it is not effective only upon the testator's death, even if the will transfers additional property into the trust upon the testator's death. When evaluating testamentary trusts, [SSA's] field offices should obtain and review a copy of the last will and testament.[13]

It is important to recognize that the POMS also includes directions for the field offices on the treatment of these third-party trusts, with the following caution included: "Be alert for situations where a trust is allegedly established with the assets of a third party but in reality is created with the trust beneficiary's property. In such cases, the trust is a grantor trust, not a third[-]party trust."[14]

B. Modification: Applicability to Special Needs Trusts

The question of whether a discretionary trust can be modified to create a special needs trust (SNT) for the beneficiary has been addressed by the courts. The history of modification of trusts for beneficiaries with disabilities has been fluid. Earlier cases, like *Harrell v. Badger*[15] and *Thomas v. Arkansas Department of Human Services*,[16] expressed disfavor for the use (and modification) of trusts to create or preserve public benefits eligibility. For example,

11. *See id.* SI 01120.200.B.1.
12. *Id.* SI 01120.200.B.15.
13. *Id.*
14. *Id.* SI 01120.200.B.16.
15. 171 So. 3d 764 (Fla. Dist. Ct. App. 2015).
16. 894 S.W.2d 584 (Ark. 1995).

in *Thomas*, the beneficiary was injured and received a settlement,[17] with the employer as the settlor of the trust and a bank as the trustee, with the trust purpose "to meet the special or supplemental needs of [the beneficiary]. It is anticipated that the primary source of . . . Beneficiary's medical, custodial and financial support shall come from governmental assistance, including Medicaid."[18] The wife's second application for Medicaid for the beneficiary was denied for excess resources due to the trust;[19] thereafter, the probate court entered an order that the SNT was not available for "medical, custodial, and financial expenses of [the beneficiary and the court ordered] the Trustee not to use trust income or corpus for such purposes or for any purpose that would render Medicaid benefits unavailable."[20] The Medicaid application was denied a third time, again for excess resources.[21] Relying heavily on the public policy against "artificial impoverishment,"[22] the court determined:

> The Guy Thomas Trust without question limits the availability of trust income and principal for purposes that Medicaid benefits would cover. Whether the limitation in the trust is in effect before the beneficiary applies for Medicaid assistance or occurs at the time of application for that assistance is of no significance under the statute. The provisions of the Guy Thomas Trust relating to the safeguarding of government benefits run afoul of the public policy of this state as expressed in § 28-69-102, and for that reason, they are void and unenforceable. In addition, the order of the Johnson County Probate Court is of little avail to the appellants. The probate court is clearly without jurisdiction to interpret a trust instrument. Because the limit on trustee discretion is unenforceable under Ark. Code Ann. § 28-69-102 and because the probate court order has no effect, the discretion in the Bank as trustee to apply trust resources for Guy Thomas's benefit is comprehensive. There is no basis for reversing the DHS [Department of Human Services] decision on this point.[23]

17. *Id.* at 585–86

18. *Id.* at 586.

19. *Id.*

20. *Id.*

21. *Id.* ("We begin by noting that the Bank as Trustee does have 'sole discretion' over payment of trust funds for Guy Thomas's benefit with the proviso that no expenditures should be made which disqualified Thomas from government assistance. That limitation, though, is in direct contravention of the public policy expressed in Ark. Code Ann. § 28-69-102.").

22. *Id.* at 588.

23. *Id.* (citations omitted).The court also addressed the argument that a third party (the employer) had established the trust but found that the public policy still applied to this case, even though the beneficiary had not established the trust. *Id.* ("But even if we accept the fact that the statute has specific reference to grantors who establish trusts in order to facilitate their own eligibility for Medicaid assistance, the public policy behind the Act is absolutely beyond dispute—trusts may not be created and used as devices to

Similarly, an early New Jersey trial court case from 1996[24] denied the modification of a nine-year-old trust into an SNT.[25] Plaintiffs had argued that the trust purpose was to "provide for the lifelong protection of [the beneficiary] and only be used to supplement other resources available to [the beneficiary] by meeting those needs which cannot be met through other sources, including but not limited to, any government or private program of financial entitlements, services, or other benefits."[26] In this case the court denied the modification because the beneficiary had "furnished the consideration needed for the creation of the trust when he exchanged his claim against defendants for settlement funds later deposited in trust. Thus, contrary to plaintiffs' argument, [the judge determined] that [the beneficiary] is the settlor of the trust . . . ," which would result in allowing the beneficiary to do indirectly what he could not do directly.[27] After reviewing precedent and noting that the Medicaid statute in effect at the time supported the trial court's decision, the court concluded that the assets were not exempt[28] and, further, one section of the Medicaid statute prohibited provisions in trusts to protect a beneficiary's eligibility for public benefits.[29]

The Arkansas Supreme Court moved away from the public policy-based denial, at least in the context of the creation of a first-party SNT.[30] In the case *In re Corn*,[31] the individual with special needs sought to create an SNT from assets passing to him on his partner's death by operation of law.[32] Although his partner had created an SNT for him, she had named him as beneficiary on both her bank accounts and life insurance, totaling about $260,000.[33] Direct receipt of these assets would render the beneficiary no longer eligible for

---

sequester resources for the purpose of qualifying individuals otherwise ineligible for Medicaid assistance. In *Walters*, we highlighted the fact that the General Assembly had voided provisions in such trusts 'to stop chicanery and to preserve the fiscal integrity of the Medicaid program.' We further held in *Walters* that § 28-69-102, which was enacted by Act 1228 of 1993, had retroactive application." (citations omitted)).

24. *In re* Lennon, 294 N.J. Super. 303 (N.J. Super. Ct. Ch. Div. 1996).

25. *Id.* at 305–06.

26. *Id.* at 306.

27. *Id.* at 309–10.

28. *Id.* at 310.

29. *Id.* One statute in effect at the time of the case, New Jersey Revised Statutes section 30:4D-6f, provided:

> Any provision in a . . . trust agreement . . . which reduces or excludes coverage or payment for goods and services to an individual because of that individual's eligibility for or receipt of Medicaid benefits shall be null and void, and no payment shall be made under this act as a result of any such provision.

Id.

30. *In re* Corn, 493 S.W.3d 311 (Ark. 2016).

31. *Id.*

32. *Id.* at 312.

33. *Id.*

Supplemental Security Income (SSI) and Medicaid.[34] The beneficiary created a (d)(4)(A) trust and sought court approval.[35] The trial court denied the petition, and on reconsideration again denying the establishment of the SNT, the trial court "found that the establishment of the trust would be against Arkansas public policy."[36]

The Arkansas Supreme Court reversed, noting that first-party SNTs are specifically recognized in the Medicaid Act, and states that participate in Medicaid are required to follow the Medicaid statute.[37] The court distinguished prior cases relied on by the trial court in its denial of the SNT from this case, as those prior cases did not involve (d)(4)(A) trusts.[38] The court determined that "the circuit court erred in finding that the establishment of a D4A trust in this case would be against Arkansas public policy."[39]

The history of modification of trusts for beneficiaries with disabilities has been fluid. Earlier cases, like *Harrell*[40] and *Thomas*,[41] favored an inability to modify third-party trusts to protect beneficiaries with disabilities. The 2007 Washington case *In re Riddell*[42] ushered in a new era.

In re Riddell[43] concerned the trial court's refusal to approve the trustee's requested trust modification and creation of an SNT on behalf of the beneficiary with special needs.[44] The trusts, which had been created by the beneficiary's grandparents, provided for the trusts to terminate on the trustee's death, with an outright distribution of a part of the trust proceeds to the beneficiary. The trustee argued modification was allowable under an unanticipated change in circumstances, that being the beneficiary's special needs. The appellate court reversed and remanded for the trial court "to reconsider an equitable deviation in light of changed circumstances and the settlors' intent that the beneficiaries receive both medical care and general support from the trust's funds."[45] As mentioned earlier, the grandparents' trust contained a termination provision on the deaths of their son/trustee and spouse, with the principal being paid to the two grandchildren, one of whom is the beneficiary with special needs.[46]

34. *Id.*
35. *Id.* at 312–13.
36. *Id.* at 313–14.
37. *Id.* at 314.
38. *Id.* at 315.
39. *Id.*
40. Harrell v. Badger, 171 So. 3d 764 (Fla. Dist. Ct. App. 2015).
41. Thomas v. Ark. Dep't of Hum. Servs., 894 S.W.2d 584 (Ark. 1995).
42. 157 P.3d 888 (Wash. Ct. App. 2007) (citations omitted).
43. *Id.* (citations omitted).
44. *Id.* at 889.
45. *Id.*
46. *Id.* at 889–90.

The trustee's argument for the creation of the SNT was that if the funds were paid to the beneficiary, those "trust funds would either be seized by the State of Washington to pay [the beneficiary's] extraordinary medical bills or [the beneficiary] would manage the funds poorly due to her mental illness and lack of judgment."[47] The trial court's denial was primarily based on the view that the creation of the SNT would be contrary to the purpose of the trust.[48] As well, the trial court took the position that "modification would only 'permit[ ] the family to immunize itself financially from reimbursing the State for costs of [the beneficiary's medical] care.'"[49]

The appellate court noted that the trial court eventually concluded that it had the power to modify the trust but chose to not do so.[50] The trustee argued that the minimum age (35) requirement for distribution to the beneficiary showed intent "that their grandchildren have a level of maturity and stability before receiving the trust distribution. [The Trustee] asserts that given [the beneficiary's] medical conditions and inability to handle her finances independently, she will never attain a level of maturity to handle the distribution of funds; therefore a special needs trust is appropriate."[51] The appellate court, after reviewing precedent that analyzed the use of equitable deviation,[52] found that the trial court did find changed circumstances (the first part of the test) and that the "primary purpose was to provide for [the beneficiary] during her lifetime. Because the trust was to terminate at age thirty-five, it was also the settlors' intent that [the beneficiary] have the money to dispose of as she saw fit, which would include any estate planning that she might choose to do."[53] The court stated:

> There is no question that changed circumstances have intervened to frustrate the settlors' intent. [The beneficiary's] grandparents intended that she have the funds to use as she saw fit. Not only is [the beneficiary] unable to manage the funds or to pass them to her son, but there is a great likelihood that the funds will be lost to the State for her medical care. It is clear that the settlors would have wanted a different result.[54]

---

47. *Id.* at 890.
48. *Id.*
49. *Id.*
50. *Id.* at 890–91.
51. *Id.* at 891–92.
52. *Id.*
53. *Id.* at 892.
54. *Id.*

The court then noted that Congress had authorized the use of SNTs in order to allow disabled persons to continue to receive governmental assistance for their medical care:

> Special needs trusts were created in order to allow disabled persons to continue receiving governmental assistance for their medical care, while allowing extra funds for assistance the government did not provide. Given this legal backdrop, the trial court should not have considered any loss to the State in determining whether an equitable deviation is allowed. The law invites, rather than discourages, the creation of special needs trusts in just this sort of situation. The proper focus is on the settlors' intent, the changed circumstances, and what is equitable for these beneficiaries.[55]

Noting that the trust here, if modified, would be a third-party SNT, which does not require a payback, the appellate court remanded "to the trial court to reconsider this matter and to order such equitable deviation as is consistent with the settlors' intent in light of changed circumstances."[56]

A few years later, the case *In re Ruby G. Owen Trust*[57] concerned the petition of the successor trustee's petition to modify the trust created for a grandchild into an SNT.[58] The grandchild became disabled subsequently to the creation of the trust.[59] "The trust allows the trustee to distribute as much income and principal to [the beneficiary] as the trustee deems advisable, but it also instructs the trustee to remain mindful of and to always consider other resources available to [the beneficiary]. According to the trust, preservation of principal is a priority."[60] The trial court denied the modification on the basis that the modification was inappropriate on public policy grounds,[61] "finding that the requested modification would violate Arkansas public policy forbidding the use of trusts to artificially sequester resources and qualify for government assistance."[62] The court stated:

---

55. *Id.* at 893.
56. *Id.*
57. 418 S.W.3d 421 (Ark. Ct. App. 2012).
58. *Id.* at 422.
59. *Id.*
60. *Id.*
61. *Id.*
62. *Id.* The appellate court noted the trial court's reliance on Arkansas Supreme Court opinions that "previously held that a trust provision that deliberately sequesters funds to qualify a beneficiary for Medicaid is void per public policy" (citing Thomas v. Ark. Dep't of Hum. Servs., 894 S.W.2d 584 (Ark. 1995); Ark. Dep't of Hum. Servs. v. Walters, 866 S.W.2d 823 (Ark. 1993)). *Id.* at 424.

> [E]ven trust provisions that do not expressly impoverish a beneficiary are void when the trust seeks to qualify a beneficiary for government benefits. Because PBNB's [the bank's] intent to modify the trust was to qualify [the beneficiary] for "public benefits," and because impoverishing her to qualify for government benefits would render those trust provisions void, the modified trust provisions would be void on public-policy grounds. The fact that the primary purpose for modifying the trust would be defeated was the reason behind the trial court's denial of [the trustee's] motion to modify the trust.[63]

In the Montana Supreme Court case *Estate of Scheidecker v. Montana Department of Public Health & Human Services*,[64] the court discussed, among other things, the ability of the beneficiary to modify the irrevocable trust under state law.[65] The beneficiary and her sister created the irrevocable trust, in which the only res was their home.[66] In denying the beneficiary's application for Medicaid, the state took the position that the trust was revocable and the asset in the trust thus available to the beneficiary.[67] On appeal, the district court reversed the Medicaid agency's position that the trust was revocable, instead holding that under the "any circumstances" test of 42 U.S.C. § 1396p(d)(3)(B), circumstances existed where distributions to the beneficiary could be made.[68]

The Montana Supreme Court reviewed the applicable statutes for modification starting with the statute that allows modification on the consent of the settlor and the beneficiaries.[69] The court determined that this statute could not apply in this case because the terms of the trust included an express waiver by the beneficiary of the right or ability to make any changes to the trust.[70] The trust terms take priority over the statute, the court notes, concluding then that "a court could not recognize as legitimate any attempt by [the beneficiary] to terminate or modify the trust under" the applicable Montana statute.[71] As far as the Montana "material purpose" statute, since the trust's material purpose was "to supplement and not supplant [Medicaid] benefits," a court would not be able to find that ending the trust would not defeat the trust's material

63. *Id.* at 425.
64. 490 P.3d 87 (Mont. 2021).
65. *Id.* at 93–94.
66. *Id.* at 89–90.
67. *Id.*
68. *Id.* at 90.
69. *Id.* at 93.
70. *Id.*
71. *Id.*

purpose.[72] The court acknowledged that Medicaid eligibility for a trust settlor is governed by the trust terms, "not by what the trustee or beneficiaries hypothetically could agree to do *despite* the terms of the trust."[73] For the argument about modification, the court then concluded that "this Court does not construe the 'any circumstances' provision in 42 U.S.C. § 1396p(d)(3)(B) to encompass a court's or agency's misinterpretation of a written instrument's terms or purposes. Such a speculative possibility does not render the trust 'available' to [the beneficiary] for the purpose of determining Medicaid eligibility."[74] The court, after further consideration, concluded that there were no circumstance under which the corpus could be used for payments to the beneficiary, and reversed and remanded the case.[75]

PRACTICE NOTE

If the beneficiary is the client and seeks reformation or modification, consider whether any changes would result in SSA considering the beneficiary to have control over the trust and thus the res (or a portion) would be available to the beneficiary.[76]

Further if the res comes from an inheritance, then that res could be viewed as the money of the beneficiary, and a third-party SNT would not be appropriate.[77] Instead, a first-party SNT would have to be created.[78]

72. *Id.* at 93–94.

73. *Id.* at 94 (citing Centers for Medicare and Medicaid Services, State Medicaid Manual, HCFA Pub. No. 45-3, Transmittal 64 § 3259 (1994)).

74. *Id.*

75. *Id.* at 97.

76. See POMS SI 01120.200.D.1.a, which states:

> Trust principal is a resource for SSI purposes if a trust beneficiary (applicant, recipient, or deemor) has legal authority to revoke or terminate the trust and then use the funds to meet his or her food or shelter needs. The trust principal is also a resource for SSI purposes if the trust beneficiary can direct the use of the trust principal for his or her support and maintenance under the terms of the trust. For the definition of revoke, see SI 01120.200.B.11. in this section.
>
> Additionally, if the trust beneficiary can sell his or her beneficial interest in the trust, that interest is a resource. For example, if the trust provides for payment of $100 per month to the trust beneficiary for spending money, and the trust does not have a valid spendthrift clause, then the trust beneficiary may be able to sell the right to future payments for a lump-sum settlement. The present value of the future payments counts as a resource. For more information on spendthrift clauses, see SI 01120.200.B.13. in this section.

77. But note that the experienced practitioner might seek language authorizing even an estate's personal representative to modify vague terms to provide clear authority for a third-party SNT. Not every testamentary bequest will prohibit interpretation of possible trust modifications.

78. The funds would be viewed to be the beneficiary's, not a third party's.

III. Reformation

It is important to note the differences between reformation and modification. As noted in the Restatement:[79]

> "Reformation" involves the use of interpretation (including evidence of mistake, etc.) in order to ascertain—and properly restate—the true, legally effective intent of settlors with respect to the original terms of trusts they have created; by way of contrast, "modification" involves a change in—a departure from—the true, original terms of the trust, whether the modification is done by a court . . . or by the beneficiaries . . . or a power holder. . . . Thus, a trust that needs no reformation—i.e., the trust instrument says what it was supposed to say—may later be modified to improve or otherwise change the trust when grounds or a power to do so exists.)[80]

Section 415 of the UTC, Reformation to Correct Mistakes, provides for reformation by the court as follows:

> The court may reform the terms of a trust, even if unambiguous, to conform the terms to the settlor's intention if it is proved by clear and convincing evidence what the settlor's intention was and that the terms of the trust were affected by a mistake of fact or law, whether in expression or inducement.

Note the comment explains the application of the section, which has typically been used to correct a mistake,

> whether the mistake is one of expression or one of inducement. A mistake of expression occurs when the terms of the trust misstate the settlor's intention, fail to include a term that was intended to be included, or include a term that was not intended to be included. A mistake in the inducement occurs when the terms of the trust accurately reflect what the settlor intended to be included or excluded but this intention was based on a mistake of fact or law.[81]

What about the case where there is no mistake, but a change in circumstances, for example a grandchild with special needs is born after the trust is created? Can the trustee seek reformation to direct the grandchild's share to an SNT? Does UTC section 412 provide the answer? Section 412, Modification or Termination Because of Unanticipated Circumstances or Inability to

---

79. Restatement (Third) of Trusts § 62 cmt. a (Am. L. Inst. 2012).

80. *See id.* § 62 reporter's notes. *See also* George G. Bogert et al., Bogert's The Law of Trusts and Trustees § 991 (2021).

81. *See* Unif. Tr. Code § 415 cmt. (Unif. L. Comm'n 2010) (citing Restatement (Third) of Property § 12.1 cmt. i (Am. L. Inst. 2003).

Administer Trust Effectively, recognizes that the court is allowed to modify the trust's dispositive provisions "if, because of circumstances not anticipated by the settlor, modification . . . will further the purposes of the trust. To the extent practicable, the modification must be made in accordance with the settlor's probable intention."[82] The comment makes note that the court's power to do these modifications is the equitable deviation doctrine, noting that the intent of this provision is to not ignore the settlor's intent as contained in the trust, but is instead "to modify inopportune details to effectuate better the settlor's broader purposes. Among other things, equitable deviation may be used to modify . . . dispositive terms due to the failure to anticipate . . . the incapacity of a beneficiary."[83]

The comment to the POMS provides this useful example:

> [A] grandparent creates a support trust for his three grandchildren to make sure they have the resources to provide for their health, housing, and quality of life. After his death, one of the grandchildren becomes permanently disabled. If the trustee petitions the court to modify the terms of the trust so that the grandchild's share is paid into a special needs trust, the settlor's intent would still be fulfilled, as the proceeds from the SNT could be used to pay for housing for the beneficiary while public benefits pays for the beneficiary's health care. Further, the SNT trustee can use the SNT funds to pay for things for the beneficiary not otherwise covered by public benefits that would enhance the beneficiary's quality of life.[84]

A New York Surrogate's Court opinion illustrates the use of reformation to a supplemental needs trust.[85] The testamentary trust was created for the testator's son who was born with special needs.[86] Previously the beneficiary had only received Social Security Disability Insurance, but on subsequent enrollment into a Medicaid day treatment program, the beneficiary was determined to be ineligible because of the testamentary trust.[87] Noting the liberal public policy of New York toward supplemental needs trusts,[88] the court found the testator's intent was to arrange for his son's care.[89] Given case law and the state's public policy, the court held that allowing reformation of the trust "into

82. *See id.* § 412(a).

83. *See id.* § 412 cmt.

84. *See* POMS SI 01120.200.B.16, Third-party trust, https://secure.ssa.gov/apps10/poms.nsf/lnx/0501120200 (last visited Dec. 11, 2022).

85. *In re* Reformation of Tr. of Kamp, 790 N.Y.S.2d 852 (N.Y. Surr. Ct. 2005). *See also In re* Est. of Newman, 856 N.Y.S.2d 500 (N.Y. Surr. Ct. 2008) (unreported).

86. *Kamp*, 790 N.Y.S.2d at 853.

87. *Id.*

88. *Id.* at 853–55 (citing legislative intent and a memo from the governor, as well as prior case law).

89. *Id.* at 856.

a supplemental needs trust accords with public policy recognized and encouraged by all three branches of government"[90] and found it in the best interest of the beneficiary to reform the trust into a supplemental needs trust.[91]

IV. Decanting

"Decanting" can be explained as follows:

> [T]rust decanting refers to the act of distributing trust property from an irrevocable trust to another trust, under the trustee's discretionary authority to make distributions to or for the benefit of its beneficiaries. The ability of a trustee to decant arises principally from the trustee's distribution powers as conferred by the trust instrument. Except where decanting is expressly allowed by statute under different circumstances, a trustee must generally possess the absolute power to invade the trust's principal in order for decanting to be expressly permitted. The practical effect is to allow a trustee with decanting power to amend an otherwise unamendable trust by transferring trust property to a second trust with different administrative or dispositive terms.[92]

Florida Statutes section 736.04117 is an example of a decanting statute.[93]

Florida was the first state to allow decanting via common law while New York was the first state to adopt a decanting statute.[94] According to the Supreme Judicial Court of Massachusetts, "decanting" typically means "the distribution of [irrevocable] trust property to another trust pursuant to the trustee's discretionary authority to make distributions to, or for the benefit of, one or more

---

90. *Id.* at 858.

91. *Id. See also In re* Rappaport, 866 N.Y.S.2d 483, 488 (N.Y. Surr. Ct. 2008) (allowing reformation based on the statute and public policy of New York, finding that doing so would not change the testator's testamentary plan and the reformation to be in the beneficiary's best interest; court noted that the beneficiary was not currently receiving public benefits or had so previously).

92. Lydia Lee Lockett & Peter Blumeyer, *Sour Grapes: When Decanting Gives Rise to Litigation*, 33 Prob. & Prop. 26 (2019).

93. Fla. Stat. § 736.04117 (2019). *See also* Amy J. Fanzlaw, *New Opportunities to Decant in Florida, Part I: Recent Changes to the Trust Decanting Statute*, 93 Fla. B.J. 31 (2019); Amy J. Fanzlaw, *New Opportunities to Decant in Florida, Part II: Successful Execution of Trust Decanting*, 93 Fla. B.J. 22 (2019).

94. *See* John Fritz, *The Wild, Wild West: The Mechanics and Potential Uses of Trust Decanting*, 19 Wyo. L. Rev. 327, 331–32 (2019) ("In 1940, Florida became the first jurisdiction to allow decanting through its common law in *Phipps v. Palm Beach Trust Co*. Phipps v. Palm Beach Tr. Co., 196 So. 299, 301 (Fla. 1940) (recognizing "the power of the individual trustee to create [a] second trust provided one or more of the descendants of the donor of the original trust are made the beneficiaries"). Fifty-two years later, in 1992, New York became the first state to codify a trustee's decanting power (citing Act of July 24, 1992, ch. 591, 1992 N.Y. Laws 3520, 3521 (codified as amended at N.Y. Est. Powers & Trusts Law § 10-6.6(b) (Consol. 2019)) (citations omitted).

beneficiaries [of the original trust]." It results in "amend[ing] an unamendable trust, in the sense that [the trustee] may distribute the trust property to a second trust with terms that differ from those of the original trust." Why should decanting be allowed, especially because the trust is irrevocable and that was the settlor's choice? Because "if a trustee has the discretionary power to distribute property to or for the benefit of the beneficiaries, the trustee likewise has the authority to distribute the property to another trust for the benefit of those same beneficiaries."[95]

Why seek to decant? There can be myriad reasons, such as a beneficiary's eligibility for public benefits, reducing taxes or costs, administrative changes, changing the trust from non-grantor to grantor, switching to another governing law, dividing the trust res into smaller trusts, minimizing liability, and changing the nature of the trust.[96]

A. Uniform Trust Decanting Act[97]

The Uniform Trust Decanting Act (UTDA) was approved by the Uniform Law Commission in 2015.[98] Decanting, that is the trustee's power to move the property from the first trust into a second trust, can serve many purposes.[99] The prefatory note offers some comments about the rise in popularity of decanting statutes:

> These statutes represent one of several recent innovations in trust law that seek to make trusts more flexible so that the settlor's material purposes can best be carried out under current circumstances. A decanting statute provides flexibility by statutorily expanding discretion already granted to the trustee to permit the trustee to modify the trust either directly or by distributing its assets to another trust. While some trusts expressly grant the trustee or another person a power to modify or decant the trust, a statutory provision can better describe the power granted, impose limits on the power to protect

95. Ferri v. Powell-Ferri, 72 N.E.3d 541, 546 (Mass. 2017).

96. *See, e.g.*, Stewart E. Sterk, *Trust Decanting: A Critical Perspective*, 38 Cardozo L. Rev. 1993, 2013–14 (2017) (discussing decanting to SNT as a cost-shifting from beneficiary to taxpayer). *See also In re* Riddell, 157 P.3d 888 (Wash. Ct. App. 2007) (reversing trial court's consideration of using Medicaid instead of private pay).

97. Unif. L. Comm'n, *Trust Decanting Act*, https://www.uniformlaws.org/committees/community-home?communitykey=5b248bac-9251-47fb-bad8-57a23f3df540&tab=groupdetails (last visited Dec. 11, 2022) (states that have adopted it include Alabama, California, Colorado, Illinois, New Mexico, North Carolina, Virginia, Washington, and West Virginia).

98. *Id.*

99. *See* Unif. Tr. Decanting Act § 2(10) (Unif. L. Comm'n 2015) ("'Decanting power' or 'the decanting power' means the power of an authorized fiduciary under this [act] to distribute property of a first trust to one or more second trusts or to modify the terms of the first trust.").

> the beneficiaries and the settlor's intent, protect against inadvertent tax consequences, provide procedural rules for exercising the power and provide for appropriate remedies. While decanting may be permitted in some situations under common law in some states, in many states it is unclear whether common law decanting is permitted, and if it is, the circumstances in which it is permitted and the parameters within which it may be exercised.[100]

Clearly, the ability to decant is a valuable tool that is used primarily for private irrevocable trusts, but it is not available in all situations[101] and there are typically limitations on the use of decanting unless specific considerations are met.[102] The UTDA highlights the limits to the use of decanting.[103] In addition to the applicable state statute, decanting may also be authorized by the terms of the trust as well as the common law.[104] The purpose of decanting is to further the intent of the settlor, although it may not on its face seem so. For example, the comment to UTDA explains:

> An exercise of the decanting power must be in accordance with the purposes of the first trust. The purpose of decanting is not to disregard the settlor's intent but to modify the trust to better effectuate the settlor's broader purposes or the settlor's probable intent if the settlor had anticipated the

100. Unif. L. Comm'n, *Trust Decanting Act*, *supra* note 97. For a discussion of "expanded discretion," see Sterk, *supra* note 96, at 2008–11.

101. *See* Unif. Tr. Decanting Act § 3(a) (Unif. L. Comm'n 2015) ("Except as otherwise provided in subsections (b) and (c), this [act] applies to an express trust that is irrevocable or revocable by the settlor only with the consent of the trustee or a person holding an adverse interest.").

102. *See* Brandon A.S. Ross, *Practical Considerations for Decanting*, 30 Prob. & Prop. 36, 37 (2016) (discussing, among other things, the typical statutory requirements for decanting, "Many state decanting statutes have the following common requirements: • The beneficiaries of the Second Trust must be beneficiaries of the First Trust, and the Second Trust cannot add beneficiaries. • The Second Trust Agreement cannot reduce the fixed rights to income, annuity, or unitrust interests granted under the First Trust Agreement. • If the First Trust qualifies for the marital or charitable deduction, the Second Trust also must qualify for that deduction. • Certain beneficiaries of the First Trust must be notified."). *See also, e.g.*, Stephanie Vara, *Two Cheers for Decanting: A Partial Defense*, 22 Quinnipiac Prob. L.J. 23 (2018).

103. See *supra* note 100, stating:

> Generally, the Uniform Trust Decanting Act permits decanting of an irrevocable, express trust in which the terms of the trust grant the trustee or another fiduciary the discretionary power to make principal distributions. . . . The act does not apply to revocable trusts unless they are revocable by the settlor only with the consent of the trustee or an adverse party. . . . The act does not apply to wholly charitable trusts. . . . With one exception, if no fiduciary has discretion to distribute principal, the act does not apply unless the court appoints a special fiduciary and authorizes the special fiduciary to exercise the decanting power. . . . The exception is that a fiduciary who is responsible for making trust distributions may decant a trust to create a special-needs trust even if the fiduciary does not have discretion over principal if the decanting will further the purposes of the first trust.

104. *See* Unif. Tr. Decanting Act § 3 cmts. (Unif. L. Comm'n 2015). *See also* Unif. Tr. Code § 111 (Unif. L. Comm'n 2010) (authorizing settlement of certain disputes through settlement agreements). *See also* Ross, *supra* note 102, at 37.

circumstances in place at the time of the decanting. The settlor's purposes generally include efficient administration of the trust. The settlor's purposes may also include achieving certain tax objectives or generally minimizing overall tax liabilities. The settlor's purposes often include avoiding fruitless, needless dissipation of the trust assets should a beneficiary develop dependencies such as substance abuse or gambling, have creditor problems, or otherwise be unfit to prudently manage assets that might be distributed from the trust. The exercise of the decanting power need not be in accord with the literal terms of the first-trust instrument because decanting by definition is a modification of the terms of the first trust.[105]

B. State Example: Florida's Decanting Statute

Florida's statute on trust decanting to a supplemental needs trust is found in Florida Statutes section 736.04117(4). This statute provides for a transfer from the first trust to the second (SNT) trust as follows:

> (a) Notwithstanding subsections (2) and (3), unless the trust instrument expressly provides otherwise, an authorized trustee who has the power under the terms of a first trust to invade the principal of the first trust to make current distributions to or for the benefit of a beneficiary with a disability may instead exercise such power by appointing all or part of the principal of the first trust in favor of a trustee of a second trust that is a supplemental needs trust if:
>
> 1. The supplemental needs trust benefits the beneficiary with a disability;
>
> 2. The beneficiaries of the second trust include only beneficiaries of the first trust; and
>
> 3. The authorized trustee determines that the exercise of such power will further the purposes of the first trust.
>
> (b) Except as affected by any change to the interests of the beneficiary with a disability, the second trusts, in the aggregate, shall grant each other beneficiary of the first trust beneficial interests in the second trusts which are substantially similar to such other beneficiary's beneficial interests in the first trust.

105. *See* Unif. Tr. Decanting Act § 4 cmts. (Unif. L. Comm'n 2015). The comments further provide:

> Therefore subsection 4(c) provides that the terms of the first trust shall be deemed to include the decanting power for purposes of determining the fiduciary duties of the authorized fiduciary. Nonetheless, the other terms of the first trust may provide insight into the purposes of the first trust and the settlor's probable intent under current circumstances.

For trusts with trust protectors, depending on the provisions of the trust or under the applicable statute, the trust protector may be able to decant the first trust into a second trust, or direct the trustee to do so.[106]

C. Decanting Cases

A New York case, *In re Kroll*,[107] asked the surrogate's court to decant from an existing trust to a supplemental needs trust.[108] The state Medicaid agency

106. *See, e.g.*, FLA. STAT. § 736.0808 (2006).

107. 971 N.Y.S.2d 863 (N.Y. Surr. Ct. 2013).

108. In some states like New York, the phrase "supplemental needs trust" is used instead of an SNT, *see, e.g.*, N.Y. EST. POWERS & TRUSTS LAW § 7-1.12 (2017). Florida Revised Statutes section 736.04117, Trustee's power to invade principal in trust, also uses "supplemental needs trust" and defines it as "a trust that the authorized trustee believes would not be considered a resource for purposes of determining whether the beneficiary who has a disability is eligible for government benefits." FLA. STAT. § 736.04117(1)(j) (2022).

The New York Estates, Powers, and Trusts Law section 7-1.12(5) provides that a "supplemental needs trust" means a discretionary trust established for the benefit of a person with a severe and chronic or persistent disability (the "beneficiary"), which conforms to all of the following criteria:

> (i) The trust document clearly evidences the creator's intent to supplement, not supplant, impair or diminish, government benefits or assistance for which the beneficiary may otherwise be eligible or which the beneficiary may be receiving, except as provided in clause (ii) of this subparagraph;
>
> (ii) The trust document prohibits the trustee from expending or distributing trust assets in any way which may supplant, impair or diminish government benefits or assistance for which the beneficiary may otherwise be eligible or which the beneficiary may be receiving; provided, however, that the trustee may be authorized to make such distributions to third parties to meet the beneficiary's needs for food, clothing, shelter or health care but only if the trustee determines (A) that the beneficiary's basic needs will be better met if such distribution is made, and (B) that it is in the beneficiary's best interests to suffer the consequent effect, if any, on the beneficiary's eligibility for or receipt of government benefits or assistance;
>
> (iii) The beneficiary does not have the power to assign, encumber, direct, distribute or authorize distributions from the trust;
>
> (iv) If an inter vivos trust, the creator of the trust is a person or entity other than the beneficiary or the beneficiary's spouse; and
>
> (v) Notwithstanding subparagraph (iv) of this paragraph, the beneficiary of a supplemental needs trust may be the creator of the trust if such trust meets the requirements of subparagraph two of paragraph (b) of subdivision two of section three hundred sixty-six of the social services law and of the regulations implementing such clauses. Provided, however, that if the trust is funded with the proceeds of retroactive payments made as a result of a court action and due the beneficiary under the federal supplemental security income program, as established under title XVI of the federal social security act, the creation of a supplemental needs trust by the beneficiary under this subparagraph shall not impair nor limit any right under applicable law of a representative payee to receive reimbursement out of such proceeds for expenses incurred on behalf of the beneficiary pending the determination of the beneficiary's eligibility for such federal supplemental security income program, nor any right under applicable law of any state or local governmental entity which provided the beneficiary with interim assistance pending the determination of the beneficiary's eligibility for such federal supplemental security income program to be repaid out of such proceeds for the amount of such interim assistance.

(citations omitted).

objected to the decanting.[109] The existing trust was set up by the grandparents of the beneficiary at the time he was an infant and he had not shown any signs of disability.[110] The trustee sought decanting because the beneficiary was significantly disabled and received SSI and Medicaid.[111] The existing trust, a discretionary trust, directed the trustee to make quarterly payments to the beneficiary who had turned 21, with subsequent distributions of the principal based on the beneficiary attaining specific age benchmarks.[112] The trustee appointed the principal of the existing trust to the SNT before the beneficiary turned 21 and the court considered whether the appointment was valid.[113] The effectiveness of the decanting hinged on the date determined to be the date the exercise of the appointment was effective.[114] The surrogate's court found that the trustee was authorized to decant the existing trust, did so properly through the exercise of the power of appointment, and effective consent had been obtained; thus, the third-party SNT was created prior to the beneficiary turning 21.[115]

The case *Ferri v. Powell-Ferri*[116] concerned the decanting of a 1983 sole benefit trust created by the father for his son, Ferri, Jr.[117] Relevant to the question of whether decanting was allowed, under the trust terms, the trustee could "pay to or segregate irrevocably" trust assets for the son-beneficiary and once the beneficiary was 35, the beneficiary could ask for distributions "up to fixed percentages of trust assets, increasing from twenty-five per cent of the principal at age thirty-five to one hundred per cent after age forty-seven."[118]

After a 15-year marriage, the beneficiary's spouse filed for divorce; six months later, unbeknownst to the beneficiary, the trustees decanted the 1983 trust through executing a declaration of trust for the beneficiary and distributed almost all of the assets from the original trust to the 2011 trust.[119] During

109. *Kroll*, 971 N.Y.S.2d at 864.

110. *Id.*

111. *Id.*

112. *Id.*

113. *Id.*

114. *Id.* at 865. The notice of the exercise of the power occurred before the beneficiary's 21st birthday, but under the statute, would not be effective until after the beneficiary's 21st birthday, absent written consent for an earlier effective date, as provided in the statute. *Id.*

115. *Id.* at 866. Like so many other things in life, timing was everything here. The court's holding that the decanting occurred before the beneficiary turned 21 avoided the designation of the SNT as a first-party SNT, necessitating the inclusion of a payback provision. *Id.* at 865–66.

116. 72 N.E.3d 541 (Mass. 2017).

117. *Id.* at 544.

118. *Id.* (citations omitted).

119. *Id.* ("The 2011 Trust is a spendthrift trust; under paragraph 1(a), the trustee exercises complete authority over whether and when to make payments to the beneficiary, if at all, and the beneficiary has no

the relevant time period, the beneficiary had a right to ask for 75 percent of the principal and during the litigation, he had a vested interest of all of the original trust's assets.[120] At the conclusion of the trustees' declaratory judgment action regarding the validity of the decanting, the trial court found in favor of the beneficiary's former wife, and as part of the relief granted, "ordered restoration of seventy-five per cent of the assets of the 2011 Trust, as they were held in the 1983 Trust; an accounting of the 2011 Trust from inception to the date of restoration; and an award of reasonable attorney's fees to [the former spouse]."[121]

On appeal, the court noted that "a trustee's decanting authority turns on the facts of each case and the terms of the instrument that establishes the trust" as well as the settlor's intent.[122] After reviewing precedent and the trust instrument, the court concluded that based on

> the extremely broad authority and discretion afforded the trustees by the 1983 Trust declaration of trust, the anti-alienation provision of the 1983 Trust, the beneficiary withdrawal rights afforded under the terms of the 1983 Trust, and the settlor's affidavit, . . . that the terms of the 1983 Trust, read as a whole, demonstrate the settlor's intent to permit decanting.[123]

The court examined the importance of trustee discretion in making distributions as an indication of authority to decant.[124] Noting the 1983 trust included three discretionary distributions, several sections empowering the trustee to make distributions, and a number of additional provisions authorizing the trustee to distribute assets, the court concluded that the trustee was given "expansive discretion" to take action,[125] especially since the trustee had stated authority to "'segregate irrevocably for later payment to' the trust beneficiary," leading the court to the conclusion that the settlor meant for the trustee to have decanting authority.[126] The court acknowledged two sections of

power to demand payment of trust assets. The spendthrift provision, in paragraph 4(b), bars the beneficiary from transferring or encumbering his interest and, as with similar provisions in the 1983 Trust, shields the trust from the beneficiary's creditors. The trustees decanted the 1983 Trust out of concern that Powell-Ferri would reach the assets of the 1983 Trust as a result of the divorce action. They did so without informing the beneficiary and without his consent.").

120. *Id.*

121. *Id.* at 544–45.

122. *Id.* at 546.

123. *Id.* at 546–47.

124. *Id.* at 547 ("A trustee's broad discretion to distribute the assets of an irrevocable trust may be evidence of a settlor's intent to permit decanting.").

125. *Id.* at 547–48.

126. *Id.* at 548.

the trust that would find against decanting authority,[127] but in examining the entire trust, and specifically

> reading the entirety of art. II in harmony, it provides that, unless and until all of the trust assets were distributed in response to the beneficiary's request for a withdrawal, the trustee could exercise his or her powers and obligations under the 1983 Trust, including the duty to decant if the trustee deemed decanting to be in the beneficiary's best interest.[128]

There are specific requirements for the trustee to be able to decant. For example, it is typical that the trustee must have the absolute power to invade the trust principal.[129] The Florida decanting statute distinguishes between when the trustee has the absolute power to invade and when the trustee does not.[130] As well, careful consideration must be given to the differences between the first and second trusts, especially regarding beneficiary rights and distributions.[131]

The federal District Court of Connecticut considered the issue of decanting in an unreported case, *Simonsen v. Bremby*.[132] The issue arose when the state Medicaid agency determined that two third-party inter vivos trusts created by the plaintiff's mother in Florida made the plaintiff ineligible for Medicaid.[133] The trustee sought and received permission from the Florida court

---

127. *Id.* at 548–49 (court pointed to an anti-alienation provision found in Article V.B and the "Beneficiary withdrawal provisions" in Article II.B of the 1983 trust).

128. *Id.* at 551 (citations omitted). But see *Hodges v. Johnson*, 177 A.3d 86, 95, 98 (N.H. 2017), where the decanting was voided due to the trustee's failure to give "due regard for the diverse beneficial interests created by the terms of the trust," which was "contrary to the statutory duty of impartiality."

129. Lockett & Blumeyer, *supra* note 92, at 28.

130. *See, e.g.*, FLA. STAT. § 736.04117(2)(3) (2022).

131. *See* Lockett & Blumeyer, *supra* note 92, at 28 (noting that "[w]hen decanting, a trustee must also consider what differences between the terms of the original trust and the newly created trust are statutorily permitted. These considerations commonly include whether the new trust may eliminate a beneficiary's mandatory withdrawal or distribution rights; whether the beneficiaries of the new trust must be the same as (or are otherwise limited to) the beneficiaries of the original trust; and whether the new trust requires the same distribution standard as the original trust. In addition, some states require notice be given to the settlors and beneficiaries of the original trust before engaging in the act of decanting."). For more on the barriers that may arise to decanting, see Michael J. Skeary, *The Power of Trust Decanting: The Authority for the Power, Its Scope, and the Fiduciary Duty and Tax Implications of Its Use*, 32 PROB. & PROP. 22 (2018).

132. 2015 WL 9451031 (D. Conn. Dec. 23, 2015), *aff'd*, 679 F. App'x 57 (2d Cir. 2017).

133. *Id.* at *1–2. The Medicaid agency considered the language of the trusts, including the following provisions:

> The trustee shall pay to my daughter or utilize for her benefit so much of the income and principal of her trust as the trustee deems necessary or advisable from time to time for her health, maintenance in reasonable comfort, education and best interests considering all of her resources known to the trustee and her ability to manage and use such funds for her benefits. In exercising its discretion the trustee shall bear in mind that my daughter has suffered severely from alcohol and drug abuse and that I do not want these trust funds to be used to support a drug or alcohol habit or any other activity which may be detrimental to her in the trustee's sole opinion.

to decant the two trusts into third-party SNTs.[134] The state Medicaid agency viewed the first trusts as support trusts, and the decanting to the second trust was a transfer for less than fair market value.[135] After reviewing the applicable regulations and the POMS, the language of the trusts, and Florida law, the federal district court entered an injunction that, among other things, prohibited the state Medicaid agency from "treating the decanting of funds from the Predecessor Trusts into the Successor Trusts as transfers of assets disqualifying Plaintiff from Medicaid."[136]

V. Directed Trusts

In 2017 the Uniform Law Commission approved the Uniform Directed Trust Act (UDTA), which at this writing has been adopted in 16 states.[137] The catalyst for this act, according to the prefatory note, was the frequently used term in a trust that gave a third party who is not the trustee "the power over some aspect of the trust's administration."[138]

Under the UDTA, a directed trust is a trust for which the terms of the trust grant a power of direction[139] and a trustee subject to direction of the third-party holding the power to direct is known as the "directed trustee."[140]

> My daughter's health, happiness and best interests are to be considered foremost in priority over those who will receive the remaining trust funds on her death. Subject to the above considerations the trustee is encouraged to be liberal in its use of the funds for her even to the extent of the full expenditure thereof.

Id.

134. *Id.* at *2.

135. *Id.*

136. *Id.* at *7. The court noted:

> In short, if a trust contains a spendthrift clause, the beneficiary has no legal right or authority to access the trust principal, and, therefore, it is not counted as an available resource for SSI, and consequently Medicaid, eligibility purposes. While the total refusal of the trustee to make any payments from a spendthrift trust's interest or principal might, under some circumstances, constitute an abuse of the trustee's discretion as conflicting with the settlor's intent, "[the SSA] do[es] not require litigation to obtain access, the property is not a resource." POMS SI § 01120.010D.7.

Id. at *6.

137. Unif. L. Comm'n, *Directed Trust Act*, https://www.uniformlaws.org/committees/community-home?CommunityKey=ca4d8a5a-55d7-4c43-b494-5f8858885dd8 (last visited Dec. 11, 2022).

138. Unif. Directed Tr. Act prefatory note (Unif. L. Comm'n 2017), https://www.uniformlaws.org/HigherLogic/System/DownloadDocumentFile.ashx?DocumentFileKey=04e5b80e-3b2e-e30b-99fe-03ab5ed4a7fe&forceDialog=1 at 1.

139. *Id.* § 2(2).

140. *Id.* § 2(3). In some states, the trust director is referred to as a trust protector.

The third party with the power to direct is known as the "trust director."[141] The powers given to the trust director can be quiet extensive, as noted in the definition:

> "Power of direction" means a power over a trust granted to a person by the terms of the trust to the extent the power is exercisable while the person is not serving as a trustee. The term includes a power over the investment, management, or distribution of trust property or other matters of trust administration. The term excludes the powers described in Section 5(b).[142]

Take note of the definition of "terms of a trust," which is not limited to the terms of the trust, but also includes "the trust's provisions as established, determined, or amended by: (i) a trustee or trust director in accordance with applicable law; [or] (ii) court order; or (iii) a nonjudicial settlement agreement."[143]

As far as the actions that may be taken by the trust director, the UDTA recognizes that, with some limitations,[144] the powers of the trust director are comprehensive, and may include, for example, powers over the res of the trust, modification, termination, reformation, or decanting of the trust, making administrative changes, and making decisions that directly affect a trustee.[145]

---

141. *Id.* § 2(9) defines "trust director" as

> a person [who] is granted a power of direction by the terms of a trust to the extent the power is exercisable while the person is not serving as a trustee. The person is a trust director whether or not the terms of the trust refer to the person as a trust director and whether or not the person is a beneficiary or settlor of the trust.

142. *Id.* § 2(5). Consider this portion of the comment to section 2(5):

> The definition confirms that a power of direction may include a power over "matters of trust administration" as well as a power over "investment, management, or distribution of trust property." These examples are meant to illustrate the potential scope of a power of direction rather than to limit it. In using the term "administration," the drafting committee intended a meaning at least as broad as that found in the context of determining a trust's "principal place of administration," such as under Section 3(b). The drafting committee also intended the terms "investment, management, or distribution" to have a meaning at least as broad as that found in Uniform Trust Code § 815(a)(2)(b) (2000), which specifies a trustee's default powers. The comment to Section 6 provides examples of the kinds of specific powers that the drafting committee contemplated would fall within the definition of a power of direction.

143. *Id* § 2(8).

144. *Id.* § 7.

145. *Id.* § 6. The comment to section 6 offers these examples:

> *Breadth of subsection (a).* Without limiting the definition of a "power of direction" in Section 2(5), the drafting committee specifically contemplated that subsection (a) would validate terms of a trust that grant a power to a trust director to:
>
> - acquire, dispose of, exchange, or retain an investment;
> - make or take loans;
> - vote proxies for securities held in trust;

A. Case Law on Trust Directors

In *Minassian v. Rachins*,[146] the trust protector's actions were upheld because the trust was ambiguous.[147] The court of appeals noted:

> [T]he trust protector's amendments were made to effectuate the settlor's intent, [and] the amendments that [the trust protector] made to the trust are within his powers. The amendments may have disadvantaged the children, but the trust protector was authorized [to] correct ambiguities with the limitation that he act *either* to benefit a group of beneficiaries *or* to further [the settlor's] probable wishes. [The trust protector] acted to correct ambiguities in a way to further the [settlor's] probable wishes. As the drafting agent, [the trust protector] was privy to what the [settlor] intended.[148]

Continuing to discuss the settlor's intent, the court of appeals noted that where an ambiguity existed in the trust or a drafting error occurred, the settlor's intent was to use the trust protector, not a court, to fix the problem.[149]

In the case *In re Eleanor Pierce (Marshall) Stevens Living Trust*,[150] the settlor amended the trust first in 2006 to name Marshall as the trust protector, and again in 2007 to amend the trust protector's powers to include removal of the trustee on the trust protector's sole discretion, with or without cause.[151] "By designing a trust protector, the settlor's interest in managing the assets for the benefit of the beneficiaries is better protected as the trust protector is

- adopt a particular valuation of trust property or determine the frequency or methodology of valuation;
- adjust between principal and income or convert to a unitrust;
- manage a business held in the trust;
- select a custodian for trust assets;
- modify, reform, terminate, or decant a trust;
- direct a trustee's or another director's delegation of the trustee's or other director's powers;
- change the principal place of administration, situs, or governing law of the trust;
- ascertain the happening of an event that affects the administration of the trust;
- determine the capacity of a trustee, settlor, director, or beneficiary of the trust;
- determine the compensation to be paid to a trustee or trust director;
- prosecute, defend, or join an action, claim, or judicial proceeding relating to the trust;
- grant permission before a trustee or another director may exercise a power of the trustee or other director; or
- release a trustee or another trust director from liability for an action proposed or previously taken by the trustee or other director.

146. 152 So. 3d 719 (Fla. Dist. Ct. App. 2014).
147. *Id.* at 721, 726.
148. *Id.* at 727.
149. *Id.*
150. 159 So. 3d 1101 (La. Ct. App. 2015).
151. *Id.* at 1110.

someone the settlor has selected 'to represent the settlor's interests in making specified trust decisions that the settlor will be unable to make.'"[152]

In *In re ABB Trust*,[153] the trust protector had the sole authority to amend the trust. The question on appeal was whether the beneficiary exerted undue influence over the settlor to get the trust protector to amend the trust to make changes to the beneficiaries.[154] The trust specified that the trust protector "assist in achieving [the settlor's] objectives" and required the trust protector to "ensure that [the trust] is construed in a manner consistent with [the settlor's] estate planning objectives."[155] The court noted that the settlor's "input remained relevant if not dispositive, under the trust terms," and one commentator considered the role of the trust protector as "an agent [who has] been chosen by the settlor to have some level of power to guide the trustee's actions."[156]

In *Robert T. McLean Irrevocable Trust v. Ponder*,[157] the trust protector was sued for breach of fiduciary duty and bad faith. At the time of the litigation, Missouri did not have a statute that created any legal duties for a trust protector.[158] The trust was silent on the timing and method for the trust protector to perform the "'authority' to remove the trustee or successors." The trust just provided that the trust protector had "authority" that is "conferred in a 'fiduciary capacity.'"[159] The appellate court, scrutinizing the language, concluded liability exists when a trust protector acts in bad faith.[160]

152. *Id.* at 1111 (citations omitted).
153. 491 P.3d 1120 (Ariz. Ct. App. 2021).
154. *Id.* at 1121, 1123.
155. *Id.* at 1126.
156. *Id.* (citations omitted).
157. 283 S.W.3d 786 (Mo. Ct. App. 2009).
158. *Id.* at 794.
159. *Id.*
160. *Id.* at 794, 795.

CHAPTER 7

Special Needs Trust Alternatives

Naming this chapter "Special Needs Trust Alternatives" is somewhat of a misnomer. The documents discussed here are definitely alternatives, but they might also be used in conjunction with a special needs trust (SNT). There are several alternatives to the use of an SNT, whether first- or third-party, that should be considered.[1] The best way to do so is to determine the purpose of the action to be taken (e.g., continue the beneficiary's eligibility for public benefits, provide asset management, etc.).

I. No SNT or Trust at All

For a third-party devise, the owner of the property may decide to make an outright gift, whether inter vivos or testamentary. Where the owner of the property is considering the creation of a first-party SNT, if the amount of money is large enough, the owner may decide to take the money outright and invest it, foregoing the possibility of public benefits eligibility.

1. Disinheriting the beneficiary is no longer considered to be a favorable planning option for individuals with disabilities. As well, giving the share of the individual with special needs to a sibling is not a reliable plan. An outright gift to the sibling with the hope that the sibling will care for the individual with special needs is just that, a hope. It is important for attorneys to help clients see the flaws in a plan like this: if parents leave money to a child with the intent that the child will use those funds for the benefit of a sibling with a disability, have the parents thought of what will happen to the money if the child gets divorced, sued, or predeceases the sibling with disabilities?

No SNT/Outright Distribution

Advantages	Disadvantages	Comments
Cheaper	No creditor protection	
Quicker	No public benefits eligibility	Unlikely eligible for public benefits at least until spend down
No payback	No oversight	Although recipient will not have a payback issue from the use of a (d)(4)(A) SNT, there may still be a payback issue down the road; does not protect against creditors seeking to attach
No limits on expenditures	No third party to manage investments	Without investment and a spending plan, when the money is gone, the money is gone
Recipient does not have to answer to a third party for distributions	Likely to run out of money sooner	If recipient runs out of money, although public benefits may kick in (and pay base costs), there will be no funds remaining to pay for extra or supplemental needs
Flexibility/freedom—can spend money on whatever owner wants to spend it on	Means the recipient may not spend the money on things the recipient really needs	Remember, a fool and their money are soon parted*

* Know Your Phrase, *A Fool and His Money Are Soon Parted*, https://knowyourphrase.com/a-fool-and-his-money-soon-parted (last visited Dec. 11, 2022) (the phrase was used by poet Thomas Tusser in "Five Hundred Pointes of Good Husbandrie" in 1557).

SNTs are designed to keep beneficiaries eligible for Medicaid and other means-tested benefits programs, but there are times when the intended trust beneficiary may not be receiving those benefits. If the intended trust beneficiary is receiving public benefits that are not means-tested and the likelihood is small that the beneficiary will ever qualify or need such benefits, an SNT may not be the best solution. If the trust beneficiary has no legal status or citizenship necessary to qualify for public benefits, it might be best to forego an SNT completely.

II. Achieving a Better Life Experience Accounts

Achieving a Better Life Experience (ABLE) accounts are established pursuant to 26 U.S.C. § 529A of the Internal Revenue Code (IRC) for eligible individuals[2] who have a disability.[3] Accounts established in a qualified ABLE plan[4] are exempt from taxation.[5] The statute limits the types of contributions that can be accepted into the account.[6] A beneficiary may only have one ABLE account but a beneficiary is not limited to establishing an account in his or her home state.[7] The total amount of annual ABLE account contributions for *all* sources is limited to an amount equal to the federal annual gift tax exclusion amount, unless the person with disabilities is working.[8] Even though

---

2. 26 U.S.C. § 529A(e)(1) defines "eligible individual" as a person who

> is entitled to benefits based on blindness or disability under title II or XVI of the Social Security Act, and such blindness or disability occurred before the date on which the individual attained age 26, or . . . a disability certification with respect to such individual is filed with the Secretary for such taxable year.

3. Note that the definition for "eligible individual" requires a disability or a disability certification, which is defined as

> a certification to the satisfaction of the Secretary by the individual or the parent or guardian of the individual that . . . certifies that the individual has a medically determinable physical or mental impairment, which results in marked and severe functional limitations, and which can be expected to result in death or which has lasted or can be expected to last for a continuous period of not less than 12 months, or is blind (within the meaning of section 1614(a)(2) of the Social Security Act), and . . . such blindness or disability occurred before the date on which the individual attained age 26, and . . . includes a copy of the individual's diagnosis relating to the individual's relevant impairment or impairments, signed by a physician meeting the criteria of section 1861(r)(1) of the Social Security Act.

26 U.S.C. § 529A(e)(2)(A). Although the individual may have a disability certification for the purpose of the ABLE account, the statute specifically states that "[n]o inference may be drawn from a disability certification for purposes of establishing eligibility for benefits under title II, XVI, or XIX of the Social Security Act." *Id.* § 529A(e)(2)(B).

4. A qualified ABLE plan is

> a program established and maintained by a State, or agency or instrumentality . . . under which a person may make contributions for a taxable year, for the benefit of an individual who is an eligible individual for such taxable year, to an ABLE account which is established for the purpose of meeting the qualified disability expenses of the designated beneficiary of the account, . . . which limits a designated beneficiary to 1 ABLE account for purposes of this section.

It also has to meet any other requirements specified in 26 U.S.C. § 529A. *Id.* § 529A(b)(1).

5. *Id.* § 529A(a).

6. *Id.* § 529A(b)(2). Contributions are after-tax dollars and grow tax free. Contributions must be in cash and may be made "in the form of cash or a check, money order, credit card, electronic transfer, Gift of Independence card, or a similar method." Program Operations Manual System (POMS) SI 01130.740.B.2.

7. 26 U.S.C. § 529A(b). While the original law passed in 2014 did stipulate that an individual had to open an account in his or her state of residency, this provision was eliminated by Congress in 2015. Regardless of where an individual might live, and whether or not that individual's state has decided to establish an ABLE program, a qualified person is free to enroll in any state's program provided that the program is accepting out-of-state residents.

8. *Id.* § 529A(b)(2)(B)(i). In 2020, the annual gift tax exclusion was $15,000. *Id.* § 2503(b)(2). The contribution limits and other provisions of § 529A were modified by the 2017 act. Specifically, the 2017 act amended § 529A(b)(2)(B) to allow a designated beneficiary described in § 529A(b)(7) to contribute, prior to January 1, 2026, an additional amount in excess of the limit in § 529A(b)(2)(B)(i) (the annual gift tax exclusion amount in § 2503(b)). This additional amount is set forth in § 529A(b)(2)(B)(ii) and is equal to

favorable tax treatment is a plus,[9] the main feature of an ABLE account that makes it useful for individuals with special needs is its favorable treatment by the Social Security Administration (SSA) for Supplemental Security Income (SSI) eligibility. ABLE accounts up to $100,000 are treated by the SSA as an exempt resource for SSI eligibility.[10] The SSA treats contributions to—and distributions from—ABLE accounts similarly to those of SNTs and are countable for SSI eligibility.[11] A distribution from an ABLE account for something other than a qualified disability expense will have tax implications for the beneficiary.[12] However, for SSI eligibility, distributions from an ABLE account are excluded from income to the designated beneficiary regardless of whether the distributions are for a qualified disability expense or for a nonqualified expense.[13]

A "qualified disability expense" is defined as

> any expenses related to the eligible individual's blindness or disability which are made for the benefit of an eligible individual who is the designated beneficiary, including the following expenses: education, housing, transportation, employment training and support, assistive technology and personal support services, health, prevention and wellness, financial management and administrative services, legal fees, expenses for oversight and monitoring, funeral and burial expenses, and other expenses, which are approved by the Secretary under regulations and consistent with the purposes of this section.[14]

Similar to a first-party SNT, the ABLE account has a payback requirement when the beneficiary dies.[15] The payback requirement for ABLE accounts is

---

the lesser of (1) the designated beneficiary's compensation as defined by § 219(f)(1) for the taxable year, or (2) an amount equal to the poverty line for a one-person household for the calendar year preceding the calendar year in which the taxable year begins.

9. 26 U.S.C. § 529A(c)(1)(B) exempts, within limits, any ABLE account distributions from the recipient's gross income as long as the distribution is for a qualified disability expense.

10. POMS SI 01130.740.C.3. To the extent an ABLE account contains more than $100,000, the excess amount will be counted as a resource for SSI. If the excess causes the beneficiary to exceed the SSI resource limit, the SSA will suspend SSI benefits without time limit. The beneficiary will continue to receive Medicaid benefits during the SSI suspension, however. *Id.* SI 01130.740.D.1.c. Once the ABLE account is below $100,000, the beneficiary's SSI eligibility will be reinstated. *Id.*

11. *Id.* SI 01130.740.C.3, SI 01130.740.C.4.

12. *See* 26 U.S.C. § 529A.

13. *Id.* § 529A(c); *see also* POMS SI 01130.740.B.8.

14. 26 U.S.C. § 529A(e)(5).

15. *Id.* § 529A(f) ("Subject to any outstanding payments due for qualified disability expenses, upon the death of the designated beneficiary, all amounts remaining in the qualified ABLE account not in excess of the amount equal to the total medical assistance paid for the designated beneficiary after the establishment of the account, net of any premiums paid from the account or paid by or on behalf of the beneficiary to a Medicaid Buy-In program under any State Medicaid plan established under title XIX of the Social Security Act, shall be distributed to such State upon filing of a claim for payment by such State. For purposes of this paragraph, the State shall be a creditor of an ABLE account and not a beneficiary.").

present whether the account is funded entirely with either first-party or third-party funds,[16] so it is important to evaluate the funding source and likelihood of a fund balance upon the death of the beneficiary to determine if the SNT or the ABLE account is a better fit for each particular beneficiary.

An ABLE account may be a good planning option, either alone or in conjunction with an SNT. Consider the following:[17]

ABLE Act Account as Alternative to SNT

Action	ABLE	SNT
Eligibility	Similar to SNT	Similar to ABLE
Limit on contributions	Limit on maximum amount annually (*see* 26 U.S.C. § 529A(b)(2), (7))	None
Number beneficiary can have	Just one ABLE account per beneficiary	Unlimited number of SNTs whether first- and/or third-party
Uses	May be bit broader than SNT	Depends on SNT terms
Medicaid payback	Yes	First-party: yes for (d)(4)(A); (d)(4)(C), yes, if joinder agreement provides; third-party: no
Can funds be added after creation?	ABLE yes (annual contribution up to ceiling)	First-party: yes unless for 65 and older; (d)(4)(C) states limitations may exist for 65 and older; third-party: yes

Some ABLE plans are national[18] while others, like Florida,[19] are limited to residents of a specific state. Some salient definitions regarding ABLE accounts include:

16. *See id. See also* ABLE Nat'l Res. Ctr., Five Things You Need to Know about ABLE Accounts, https://www.ablenrc.org/wp-content/uploads/2019/07/ANRC-5-Things-to-Know-about-ABLE-2018.pdf.

17. Based on chart from ABLE Nat'l Res. Ctr. & Special Needs All., ABLE Account, Special Needs, and Pooled Trust Comparison Chart (2022), https://www.ablenrc.org/wp-content/uploads/2022/11/2022_SNT_ABLE_comparison.pdf.

18. See, for example, Ohio's ABLE plan, known as STABLE, which is available at ABLE Nat'l Res. Ctr., *Ohio*, https://www.ablenrc.org/state-review/ohio/ (last visited Dec. 11, 2022); Stable Acct., *Do I Have to Be a Resident of Ohio to Open a STABLE Account?*, https://stableaccount.com/faqs/do-i-have-to-be-a-resident-of-ohio-to-open-a-stable-account (last visited Dec. 19, 2022).

19. *See, e.g.*, ABLE National Resource Center, *Florida*, https://www.ablenrc.org/state-review/florida/ (last visited Dec. 11, 2022); ABLE United Program Description and Participation Agreement (2019), https://www.ablenrc.org/wp-content/uploads/2019/08/ABLE-United-Disclosure-Statement.pdf.

1. **Designated beneficiary**. This is the owner of the ABLE account and was either an eligible person when the ABLE account was created or replaced the former designated beneficiary as the designated beneficiary.[20]
2. **Eligible person**. A person is eligible if, during the taxable year, the person was entitled to Social Security Disability Insurance (SSDI) benefits and the disability started prior to the person turning 26, or a disability certification was filed with the Internal Revenue Service during that year.[21] As the SSA Program Operations Manual System (POMS) provides, the person must be eligible for SSI based on a disability that started before age 26 or eligible for Disability Insurance Benefits, Childhood Disability Benefits, or Disabled Widow(er)'s Benefits with the disability starting before 26.[22]
3. **Qualified disability expense**. This is any expense that is connected to the eligible person's disability and is incurred to benefit that person who is the ABLE account designated beneficiary. These expenses can include expenses for housing, education, assistive technology, health care, transportation, financial management, and more.[23] The POMS further explains housing expenses, but notes that there is a difference: "Housing expenses for purposes of an ABLE account are similar to household costs for in-kind support and maintenance purposes. However, for ABLE purposes, food is considered a qualified disability expense (basic living expense), but not a housing expense."[24]

The best option may be to use an ABLE account in conjunction with an SNT. A trustee may make contributions to an ABLE account for a trust beneficiary without incurring a reduction in SSI for in-kind support and maintenance (ISM).[25]

III. Qualified Disability Trusts

As a general rule, trusts are required to pay income tax on income the trust receives annually. The trust tax rates are compressed compared to the personal tax rates. A non-grantor trust reaches the maximum (37 percent) tax bracket

20. POMS SI 01130.740.A.3.
21. 26 U.S.C. § 529A(e)(2).
22. POMS SI 01130.740.B.3.
23. 26 U.S.C. § 529A(e)(5).
24. POMS SI 01130.740.B.9.
25. POMS SI 01130.740.B.2 states that contributions to an ABLE account "may be made by any person." And a "person" is defined by the IRC to include "an individual, trust, estate, partnership, association, company or corporation."

at just $13,450 of taxable income annually.[26] Compare that to the tax rate for a single taxpayer (including any income attributed to the taxpayer for earnings in a grantor trust): the highest (37 percent) marginal tax rate will not apply to that single taxpayer until 2022 earnings of $539,900.[27] A married couple filing a joint tax return will not reach the highest tax bracket until they have combined earnings of $647,850.[28]

To make the income tax treatment of trusts even worse, income taxed at the trust level will not benefit from the individual beneficiary's standard deduction.[29] Instead of that deduction (of $12,950 for a single taxpayer, and $29,500 for a married couple filing jointly), the non-grantor trust is eligible for an exemption of just $100 (for a "simple" trust) or $300 (for a "complex" trust).[30]

The IRC allows for certain types of disability trusts to qualify for a special personal exemption. Trusts that meet the requirements of IRC § 642(b)(2)(C) are referred to as qualified disability trusts (QDTs). A QDT receives an exemption equal to the personal/dependent exemption. Thus, if a trust has QDT status, no income tax will be due on the first $4,400 in 2022 of income the trust generates.[31] The IRC definition of a "qualified disability trust" is somewhat confusing because it references the transfer penalty rules, and specifically self-settled SNTs, rather than giving an outright definition.[32] Yet self-settled trusts

26. Rev. Proc. 2021-45, https://www.irs.gov/pub/irs-drop/rp-21-45.pdf. *See* § 3.01 tbl.5.

27. *Id.* § 3.01 tbl.3.

28. *Id.* § 3.01 tbl.1.

29. *Id.* § 3.15.

30. I.R.C. § 642(b)(2).

31. *See* Internal Revenue Service (IRS), 2022 Form 1041-ES. The exemption amount is based on the "personal exemption" that applied to individuals—in addition to a (lower) standard deduction—prior to the Tax Cut and Jobs Act of 2017. The personal exemption continues to apply to QDTs and so is calculated each year even though the code section was eliminated for tax years 2018 to 2025.

32. IRC § 642(b)(2) states:

(C) Disability trusts

(i) In general. A qualified disability trust shall be allowed a deduction equal to the exemption amount under section 151(d), determined—

(I) by treating such trust as an individual described in section 68(b)(1)(C), and

(II) by applying section 67(e) (without the reference to section 642(b)) for purposes of determining the adjusted gross income of the trust.

(ii) Qualified disability trust. For purposes of clause (i), the term "qualified disability trust" means any trust if—

(I) such trust is a disability trust described in subsection (c)(2)(B)(iv) of section 1917 of the Social Security Act (42 U.S.C. 1396p), and

(II) all of the beneficiaries of the trust as of the close of the taxable year are determined by the Commissioner of Social Security to have been disabled (within the meaning of section 1614(a)(3) of the Social Security Act, 42 U.S.C. 1382c(a)(3)) for some portion of such year.

A trust shall not fail to meet the requirements of subclause (II) merely because the corpus of the trust may revert to a person who is not so disabled after the trust ceases to have any beneficiary who is so disabled." I.R.C. § 642(b)(2)(C).

will be grantor trusts, and not required (or even permitted) to file as separate taxable entities, so the "qualified disability trust" provision will only be relevant to third-party SNTs.

If an SNT is treated as a "grantor" trust, the trust income tax rules do not apply.[33] A grantor trust passes all income of the trust through to the grantor, who will then pay taxes at the grantor's own personal tax rate (often with a standard deduction not available to a trust), rather than the compressed tax rates imposed on trusts.[34] Historically, if a trust could not avail itself of grantor trust status, however, it was subject to the compressed tax rates and minimal exemption amounts.

A. Elements

The statutory definition of a "qualified disability trust" is a trust that is "a disability trust described in subsection (c)(2)(B)(iv) of section 1917 of the Social Security Act (42 U.S.C. § 1396p),"[35] and all of whose beneficiaries are "determined by the Commissioner of Social Security to have been disabled (within the meaning of § 1614(a)(3) of the Social Security Act, 42 U.S.C. 1382c(a)(3)) for some portion of such year."[36] The code continues that "a trust shall not fail to meet the requirements of subclause (II)—that all of the beneficiaries must be disabled—merely because the corpus of the trust may revert to a person who is not so disabled after the trust ceases to have any beneficiary who is so disabled."[37]

To qualify as a QDT, all of the beneficiaries must receive benefits under SSI or SSDI.[38] This is not true of all trusts qualified as an SNT under § 1396p(c)(2)(B)(iv), which can be established without a finding of disability so long as the person could meet the disability standard as prescribed by the SSA.[39] Thus, a trust for a federal retiree with a disability who is not qualified for SSA benefits could not qualify as a QDT, but the trust might meet the definition of an SNT as prescribed by 42 U.S.C. § 1396p.

---

33. The IRS uses the term "grantor trust" "to describe any trust over which the grantor or other owner retains the power to control or direct the trust's income or assets." IRS, *Abusive Trust Tax Evasion Schemes—Questions and Answers*, https://www.irs.gov/businesses/small-businesses-self-employed/abusive-trust-tax-evasion-schemes-questions-and-answers (last updated Oct. 27, 2022).

34. I.R.C. § 671.

35. *Id.* § 642(b)(2)(c)(ii)(I).

36. *Id.* § 642(b)(2)(c)(ii)(II).

37. *Id.*

38. *Id.* § 642(b)(2)(c)(i).

39. The SSA makes disability determinations only when a person seeks benefits because he or she is disabled and meets the other program requirements for SSI or SSDI. 20 C.F.R. § 404.1520 (2012).

A grantor trust cannot be a QDT.[40] The trust must be a taxpaying entity; because a grantor trust does not file a separate return, it will not qualify.[41] Self-settled SNTs are always grantor trusts because the trustee has discretion to use all trust income and principal for the benefit of the beneficiary—even if that discretion is unexercised.[42]

Grantor trust status can sometimes also apply to third-party SNTs. If the beneficiary is a person with a disability and not the original funding source, the grantor trust rules may still cause treatment of the trust as a grantor trust to the original trust creator or donor—even if the SNT is irrevocable and the grantor has retained no remainder interest.[43] In such a case, QDT treatment will not be available to the trust because it is not the taxable entity.

The trust must be established for the benefit of individuals with disabilities who are under age 65 at the time of the trust creation. Under § 1396p(c)(2)(B)(iv), a trust must be established for the benefit of only one trust beneficiary. Thus, a grandparent with more than one grandchild with a disability could not establish a single SNT for the benefit of the group of grandchildren with disabilities and still receive the benefits of § 1396p(c)(2)(B)(iv). The IRC provision, however, requires that "all of the beneficiaries" be determined to be disabled.[44] Since the statute expressly authorizes multiple beneficiaries, the sole benefit requirement cannot apply to QDTs, which should still receive favorable tax treatment even though they may not meet the more restrictive Social Security requirements.

B. Taxation of Distributions

In addition to the possibility of qualifying for QDT status, there is another important tax-related benefit to understand in analyzing, drafting, and administering SNTs. The actual distributions from a non-grantor trust are conclusively presumed to carry out "distributable net income" (DNI) of the

40. Ron M. Landsman & Robert Fleming, Special Needs All., What Is a "Qualified Disability Trust" for Federal Income Tax Purposes?, https://www.specialneedsalliance.org/wp-content/uploads/2016/04/Qualified-Disability-Trust.pdf.

41. *Id.*

42. IRC § 673 gives grantor trust status to any portion of a trust in which there is a reversionary interest of as much as 5 percent of the value of the trust. Because the value of the reversionary share is calculated by "assuming the maximum exercise of discretion in favor of the grantor," self-settled SNTs are always grantor trusts; the only way to avoid such treatment (which ordinarily one would not want to avoid) would be to provide that the trustee have no discretion to use more than 5 percent of the value of the trust for the benefit of the grantor—over the entire life of the trust. I.R.C. § 673(c).

43. IRC §§ 671–678 outline the types of control retained by a grantor that would cause the trust to be treated as a grantor trust as to the original settlor/donor.

44. I.R.C. § 642(2)(c)(ii)(II).

trust.[45] This has an important practical effect: trust income is not taxed at the compressed marginal rates to the extent that it is distributed to, or distributed for the benefit of, the beneficiary. Such distributions are taxed to the beneficiary, who can then fully utilize not only the more gradual marginal tax rate increases, but also the standard deduction (or, if more favorable, the itemized deductions available to the individual). And, to make the benefit even sweeter, the QDT still retains the personal exemption, effectively further reducing the total tax liability.

C. Analysis

Using the QDT tax provisions will generally be a good idea for third-party non-grantor SNTs. There may be, however, good uses for the QDT tax provisions even when an SNT is not the appropriate tool.

In a typical SNT, one disabled individual is named as the beneficiary for the duration of life. Consider a situation where grandparents have a two-year-old grandchild receiving SSI because the grandchild has a total disability, but the disability can be cured with a major surgery. The surgery cannot be performed until the child reaches age ten when her body is more able to recover from such a major surgery. The grandparents have three other grandchildren for whom they would like to provide. A trust that provides for the grandchild with the disability until she is age 18, and then provides for all grandchildren, could receive QDT status so long as the first beneficiary receives SSI. Unlike the "sole benefit" requirement in the public benefits provision, which requires that the interest of the beneficiary with a disability terminate only at death, the QDT provision permits reversion after the trust ceases to have any beneficiary with a disability.

Next consider a family with four adult children; three of the children receive SSDI benefits. The three children receiving SSDI benefits do not need to adhere to the SNT rules because they are not receiving means-tested benefits. The child who is not receiving SSDI benefits has agreed to serve as trustee for a trust established for her siblings, but would prefer to manage only one trust for the whole—not three separate trusts. The parents establish a single trust for the benefit of their three children that meets the QDT tax provisions because the IRC provision permits multiple beneficiaries so long as each has a disability determination by the SSA.

---

45. *Id.* § 661.

IV. Sole Benefit Trusts

A sole benefit trust (SBT) is a trust that, when properly drafted, does not create a transfer penalty for the settlor under the Medicaid Long Term Care rules.[46] It can be the perfect planning tool for a Medicaid spend down when trying to qualify an applicant for Medicaid Long Term Care, in certain circumstances. If correctly drafted, transfers of the applicant's assets to an SBT could allow Medicaid eligibility (without a transfer penalty) while also maintaining eligibility for means-tested benefits for the trust beneficiary.

In most states, an individual must have less than $2,000 in countable assets to be eligible for Medicaid.[47] Medicaid imposes a five-year "look back" period wherein the applicant is penalized for transfers made when the applicant received less than fair market value in return. Some transfers are exempt from this penalty: transfers to the applicant's spouse, transfers to a child who is under age 21, and transfers to a child who is blind or has a disability are all exempt.[48] An often lesser used transfer exemption is a transfer to a trust for the sole benefit of any individual who is under age 65 and who does or would meet the SSA's criteria for total and permanent disability.

This may sound like a hidden loophole that allows two people to qualify for benefits with just one trust. But, there are some pitfalls to avoid for beneficiaries who receive certain types of government benefits. An SBT for this purpose combines the aspects of both first- and third-party SNTs. It is established with the funds of someone other than the beneficiary (third-party). The beneficiary must be under the age of 65 and the trust must be for the "sole benefit" of the beneficiary (first-party). It is important to note that the term "sole benefit trust" is merely descriptive: many trusts that contain the provisions that allow them to qualify as SBTs are considered standard SNTs—however, not all SNTs are SBTs. The statute[49] exempts from transfer penalties any transfer "to a trust (including a trust described in subsection (d)(4) of this section) established solely for the benefit of" a disabled person who is either under age 65 or the transferor's child of any age.[50] While the statute clearly articulates

46. *See, e.g.*, Howard S. Krooks, The Sole Benefit Trust—Whatever Happened to This Planning Tool?, Presentation at the New York State Bar Association Elder Law Section Summer Meeting (July 19, 2019), https://nysba.org/NYSBA/Meetings%20Department/Section%20Meetings/Elder%20Law/ELDSU19/ELDSU19%20Materials/Full.KrooksSole%20Benefit%20Trusts%20-Panel%205pdf.pdf.

47. *See, e.g.*, POMS SI 01110.003, Resources limits for SSI benefits, https://secure.ssa.gov/apps10/poms.nsf/lnx/0501110003 (last visited Dec. 11, 2022).

48. *See, e.g., id.* SI 01150.122, SI 01150.123.

49. 42 U.S.C. § 1396p(c)(2)(B).

50. *Id.* § 1396p(c)(2)(B)(iii).

the requirements of a (d)(4)(A) trust—including the payback requirement—it is silent as to what requirements apply to the other types of trusts that might qualify as "solely for the benefit of."[51]

A. Elements

The Centers for Medicare and Medicaid Services (CMS) State Medicaid Manual defines "sole benefit" as follows:

> A transfer is considered to be for the sole benefit . . . if the transfer is arranged in such a way that no individual or entity except the spouse, blind or disabled child, or disabled individual can benefit from the assets transferred in any way, whether at the time of the transfer or at any time in the future.[52]

An SBT could be established by a Medicaid applicant for the sole benefit of the community spouse without incurring a penalty. An SBT can also be created for a child—of any age—who is blind or who meets the disability criteria as established by the SSA. SSA defines "disability" as being "unable to engage in any substantial gainful activity by reason of any medically determinable physical or mental impairment which can be expected to result in death or which has lasted or can be expected to last for a continuous period of not less than twelve months."[53] The individual's impairment(s) must be severe enough to prevent him or her from performing not only the individual's previous job, but, considering his or her age, education, and experience, any other job that exists in the national economy.[54] Lastly, a Medicaid applicant can establish an SBT for any individual under age 65 who is disabled.[55]

To be considered "for the sole benefit of" an individual, the trust must require distributions to be actuarially sound based on the life expectancy of the beneficiary.[56] To be actuarially sound, the minimum distribution standard must provide for the complete distribution of the trust principal within the

51. *See generally id.* § 1396p.

52. CMS, The State Medicaid Manual ch. 3 § 3257, *available for download at* https://www.cms.gov/Regulations-and-Guidance/guidance/Manuals/Paper-Based-Manuals-Items/CMS021927.html.

53. 42 U.S.C. § 1382c(a)(3)(A); SSA, Social Security Handbook § 602, https://www.ssa.gov/OP_Home/handbook/handbook.06/handbook-0602.html (last revised Apr. 19, 2017).

54. *See* SSA, *supra* note 53, § 603.1, https://www.ssa.gov/OP_Home/handbook/handbook.06/handbook-0603.html#S0603-1 (describing these requirements as "substantially gainful activity").

55. *See* POMS SI 01120.203, https://secure.ssa.gov/poms.nsf/lnx/0501120203 (last visited Dec. 11, 2022) (outlining the provisions of an SBT).

56. Texas, where one of the co-authors resides, requires the trust to make distributions that are actuarially sound. Tex. Dep't of Health & Hum. Servs., Medicaid for the Elderly and People with Disabilities Handbook § I-3300 (2009), https://www.hhs.texas.gov/handbooks/medicaid-elderly-people-disabilities-handbook/i-3300-sole-benefit-requirements http://www.dads.state.tx.us/handbooks/mepd/. *See also* POMS SI 01120.201.

beneficiary's anticipated life expectancy.[57] The trustee can deplete the trust more rapidly, but the trust document must provide for minimum payments that are actuarially sound. One possible distribution standard would be to include minimum required distributions that are based on the beneficiary's life expectancy with trustee discretion to exceed the minimum standard. This would allow the trustee some flexibility in the event the beneficiary would be better served with larger distributions.

Some state Medicaid authorities have placed additional requirements on SBTs. Some states also require a payback provision to be included. Additionally, some states require the beneficiary's estate to be the sole remainder beneficiary.[58] These requirements are absent from the federal statute and the CMS manual. Ostensibly, these requirements ensure that the trust is solely for the benefit of the beneficiary, but appear to be more restrictive than the federal law.

In states without these extra hurdles, an SBT may be a solution for a penalty-free Medicaid spend down while also benefiting a disabled individual.

B. Analysis

An obvious use of the SBT is when a would-be beneficiary only receives SSDI. SSDI is a federal benefit program without income and asset restrictions. If a person with disabilities is receiving SSDI and will never qualify for SSI payments because he or she receives more than the maximum SSI payment, the person could easily be the beneficiary of an SBT because the mandatory actuarially sound distributions will not negatively impact SSDI benefits. In this circumstance, an applicant for Medicaid Long Term Care could transfer assets—penalty free—to an SBT for the SSDI recipient with no negative impact on the SSDI recipient's benefits. A true win-win.

The scenario is more complicated when the would-be beneficiary is an SSI recipient. Cash received from the trust will reduce SSI benefits dollar for dollar.[59] Therefore, it will be necessary to structure the minimum distributions so that they will not be income (under the SSI rules) to the beneficiary. An SBT for an SSI recipient could require the trustee to satisfy the minimum distribution requirements first with distributions that do not constitute income

---

57. *See* Jane Skelton, *Consider Sole Benefit Trusts for Medicaid Spend Down*, Special Needs All., https://www.specialneedsalliance.org/blog/consider-sole-benefit-trusts-for-medicaid-spend-down/ (last visited Dec. 11, 2022). *See, e.g.*, Krooks, *supra* note 46.

58. *See, e.g.*, N.Y. Comp. Codes R. & Regs. tit. 18, § 360-4.4(C)(2)(v) (1996); *see also, e.g.*, Krooks, *supra* note 46.

59. POMS SI 01120.200.E.1.a, https://secure.ssa.gov/poms.nsf/lnx/0501120200 (last visited Dec. 11, 2022).

(for SSI eligibility purposes) to the beneficiary. If the minimum required distribution cannot be satisfied under the first requirement, the trustee would next be required to make distributions that constitute ISM. The receipt of, or right to receive, food or shelter is referred to by SSA as "in-kind support and maintenance." The trust beneficiary's SSI benefits will be reduced if he or she receives ISM because SSI benefits are specifically intended to pay for a person's food and shelter. If an SSI recipient receives those goods or services from another source then, theoretically, less SSI income is needed.[60] When a trustee distributes ISM to the beneficiary, SSI benefits will be reduced, but not on a dollar-for-dollar basis as with cash.[61]

If a potential Medicaid applicant owns a brokerage account with a balance of $500,000, the applicant could fund an irrevocable trust for the sole benefit of her 52-year-old son who is disabled and receives SSDI benefits. According to the SSA's actuarial tables, a 52-year-old male has a life expectancy of 28.18 years of remaining life (age 80.18).[62] Thus, the SBT must provide for minimum annual payments of $17,743.08 ($500,000 ÷ 28.18 = $17,743.08). The trust is irrevocable and not a countable asset to the applicant. The trust requires minimum annual distributions of $17,743.08 and, thus, is actuarially sound. Because SSDI is not a means-tested program, monthly trust disbursements to (or for the benefit of) the applicant's son do not affect his benefits. Because the trust meets the requirements of an SBT, the applicant will not receive a transfer penalty for the trust funding.

Now consider a Medicaid applicant who owns $100,000 in real property and a bank account with $100,000. She creates an irrevocable trust for her 35-year-old granddaughter who receives SSI benefits. According to the actuarial tables, a 35-year-old female has 47.49 years of remaining life (age 82.49). The trust provides that the trustee make minimum annual distributions of $4,211.41 ($200,000 ÷ 47.49 = $4,211.41). The trust is irrevocable and does not result in a transfer penalty for the applicant because the minimum distributions are actuarially sound. Any cash received by the granddaughter will reduce her SSI payment dollar for dollar. So long as the applicant's

---

60. There are sometimes rather fine distinctions between allowable in-kind income and countable ISM. For example, you can pay for some travel arrangements but not others: a plane ticket (in-kind income)—but not a hotel room because that is shelter (ISM). You can pay for some entertainment expenses but not others: a movie pass (in-kind income) but not a restaurant meal because that is food (ISM). *See id.* SI 00815.001.C and D.

61. Instead, the formula the SSA uses to reduce the SSI benefits for a person who receives ISM depends on two further factors: the household and living arrangement of the SSI recipient. The formula will either be the presumed maximum value or the one-third reduction rule. *Id.* SI 00835.300.

62. SSA, *Actuarial Life Table 2017*, https://www.ssa.gov/oact/STATS/table4c6_2017_TR2020.html (last visited Dec. 11, 2022).

granddaughter continues to receive an SSI check of at least $1 per month, she remains eligible for Medicaid.

V. Settlement Protection/Preservation Trusts

A settlement protection trust is a support trust commonly used for plaintiffs who are not receiving means-tested public benefits. They are designed to hold settlement or lawsuit proceeds and are used to provide for the health, education, maintenance, and support of the beneficiary.

If a beneficiary is not eligible for means-tested public benefits, or when an SNT is not in the beneficiary's best interest, a settlement protection trust may be the best choice. Using a trust instead of having the plaintiff receive the money outright is sometimes advantageous. A major concern for many personal injury attorneys is that personal injury settlements often dump significant assets into the hands of an individual who is not experienced in managing such sums. Without proper support, education, and guidelines, even large settlements may only last a few years. Many plaintiffs face pressure from family or friends to use settlement proceeds unwisely. Establishing a settlement protection trust can prevent the assets from being spent under undue influence and can protect the beneficiary. Using a support trust also allows for the money management to be handled by an expert.

Just as SNTs can accept periodic payments from qualified structured settlements,[63] settlement protection trusts can be designed so that the payments from the structured settlement go into the trust. Doing so helps protect the structured settlement from being sold by the beneficiary at a deep discount at a later date.[64]

Under this type of trust, distributions can be flexible. A trustee can assist the beneficiary in establishing a budget and the trustee will provide the beneficiary with cash to cover the individual's monthly expenses. The trustee can arrange for a care manager and can provide the beneficiary with a team of experts to handle tax preparation; buying, building, or modifying a home; purchasing a vehicle; job coaching; and any other obstacle that a beneficiary may face. If there is sufficient money, the goal is usually to ensure that the money lasts for the lifetime of the beneficiary.

---

63. *See, e.g.*, Thomas Begley, Jr. & Andrew Hook, Representing the Elderly or Disabled Client § 16.07 (2021).

64. Plaintiffs sometimes rely on these factoring transactions to satisfy an emergency when the plaintiff has spent the cash portion of a settlement. These transactions are usually not advantageous to the beneficiary and they can usually be avoided with a trust.

If the beneficiary is a minor, a court may order the settlement proceeds into a trust that remains under the court's continued jurisdiction until the beneficiary reaches the age of majority.[65] In the case of an incapacitated person, the trust can last for the duration of the lifetime of the beneficiary. These trusts, if established by a court, are established under state law and each state may differ on requirements for court approval of distributions of income or principal.[66]

In many large settlements, a plaintiff may be receiving means-tested benefits, but those benefits can sometimes be replaced by private insurance. In these cases, it is often beneficial to consider giving up the public benefits in exchange for greater autonomy and flexibility for the beneficiary. Under such circumstances, a settlement protection trust may be the appropriate tool.

VI. Health Insurance under the Affordable Care Act

The Affordable Care Act (ACA) is the comprehensive health care reform signed into law in 2010.[67] The act includes a list of health-related provisions intended to extend health insurance coverage to Americans who have historically been without insurance. The act expands Medicaid eligibility,[68] creates health insurance exchanges,[69] and also prevents insurance companies from denying coverage based on preexisting conditions.[70] The expansion of coverage is provided through health insurance exchanges where private health insurance companies list their health plans with the exchange and buyers can compare policies to choose the most appropriate plan. There are both public and private insurance exchanges.[71] Private health insurance exchanges typically serve large employers providing job-based health insurance for employees. The public health insurance exchanges are maintained by the U.S. government to allow

65. Note that some states allow for the continuance of the trust to some date after age of majority. *See, e.g.*, Tex. Prop. Code Ann. § 142.005(b)(4) (2019).

66. In Texas, if the trust was established by the district court under section 142.005 of the property code, there is no express requirement of annual accountings.

67. The ACA is not one single health care bill that became law, but is actually composed of two laws: Patient Protection and Affordable Care Act (ACA) (Pub. L. No. 111-148, 124 Stat. 119) and Health Care and Education Reconciliation Act of 2010 (HCERA) (Pub. L. No. 111-152, 124 Stat. 1029).

68. *See, e.g.*, Nat'l Fed'n of Indep. Bus. v. Sebelius, 567 U.S. 519 (2012).

69. Louise Norris, *Health Insurance Marketplaces by State*, Healthinsurance.org (Aug. 24, 2022), https://www.healthinsurance.org/health-insurance-marketplaces/ (explaining how health insurance varies from state to state).

70. U.S. Dep't of Health & Hum. Servs., *Can I Get Coverage if I Have a Pre-existing Condition?*, https://www.hhs.gov/answers/health-insurance-reform/can-i-get-coverage-if-i-have-a-pre-existing-condition/index.html (last reviewed Aug. 4, 2017).

71. *See, e.g.*, HealthCare.gov, *Special Enrollment Periods through January 15, 2023*, https://www.healthcare.gov/screener/ (last visited Dec. 11, 2022).

individuals and families to purchase plans that comply with the requirements of the ACA. By using the public exchange, a person may be eligible to receive premium subsidies and cost-sharing subsidies that help make the plans more affordable for enrollees.

It is possible to shop for an ACA plan without accessing the exchange by using a broker or purchasing directly through an insurance company. However, the premium and cost-sharing subsidies are not available, if one does not purchase coverage through an exchange. Generally, the plans themselves will be similar on or off the exchange because insurance companies cannot sell noncompliant major medical health plans in the individual market even if sold outside of an exchange. All U.S. citizens and legally present residents who are not in prison are eligible to purchase coverage through the exchange unless the individual is eligible for premium-free Medicare Part A. The ACA prevents non-lawfully present immigrants from enrolling in coverage through the exchanges.[72] Beneficiaries without legal status are also not eligible for Medicaid under federal guidelines, making the two major cornerstones of coverage expansion under the ACA unavailable to undocumented immigrants. However, if a trust can afford it, a trustee for an undocumented person can purchase an unsubsidized insurance policy through a broker or directly from an insurance provider.

It is important to understand that if a beneficiary is lawfully present, the beneficiary can enroll in a plan through the exchange even if some members of the beneficiary's family are not lawfully present. Family members who are not applying for coverage are not asked for details about their immigration status.[73] And HealthCare.gov clarifies that immigration details provided to the exchange during the enrollment and verification process are not shared with any immigration authorities.[74]

A few states have implemented programs to cover undocumented immigrants, particularly children or pregnant women. Oregon, for example, has established the "Cover All Kids" program that provides coverage to children in households with income up to 305 percent of the poverty level, regardless

72. *See* 42 U.S.C. § 18032(f)(3).

73. *See* KFF, *Can Family Members in Families with Mixed Immigration Status, Where Some Family Members Are Citizens or Lawfully Present and Others Are Undocumented, Enroll in Medicaid or CHIP or Receive Help Buying Coverage through the Marketplaces?*, https://www.kff.org/faqs/faqs-health-insurance-marketplace-and-the-aca/can-family-members-in-families-with-mixed-immigration-status-where-some-family-members-are-citizens-or-lawfully-present-and-others-are-undocumented-enroll-in-medicaid-or-chip-or-receive-help-buying/ (last visited Dec. 11, 2022) (explaining "[n]on-applicants, such as a parent applying for a child, do not have to provide citizenship or immigration status").

74. *See* HealthCare.gov, *Immigration Status and the Marketplace*, https://www.healthcare.gov/immigrants/immigration-status/ (last visited Dec. 11, 2022).

of immigration status.[75] California has a similar program for children, and in fact now provides Medi-Cal (Medicaid) coverage to undocumented children, young people up to age 25, and those age 50 or older.[76] New York covers children and pregnant women in its Medicaid program regardless of income, and covers emergency care for other undocumented immigrants in certain circumstances.[77]

All health insurance policies offered must conform to one of five benefit tiers: catastrophic, bronze, silver, gold, or platinum.[78] Both on- and off-exchange, a policy's benefit tier describes the percentage of covered health care expenses the plan will pay, otherwise known as the actuarial value (AV) of the plan.[79] An ACA-compliant policy must cover the following essential health benefits:

a. Ambulatory care (outpatient care)
b. Emergency services
c. Hospitalization
d. Maternity and newborn care
e. Mental health care, including treatment for substance use disorders
f. Prescription drugs
g. Rehabilitation services and habilitative services, including devices
h. Laboratory services
i. Preventive care
j. Pediatric vision and dental care (coverage for adult dental and vision services is not required; the rules for pediatric dental coverage are a little different from the other essential health benefits)

While all plans are required to cover these essential health benefits, the percentage of coverage will depend on the tier of each particular policy.[80]

75. *See* Or. Health Auth., *OHP Covers Me!*, https://www.oregon.gov/oha/HSD/OHP/Pages/OHPcoversme.aspx (last visited Dec. 11, 2022).

76. *See* Press Release, Off. of Cal. Governor Gavin Newsom, Medi-Cal Expansion Provided 286,000 Undocumented Californians with Comprehensive Health Care (Oct. 19, 2022), https://www.gov.ca.gov/2022/10/19/medi-cal-expansion-provided-286000-undocumented-californians-with-comprehensive-health-care/.

77. *See* N.Y.C. Off. of Citywide Health Ins. Access, *Immigrants*, https://www1.nyc.gov/site/ochia/find-what-fits/immigrants.page (last visited Dec. 11, 2022).

78. *See* HealthCare.gov, *How Insurance Companies Set Health Premiums*, https://www.healthcare.gov/how-plans-set-your-premiums/ (last visited Dec. 11, 2022).

79. *See, e.g.*, HealthCare.gov, *The Health Plan Categories: Bronze, Silver, Gold & Platinum* [hereinafter *Health Plan Categories*], https://www.healthcare.gov/choose-a-plan/plans-categories/ (last visited Dec. 11, 2022); HealthCare.gov, *Actuarial Value*, https://www.healthcare.gov/glossary/actuarial-value/ (last visited Dec. 11, 2022).

80. See *Health Plan Categories*, *supra* note 79, for a table of percentages.

TABLE OF APPENDICES

These forms have been provided for illustrative purposes only. We do not practice in every state, and even forms directed at federal programs or agencies may need to be modified in your particular circumstances. Use these forms as starting points for your drafting and adaptation, rather than as final documents.

APPENDIX A

Self-Created Special Needs Trust

The [Beneficiary Full Name] Special Needs Trust

THIS TRUST AGREEMENT is made and entered into this [date] day of [month], [year], by [Beneficiary Full Name], (hereinafter referred to as Grantor) regarding [Beneficiary Full Name] and [Trustee Name] (hereinafter referred to as Trustee). The Beneficiary is [Beneficiary Full Name], a person with a disability, as defined in the Social Security Act, § 1614(a)(3), 42 U.S.C. § 1382c(a)(3) (hereinafter referred to as Beneficiary). The Trustee is [Trustee Name]. This Trust is created, established, and funded for the purpose of providing for the special and supplemental needs of [Beneficiary Full Name], the sole Beneficiary hereof. The Trust created, established, and funded hereunder shall be known as the [Beneficiary Full Name] SPECIAL NEEDS TRUST.

ARTICLE I

PURPOSE

It is the principal purpose and the intent of the Grantor and parties herein to provide a system for fund handling, fiscal management, investment and disbursement, respite care, personal attendant services, advocacy, social development services, habilitation care management, and moral guidance for [Beneficiary Full Name].

It is my secondary intention to provide for a continuing conservation and enhancement of the funds in this Trust to supplement all other financial funds and service benefits to which I might be eligible as a result of my disability from any local, county, state, or federal agency, or through any public or private for-profit or nonprofit corporations or agencies. It is further my intention to create, establish, and fund a purely discretionary supplemental non-support care fund and not to displace financial assistance that may otherwise be available to me.

I was born on [Beneficiary date of birth]. I currently need and will continue to need in the future extensive medical, nursing, rehabilitation, and hospital care. In creating, establishing, and funding this Trust in addition to the aforementioned purposes it is also my intention to create, establish, and fund a supplemental needs trust wherein all of my funds can be administered in an efficient and coordinated fashion.

ARTICLE II

TRUST FUNDING

2-1 Initial Trust Funding. This Trust shall be initially funded with the assets described in Exhibit [#] attached hereto. By execution hereof, I hereby assign, convey, transfer, and deliver the described assets to Trustee on even date herewith.

2-2 Additions to Trust. Other property, real or personal, may be transferred to Trustee by anyone with the consent of the Trustee. All property held by the Trustee may be referred to herein as the "Trust estate."

ARTICLE III

REVOCATION

This Trust shall be irrevocable. The Beneficiary shall have no power or right, whether alone or in conjunction with others, in whatever capacity, to alter, amend, revoke, or terminate this Trust, or any of the terms of this Trust agreement, in whole or in part, or to designate the persons who shall possess or enjoy the Trust estate, except as is set out in this instrument.

ARTICLE IV

DISPOSITION OF TRUST ESTATE

During my lifetime, the Trust estate shall be held, administered, and distributed as follows:

4-1 Introduction. I suffer from a disability that substantially impairs my ability to provide for my own care and custody and that constitutes a substantial disability. I reside in [City, State]. I need ongoing assistance in my activities of daily living. It is not expected that I will experience significant improvement in my impaired development in the future. The severity of my disability will cause me to require continuing support, assistance, and supervision for the remainder of my life. It is the intent of the parties hereto in creating, establishing, and funding this Trust that it continue in existence as a supplemental (and emergency) fund to public assistance for me throughout my life. Currently, there exist basic living needs such as dental care, and special equipment that public benefit programs for the disabled do not provide. It is vitally important that I continue to have these programs in order to maintain a level of human dignity and humane care. If this Trust were to be invaded by creditors, subjected to any liens or encumbrances, or cause assistance benefits to be unavailable or terminated, it is likely that the Trust corpus would be depleted prior to my death, especially because the cost of care for persons with disability (not including any emergency needs) is high. In this event, there would be no coverage for emergencies or supplementation for basic needs. The following trust provisions should be interpreted by the Trustee in light of these concerns and stated intent.

4-2 Special Non-Support Needs. The Trustee shall apply for my benefit for my lifetime, such amounts from the principal or income, up to the whole thereof, as the Trustee in the Trustee's sole and absolute discretion may from time to time deem necessary or advisable for the satisfaction of my supplemental non-support needs, if any. Any income not distributed shall be added annually to principal. Distributions shall be limited so that I am not disqualified from receiving public benefits to which I am otherwise entitled, and this Trust shall be administered so as to supplement not supplant such benefits. The Trustee may, however, make distributions that would reduce public benefits without terminating my eligibility for such benefits. The Trustee may make a distribution that would be considered income to a Beneficiary eligible for benefits under the Supplemental Security Income (SSI) program that would result in a reduction of benefits to the Beneficiary under the "Presumed Maximum Value Rule" or the "One-Third Reduction Rule" so long as such distribution will not cause the Beneficiary to be disqualified from the program.

4-3 Trustee Guidelines. It is my intention to create, establish, and fund a supplemental and emergency fund for my special non-support needs and not to displace assistance that may otherwise be available to me. As used in this instrument, "special non-support needs" refers to the requisites for maintaining my good health, safety, and welfare when in the discretion of the Trustee such requisites are not being provided by any public agency, office, or department of any city, county, or state government, or by the federal government or any other public or private agency, or are not otherwise being provided by other sources of income available to me. The Trustee may purchase, hold, and maintain assets in the name of the Trust or in such other manner as the Trustee deems appropriate (such as business interest, residence, or automobile) that the Trustee deems in its sole discretion to be reasonably needed for my special needs, notwithstanding any restrictions under this agreement or under the law that might otherwise make these types of assets improper investments of the Trust estate. The Trustee may not make a distribution that discharges a legal or contractual obligation of the Trustee.

4-4 Spendthrift. This is a discretionary non-support spendthrift trust. No interest in the principal or income of this Trust shall be anticipated, assigned, or encumbered, or shall be subject to any creditor's claim or to legal process, prior to my actual receipt of the funds. Furthermore, because this Trust is to be conserved and maintained for my supplemental non-support needs, no part of the Trust estate, neither principal nor undistributed income, shall be construed as part of my "estate" or be subject to the claims of voluntary or involuntary creditors for the provision of care and services, including residential care, by any public entity, office, department, or agency of any city, county, or state government, or by the federal government or any other public or private agency. Under no circumstances can I compel a distribution.

4-5 Public Benefits. Because I am a person with a disability, the Trustee shall, in the exercise of the Trustee's best judgement and fiduciary duty, seek support and maintenance for me from all available public resources, including Supplemental Security Income (SSI), federal Social Security Disability Insurance (SSDI), and any other appropriate state or local agency serving people with disabilities. Further, the Trustee should cooperate with me, my guardian, or legal representative to seek support and maintenance from all available resources. In making distributions to me, as herein defined, the Trustee shall take into consideration the applicable resource limitations of the public assistance programs for which I am eligible.

It is recognized that the Trustee is not licensed or skilled in the field of social sciences. The Trustee may seek counsel and assistance of any state and local agencies that are established to assist the disabled. The Trustee should use any available resources, including consultants, to assist in identifying programs that may be of social, financial, developmental, or other assistance to me. The trustee shall not in any event, however, be liable to me or the remainder beneficiary of this Trust or any other party for acts undertaken as Trustee in good faith. The Trustee shall not be liable for failure to identify all programs or resources that may be available to me.

4-6 Supplemental. No part of the corpus of the Trust created, established, and funded herein shall be used to supplant or replace public assistance benefits of any city, county, state, federal, or other governmental agency that has a legal responsibility to serve persons with disabilities that are the same or similar to the impairment(s) of the Beneficiary herein. No part of the Trust shall be used to supplant or replace benefits due from any insurance carrier under any insurance policy covering the Beneficiary. For purposes of determining my public assistance eligibility, no part of the principal or undistributed income of the Trust estate shall be considered available to me. In the event the Trustee is requested to release principal or income of the Trust to or on my behalf to pay for benefits, medication, or services that such public assistance is otherwise authorized to provide (were it not for the existence of this Trust), or in the event the Trustee is requested to petition the court or any other administrative agency for the release of Trust principal, interest, or income for this purpose, the Trustee is authorized and directed to deny such request. The Trustee is authorized, in the Trustee's sole discretion, to take whatever administrative or judicial steps may be necessary to continue my eligibility for public assistance programs, including obtaining instructions from a court of competent jurisdiction ruling the Trust corpus is not available to me for such eligibility purposes. Any expenses of the Trustee in this regard, including reasonable attorney's fees, shall be a proper charge to the Trust estate. In carrying out the provisions of this Trust, the Trustee shall be mindful of my probable future needs but not of the Trust remainder beneficiary(s).

4-7 Professional Care Manager. The trustee is encouraged to consider retaining the services of a Professional Care Manager to assist in providing my required care. The Professional Care Manager should be medically certified, medically trained, or approved to provide care. The purpose of the Professional Care Manager would be to coordinate other agencies or professionals or home-health aides or personal-care providers or homemakers or any other services that the Professional Care Manager and Trustee feel are in my best interests.

The primary purpose of this Trust is to provide funds to be spent on my behalf. The Trustee shall pay all costs in connection with the Professional Care Manager.

4-8 Residence. The Trustee may acquire, hold, and maintain any residence (whether held as real property, condominium, or cooperative apartment) for investment or for my use and benefit, as the Trustee, in the exercise of sole and absolute discretion, shall determine. If the Trustee holds a residence for me, then I may live in the residence rent free. The Trustee may file residential real estate property tax exemptions pursuant to [Statute #] of the [State Law/Code].

If the Trustee, in the exercise of sole and absolute discretion, shall determine that it would be in my best interests to maintain a residence for my use but that the residence owned by the Trustee should not be used for such purpose, the Trustee shall be authorized to sell said residence and to apply the net proceeds of sale to the purchase of such other residence or residences or to make such other arrangements as the Trustee, in the exercise of sole and absolute discretion, shall deem suitable for the purpose.

Any proceeds of sale not needed for reinvestment in a residence as provided above are to be added to the principal of the Trust and thereafter held, administered, and disposed of as a part thereof. The Trustee shall use the proceeds to pay all carrying charges of such residence, including but not limited to any taxes, assessments, and maintenance thereon, and all expenses of the repair and operation thereof, including the employment of household help other expenses incident to the maintenance of a household for my benefit, to expend such amounts as the Trustee, in the exercise of sole and absolute discretion, shall determine to be necessary to maintain my current life style, including, but not limited to, providing for my personal care and comfort in any manner whatsoever.

4-9 Burial. I desire but do not mandate that the Trustee purchase or make suitable arrangements for a burial plan or burial arrangements for me. These arrangements may include all burial services and a place of burial including a plot or mausoleum or crypt or services for cremation. The arrangements may be in any form selected by the Trustee. The Trustee is specifically authorized to purchase a prepaid burial plan and to distribute said plan to me so that the arrangements are owned by me and are not considered the property of the Trust. These arrangements may be as comprehensive as the Trustee shall determine and include transportation expenses for my body to the appropriate internment location, flowers, opening and closing of the grave, and any other services to provide for my last expenses.

4-10 Government Benefits Advisor. The Trustee shall have the power to retain legal and professional assistance in administering this Trust and fulfilling its purposes. In particular, in making a determination whether to distribute income or principal to or for a beneficiary under the provisions of this Trust, the Trustee may engage a professional advisor knowledgeable on the subject of the availability of funds or benefits from government or other sources on account of my mental or physical disability or handicap, to advise the Trustee concerning the availability of such funds or benefits.

The Trustee shall be entitled to rely on the advice and information obtained from such advisor and shall not be liable for any act or omission on the part of the Trustee attributable thereto. The reasonable costs and expenses of administering the Trust, including the retention of legal and professional assistance, shall be paid first out of the Trust's income and then out of principal.

4-11 Trust Termination. This Trust shall terminate upon my death. Any assets remaining in the Trust upon my death shall first be used to reimburse the "state" or any agency acting on its behalf, for the total amount of medical assistance paid on behalf of the Beneficiary under the state Medicaid plan and as required by applicable law. If I have received medical assistance from more than one state, each state that provided medical assistance shall be repaid. If the Trust has insufficient assets to repay all medical assistance benefits received, then each state shall be paid its proportionate share of the remaining Trust assets. It is the intention of the Grantor to create a vested remainder in the "state." Assets remaining in the Trust after such reimbursement shall be distributed as set forth in 4-12 below.

4-12 Termination upon Death. After reimbursement of the State as set forth in 4-11 above the Trustee shall distribute the remaining Trust estate to the duly appointed Executor of my Last Will and Testament. In the event that I have not validly executed a Last Will and Testament, or my Last Will and Testament is not admitted to probate, the remaining Trust estate shall be distributed to those persons who would be my heirs had I died intestate. The distribution of Trust property, for purposes of this section, shall be determined by the laws of descent and distribution for intestate estates by the [State Law/Code] in effect at the time of any distribution under this section.

4-13 Expenses. Upon my death, the Trustee may pay any death taxes that may by reason of my death be due regarding assets passing in accordance with these Trust provisions or otherwise, and expenses related to administration and distribution of the Trust estate if, in the Trustee's discretion, other satisfactory provisions have not been made for the payment of such expenses. The Trustee shall make no payments for obligations incurred for my health, support, and maintenance if the Trustee shall determine in its discretion that payment therefore is the obligation of any city, county, state, federal, or other governmental agency that has a legal responsibility to serve persons with disabilities that are the same or similar to my impairment(s).

4-14 Tax Provision. The Trustee hereunder shall pay any income tax liability of mine that results from income received by the Trust properly reported on my income tax return. The Trustee is authorized to pay the costs of my tax preparation for the annual income tax return. The funds used to pay any such income tax liability shall be paid directly to the appropriate tax authority and shall not be available to me. I shall not have any right to or interest in any such funds paid by the Trustee. Any such funds are not a resource of mine and should not be treated as a distribution of income for purposes of Medicaid qualification.

In the event of a tax refund any amount refunded shall be paid directly to the Trustee to the extent such refund is attributable to amounts previously paid by the Trustee. For purposes of determining whether an amount is attributable to such prior payments, any refund (including interest thereon) shall be attributed to amounts previously paid by the Trustee to the extent the Trustee made any tax payment for the relevant tax year that has not been previously refunded. For purposes of determining whether an amount previously paid has been previously refunded, any interest included as part of a refund shall not be used to offset a previous payment by the Trustee.

My agent, guardian, or I shall execute any letters, powers of attorney, or other documents required or requested by the taxing authority in order to allow payment of any refund to the Trustee.

4-15 Separate Fund. All public assistance benefits I receive and all my other earnings shall not be commingled with Trust assets but shall be separately held by the Trustee. Nothing in this provision shall be construed to require the addition to the Trust estate of either public assistance benefits or earnings received by, or on behalf of, any beneficiary herein.

4-16 No Perpetual Trusts. Unless terminated at an earlier date under the foregoing provisions, any trust created under this agreement shall cease on the date that is 21 years after the decease of the last to survive of the beneficiaries alive or in being at the time of the creation of the Trust and thereupon the Trustee shall distribute and deliver all of the balance of any share of the Trust estate or any portion thereof then held for the benefit of a living beneficiary of said Trust to such beneficiary or to my legal representative.

ARTICLE V

TRUSTEE PROVISIONS

The provisions of this Article govern the fiduciary relationship of the Trustee. When used in this instrument, where the context permits, the term "Trustee" means the trustee or co-trustees from time to time serving and the "estate" of the Trust means the particular trust estate being administered by the Trustee.

5-1 Trustee Compensation. An individual or entity serving as Trustee shall be reimbursed from the estate for the reasonable costs and expenses incurred in connection with the administration of the estate. The Trustee shall be entitled to receive fair and reasonable compensation for services as Trustee to be paid from the Trust's income, corpus, or both. In determining the fair and reasonable compensation of the Trustee the following factors shall be considered: (1) the duties, responsibilities, risks, and potential liabilities undertaken; (2) the nature of the estate; (3) the time and effort involved; and (4) the customary and prevailing charges for services of a similar character at the time and at the place such services are performed.

5-2 Trustee Liability. No Trustee shall have any duty (1) to investigate the prior acts or failures to act of a Predecessor Fiduciary (including a predecessor

Trustee under this instrument or a personal representative or trustee of any estate or trust from which distributions may be made to the Trustee); (2) to request a formal accounting by a Predecessor Fiduciary; or (3) to investigate any accountings provided by a Predecessor Fiduciary. No Trustee shall be personally liable for any act or failure to act of a Predecessor Fiduciary, or for the failure to contest any accounting provided by a Predecessor Fiduciary. However, the preceding shall not apply to any Trustee to the extent that the Trustee (1) has received a request from a beneficiary having a material interest in its estate to secure such an accounting or to conduct such an investigation, or (2) has actual knowledge of facts that would lead a reasonable person to believe that, as a consequence of any act or omission of a Predecessor Fiduciary, a material loss has occurred or will occur.

An individual or entity serving as Trustee shall be entitled to reimbursement from the estate for any liability or expense, whether in contract, tort, or otherwise, reasonably incurred by the Trustee in the administration of the estate.

5-3 Ancillary or Corporate Trustee. The Trustee, to the extent permitted by applicable law, may appoint (and remove) any Qualified Corporation (meaning any corporation having trust powers that is qualified and willing to serve under this instrument and that has, as of the relevant time, either (1) a minimum capital and surplus of at least five million dollars ($5,000,000 U.S.), or (2) at least 50 million dollars ($50,000,000 U.S.) in trust assets under administration, hereinafter referred to as an Ancillary or Corporate Trustee) to act as Ancillary Trustee on such terms as the Trustee may deem appropriate. If the corpus of this Trust were to ever exceed a value of more than four hundred thousand dollars ($400,000 U.S.) and if the then-acting Trustee is a noncorporate fiduciary, then the Trustee shall appoint an Ancillary Trustee to manage and invest the assets of the Trust. The acting Trustee shall retain any and all powers granted in this Trust except for any powers delegated to the Ancillary Trustee concerning the management and investment of the Trust assets. It is the Grantor's intention by this paragraph to allow the Trustee to assign any and all fiduciary responsibility and liability for the management and investment of the Trust assets to the Ancillary Trustee. The Trustee is authorized to execute any documents or contractual arrangements necessary to accomplish this task. The Trustee shall always be responsible for all other administrative decisions including decisions concerning disbursements from the Trust. This paragraph is intended to relieve the noncorporate Trustee of the burden and liability for managing and investing the assets of the Trust. If the then-sole-acting Trustee is a Corporate Trustee, then the Corporate Trustee shall exercise all of the powers of the Trustee.

5-4 Reorganization or Insolvency of Corporate Trustee. If a corporation nominated to serve or serving as the Trustee shall ever change its name, or shall merge or consolidate with or into any other bank or trust company, such corporation shall be deemed to be a continuing entity and shall continue to be eligible for appointment, or shall continue to act as the Trustee.

ARTICLE VI

ADMINISTRATIVE PROVISIONS

6-1 Investment Authority. The Trustee shall invest the assets of the estate in proper and prudent investments with due regard to reasonable diversification, considering the entire portfolio of its estate (and the entire portfolio of any collective investment vehicle, as the case may be) rather than on an individual asset basis. To the extent consistent with the foregoing; (1) a corporate entity serving as Trustee may deposit funds with itself and may place funds under its administration in common trust funds; and (2) the Trustee may acquire securities, real estate, life insurance, oil, gas, and other mineral interests, and other investments.

6-2 Management Authority. The Trustee may exercise the managerial powers of an individual with respect to matters affecting the estate and the broadest managerial discretion that is consistent with the reasonable and prudent management and administration of the estate, including the following managerial authorities: (1) the Trustee may manage, sell, lease (for any term, even if beyond the anticipated term of the estate), partition, improve, repair, insure, and otherwise deal with all property of the estate; (2) the Trustee may form, reorganize, or dissolve corporations, give proxies to vote securities, enter into voting trusts, and generally exercise all rights of a stockholder; (3) the Trustee may take whatever action, if any, the Trustee considers best to collect the proceeds of life insurance policies and employee benefit plans as well as any other property that may be tendered to the Trustee; (4) the Trustee may pay all taxes and all reasonable expenses, including reasonable compensation to the agents and counsel (including investment counsel) of the Trustee; (5) the Trustee may employ and compensate advisors and agents and delegate to an agent any authorities (including discretionary authorities); (6) the Trustee may institute and defend suits and release, compromise, or abandon claims; (7) the Trustee may hold title to any property in the name of one or more nominees without disclosing the fiduciary relationship; (8) the Trustee may lend money to any entity with or without security, endorse, guarantee, provide security for, or otherwise become obligated with respect to the debts of any entity, provided that all such transactions (except those for the benefit of any beneficiaries of the particular estate involved) must be on commercially reasonable terms; (9) the Trustee may assume, renew, and extend any indebtedness previously created and borrow for any purpose (including the payment of taxes or expenses) from any source (including a Trustee individually) at the then usual and customary rate of interest, and mortgage or pledge any property of the estate to any such lender; (10) the Trustee may make partial distributions to any beneficiary, including any trust created by this instrument, whether or not the administration of the estate is complete; (11) the Trustee may retain, sell, or distribute in kind any personal residence and any furnishings of such residence; (12) the Trustee may store personal effects given to a minor or other incapacitated beneficiary for later distribution to such individual, or sell such property and add the proceeds of sale to a trust of which individual is a beneficiary; (13) the Trustee may divide, allocate, or distribute property of the estate in undivided interests, non pro rata, and either wholly or partly in kind; (14) for administrative and investment purposes only, the Trustee may hold separate estates under this or any other instrument in one or more common accounts in which such estates have undivided interests; (15) the Trustee may allocate receipts and disbursements between principal and income in a reasonable manner, and may establish a reasonable reserve for depreciation or depletion and fund such reserve by appropriate charges against income of the estate; (16) the Trustee may take all appropriate action to deal with any environmental hazard and comply with any environmental law, regulation, or order, and may institute, contest, or settle legal proceedings concerning environmental hazards; and (17) the Trustee may distribute income or principal to the Beneficiary's qualified ABLE account under section 529A of the Internal Revenue Code. All distributions of principal and income shall be made in cash directly to the Beneficiary's qualified ABLE account. A distribution for the Beneficiary's benefit to a qualified ABLE account shall not exceed such annual contribution limits (from all sources) as imposed by section 529A(b)(2)(8) and the aggregate excess limitations (from all sources) as imposed by section 529A(b)(6).

6-3 Records, Books of Account, and Reports. The Trustee shall maintain proper books of account, which shall at all reasonable times be open for inspection or audit by me, or any court-appointed guardian for me. The Trustee shall make a written financial report, at least annually, to me, or any court-appointed guardian for me. The Trustee's usual computer statements shall suffice for any accounting. The Trustee shall not be accountable to any person interested in this Trust for the manner in which, in good faith, it carries out its discretion to supplement my needs (including any decision it may make not to incur the expense of detailed analysis of alternative choices) and, even though its decision in this regard may result in decreased distributions to the contingent beneficiaries of this Trust, there shall in no event be any compensation readjustments or reimbursements by the Trustee by reason of the manner in which the Trustee thus carries out the Trustee's discretion.

6-4 Applicability of [State Law/Code]. To the extent consistent with the other provisions of this instrument, the Trustee shall have the powers, duties, and liabilities of trustees set forth in [State Law/Code], as amended and in effect from time to time. However, any legislation enacted subsequent to the date of this instrument that limits a Trustee's duties or liability to the beneficiaries of the estate shall be inapplicable to every trust created under this instrument, and the Trustee's acceptance of office under this instrument shall constitute an irrevocable agreement that no such subsequent legislation shall be applicable.

6-5 Additional Transfers of Property. Any additional transfer of property to this Trust shall be absolute; provided, however, that the duties of the Trustee shall not be increased by virtue of any such transfer without the consent of the Trustee.

6-6 Majority Controls. All actions taken by Trustees hereunder shall be taken only with the agreement of a majority of Trustees, which majority shall include the Corporate Trustee if one is then acting.

6-7 Resignation. Any Trustee may resign by giving thirty (30) days written notice to a beneficiary. If a beneficiary is legally incapacitated, the notice shall be delivered to that beneficiary's legal representative.

6-8 Removal of Trustee. Any interested person herein, including, but not limited to the Beneficiary's legal representative, the Beneficiary's parent, or contingent beneficiaries, may petition any court of competent jurisdiction for removal of any Trustee; the decision on whether to remove any Trustee shall be in the exclusive discretion and control of the court.

6-9 Appointment of Successors. In the event that [Trustee Name] shall resign, is removed, or otherwise fails or ceases to act as Trustee for any reason, [Successor Trustee Name] shall be named Successor Trustee. In the event that [Successor Trustee Name] shall resign, is removed, or otherwise fails or ceases to act as Trustee for any reason, any court of competent jurisdiction shall have the power to fill any vacancy in the Trusteeship.

ARTICLE VII

GENERAL PROVISIONS

7-1 State; State Plan. References to the "state" means the state of [______] and all other states, if any, that may ever pay medical assistance on my behalf under a state plan. References to a "state plan" mean any plan under Title 42 of the U.S. Code Annotated (The Public Health and Welfare), chapter 7 (Social Security), subchapter XIX (Grants to States for Medical Assistance Programs) and any other "plans" for purposes of 42 U.S.C. § 1396p(d)(4).

7-2 Execution. The Trustee hereby accepts the Trust herein created, established, and funded and covenants and agrees to and with the Grantor in consideration thereof that the Trustee will execute the same as herein provided.

7-3 Pronouns, Singular and Plural. Unless the context requires otherwise, words denoting the singular may be construed as denoting the plural, and words of the plural may be construed as denoting the singular, and words of one gender may be construed as denoting such other gender or no gender as is appropriate.

7-4 Execution in Counterparts. This document may be executed in any number of counterpart signature pages, all of which together will constitute the entire, original document.

By: ______________________________

[Full Name], Grantor

State of [State Name]
County of [County Name]

SUBSCRIBED AND ACKNOWLEDGED before me by [Full Name], as Grantor, on this [date] day of [month], [year].

____

Notary Public, State of [State Name]

TRUSTEE'S ACCEPTANCE:

By: ___________________________________

[Trustee Name]

Title: Trustee

State of [State Name]

County of [County Name]

SUBSCRIBED AND ACKNOWLEDGED before me by [Trustee Name], as Trustee, on this [date] day of [month], [year].

____

Notary Public, State of [State Name]

Exhibit [#]

The foregoing Trust shall be funded with $____.

APPENDIX B

Third-Party Inter Vivos Trust

The [Beneficiary Full Name] Special Needs Trust

THIS TRUST AGREEMENT is made and entered into this [date]day of [month], [year], by [Parent #1 Name] and [Parent #2 Name], Parents of [Beneficiary Name] (hereinafter referred to as Grantors). [Beneficiary Name] is a person with a disability, as defined in the Social Security Act, § 1614(a)(3), 42 U.S.C. § 1382c (a)(3) (hereinafter referred to as Beneficiary). The Trustees are [Parent #1 Name] and [Parent #2 Name]. This Trust is created, established, and funded for the purpose of providing for the special and supplemental needs of [Beneficiary Name], the sole Beneficiary hereof. The Trust created, established, and funded hereunder shall be known as the [Beneficiary Name] SPECIAL NEEDS TRUST.

ARTICLE I

PURPOSE

It is the principal purpose and the intent of the Grantors and parties herein to provide a system for fund handling, fiscal management, investment and disbursement, respite care, personal attendant services, advocacy, social development services, habilitation care management, and moral guidance for [Beneficiary Name].

It is the secondary intention of the Grantors and parties hereto to provide for a continuing conservation and enhancement of the funds in this Trust to supplement all other financial funds and service benefits to which [Beneficiary Name] might be eligible as a result of [Beneficiary Name]'s disability from any local, county, state, or federal agency, or through any public or private for-profit or nonprofit corporations or agencies. It is further the intention of the Grantors to create, establish, and fund a purely discretionary supplemental non-support care fund and not to displace financial assistance that may otherwise be available to [Beneficiary Name].

[Beneficiary Name] was born on [date]. [Beneficiary Name] currently needs and will continue to need in the future medical, nursing, rehabilitation, and hospital care. [Beneficiary Name] is not currently the beneficiary of a trust or trusts. In creating, establishing, and funding this Trust, in addition to the aforementioned purposes, it is also the Grantors' intention to create, establish, and fund a supplemental needs trust wherein all of [Beneficiary Name]'s funds can be administered in an efficient and coordinated fashion.

ARTICLE II

TRUST FUNDING

2-1 Initial Trust Funding. This Trust shall be initially funded with the assets described in Exhibit [#] attached hereto. By execution hereof, the Grantors hereby assign, convey, transfer, and deliver the described assets to Trustees on even date herewith.

2-2 Additions to Trust. Other property, real or personal, may be transferred to the Trustees by anyone with the consent of a Trustee. All property held by the Trustees may be referred to herein as the "Trust estate."

ARTICLE III

REVOCATION

This Trust shall be irrevocable. The Beneficiary shall have no power or right, whether alone or in conjunction with others, in whatever capacity, to alter, amend, revoke, or terminate this Trust, or any of the terms of this Trust agreement, in whole or in part, or to designate the persons who shall possess or enjoy the Trust estate, except as is set out in this instrument.

ARTICLE IV

DISPOSITION OF TRUST ESTATE

During the lifetime of [Beneficiary Name], the Trust estate shall be held, administered, and distributed as follows:

4-1 Introduction. [Beneficiary Name] suffers from [disability], which impairs [Beneficiary Name]'s ability to provide for [his/her/their] own care and custody and which constitutes a substantial handicap. [Beneficiary Name] resides in [City, State] and needs ongoing assistance within [his/her/their] activities of daily living. It is not expected that [Beneficiary Name] will experience significant improvement in [his/her/their] impaired development in the future. The severity of [Beneficiary Name]'s disability will cause [him/her/them] to require continuing support, assistance, and supervision for the remainder of [his/her/their] life. It is the intent of the parties hereto in creating, establishing, and funding this Trust that it continue in existence as a supplement (and emergency) fund to public assistance for [Beneficiary Name] throughout [Beneficiary Name]'s life. Currently, there exist basic living needs such as dental care and special equipment that public benefit programs for people with disabilities do not provide. It is vitally important that [Beneficiary Name] continue to have these programs in order to maintain a level of human dignity and human care. If this Trust were to be invaded by creditors, subjected to any liens or encumbrances, or cause assistance benefits to be unavailable or terminated, it is likely that the Trust corpus would be depleted prior to [Beneficiary Name]'s death, especially because the cost of care for persons with disabilities (not including any emergency needs) is high. In this event, there would be no coverage for emergencies or supplementation for basic needs. The following trust provisions should be interpreted by the Trustees in light of these concerns and stated intent.

4-2 Special Non-Support Needs. The Trustees shall apply for the benefit of [Beneficiary Name], for [Beneficiary Name]'s lifetime, such amounts from the principal or income, up to the whole thereof, as the Trustees in their sole and absolute discretion may from time to time deem necessary or advisable for the satisfaction of the Beneficiary's supplemental non-support needs, if any. Any income not distributed shall be added annually to principal. Distributions shall be limited so that the Beneficiary is not disqualified from receiving public benefits to which [Beneficiary Name] is otherwise entitled, and this Trust shall be administered so as to supplement not supplant such benefits. The Trustees may, however, make distributions that would reduce public benefits without terminating the Beneficiary's eligibility for such benefits. The Trustees may make a distribution that would be considered income to a Beneficiary eligible for benefits under the Supplemental Security Income (SSI) program that would result in a reduction of benefits to the Beneficiary under the "Presumed Maximum Value Rule" or the "One-Third Reduction Rule" so long as such distribution will not cause the Beneficiary to be disqualified from the program.

4-3 Trustee Guidelines. It is the intention of the Grantors to create, establish, and fund a supplemental and emergency fund for the special non-support needs of the Beneficiary and not to displace assistance that may otherwise be available to [him/her/them]. As used in this instrument, "special non-support needs" refers to the requisites for maintaining the Beneficiary's good health, safety, and welfare when in the discretion of the Trustees such requisites are not being provided by any public agency, office, or department of any city, county, or state government, or by the federal government or any other public or private agency, or are not otherwise being provided by other sources of income available to [him/her/them]. The Trustees may purchase, hold, and maintain assets in the name of the Trust or in such other manner as the Trustees deem appropriate (such as business interest, residence, or automobile) that the Trustees deem in their sole discretion to be reasonably needed for the special needs of the Beneficiary, notwithstanding any restrictions under this agreement or under the law that might otherwise make these types of assets improper investments of the Trust estate. The Trustees may not make a distribution that discharges a legal or contractual obligation of the Trustees.

4-4 Spendthrift. This is a discretionary non-support spendthrift trust. No interest in the principal or income of this Trust shall be anticipated, assigned, or encumbered, or shall be subject to any creditor's claim or to legal process, prior to its actual receipt by the Beneficiary. Furthermore, because this Trust is to be conserved and maintained for the supplemental non-support needs of the Beneficiary who may be medically disabled or impaired throughout [his/her/their] lifetime, no part of the Trust estate, neither principal nor undistributed income, shall be construed as part of the Beneficiary's "estate" or be subject to the claims of voluntary or involuntary creditors for the provision of care and services, including residential care, by any public entity, office, department, or agency of any city, county, or state government, or by the federal government or any other public or private agency. Under no circumstances can the Beneficiary compel a distribution.

4-5 Public Benefits. Because [Beneficiary Name] has a disability and is unable to maintain and support [himself/herself/themselves] independently, the Trustees shall, in the exercise of the Trustees' best judgement and fiduciary duty, seek support and maintenance for the Beneficiary from all available public resources, including Supplemental Security Income (SSI), federal Social Security Disability Insurance (SSDI), and any other appropriate state or local agency serving people with disabilities. Further, the Trustees should cooperate with the Beneficiary's guardian or legal representative to seek support and maintenance for the Beneficiary from all available resources. In making distributions to the Beneficiary for [his/her/their] special needs, as herein defined, the Trustees shall take into consideration the applicable resource limitations of the public assistance programs for which the Beneficiary is eligible.

It is recognized that the Trustees are not licensed or skilled in the field of social sciences. The Trustees may seek counsel and assistance of any state and local agencies that are established to assist the disabled. The Trustees should use any available resources, including consultants, to assist in identifying programs that may be of social, financial, developmental, or other assistance to the Beneficiary. Trustees shall not in any event, however, be liable to the Beneficiary or the remainder beneficiary of this Trust or any other party for acts undertaken as Trustee in good faith. The Trustees shall not be liable for failure to identify all programs or resources that may be available to the Beneficiary because of [his/her/their] disabilities.

4-6 Supplemental. No part of the corpus of the Trust created, established, and funded herein shall be used to supplant or replace public assistance benefits of any city, county, state, federal, or other governmental agency that has a legal responsibility to serve persons with disabilities that are the same or similar to the impairment(s) of the Beneficiary herein. No part of the Trust shall be used to supplant or replace benefits due from any insurance carrier under any insurance policy covering the Beneficiary. For purposes of determining the Beneficiary's public assistance eligibility, no part of the principal or undistributed income of the Trust estate shall be considered available to said Beneficiary. In the event the Trustees are requested to release principal or income of the Trust to or on behalf of the Beneficiary to pay for benefits, medication, or services that such public assistance is otherwise authorized to provide (were it not for the existence of this Trust), or in the event the Trustees are requested to petition the court or any other administrative agency for the release of Trust principal, interest, or income for this purpose, the Trustees are authorized and directed to deny such request. The Trustees are authorized, in the Trustees' sole discretion, to take whatever administrative or judicial steps may be necessary to continue the public assistance program eligibility of the Beneficiary, including obtaining instructions from a court of competent jurisdiction ruling the Trust corpus is not available to the Beneficiary for such eligibility purposes. Any expenses of the Trustees in this regard, including reasonable attorney's fees, shall be a proper charge to the Trust estate. In carrying out the provisions of this Trust, the Trustees shall be mindful of the probable future needs of the Beneficiary but not of the Trust remainder beneficiary(s).

4-7 Professional Care Manager. The Trustees are encouraged to consider retaining the services of a Professional Care Manager to assist in providing [Beneficiary Name]'s required care. The Professional Care Manager should be medically trained or approved to provide care. The purpose of the Professional Care Manager is to coordinate other agencies or professionals or home-health aides or personal-care providers or homemakers or any other services that the Professional Care Manager and Trustees feel are in [Beneficiary Name]'s best interests.

The primary purpose of this Trust is to provide funds to be spent on [Beneficiary Name]'s behalf. It is the Grantors' intention to benefit [Beneficiary Name] to the fullest extent possible, rather than the remainder beneficiary(s). The Trustees shall pay all costs in connection with the Professional Care Manager.

4-8 Residence. The Trustees may acquire, hold, and maintain any residence (whether held as real property, condominium, or cooperative apartment) for investment or for [Beneficiary Name]'s use and benefit, as the Trustees, in the exercise of sole and absolute discretion, shall determine. If the Trustees hold a residence for the Beneficiary, then the Beneficiary may live in the residence rent free.

If the Trustees, in the exercise of sole and absolute discretion, shall determine that it would be in [Beneficiary Name]'s best interests to maintain a residence for [his/her/their] use but that the residence owned by the Trustees should not be used for such purpose, the Trustees shall be authorized to sell said residence and to apply the net proceeds of sale to the purchase of such other residence or residences or to make such other arrangements as the Trustees, in the exercise of sole and absolute discretion, shall deem suitable for the purpose.

Any proceeds of sale not needed for reinvestment in a residence as provided above are to be added to the principal of the Trust and thereafter held, administered, and disposed of as a part thereof. The Trustees shall use the proceeds to pay all carrying charges of such residence, including but not limited to any taxes, assessments, and maintenance thereon, and all expenses of the repair and operation thereof, including the employment of household help and other expenses incident to the maintenance of a household for [Beneficiary Name]'s benefit, to expend such amounts as the Trustees, in the exercise of sole and absolute discretion, shall determine to be necessary to maintain [his/her/their] current life style, including, but not limited to, providing for [Beneficiary Name]'s personal care and comfort in any manner whatsoever.

4-9 <u>Burial</u>. Grantors desire, but do not mandate, that the Trustees purchase or make suitable arrangements for a burial plan or burial arrangements for the Beneficiary. These arrangements may include all burial services and a place of burial including a plot or mausoleum or crypt or services for cremation of the Beneficiary. The arrangements may be in any form selected by the Trustees. The Trustees are specifically authorized to purchase a prepaid burial plan and to distribute said plan to the Beneficiary so that the arrangements are owned by the Beneficiary and are not considered the property of the Trust. These arrangements may be as comprehensive as the Trustees shall determine and include transportation expenses of the Beneficiary's body to the appropriate internment location, flowers, opening and closing of the grave, and any other services to provide for the last expenses of the Beneficiary.

4-10 <u>Government Benefits Advisor</u>. The Trustees shall have the power to retain legal and professional assistance in administering this Trust and fulfilling its purposes. In particular, in making a determination whether to distribute income or principal to or for a beneficiary under the provisions of this Trust, the Trustees may engage a professional advisor knowledgeable on the subject of the availability of funds or benefits from government or other sources on account of a beneficiary's mental or physical disability or handicap, to advise the Trustees concerning the availability of such funds or benefits.

The Trustees shall be entitled to rely on the advice and information obtained from such advisor and shall not be liable for any act or omission on the part of the Trustees attributable thereto. The reasonable costs and expenses of administering the Trust, including the retention of legal and professional assistance, shall be paid first out of the Trust's income and then out of principal.

4-11 Termination upon Death. This Trust shall terminate upon the death of the Beneficiary. Upon termination of this Trust, all of the remaining unappointed property shall be distributed to [Parent #1 Name] and [Parent #2 Name], in equal shares. If only one survives, the remaining trust shall be paid out to the survivor of the two. If neither [Parent #1 Name] nor [Parent #2 Name] survive, then the remaining trust estate shall be distributed to [Remainder Beneficiary]. If [Remainder Beneficiary] does not survive, the remaining trust estate shall be paid to [Beneficiary Name]'s heirs at law as determined by the laws of the state in which [he/she/they] resides at [his/her/their] death.

4-12 Expenses. Upon the death of [Beneficiary Name], the Trustees may pay any death taxes that may by reason of said Beneficiary's death be due regarding assets passing in accordance with these Trust provisions or otherwise, and expenses related to administration and distribution of the Trust estate if, in the Trustees' discretion, other satisfactory provisions have not been made for the payment of such expenses. The Trustees shall make no payments for obligations incurred for said Beneficiary's health, support, and maintenance if the Trustees shall determine in their discretion that payment therefore is the obligation of any city, county, state, federal, or other governmental agency that has a legal responsibility to serve persons with disabilities that are the same or similar to the impairment(s) of the Beneficiary herein.

4-13 Tax Provision. The Trustees hereunder shall pay any income tax liability of the Beneficiary that results from income received by the Trust properly reported on the income tax return of the Beneficiary. The funds used to pay any such income tax liability shall be paid directly to the appropriate tax authority and shall not be available to the Beneficiary. The Beneficiary shall not have any right to or interest in any such funds paid by the Trustees. Any such funds are not a resource of the Beneficiary and should not be treated as a distribution of income for purposes of Medicaid qualification.

In the event of a tax refund, any amount refunded shall be paid directly to the Trustees to the extent such refund is attributable to amounts previously paid by the Trustees. For purposes of determining whether an amount is attributable to such prior payments, any refund (including interest thereon) shall be attributed to amounts previously paid by the Trustees to the extent the Trustees made any tax payment for the relevant tax year that has not been previously refunded. For purposes of determining whether an amount previously paid has been previously refunded, any interest included as part of a refund shall not be used to offset a previous payment by the Trustees.

The Beneficiary or [his/her/their] guardian shall execute any letters, powers of attorney, or other documents required or requested by the taxing authority in order to allow payment of any refund to the Trustees.

4-14 Separate Fund. All public assistance benefits for the Beneficiary of this Trust and all earnings of the Beneficiary of this Trust shall not be commingled with other Trust assets but shall be separately held by the Trustees. Nothing in this provision shall be construed to require the addition to the Trust estate of either public assistance benefits or earnings received by, or on behalf of, any beneficiary herein.

4-15 No Perpetual Trusts. Unless terminated at an earlier date under the foregoing provisions, any trust created under this agreement shall cease on the date that is 21 years after the decease of the last to survive of the beneficiaries alive or in being at the time of the creation of the Trust and thereupon the Trustees shall distribute and deliver all of the balance of any share of the Trust estate or any portion thereof then held for the benefit of a living beneficiary of said Trust to such beneficiary or [his/her/their] legal representative.

ARTICLE V

TRUSTEE PROVISIONS

The provisions of this Article govern the fiduciary relationship of the Trustees. When used in this instrument, where the context permits, the term "Trustee" means the trustee or co-trustees from time to time serving and the "estate" of the Trust means the particular trust estate being administered by the Trustees.

5-1 Trustee Compensation. An individual or entity serving as Trustee shall be reimbursed from the estate for the reasonable costs and expenses incurred in connection with the administration of the estate and the Trustees shall be entitled to receive fair and reasonable compensation for services as Trustee to be paid from the Trust's income, corpus, or both. The Trustees shall also be reimbursed for all reasonable expenses incurred in connection with the administration of the Trust considering (1) the duties, responsibilities, risks, and potential liabilities undertaken; (2) the nature of the estate; (3) the time and effort involved; and (4) the customary and prevailing charges for services of a similar character at the time and at the place such services are performed.

5-2 Trustee Liability. No Trustee shall have any duty (1) to investigate the prior acts or failures to act of a Predecessor Fiduciary (including a predecessor Trustee under this instrument or a personal representative or trustee of any estate or trust from which distributions may be made to the Trustee); (2) to request a formal accounting by a Predecessor Fiduciary; or (3) to investigate any accountings provided by a Predecessor Fiduciary. No Trustee shall be personally liable for any act or failure to act of a Predecessor Fiduciary, or for the failure to contest any accounting provided by a Predecessor Fiduciary. However, the preceding shall not apply to any Trustee to the extent that the Trustee (1) has received a request from a beneficiary having a material interest in its estate to secure such an accounting or to conduct such an investigation, or (2) has actual knowledge of facts that would lead a reasonable person to believe that, as a consequence of any act or omission of a Predecessor Fiduciary, a material loss has occurred or will occur.

An individual or entity serving as Trustee shall be entitled to reimbursement from the estate for any liability or expense, whether in contract, tort, or otherwise, reasonably incurred by the Trustee in the administration of the estate.

5-3 Ancillary or Corporate Trustee. The Trustees, to the extent permitted by applicable law, may appoint (and remove) any Qualified Corporation (meaning any corporation having trust powers that is qualified and willing to serve under this instrument and that has, as of the relevant time, either (1) a minimum capital and surplus of at least five million dollars ($5,000,000 U.S.), or (2) at least 50 million dollars ($50,000,000 U.S.) in trust assets under administration, hereinafter referred to as an Ancillary or Corporate Trustee) to act as Ancillary Trustee on such terms as the Trustees may deem appropriate. If the corpus of this Trust were to ever exceed a value of more than one hundred thousand dollars ($100,000 U.S.) and if the then-acting Trustees are noncorporate fiduciaries, then the Trustees shall appoint an Ancillary Trustee to manage and invest the assets of the Trust. The acting Trustees shall retain any and all powers granted in this Trust except for any powers delegated to the Ancillary Trustee concerning the management and investment of the Trust assets. It is the Grantors' intention by this paragraph to allow the Trustees to assign any and all fiduciary responsibility and liability for the management and investment of the Trust assets to the Ancillary Trustee. The Trustees are authorized to execute any documents or contractual arrangements necessary to accomplish this task. The Trustee shall always be responsible for all other administrative decisions including decisions concerning disbursements from the Trust. This paragraph is intended to relieve the noncorporate Trustees of the burden and liability for managing and investing the assets of the Trust. If the then-sole-acting Trustee is a Corporate Trustee, then the Corporate Trustee shall exercise all of the powers of the Trustee.

5-4 Reorganization or Insolvency of Corporate Trustee. If a corporation nominated to serve or serving as the Trustee shall ever change its name, or shall merge or consolidate with or into any other bank or trust company, such corporation shall be deemed to be a continuing entity and shall continue to be eligible for appointment, or shall continue to act as the Trustee.

ARTICLE VI

ADMINISTRATIVE PROVISIONS

6-1 Investment Authority. The Trustees shall invest the assets of the estate in proper and prudent investments with due regard to reasonable diversification, considering the entire portfolio of its estate (and the entire portfolio of any collective investment vehicle, as the case may be) rather than on an individual asset basis. To the extent consistent with the foregoing; (1) a corporate entity serving as Trustee may deposit funds with itself and may place funds under its administration in common trust funds; and (2) the Trustee may acquire securities, real estate, life insurance, oil, gas, and other mineral interests, and other investments.

6-2 Management Authority. The Trustees may exercise the managerial powers of an individual with respect to matters affecting the estate and the broadest managerial discretion that is consistent with the reasonable and prudent management and administration of the estate, including the following managerial authorities: (1) the Trustees may manage, sell, lease (for any term, even if beyond the anticipated term of the estate), partition, improve, repair, insure, and otherwise deal with all property of the estate; (2) the Trustees may form, reorganize, or dissolve corporations, give proxies to vote securities, enter into voting trusts, and generally exercise all rights of a stockholder; (3) the Trustees may take whatever action, if any, the Trustees consider best to collect the proceeds of life insurance policies and employee benefit plans as well as any other property that may be tendered to the Trustees; (4) the Trustees may pay all taxes and all reasonable expenses, including reasonable compensation to the agents and counsel (including investment counsel) of the Trustees; (5) the Trustees may employ and compensate advisors and agents and delegate to an agent any authorities (including discretionary authorities); (6) the Trustees may institute and defend suits and release, compromise, or abandon claims; (7) the Trustee may hold title to any property in the name of one or more nominees without disclosing the fiduciary relationship; (8) the Trustees may lend money to any entity with or without security, endorse, guarantee, provide security for, or otherwise become obligated with respect to the debts of any entity, provided that all such transactions (except those for the benefit of any beneficiaries of the particular estate involved) must be on commercially reasonable terms; (9) the Trustees may assume, renew, and extend any indebtedness previously created and borrow for any purpose (including the payment of taxes or expenses) from any source (including a Trustee individually) at the then usual and customary rate of interest, and mortgage or pledge any property of the estate to any such lender; (10) the Trustees may make partial distributions to any beneficiary, including any trust created by this instrument, whether or not the administration of the estate is complete; (11) the Trustees may retain, sell, or distribute in kind any personal residence and any furnishings of such residence; (12) the Trustees may store personal effects given to a minor or other incapacitated beneficiary for later distribution to such individual, or sell such property and add the proceeds of sale to a trust of which individual is a beneficiary; (13) the Trustees may divide, allocate, or distribute property of the estate in undivided interests, non pro rata, and either wholly or partly in kind; (14) for administrative and investment purposes only, the Trustees may hold separate estates under this or any other instrument in one or more common accounts in which such estates have undivided interests; (15) the Trustees may allocate receipts and disbursements between principal and income in a reasonable manner, and may establish a reasonable reserve for depreciation or depletion and fund such reserve by appropriate charges against income of the estate; and (16) the Trustees may take all appropriate action to deal with any environmental hazard and comply with any environmental law, regulation, or order, and may institute, contest, or settle legal proceedings concerning environmental hazards; and (17) the Trustee may distribute income or principal to the Beneficiary's qualified ABLE account under section 529A of the Internal Revenue Code. All distributions of principal and income shall be made in cash directly to the Beneficiary's qualified ABLE account. A distribution for [his/her/their] benefit to a qualified ABLE account shall not exceed such annual contribution limits (from all sources) as imposed by section 529A(b)(2)(8) and the aggregate excess limitations (from all sources) as imposed by section 529A(b)(6).

6-3 Records, Books of Account, and Reports. The Trustees shall maintain proper books of account, which shall at all reasonable times be open for inspection or audit by [Beneficiary Name], or any court-appointed guardian for the Beneficiary, or [his/her/their] caregiver(s). The Trustees shall make a written financial report, at least annually, to [Beneficiary Name], or any court-appointed guardian for the beneficiary, or [his/her/their] caregiver(s). The Trustees' usual computer statements shall suffice for any accounting. The Trustees shall not be accountable to any person interested in this Trust for the manner in which, in good faith, it carries out its discretion to supplement the needs of the primary beneficiary (including any decision it may make not to incur the expense of detailed analysis of alternative choices) and, even though its decision in this regard may result in decreased distributions to the contingent beneficiaries of this Trust, there shall in no event be any compensation readjustments or reimbursements by the Trustees by reason of the manner in which the Trustees thus carry out their discretion.

6-4 Applicability of [State] Trust Code. To the extent consistent with the other provisions of this instrument, the Trustee shall have the powers, duties, and liabilities of trustees set forth in the [State] Trust Code, as amended and in effect from time to time. However, any legislation enacted subsequent to the date of this instrument that limits a Trustee's duties or liability to the beneficiaries of the estate shall be inapplicable to every trust created under this instrument, and the Trustees' acceptance of office under this instrument shall constitute an irrevocable agreement that no such subsequent legislation shall be applicable.

6-5 Additional Transfers of Property. Any additional transfer of property to this Trust shall be absolute; provided, however, that the duties of the Trustees shall not be increased by virtue of any such transfer without the consent of the Trustees.

6-6 Actions by Co-Trustees. When multiple Trustees are serving, each Trustee shall have the authority to act alone and independently of the other Trustees then serving, without the necessity of consultation with or approval of any other Co-Trustee. Any writing signed by a Co-Trustee with the authority to act alone and independently shall be valid and effective for all purposes as if signed by all such Trustees.

6-7 Resignation. Any Trustee may resign by giving thirty (30) days written notice to a beneficiary. If a beneficiary is legally incapacitated, the notice shall be delivered to that beneficiary's legal representative.

6-8 Removal of Trustee. Any interested person herein, including, but not limited to the Beneficiary's legal representative, the Beneficiary's parent, or contingent beneficiaries, may petition any court of competent jurisdiction for removal of any Trustee; the decision on whether to remove any Trustee shall be in the exclusive discretion and control of the court.

6-9 Appointment of Successors. In the event that [Parent #1 Name] and [Parent #2 Name] shall both resign, are removed, or otherwise fail or cease to act as Trustees for any reason, then Grantors hereby appoint [Name of Successor Trustee] as Successor Trustee. In the event that [Name of Successor Trustee] shall resign, is removed, or otherwise fails or ceases to act as Trustee for any reason, then Grantors hereby appoint [Name of Second Successor Trustee] as second Successor Trustee. In the event that [Name of Second Successor Trustee] shall resign, is removed, or otherwise fails or ceases to act as Trustee for any reason, then Grantors hereby appoint [Name of Third Successor Trustee] as third Successor Trustee. Any court of competent jurisdiction shall have the power to fill any vacancy in the Trusteeship resulting from the death, resignation, removal, or incapacity of a Trustee.

ARTICLE VII

GENERAL PROVISIONS

7-1 State; State Plan. References to the "state" means the state of [State Name] and all other states, if any, that may ever pay medical assistance on Beneficiary's behalf under a state plan at a time when the existence of this Trust, were it not described in 42 U.S.C.A. § 1396p(d)(4), would disqualify [Beneficiary Name] for state plan benefits. References to a "state plan" means any plan under Title 42 of the U.S. Code Annotated (The Public Health and Welfare), chapter 7 (Social Security), subchapter XIX (Grants to States for Medical Assistance Programs) and any other "plans" for purposes of 42 U.S.C. § 1396p(d)(4).

7-2 Execution. The Trustee hereby accepts the Trust herein created, established, and funded and covenants and agrees to and with the Grantor in consideration thereof that the Trustee will execute the same as herein provided.

7-3 Pronouns, Singular and Plural. Unless the context requires otherwise, words denoting the singular may be construed as denoting the plural, and words of the plural may be construed as denoting the singular, and words of one gender may be construed as denoting such other gender or no gender as is appropriate.

7-4 Execution in Counterparts. This document may be executed in any number of counterpart signature pages, all of which together will constitute the entire, original document.

By: ________________________________

[Parent #1 Name], Grantor and Trustee

By: ________________________________

[Parent #2 Name], Grantor and Trustee

State of [State Name]
County of [County Name]

SUBSCRIBED AND ACKNOWLEDGED before me by [Parent #1 Name], as Grantor and Trustee, on this [date] day of [month], [year].

____

Notary Public, State of [State Name]

State of [State Name]
County of [County Name]

SUBSCRIBED AND ACKNOWLEDGED before me by [Parent #2 Name], as Grantor and Trustee, on this [date] day of [month], [year].

____

Notary Public, State of [State Name]

Exhibit [#]

The foregoing Trust shall be funded with $____.

APPENDIX C

Checklist for First-Party Special Needs Trust Considerations for Interview and Drafting

- ❑ What is the beneficiary's legal name and any alias?
- ❑ What is the beneficiary's age?
- ❑ What is the beneficiary's family status (married, single, children, siblings)?
- ❑ Is the proposed beneficiary disabled as defined in 42 U.S.C. § 1382c(a)(3)?
    - Age of onset?
- ❑ Is the beneficiary currently receiving public benefits?
    - If so, which ones?
- ❑ Is it likely the beneficiary will require public benefits in the future?
- ❑ Will the beneficiary need a caregiver? If so, who will serve in that role and at what cost?
    - If the caregiver is the parent, who will become the caregiver if the parent becomes unable to care for the beneficiary?
- ❑ What is the beneficiary's health prognosis for the future?
- ❑ What is the beneficiary's life expectancy?
- ❑ Is the beneficiary mentally competent?
- ❑ Has a conservator, guardian, or guardian ad litem been appointed?
- ❑ Is anyone in the beneficiary's household or immediate family receiving public benefits? If so, who?
- ❑ Does the beneficiary have any income? If so, from what source?
- ❑ Has someone made an application for public benefits that is still pending?
- ❑ What kinds of services does the beneficiary now need that the beneficiary is not receiving?
- ❑ Where would the beneficiary like to be in two years?
- ❑ Will there need to be unusual or big-ticket expenditures (e.g., house, van that accommodates wheelchair, tuition for beneficiary)?
- ❑ Where does the beneficiary live and with whom?
- ❑ If the beneficiary is living with caretakers, what kinds of equipment, personal property, real property, or renovations are requested?
- ❑ Does the beneficiary presently have any estate planning documents?

- ❑ Does the beneficiary or do the parents or spouse of the beneficiary have estate planning documents?
- ❑ What is the source of funds to establish the special needs trust (SNT)?
- ❑ Is the money for the trust the proposed beneficiary's?
- ❑ What is the purpose of the trust (supplement not supplant)?
- ❑ Will the trust assets be used for the sole benefit of the beneficiary?
- ❑ The trust will be irrevocable?
- ❑ The trust will be discretionary?
- ❑ Who will establish the trust?
  - Individual
  - Parent
  - Grandparent
  - Guardian
  - Court. If so, what language is required through state statute and/or court rule?
- ❑ Who will be the trustee?
  - Family or professional?
  - Does proposed trustee understand SNT distribution standard?
- ❑ Who will be the successor trustee?
  - Family or professional?
  - Does proposed successor trustee understand SNT distribution standard?
- ❑ Will the trustee have the power to make distributions that will render the beneficiary ineligible for public benefits?
- ❑ Will the trust include a trust director (sometimes known as the trust protector)?
- ❑ Will the trustee receive compensation for serving? At what rate?
- ❑ Will the trust contain payback language?
- ❑ Will the trust contain special needs language?
- ❑ Does the beneficiary have any financial obligations (e.g., mortgage, spousal support, child support, student loans)?
- ❑ Is there a need for a Medicare set-aside?
- ❑ Other?

APPENDIX D

Client Interview Questionnaire

Public Benefits Intake

FLEMING & CURTI PLC

Your Name	aka	Already a client?
Finley Doe	Fin	No
Name as you would sign a legal document *Signing name, e.g.John Q. Adams vs. John Quincy Adams*	AKA, Alias, Call Me *Other names you use or have used in the past*	*Have we previously represented you?*

Prefix	Your First Name	Your Middle Name	Your Last Name	Suffix
	Finley		Doe	

Your Address	Address second line	City	State	Zip
135 Anywhere		Benson	AZ	85602

DOB	Place of Birth	Preferred pronouns	U.S. Citizen	Your County
1/1/1960		they/them/theirs	⊙ Yes ○ No	Cochise

Self-employed?	Occupation	Employer
No	Retired	
Are you self-employed?		

Home Phone	Work Phone	MobilePhone

Home Email	Work Email	Website

Benefits Applicant's Name

Title	First	Middle	Last	Suffix
	Skylar		Doe	

Their Address	Other names used
unknown	Sky, Skyy

Their DOB
1/1/1985

Their Place of Birth

U.S. Citizizen (2)
⊙ Yes ○ No

Preferred pronouns
they/them/theirs

Their Phone

Phone type

Their Email Address

Benefits SkylarDoe is currently receiving
☐ Supplemental Security Income (SSI) ☐ Social Security Disability Income (SSDI) ☐ Social Security retirement ☐ Private disability/pension income ☐ Medicaid ☐ Medicaid Long Term Care ☐ Medicare ☐ Medicare Advantage Plan ☐ Section 8 or housing subsidy ☐ SNAP or "food stamps"
☐

Occupation
None

Reason for contacting Fleming & Curti, PLC

Trying to preserve eligibility for public benefits

Describe what you see as the primary reason for contacting our office (e.g.: qualifying for ALTCS, dealing with an inheritance, etc.).

Children

Does Skylar Doe have any children?

No

Other information

Please tell us about recent medical history, living arrangements and other information that will help explain the current situation and concerns about Skylar Doe:

Details
Sky has lots of problems, both medical and mental. They are clearly disabled.
Special family details

Insert and format text, links, and images here.

Types of Assets

Next we want to collect information about Skylar Doe's assets. Precise values are not important for this listing. Please just give us the best information you have readily available. At the end, we'll give you a chance to upload documents (statements, beneficiary designations, deeds, etc.) to give us more detailed information. We'll start with identifying which types of assets Skylar Doe owns:

Types of assets
☑ Real Estate ☑ Bank Accounts ☑ Retirement Accounts ☑ Other Stock/Bond Investments ☑ Life Insurance ☑ Business Interests ☑ Tangible Personal Property (of significant value)

Real Estate

Real Property 1

Type | **Description** | **ID #**

Property Address | **Title held by:**

County | **Current Mortgage Balance** | **Value**

Approximate mortgage balance

Approximate (net) value of property

Total Real Property
$0.00

Banking

Bank Account 1

Type | **Description** | **ID #**

Owner | **Title %**

Contact Name | **Contact Tele.** | **Value**

Approximate balance in account

Total Banking
$0.00

Retirement

Retirement Account 1

Type | **Description** | **ID #**

Address | **Title %**

Contact Name | **Contact Tele.** | **Value**

Approximate value of retirement account

Total Retirement
$0.00

Other Investments

Investment - Brokerage account, Stocks, Bonds, etc. 1

Type **Description** **ID #**

Owner **Title %**

County **Current Mortgage Balance** **Value**

Contact Name **Contact Tele.**

Total Investment
$0.00

Life Insurance

Life Insurance Policy 1

Type **Description** **ID #**

Name of Company

Beneficiary **Owner**

Contact Name **Contact Tele.** **Death Benefit** **Value**

Cash Surrender Value

Total Insurance
$0.00

Business Interests

Business Interest 1

Type **Description** **ID #**

Name of Entity

Owner

Title %

Date

Cost or Other Basis

Value

Approximate value of your interest in this business

Contact Name

Contact Tele.

Copy of Agreement

Total Business Interests
$0.00

Tangible Personal Property

Only include individual items or collections with significant value. List vehicles and other individual items worth over approx. $25,000

Personal Property Items 1

Type

Description

ID #

Loans Made by You

Owner

Title %

Date

Cost or Other Basis

Value

Fair Market Value

Contact Name

Contact Tele.

Total Tangible Personal Property
$0.00

Inheritances

Describe expected future inheritances

Do you expect family (or others) to leave assets directly to Skylar Doe in the near or longer-term future?

Debts

Debts (that Skylar Doe owes)

Loan 1

Type

Name of Creditor

ID #

Manner of Payment

demand installment, open, line of credit

Collateral Security

Description of Collateral Security

Amount of Debt

Amount of Debt (excluding mortgages on real estate interests)

Provide detail as to any such liability in excess of $10,000.

Contact Name

Contact Tele.

Total Debts

$0.00

Gifts Skylar Doe has made in the past five years

Gift 1

Year

Description

Recipient

Total Gifts in Excess of 10,000.

Attach Document(s)

Document(s) 1

Doc Type **Document Title**

Document Date **Client Name**

Comment

Memo/Note

Upload File

You can upload documents with your questionnaire by dragging and dropping above. We would like to see these documents:

1. Your existing will, powers of attorney, living will, and any trust agreements
2. Life insurance and annuity policies (a recent statement will suffice)
3. Statements of account for savings and checking accounts
4. Brokerage statements for stocks, bonds, and securities or copies of certificates and bonds
5. Guardianship documents, if you have been named as guardian or a spouse or chld has a guardian appointed
6. Employee or retiree benefit statements (IRA's, Keoghs, or other retirement plan), including current beneficiary designation
7. Business papers: operating agreement, partnership agreement, corporate minute books, buy/sell agreements

In addition, we need to see your current beneficiary designations for retirement accounts, brokerage, bank and other financial accounts and real estate. You may need to visit your financial institution's online portal to download these beneficiary designations, or request them from your broker, banker or retirement plan administrator

APPENDIX E

Social Security Administration Notice Letter for Self-Settled Trust with Payback Language Based on SSA Step-Action from the Program Operations Manual System

[DATE]
VIA CMRRR

Social Security Administration
[Regional Office]
[Address]

Re: THE [Beneficiary Name] SPECIAL NEEDS TRUST
Social Security Number: [#]

To Whom It May Concern:

Enclosed please find the copy of the [Beneficiary Name] Special Needs Trust, which has been provided for your records, and a copy of the proof of funding of the trust.

This trust is a **self-settled special needs trust** and the Beneficiary funded the trust with [his/her/their] own money. The trust meets the requirements of 42 U.S.C. § 1396p(d)(4)(A).

The assets in the trust are not a countable resource for Supplemental Security Income eligibility purposes. This trust is a fully discretionary trust. The Beneficiary cannot compel a distribution from the trust. As such, the assets contained in the trust are not an available resource under the Program Operations Manual System (POMS) **SI 01120.203, Exceptions to Counting Trusts Established on or after January 1, 2000.**

In support of a finding that this trust meets the requirements of 42 U.S.C. § 1396p(d)(4)(A), please consider the following sections of the POMS that apply to trusts on or after December 13, 2016:

> SI 01120.203 Exceptions to Counting Trusts Established on or after January 1, 2000
>
> > I. Procedure For Developing Exceptions To Resource Counting
> >
> > > **2. Special needs trusts under Section 1917(d)(4)(A) of the Act on or after December 13, 2016**

This section of the POMS contains a step-action chart to determine whether a trust is compliant with the requirements of the law. The chart asks the following questions:

1. Does the trust contain the assets of an individual who was under age 65 when the trust was established? (See SI 01120.203B.2. in this section.)

    [I/We] believe the section that requires the establishment of the trust for an individual who is under the age of 65 is SI 01120.203C.1, **General rules for special needs trusts established on or after December 13, 2016**, as this trust was established after December 13, 2016, and "contains the assets of an individual who is under age 65 and is disabled,"

    The answer is yes, the birth date of the Beneficiary is [Beneficiary date of birth]. The date the trust was signed was [date trust signed]. The Grantor [Grantor Name] was [age] years old at the time of the creation and establishment of the trust. *A copy of the birth certificate of the Beneficiary is attached as Exhibit [#].*

2. Does the trust contain the assets of a disabled individual? (See SI 01120.203B.4. in this section.)

[I/We] believe the section that requires the establishment of the trust for an individual who is disabled is SI 01120.203C.1, **General rules for special needs trusts established on or after December 13, 2016**, as this trust was established after December 13, 2016, and "contains the assets of an individual who is under age 65 and is disabled."

The answer is yes, on the date the trust was funded the Beneficiary was receiving Supplemental Security Income (SSI) benefits as a result of having previously been found disabled by the Social Security Administration. *Attached to this letter as Exhibit [#] is a copy of the award letter showing the date eligibility for SSI benefits was granted.*

3. Is the disabled individual the sole beneficiary of the trust? (See SI 01120.203B.5. in this section.)

[I/We] believe the section that refers to the trust being established for the sole benefit of the Beneficiary is actually SI 01120.203B.6, **Established for the benefit of the individual**.

The answer is yes, [Beneficiary Name] is the only and sole Beneficiary of the trust. On page [#] paragraph [#] of the trust it states:

> This Trust is created, established, and funded for the purpose of providing for the special and supplemental needs of [Beneficiary Name], the sole Beneficiary hereof.

4. Did the individual, a parent, a grandparent, a legal guardian, or a court establish the trust? (See SI 01120.203B.6. in this section.)

[I/We] believe the section that requires the establishment of the trust by certain entities is SI 01120.203C.1, **General rules for special needs trusts established on or after December 13, 2016**, as this trust was established after December 13, 2016.

The answer is yes, included with this letter is a copy of the trust as it was signed, created, and established by Grantor/Beneficiary. The signature of the Grantor/Beneficiary is on page [#].

5. Does the trust provide specific language to reimburse any State(s) for medical assistance paid upon the individual's death as required in SI 01120.203B.10. in this section?

> The answer is yes, on page [#] at paragraph [#], <u>Trust Termination</u>, the trust states:
>
> > This Trust shall terminate upon the death of the Beneficiary. Any assets remaining in the Trust upon the death of the Beneficiary shall first be used to reimburse the "State" or an agency acting on its behalf, for the total amount of medical assistance paid on behalf of the Beneficiary during the Beneficiary's lifetime under the State Medicaid plan and as required by applicable law. If the Beneficiary has received medical assistance from more than one state, each state that provided medical assistance shall be repaid. If the Trust has insufficient assets to repay all medical assistance benefits received, then each state shall be paid its proportionate share of the remaining Trust assets.

6. Verify if the trust contains any early termination provisions as described in SI 01120.199. If the trust does not contain any early termination provisions, go to Step 7.

If the trust contains any early termination provisions, does it meet the early termination criteria in SI 01120.199F that would make early termination acceptable?

> The trust does not contain any early termination provision. On page [#] paragraph [#], Trust Termination is the only provision in the trust that speaks to termination and it states:
>
> > "This Trust shall terminate upon the death of the Beneficiary."

7. The trust meets the special needs trust exception to the extent that the assets of the individual were put in trust prior to the individual's attaining age 65. Any assets placed in the trust after the individual attained age 65 are not subject to this exception, except as provided in SI 01120.203B.3. in this section.

> The assets were deposited into the trust on [date] and a copy of the deposit slip is included with this transmittal.
>
> The age of the Grantor/Beneficiary on the date the assets were deposited into the trust is set forth in Step 1 above.

8. Evaluate the trust under SI 01120.200D.1.a. to determine if it is a countable resource.

SI 01120.200.D. Policy For Trusts As Resources

1. Trusts that are resources

a. When trusts are resources

Trust principal is a resource for SSI purposes if a trust beneficiary (applicant, recipient, or deemor) has legal authority to revoke or terminate the trust and then use the funds to meet his or her food or shelter needs. The trust principal is also a resource for SSI purposes if the trust beneficiary can direct the use of the trust principal for his or her support and maintenance under the terms of the trust. For the definition of revoke, see SI 01120.200B.11. in this section.

Additionally, if the trust beneficiary can sell his or her beneficial interest in the trust, that interest is a resource. For example, if the trust provides for payment of $100 per month to the trust beneficiary for spending money, and the trust does not have a valid spendthrift clause, then the trust beneficiary may be able to sell the right to future payments for a lump-sum settlement. The present value of the future payments counts as a resource. For more information on spendthrift clauses, see SI 01120.200B.13. in this section.

Article [#] on page [#] of the trust states:

REVOCATION. This Trust shall be irrevocable. The Beneficiary shall have no power or right, whether alone or in conjunction with others, in whatever capacity, to alter, amend, revoke, or terminate this Trust, or any of the terms of this trust agreement, in whole or in part, or to designate the persons who shall possess or enjoy the Trust estate, except as is set out in this instrument.

Paragraph [#] on page [#] of the trust states:

[Paragraph #] Spendthrift. This is a discretionary non-support spendthrift trust. No interest in the principal or income of this Trust shall be anticipated, assigned, or encumbered, or shall be subject to any creditor's claim or to legal process, prior to its actual receipt by the Beneficiary. Furthermore, because this Trust is to be conserved and maintained for the supplemental non-support

> needs of the Beneficiary who may be medically disabled or impaired throughout his lifetime, no part of the Trust estate, neither principal nor undistributed income, shall be construed as part of the Beneficiary's "estate" or be subject to the claims of voluntary or involuntary creditors for the provision of care and services, including residential care, by any public entity, office, department, or agency of any city, county, or state government, or by the federal government or any other public or private agency.
>
> Under no circumstances can the Beneficiary compel a distribution.

Based on the analysis that is set forth in SI 01120.203, Exceptions to Counting Trusts Established on or after January 1, 2000, I. Procedure For Developing Exceptions To Resource Counting, 2. Special needs trusts under Section 1917(d)(4)(A) of the Act on or after December 13, 2016, [I/We] believe the funds in the trust should not be a countable resource to the Beneficiary for eligibility purposes as set forth in the POMS.

The trust meets the requirements of 42 U.S.C. § 1396p(d)(4)(A) and SI 01120.203, Exceptions to Counting Trusts Established on or after January 1, 2000.

We thank the agency for its diligent work and consideration of our request to approve the trust. Most importantly, we state our belief that the trust meets all the requirements of 42 U.S.C. § 1396p(d)(4)(A) and that the assets contained in the trust should not be considered countable resources of the Beneficiary.

In the event that your agency would conclude that the assets in the trust would be a countable resource to the Beneficiary, we would request that you notify our office immediately.

Yours very truly,

Enclosures [#]

APPENDIX F

Social Security Administration Letter for Third-Party Special Needs Trust, No Payback

[DATE]

VIA CMRRR

Social Security Administration
[Regional Office]
[Address]

Re: [NAME OF THE TRUST]
Social Security Number: [#]

To Whom It May Concern:

Enclosed please find the copies of the [NAME OF THE TRUST] that was created under the Last Will and Testament of [Testator]. Please also find copies of the order admitting the Will to probate and authorizing letters testamentary and proof of funding trust created under the Will of [Testator].

This Trust is a fully discretionary trust. The Beneficiary cannot compel a distribution from the Trust. As such, the assets contained in the Trust are not an available resource under the Program Operations Manual System (POMS) SI 01120.200.D.2. The money that funded the Trust did not belong to the Beneficiary prior to the funding of the Trust. This Trust meets the definition of a third-party trust under the POMS SI 01120.200.B.16. The relevant POMS sections are included below.

We believe the funds in the Trust should not be a countable resource to [Beneficiary Name] for eligibility purposes as set forth in the POMS. In the event that your agency would conclude that the assets in the Trust would be a countable resource to [Beneficiary Name], we would request that you notify our office immediately.

Yours very truly,

Cc: [Client Name]
Enclosures [#]

SI 01120.200 Information on Trusts, Including Trusts Established Prior to January 01, 2000, Trusts Established with the Assets of Third Parties, and Trusts Not Subject to Section 1613(e) of the Social Security Act

A. Introduction To Trusts

A trust is a legal arrangement involving property and ownership interests. Property held in trust may or may not be considered a resource for SSI purposes. The general rules concerning resources apply when evaluating the resource status of property held in trust.

1. Applicability of policy instructions

Generally, these instructions apply to trusts not subject to the trust provisions in Section 1613(e) of the Social Security Act, which we evaluate using instructions in SI 01120.201 through SI 01120.204. However, trusts that meet the requirements of SI 01120.203 must also meet the requirements of this section. Use these instructions to evaluate the following types of trusts:

a. Trusts established prior to January 01, 2000 that contain assets of the individual

This includes trusts established before January 01, 2000 that contain assets of the individual, any of which were transferred before January 01, 2000.

If the trust was established prior to January 01, 2000, but no assets of the individual were transferred to the trust prior to January 01, 2000, see SI 01120.201.

b. Trusts that contain assets of third parties

This includes trusts that are:

• established before January 01, 2000 that contain assets of third parties;

• established on or after January 01, 2000 that contain only assets of third parties, or the portion of a commingled trust attributable to assets of third parties; and

• Indian Gaming Regulatory Act (IGRA) trusts established by the Indian tribes that meet the criteria in SI 01120.195F.

NOTE: Trusts established on or after January 01, 2000 that contain assets of a Supplemental Security Income (SSI) applicant, recipient, or spouse (or the portion of a commingled trust attributable to assets of an SSI claimant, recipient, or spouse) must be evaluated under SI 01120.201 through SI 01120.204.

SI 01120.200

B. Glossary Of Terms

1. Discretionary trust

A **discretionary trust** is a trust in which the trustee has full discretion as to the time, purpose, and amount of all distributions. The trustee may pay all or none of the trust as he or she considers appropriate to, or for the benefit of, the trust beneficiary. The beneficiary has no control over the trust.

SI 01120.200

B. Glossary Of Terms

16. Third-party trust

A **third-party trust** is a trust established with the assets of someone other than the trust beneficiary (or his or her spouse). For example, a grandparent can establish a third party trust using his or her assets, with a grandchild as the trust beneficiary. Be alert for situations where a trust is allegedly established with the assets of a third party but in reality is created with the trust beneficiary's property. In such cases, the trust is a grantor trust, not a third party trust.

SI 01120.200

D. Policy For Trusts As Resources

2. Trusts that are not resources

If an individual does not have the legal authority to revoke or terminate the trust or direct the use of the trust assets for his or her own support and maintenance, the trust principal **is not** the individual's resource for SSI purposes.

The revocability of a trust and the ability to direct the use of the trust principal depend on the terms of the trust agreement and on State (or Tribal) law. If a trust is irrevocable by its terms and under State law, and the trust beneficiary cannot control or direct use of the trust assets for the trust beneficiary's support and maintenance, the trust **is not** a resource.

APPENDIX G[1]

Social Security Administration Step-Action from the Program Operations Manual System: SI 01120.203 Exceptions to Counting Trusts Established on or after January 1, 2000

1. Provided as an illustration only. Be sure to consult the Program Operations Manual System (POMS) for the most current version.

I. Procedure For Developing Exceptions To Resource Counting

2. Special needs trusts under Section 1917(d)(4)(A) of the Act on or after December 13, 2016[2]

STEP	ACTION
1	Does the trust contain the assets of an individual who was under age 65 when the trust was established? (See SI 01120.203B.2. in this section.) • If **yes**, go to **Step 2**. • If **no**, go to **Step 9**.
2	Does the trust contain the assets of a disabled individual? (See SI 01120.203B.4. in this section.) • If **yes**, go to **Step 3**. • If **no**, go to **Step 9**.
3	Is the disabled individual the sole beneficiary of the trust? (See SI 01120.203B.6. in this section.) • If **yes**, go to **Step 4**. • If **no**, go to **Step 9**.
4	Did the individual, a parent, a grandparent, a legal guardian, or a court establish the trust? (See [SI 01120.203C.2.] in this section.) • If **yes**, go to **Step 5**. • If **no**, go to **Step 9**.
5	Does the trust provide specific language to reimburse any State(s) for medical assistance paid upon the individual's death as required in SI 01120.203B.10. in this section? • If **yes**, go to **Step 6**. • If **no**, go to **Step 9**.
6	Verify if the trust contains any early termination provisions as described in SI 01120.199. If the trust does not contain any early termination provisions, go to **Step 7**. If the trust contains any early termination provisions, does it meet the early termination criteria in SI 01120.199F that would make early termination acceptable? • If **yes**, go to **Step 7**. • If **no**, go to **Step 9**.

2. POMS SI 01120.203, https://secure.ssa.gov/apps10/poms.nsf/lnx/0501120203 (last visited Dec. 11, 2022).

STEP	ACTION
7	The trust meets the special needs trust exception to the extent that the assets of the individual were put in trust prior to the individual's attaining age 65. Any assets placed in the trust after the individual attained age 65 are not subject to this exception, except as provided in SI 01120.203B.3. in this section. Go to **Step 8** for treatment of assets placed in trust prior to age 65. Go to **Step 9** for treatment of assets placed in trust after attaining age 65.
8	Evaluate the trust under SI 01120.200D.1.a. to determine if it is a countable resource.
9	The trust (or portion thereof) does not meet the requirements for the special needs trust exception. Consider if the pooled trust exception in SI 01120.203D in this section applies. If neither exception applies, determine whether the undue hardship waiver applies under SI 01120.203K in this section.

APPENDIX H

Third-Party Special Needs Trust Information Schedule[1]

1. © Richard Courtney, Esq., *A Lawyer's Guide to Working with Special Needs Clients* (ABA), reprinted with permission.

THIRD PARTY SPECIAL NEEDS TRUST INFORMATION SCHEDULE

Client(s): ____

Explanation: The purpose of a "special needs trust" (SNT) is to hold money or other assets of a disabled person (the "beneficiary") that would disqualify that person from receiving SSI and/or Medicaid benefits. Assets held in a properly handled SNT will not be counted as assets by those programs. Payments made from such trusts directly to the beneficiary or for the beneficiary's food, clothing or shelter (rent/mortgage payments, utilities, property taxes, garbage or sewer fees) will be treated as income to the beneficiary, and therefore must be limited so as not to exceed the income limits of the SSI and/or Medicaid programs. Payments from the SNT for any other purposes (home repairs/maintenance/improvements, home furnishings, vehicle purchase/repairs/modification, therapies, recreation, entertainment, etc.) will not affect the beneficiary's public benefit payments.

Third party SNT: A SNT may be created by the parents, spouse or anyone else who wishes to establish a fund that can later receive gifts of money or assets for the disabled beneficiary by lifetime gift(s) or by last will and testament gifts. The assets in this type trust will be used for the disabled beneficiary's needs during his/her lifetime, and the assets remaining in the trust at the death of the beneficiary will be distributed to the persons and in the manner prescribed in the trust (such as other children or family, non-profit groups, etc.). This trust, called a **"third party"** trust, will not provide for any recovery by Medicaid, thus permitting all the trust assets to be distributed to the designated remainder beneficiaries at the death of the disabled primary beneficiary.

This type SNT is unlike a **"self-settled"** trust, into which the disabled beneficiary puts his/her own money or assets and which, by law, must provide that at the beneficiary's death, Medicaid will be first in line to recover from the trust assets the amount Medicaid has paid for the beneficiary's medical care. Such "self-settled" trusts are created to hold the assets already owned by the beneficiary **or** that the beneficiary is to receive through a lawsuit settlement, inheritance or life insurance settlement.

The information requested in this form is necessary for us to prepare a **third party** special needs trust most appropriate for the needs of the disabled beneficiary. If the beneficiary owns or is entitled to receive assets in his/her own name, please ask us for the Self-Settled Special Needs Trust Information Form.

NOTE: "**Beneficiary**" refers to the disabled person/spouse/child.

"**Settlor**" refers to the person(s) who is/are creating the trust (signing the trust agreement) for the benefit of the disabled beneficiary.

"Remainder beneficiary(ies)" refers to the person(s) who are to receive the trust assets remaining in the trust at the death of the primary disabled beneficiary.

A. Settlor(s) Information:

Name(s): ______________________________

Address: ______________________________

Date of Birth: ______________ Social Security No.: ______________

Telephone: ____________ Fax: ____________ Email: ____________

Relationship to Beneficiary: ______________________________

B. Beneficiary Information:

Name: ______________________________

Address: ______________________________

Date of Birth: ______________ Social Security No.: ______________

Telephone: ____________ Fax: ____________ Email: ____________

Beneficiary's Physical/Mental Disability(ies) (Diagnosis, description and duration):

____

____

____

Beneficiary's Spouse (if married):

Name: ______________________________

Residence Address: ______________________________

Date of Birth: ______________ Social Security No.: ______________

Telephone: ____________ Fax: ____________ Email: ____________

Beneficiary's Parent(s):

Father: ______________________________

Address: ______________________________

Telephone: ______________ Social Security No.: ______________

Mother: ______________________________

Address: ______________________________

Telephone: ______________ Social Security No.: ______________

Date, place and cause number of divorce of parents, if applicable (**enclose copy of divorce decree**):

____

Is Beneficiary the subject of a guardianship or conservatorship? _______Yes ________ No

If yes: County ______________________________________ Case No. ______________________

Guardian Name: ____________________________________ (Attach **copy of Decree** appointing)

Address: ____ Phone: _________________

Relationship to Beneficiary: ____

Beneficiary's residence: _____ Owns home/condo ____ Live w/ parents/family

____ Rent apartment/home _____ Nursing home _____ Assisted living facility ____ Group home

Beneficiary's Income and Benefits:

Does Beneficiary currently receive:

______ Social Security Disability payments ($ ________________ per month)

______ Supplemental Security Income (SSI) ($ _______________ per month)

______ Medi**care** for medical expenses (since date: ________________________)

______ Medi**caid** for medical expenses (since date: ________________________)

Does Beneficiary receive **other income or assistance** from any source (such as public housing, Food Stamps, etc.)? ______ Yes ______ No If yes, specify:

$ __________ per month/____________ from ____

$ __________ per month/____________ from ____

Beneficiary's Resources (Assets):

Does Beneficiary own (in sole or part interest): (indicate by "Y" or "N")

______ Residence _______ Automobile ______ Home furnishings ______ Funeral Plan

______ Burial Plot _______ Life Insurance ______ Other Real Estate (value $____________)

______ Checking/Savings/CD/Brokerage Accounts (total $_______________________________)

______ Other Assets (list and values): ____

____

C. Does Beneficiary expect to receive (indicate "Y" or "N"):

______ Lawsuit settlement (attach copy of Complaint and any Order dismissing any party)

______ Inheritance distribution (attach copy of Petition and Order Closing Estate)

______ Life insurance settlement (attach copy of policy)

D. Trustee Information

There must be at least one Trustee who is capable of (1) handling the funds of the trust for the sole benefit of Beneficiary, (2) understanding the trust rules and requirements of Medicaid and SSI, (3) managing the trust assets within the guidelines of the "prudent investor" standards of Mississippi law, and (4) comparing, engaging and supervising appropriate investment advisors to invest the trust funds. Also, if there is a court-appointed conservator or guardian for the beneficiary, the court may require the Trustee to file annual accountings of the trust assets and to obtain and file a trustee's bond with the court. It is advisable to name one or more successor Trustees who would serve if the initial Trustee becomes unable to serve.

Initial Trustee: ____________________

Address: ____________________

Phone(s): ____________________ Fax: ____________________

Initial Co-Trustee (if applicable): ____________________

Address: ____________________

Phone(s): ____________________ Fax: ____________________

First Successor Trustee: ____________________

Address: ____________________

Phone(s): ____________________ Fax: ____________________

Second Successor Trustee: ____________________

Address: ____________________

Phone(s): ____________________ Fax: ____________________

If no individual Trustee is willing or able to serve, do you want a corporate Trustee (such as a bank) to serve? ____ Yes ______ No If so:

Corporate Trustee: ____________________

Address: ____________________

Phone(s): ____________________ Fax: ____________________

E. Trust Protector / Trust Advisor

In some situations, it may be advisable to appoint an independent person (not the Beneficiary or Beneficiary's spouse or child) to serve as Trust Protector or Trust Advisor. Such situations may include where there is a corporate Trustee or an individual Trustee who may lack some sophistication for handling all the trust matters. The Trust Protector would be given, in the trust document, the authority to remove a Trustee who is not being responsive to the Beneficiary's needs or who is endangering the Beneficiary's public benefits through improper handling of the trust. The Trust Protector (or Trust Advisor) could also have the ability to make amendments to the trust to comply with changing laws and regulations, revise the trustee's investment powers, recommend disbursements for the Beneficiary's benefit, etc.

Trust Protector: ______________________________

Address: ______________________________

Phone(s): ______________________ Fax: ______________________

Relationship to Settlor(s): ______________________________

F. Special Needs Provisions

While the Trustee will have broad and complete discretion to meet the needs of the Beneficiary, the trust can specify various physical, medical care, therapy, recreational, travel and entertainment needs to be paid from the trust. SPECIFY BELOW any particular needs or services you would want the trust to provide.

______ Attendants / Caretaker services ______________________

______ Equipment (wheelchair, walker, computer talking devices, etc.)

______ Therapies ______________________________

______ Travel / Recreation ______________________________

______ Other ______________________________

____

____

G. Distributions After Beneficiary's Death

The SNT should direct that, following the death of the disabled beneficiary, the assets remaining in the trust will be distributed to named individuals or organizations or held in trust for young remainder beneficiaries (such as grandchildren) until certain ages. If such assets may be left to minor or disabled remainder beneficiaries, it is advisable to leave their shares in trust for them in order to prevent the need for a court-ordered guardianship. You may also allow the disabled beneficiary to decide who will receive the assets remaining in his/her trust by naming them in his/her last will and testament (if the disabled beneficiary does not have a valid will at his/her death, then the assets will pass to persons as otherwise designated in the trust document). Please name or describe below the remainder beneficiaries to whom you wish the assets distributed.

Do you want to allow the disabled beneficiary to designate who will receive the remaining trust funds in his/her last will and testament? Yes _____ No _____

Named Remainder Beneficiary(ies) and Relationship to Settlor: ____________________________

____

____

Described Remainder Beneficiary(ies) (such as "settlor's surviving children", etc.): ___________

____

____

Do you want the share for any **minor child or grandchild** to be held in trust for that child / grandchild? Yes ______ No ______

a. If "Yes", indicate how you would like the trustee to make distributions to / for that child:

____ to pay for general health, education, maintenance and support for him/her

or

____ to pay medical expenses not covered by other insurance

____ to pay education expenses, including college / vocational / graduate school

____ to purchase a car for him/her at certain ages or up to a certain purchase price

____ to provide summer trips, camps or other cultural experiences

____ to provide a cash award of some amount for good grades during each semester

____ to pay for a wedding, the purchase of a first house, or starting a business

____ to pay a monthly / quarterly income to the child / grandchild starting after age 21

b. The trustee must distribute the principal amount of the trust at one or more times in the future. How would you like the trust to be distributed:

____ distribute all to ____ at age _________

____ distribute all to ____ at age _________

____ distribute all to ____ at age _________

____ distribute all to each child / grandchild at age ____ 21 ____ 25 ____ other (______)

____ distribute ______% at age ______, then distribute ______% at age ______, then distribute ______% at age ______

Notes:

APPENDIX I

Caregiver Letter

[Current Date]

[Parent(s) Name]
[Parent(s) Address]

Re: [Name of Trust]

Dear [Parent(s) Name]:

The purpose of this letter is to summarize how [Beneficiary Name]'s trust will work and what some of the goals of the trust will be. I also would like to explain a few of the potential limitations of the trust, especially with regard to benefits that might be available from resources other than your own.

When a person or entity such as the court (who is called the grantor) places money into a trust, he or she is giving someone else (the trustee) the right to manage the money for the benefit of a third person (the beneficiary).

The documents creating the trust (the Trust and Schedule [#]) have general rules about when the trust's money can be spent and on what it can be spent. [Beneficiary's Name]'s trust gives the trustee broad discretionary authority with regard to distributions. (Any subsequent independent trustee would have the same authority.) Furthermore, except in very limited circumstances, once the trust is created it cannot be changed or terminated.

If you think that [Beneficiary Name] needs something and that the trust should pay for it, you can request that the trustee release funds for that purpose. However, [Beneficiary Name] cannot force the independent trustee to release money if the trustee does not think that the trust allows [him/her/them] to do so. You should make sure that you understand how the trust's money is invested.

The trust must always have an "independent trustee." The independent trustee is responsible for determining when the trust's money can be released, how much can be released, to whom it can be released, and for what purposes it can be released. (This is explained in Article [#], Sections [#] and [#].) The trust does not require any trustee to post a bond.

The "Disposition of the Trust Estate" provisions are found in Article [#], Sections [#] through [#] of the trust. Furthermore, the independent trustee always has the authority to make additional distributions to [Beneficiary Name].

The trustee is required to reimburse the state for any Medicaid-type benefits that [Beneficiary Name] received during [his/her/their] lifetime. It does not matter whether [Beneficiary Name] received these benefits before or after the trust was created. The trustee will use the money remaining in the trust if [he/she/they] [is/are] no longer alive for this purpose. Although we could have drafted a trust that did not require that the state be reimbursed, it would have disqualified [Beneficiary Name] from receiving Medicaid benefits.

[Beneficiary Name]'s trust gives [him/her/them] a general power of appointment. This means that [Beneficiary Name] can decide who should receive any remaining trust assets if [he/she/they] [is/are] no longer alive. However, [Beneficiary Name] can only make this choice in [his/her/their] will, and the will must make a specific reference to the trust and to the power of appointment. (The existence of the general power of appointment will cause the trust property to be included in [Beneficiary Name]'s estate for tax purposes.) If [Beneficiary Name] does not exercise [his/her/their] power of appointment, then the remaining assets will pass to [his/her/their] heirs. This part of the trust is found in Article [#], Sections [#] through [#].

One of the trustee's objectives should be to invest the assets so that the amount of money in the trust increases in the future. HOWEVER, BECAUSE MOST INVESTMENTS INCLUDE SOME DEGREE OF RISK, A TRUSTEE CANNOT GUARANTEE THE PERFORMANCE OF THE TRUST'S INVESTMENT NOW OR AT ANY POINT IN THE FUTURE. Furthermore, as a general rule, the trustee will not be liable if the investments do not perform as well as expected. The trustee would only be liable if [he/she/they] acted in bad faith and if [his/her/their] action constituted gross misconduct. This standard applies to any situation in which the trustee is given discretion. (You should also carefully read Article [#], Sections [#] and [#] of the Administrative Provisions. They deal with this and other related issues.)

One of the goals of this trust is to help ensure that [Beneficiary Name] is eligible for government assistance such as Medicaid, if [he/she/they] otherwise [qualifies/qualify] for such assistance. However, it is important for you to understand that the Medicaid eligibility requirements are continuously changing. Federal legislation was enacted that is designed to prohibit, in most cases, a person's receiving Medicaid benefits if assets are being held for the person in a trust. Although the legislation includes an exception for trusts designed for disabled individuals, I am not certain how [State Name] will apply the federal law or how it will view [Beneficiary Name]'s trust.

IN SUMMARY, I CANNOT GUARANTEE THAT [Beneficiary Name] IS OR WILL BE ELIGIBLE FOR GOVERNMENT ASSISTANCE SUCH AS MEDICAID.

The trust may disqualify [Beneficiary Name] from receiving future Supplemental Security Income (SSI) benefits. In order to avoid this result, the trust should prohibit the trustee from using any money for [Beneficiary Name]'s food or shelter.

The existence of [Beneficiary Name]'s trust *must* be reported to Medicaid (and the [Program Name] program, if applicable). Although the trust did not exist when [he/she/they] originally made application, there is a continuing obligation to report *changes* in [his/her/their] and your financial assets and income. As the person who signs the application on [Beneficiary Name]'s behalf, you are responsible for reporting these changes in [his/her/their] assets and income. It is your responsibility to send your caseworker a copy of the trust and to make sure that all disbursements from [his/her/their] trust are reported to the caseworker. You should discuss the reporting of the disbursements with the trustee. However, you must understand that it is ultimately your responsibility to do the reporting.

It is important for you to understand the issues that I discussed in this letter. Because I only summarized a few of the trust's provisions, you should carefully read the Declaration of Trust, and you should make sure that you understand this document. I will answer any questions that you may have.

Finally, it is important that you, as caregivers, give some thought to updating your wills and powers of attorney as soon as practicable. Some trusts even provide for the trust to pay for preparation of estate planning documents.

The beneficiary is only partly covered when a trust is in place. If [his/her/their] caregivers do not have adequate provisions in place regarding guardianship, estate plans, and contingency plans in the event of their incapacity or death, the consequences to the beneficiary could be devastating *and* expensive. As an example, if the primary caregiver passes away unexpectedly, without any provisions in place, another family member may be forced to step into the role of caregiver, who may or may not be qualified to do so, or have the best interests in mind for the beneficiary. That would result in costly emergency litigation, the cost of which will be borne by the trust. With a little planning, that can all be avoided.

I cannot stress enough how important it is for these issues to be discussed and resolved by the caregivers.

If you do not have any questions, then I ask you to sign this letter and return it to me. By signing it, you are acknowledging that you received a copy of it and that you understand the issues I addressed. The enclosed copy of this letter is for your records. Please return this signed original in the enclosed self-addressed, stamped envelope.

Again, please call me if you have any questions whatsoever.

Very truly yours,
[Firm Name]

[Attorney Name]

[Day, Month][[: ______________________________, [Year]

____

[Parent(s) Name]

Enc.

APPENDIX J

Trustee Letter

[Current Date]

[Trust Officer Name and Title]
[Address]

Re: Special Needs Trust of [Beneficiary Name]

Dear [Trust Officer Name]:

This correspondence is to advise you as trustee as to how distributions from the [Trust Name] could be made such that [Beneficiary Name] will maintain [his/her/their] eligibility for Supplemental Security Income (SSI), and as a result of the SSI eligibility, keep [his/her/their] Medicaid benefits.

As an SSI beneficiary, [Beneficiary Name] receives a monthly cash payment for support because [he/she/they] [is/are] aged, blind, or disabled and [his/her/their] assets and income are low enough to meet a "means test." SSI is intended to pay for the beneficiary's food and shelter.

As you are aware, any money that is disbursed from the trust will affect [Beneficiary Name]'s SSI benefits. The Social Security Administration (SSA) receives a report from the Internal Revenue Service (IRS) that they cross-match with the recipient's Social Security number and compare the income reported to the IRS against the income reported by the recipient.

The key to maintaining the eligibility for SSI lies in how the distributions from the trust are made and whether they are made in the form of cash to the recipient or paid directly to vendors for [his/her/their] benefit.

To achieve the desired result, you must purchase goods and services for [his/her/their] benefit in a manner so that these purchases comply with the SSI rules for determining when disbursements from the trust will be counted as income to [him/her/them] that will affect [his/her/their] eligibility.

<u>SSI Rules</u>

The SSA will categorize any distribution made to or for the beneficiary as some form of income, subject to their "income rules." Then, if the income buys some kind of asset (or becomes an asset itself), the asset will be subject to separate "resource rules."

SSI rules will treat distributions made from the trust as either

(1) direct "income" to the beneficiary;

(2) "not income"; or

(3) "in-kind support and maintenance."

If the distribution becomes an asset, SSI rules will treat it as either a "countable resource" or an "excluded resource." Each of these categories is explained in detail below. Classifying the disbursements from the trust as "income" or as a "resource" will usually make a big difference to the beneficiary's eligibility and benefit levels, so it is important to have some understanding of them.

To be sure that the distributions fall into the desired category, you must maintain very accurate records of how the trust funds are spent. These records will be needed if the SSA or the [State Medicaid Agency Name] want verification of the expenditures that have been made. It is not unusual for the agencies to make a demand for verification, and you should expect it; however, you can appeal any unreasonable demands for verification.

<u>SSI Rules</u>: Assets

(1) Countable Resources

Generally, a "countable resource" is any asset considered by SSI rules (therefore a resource is sometimes called a "countable asset"). It could be tangible, like a second car, or it could be intangible, like a savings account. An SSI recipient is allowed to have only $2,000 or less in "resources." If resources exceed $2,000 during any whole calendar month (even by a few cents), the beneficiary's public benefits may be terminated. The determination of the asset level is always done at 12:01 a.m. on the first day of the month.

Income that is received during the month is considered "income" throughout the calendar month of receipt, even if it is deposited in a bank account. If, at the end of the month, it is still in the account, it becomes a "resource" in the next month, and is then subject to "resource" rules.

(2) Excluded Resources

The beneficiary is allowed to have certain exempt assets. These exempt assets are not counted in determining eligibility, and the beneficiary's ownership of them will not jeopardize [his/her/their] SSI benefits. Therefore, you may freely purchase exempt assets for the beneficiary and give them to the beneficiary (except food and shelter, as explained below). You should not give the beneficiary the money to purchase exempt assets [himself/herself/themselves]—payments of money are always considered countable income as explained below.

The following assets are exempt:

- A home, including adjacent land, if the beneficiary lives in it or intends to return to it
- Household goods (furniture, furnishings, household equipment, household supplies) and personal effects (toiletries, items of personal care and education, clothing and jewelry); however, giving the beneficiary food is in-kind support, as explained below—all of the abovementioned items are subject to the limit of a total value of $2,000
- One automobile (or other vehicle) limited in value to $4,500—unless needed for specific or regular medical treatments, modified for handicapped use, or especially needed for essential daily activities
- Life insurance with cash surrender value of less than $1,500 if its face value is more than $1,500, and all term life insurance
- A burial plot, or other burial space, worth any amount
- A revocable burial fund, worth up to $1,500

All the assets above are specifically exempted by law. You might note a number of common and useful items are not specifically mentioned as exempt in the SSI regulations, but are not counted because they are included among "personal effects" or are services. These include:

- Recreational equipment, games, and crafts
- Books and magazines
- Telephone, answering machine, etc.

- Television, radio, and cable service
- Musical instruments and stereo
- Travel and education
- Recreation and entertainment
- Some home maintenance, such as gardening and mowing
- Some home repairs
- Some plane tickets

There is little litigation as to what is exempt or not. However, if an item is determined to be not exempt and a request for reconsideration asking for continued benefits is filed within ten days of the denial of benefits, you can litigate the exemption without losing benefits. The downside to this strategy is that it can take as long as two years to get a final decision from an administrative law judge. This can mean if the reconsideration is lost that there would be a large overpayment. That is, the SSA would demand that the money paid during the period that the appeal is pending be repaid. However, this is not as bad as it sounds because the SSA recovers overpayments at 10 percent of the person's monthly check, or about $48 for most people.

<u>SSI Rules</u>: Income

Direct Income

Any money you give to the beneficiary directly will be considered income to the beneficiary, and will reduce [his/her/their] SSI benefits on a dollar-for-dollar basis. As a result, you should avoid making direct payments to the beneficiary, since there will be no net advantage from doing so. If your actions reduce the beneficiary's SSI benefits to nothing, then both the beneficiary's SSI and Medicaid benefits will be jeopardized, because the Medicaid benefits depend on SSI eligibility.

You may not reimburse the beneficiary for purchases [he/she/they] [has/have] made, even if the purchases are for exempt assets. The payment will simply be counted as direct income. In addition, SSI rules say that if you give the beneficiary anything that is equivalent to cash (e.g., a winning lottery ticket, bus ticket, or postage stamps), it will be counted.

Not Income

(a) Services and resources

Other kinds of distributions from the trust are "not income" because they are not cash, nor are they food or shelter.

Examples of benefits that are "not income" include payments you make for certain kinds of medical care and social services. Also, bills you pay for the beneficiary to receive services are not income. However, if the beneficiary receives any asset as a result of you paying the bill, the value [he/she/they] receive[s] is counted under the "in-kind income" rules discussed below.

(b) In-kind income

Generally speaking, "in-kind income" exists when you give the beneficiary something other than money. In most cases, it is safe to provide such income to the beneficiary. This is because the value of any non-cash item (other than food or shelter) is not counted as income if the item will become an exempt asset when it is retained into the following month.

As a result, you may give the beneficiary most of the exempt assets mentioned above (such as books, furniture, or recreational equipment). For example, if you give the beneficiary a television, it will not be counted as income in the month received. This is because it would be an exempt household item if retained into the following month (assuming its value does not cause the total value of household goods and personal effects to exceed $2,000).

There are three ways that you can distribute allowable in-kind income. The safest (but least convenient) way is to distribute these services or goods directly to the beneficiary personally. In other words, you can buy the television and deliver it to the beneficiary. Alternatively, you also may make a direct payment to "providers" (such as an appliance store) who then in turn provides the goods or services to the beneficiary. Finally, you can give the beneficiary the right to obtain the goods and services (e.g., a voucher). This last method may be risky, however, if [he/she/they] can convert the right into cash. Then it would be considered a cash equivalent like a winning lottery ticket. **When you give the beneficiary any right to receive services or goods it should *always be* nontransferable and nonrefundable.**

One safe way to use the voucher approach is to buy the voucher with a credit card provided by the trust. Then, any refund would be credited to the trust rather than to the beneficiary. As a result, the beneficiary can show that [he/she/they] cannot refund the item to obtain cash.

Of course, you may also give the beneficiary services (such as telephone service, massage therapy, or a nonrefundable airline ticket). None of these will be counted against the beneficiary's SSI benefits, because there is no way to convert them into cash.

Income

In-Kind Support and Maintenance

As mentioned above, problems arise when "in-kind income" consists of food or shelter. The receipt, or right to receive, food or shelter is known technically as "in-kind support and maintenance," or ISM. **The beneficiary's SSI benefits will be reduced if [he/she/they] receive[s] ISM.**

The theory here is that, because SSI benefits are specifically intended to pay for a person's food and shelter, if that person receives those goods or services from another source, then less SSI income is needed. As a result, if you pay the beneficiary's rent, grocery bill, or meals (e.g., a restaurant meal), you would be providing ISM to the beneficiary. Thus, you are also (in theory) reducing [his/her/their] need for SSI.

There are sometimes rather fine distinctions between allowable in-kind income and countable ISM. For example, you can pay for some travel arrangements but not others (e.g., a charged plane ticket—but not a hotel room, because that is shelter). You can pay for some entertainment expenses but not others (e.g., a movie pass but not a restaurant meal, because that is food). Note also that you can pay for certain medications and alternative health treatments if they are not covered by Medicaid or other benefit programs.

Medical care and services paid directly to the vendor will not be considered income. A particularly useful form of transfer is vendor payment for medical care and services and probably medical equipment. It is not only not income but it is also exempt as a resource. Of course, it would be foolish to purchase exempt medical care and services and equipment paid for by Medicaid. If the trust were to provide services or equipment that could be provided by Medicaid, then the authorities might try to have the trust declared to be a primary payer and require the trust to pay for bills prior to Medicaid paying them.

If you do give ISM to the beneficiary, [his/her/their] SSI benefits will be reduced as well, but not on a dollar-for-dollar basis as with cash. Instead, the formula the SSA uses to reduce the SSI benefits for a person who receives ISM depends on two further factors: the household and the living arrangement of the SSI recipient.

Presumed Maximum Value Rule

If the beneficiary lives in [his/her/their] own household, or lives in someone else's household but does not receive both food and shelter from that household, then the Presumed Maximum Value (PMV) rule applies. In general, under the PMV rule, the value of the ISM is the lesser of

a. its actual value; or

b. its "presumed" value of one-third of the federal benefit portion.

The reduction applies to any month in which ISM is received, regardless of the actual value of the total food or shelter received in that month. Note there is a balancing of the ISM under this rule, and the reduction is the lesser of the actual amount or the "presumed value."

For example, if you directly pay the beneficiary's rent, [his/her/their] SSI benefits will only be reduced by one-third, even if the rent payment was $800. One dramatic result of this rule is that you could buy a house for the beneficiary to live in and then give it to the beneficiary. The beneficiary only would lose one-third of [his/her/their] monthly SSI benefits, because the "presumed value" (one-third of the SSI check) is less than the actual value of $800. The reduction would occur only in the one month the beneficiary receives the house. It would be considered ISM for "shelter" in the month of receipt. And in the following month, the home would be an exempt asset.

Ownership of a home by the beneficiary, however, may cause some greater problems, particularly if you expect to help support the home from the trust. For example, ISM would arise in each month you pay the beneficiary's mortgage payments, property taxes, insurance required by the mortgage lender, or utilities (garbage, water, gas, and electricity). Interestingly, no ISM exists if you pay for the beneficiary's phone, cable television, or voluntary home insurance—these are not considered "shelter" by the SSA.

On the other hand, if the actual value of the ISM is below one-third (e.g., you buy only one restaurant meal for the beneficiary), then the SSI reduction can be adjusted from one-third to reflect the actual value of the ISM the beneficiary actually received. One-third is only a "presumed" value. In this case, however, you would have provided no net benefit to the beneficiary, because the value of your purchase will exactly equal the reduction in [his/her/their] SSI benefits. In addition, you will have the burden of having to demonstrate the actual value.

In-Kind Support and Maintenance: One-Third Reduction Rule

The PMV rule does not apply if the beneficiary lives in someone else's household and receives both food and shelter from that household. Instead, the One-Third Reduction rule applies and the federal benefit portion of the beneficiary's SSI benefits is reduced by a flat one-third. This is often referred to as the "one-third cut back" rule.

However, no other ISM is counted, no matter how much. As a result, the value of shelter (rent) you pay directly to the landlord on behalf of the beneficiary is not counted as additional income to what is already deemed received by the beneficiary when living in another's household. You must remember, however, that other income that is not ISM will still be counted.

SSI Rules:

(1) Planning under the PMV and One-Third Reduction Rules

Taking all these rules into account, you should generally provide ISM (food or shelter) for the beneficiary only if the total value of such income in a given month exceeds one-third of the beneficiary's benefits. You must exercise your discretion regularly and knowledgeably.

The beneficiary's rent or mortgage is a good example: if the PMV rule applies and you pay the rent (e.g., $800), the beneficiary would receive $800 in ISM, but sustain a loss of only one-third in monthly SSI benefits.

In taking advantage of these ISM rules, however, you must be careful that the beneficiary does not retain too much of [his/her/their] SSI income at the end of the month. The reason is that the income [he/she/they] receive[s] from SSI this month will be considered as a resource next month unless spent. Once [he/she/they] [has/have] $2,000 or more in nonexempt resources, [he/she/they] will lose [his/her/their] SSI eligibility, and probably [his/her/their] Medicaid eligibility as well.

Another planning problem arises if the beneficiary receives only a small SSI check each month. Since SSI is a supplemental income program, the greater the beneficiary's other income (such as from Social Security disability benefits or otherwise), the less SSI that the beneficiary will receive. If [he/she/they] receive[s] only a small amount of SSI each month, then the reduction in SSI benefits due to the receipt of ISM may be fatal to the beneficiary's SSI and Medicaid benefits. For example, if the beneficiary living alone only receives $200 per month in SSI, the imposition of a one-third reduction of the [year] SSI federal rate of [current $ #], or [current $ # for PMV] PMV reduction must be avoided. Otherwise, the reduction will wipe out the entire SSI benefit, and Medicaid coverage will end along with it.

(2) Summary of Payment

In order to provide the most net benefit to the beneficiary, you should not make any cash distributions to [him/her/them]. You should instead, in your discretion, pay for and distribute services and exempt assets that are not food or shelter, and are not ISM (food and shelter), but only if: the total value in a given month exceeds the loss in SSI benefits calculated under the PMV or One-Third Reduction rules, and the beneficiary is able to sustain the reduction without reducing [his/her/their] SSI benefits to $0.

Medicaid Rules

[Beneficiary Name] is automatically entitled to [his/her/their] Medicaid benefits because [he/she/they] receive[s] SSI. Although Medicaid has its own income and resource eligibility rules, these rules do not generally apply in [his/her/their] case, because of the automatic Medicaid eligibility for SSI recipients. However, you must be responsive to requests for information from the [State Medicaid Agency Name] regarding expenditures from the trust.

REPORTING REQUIREMENTS

SSI Rules

The SSI program requires periodic reports for all SSI recipients. These reports must be completed if eligibility is to continue. In addition, you or the beneficiary must report to the SSA the existence of the trust and provide a copy of it if requested. We know they are aware of the trust but we should formally report it if that has not already been done. Finally, you or the beneficiary must report all of the following:

- A change in the beneficiary's address, or eligibility for other governmental benefits
- A change in [his/her/their] living arrangements (e.g., adding or losing a roommate)
- A change in [his/her/their] income (including the receipt of any direct distribution or ISM from you)
- A change in any (countable) resources
- A change in the beneficiary's marital status
- Admission to or discharge from any health facility or public facility, such as a hospital or nursing home
- Any intended trip outside the United States

The report may be brief, but it should be in writing to the SSA, and it should include the beneficiary's name and Social Security number, your name, and a description of the event that triggered the report and the date it happened. The report is due within ten days after the end of the month in which the event occurred.

Should you fail to make a required report in a timely fashion, the SSI program is entitled to reimbursement for all SSI benefits incorrectly paid to the beneficiary. In addition, for each report that is filed late, depending on how late the report is, the SSA is entitled to assess a penalty of up to $100.

You may be in doubt sometimes about what to report. As a practical matter, it is safer to report and explain a distribution to the beneficiary currently than to be discovered later by the SSA's Income and Eligibility Verification System (IEVS). At that point, the explanation then will have to be made to a skeptical investigations unit.

Note: If your trust is required to file tax returns, the IRS will know about all income distributed from the trust, and they regularly send reporting information to SSI and Medicaid.

You should file all reports on time as required by the governmental agencies and in the proper fashion. The SSA may require the trustee to appear at the annual redetermination of eligibility for the beneficiary.

<u>Protecting Benefits</u>

In administering the trust, pay attention to any notice regarding change of benefits and keep reasonably informed of new developments. If SSI or Medicaid notifies you or the beneficiary that it intends to reduce or eliminate the beneficiary's benefits, you should appeal in writing **within ten days**. If you act quickly, the SSI and Medicaid benefits will continue and not be suspended during the appeal. Although you are allowed up to 60 days to appeal an SSI decision, and 90 days to appeal a Medicaid decision, asking for an appeal <u>after</u> ten days have passed will result in the <u>loss</u> of SSI and Medicaid benefits while you await the results of the appeal.

You must also stay informed about changes in the beneficiary's benefits in order to make intelligent decisions as trustee of the trust. Failure to learn about a change in benefits can have catastrophic results (e.g., if the PMV penalty exceeds the SSI benefit level). SSI is a federal program run by the SSA, and the federal contribution in [State Name] is [#] percent of the SSI benefit.

Make sure the SSI and Medicaid programs have your address, in addition to the beneficiary's address, and request that you receive copies of all communications affecting the beneficiary's benefits. Be sure to keep copies of all correspondence from each benefit agency. This will help in determining the applicable rules on eligibility, reporting, and appeals.

The rules presented in this letter are very complex and technical in nature. It can be overwhelming for most people when first confronted with the requirements they impose. However, it helps to keep in mind the intent of the settlor of the trust. The purpose is to enrich the life of the beneficiary by providing for "extras" because the public benefits the beneficiary receives only allow a meager existence. The difficult tasks required to carry out the intentions of the settlor are themselves meager when measured against the wonderful benefits the trust can bring to the life of the beneficiary. Always keep in mind the fact that your efforts are making a tremendous difference in the quality of life of the beneficiary.

Additionally, our office can assist you with the annual accountings of the trust if required by the court.

While the court may have no annual reporting/accounting requirement at this time, you should keep in mind that at some point down the road, you may receive a notification from them asking for these documents, because their rules and policies change from time to time. In that event, we can assist you with that work and all you have to do is call us.

Finally, as trustee, you will have a relationship with the beneficiary and caregivers. It is important that you encourage the caregivers to update their wills and powers of attorney as soon as practicable. Some trusts even provide for the trust to pay for preparation of estate planning documents.

The beneficiary is only partly covered when a trust is in place. If [his/her/their] caregivers do not have adequate provisions in place regarding guardianship, estate plans, and contingency plans in the event of their incapacity or death, the consequences to the beneficiary could be devastating ***and*** expensive. As an example, if the primary caregiver passes away unexpectedly, without any provisions in place, another family member may be forced to step into the role of caregiver, who may or may not be qualified to do so, or have the best interests in mind for the beneficiary. That would result in costly emergency litigation, the cost of which will be borne by the trust. With a little planning, that can all be avoided.

We cannot stress enough how important it is for these issues to be discussed and resolved with your clients. In addition to creating special needs trusts, our office can assist your clients with preparation of wills, powers of attorney, and guardianships to prepare for any contingency and ensure the care of the beneficiary.

Our office is willing and ready to provide any further service in order to assure that protection of the trust fund is maintained and that the settlor's intent is fulfilled. Please let us know if we can help you.

Very truly yours,
[Firm Name]

[Attorney Name]

Enclosures

cc: [Parent/Caregiver Name]

APPENDIX K

Choosing a Trustee Letter

[DATE]

[Client Name]
[Client Address]

Re: [Name of Proposed Trust]

Dear [Client Name]:

We have met and discussed the importance of creating a trust for the benefit of [Beneficiary Name]. The selection of the trustee is one of the most important aspects in the creation and ongoing administration of the trust. To achieve the best results, the trustee must administer the trust in compliance with the eligibility rules of the benefit programs from which the beneficiary seeks to obtain eligibility. Because a special needs trust must be carefully drafted and administered with great skill, one person or institution may not have all the skills needed to do the job. Choosing a team to administer a special needs trust may often be the best approach.

Finding the "ideal trustee" is a near impossible task. The role of the trustee requires a long-term commitment; a keen sensitivity to the individual's disabilities; involvement in monitoring the beneficiary's services and advocating for medical and financial entitlements; and prudently investing and distributing the trust funds. The trustee also has to comply with a number of very complicated laws, including the Prudent Investor Act, the Principal and Income Act, the Social Security Administration requirements concerning distributions from the trust, and the general laws pertaining to serving as trustee. You can achieve success, however, if you take all of the attributes of the ideal trustee and develop a system of checks and balances that creates a stable environment to enrich your beneficiary's life—beyond just protecting public benefits.

A Trustee's Job Is Complex:

A trustee holds legal title to trust assets in a fiduciary capacity for the sole benefit of the beneficiary. Traditionally, a trustee's job was to invest trust assets wisely, to handle tax matters, to keep good accounts, to avoid commingling personal assets with trust assets, to avoid conflicts of interest, to act impartially and loyally towards beneficiaries, and to follow the distribution standards set out in the trust. For example, a simple trust might direct the trustee to distribute all income to the grantor's spouse and at the spouse's death distribute the principal to the grantor's children. A traditional trust might also have a spendthrift provision to protect trust assets from a beneficiary's creditors.

A trustee of a special needs trust has all the traditional trustee duties plus a primary duty to supplement, not supplant, means-tested government benefits. Instead of clear instructions about distributions, the special needs trustee has complete discretion to make—or not make—distributions for the beneficiary's special needs.

Basically, a beneficiary of a special needs trust can have no control whatsoever over trust distributions. Special needs trusts are drafted this way so that the assets will be considered "unavailable" for means-tested government benefit programs. If a beneficiary could demand distributions, Supplemental Security Income (SSI) or Medicaid could declare the beneficiary ineligible because of excess "available resources." "If you can get it, they can count it" is the classic rule. Whether serving as trustee of a self-settled special needs trust funded with the beneficiary's own funds or as trustee of a third-party special needs trust funded by others, a special needs trustee must have a thorough knowledge of the means-tested benefits the beneficiary receives in order to supplement those benefits, not jeopardize them.

All trusts have certain duties concerning handling investments, tax planning, and maintaining books. The discretionary nature of a special needs trust intensifies those needs, especially when a beneficiary needs assistance advocating for his or her needs. Oddly enough, the trustee may have no legal obligation to make a single distribution from the trust, but does have the duty to make "prudent investments." The trustee has a duty to oversee the investments in the trust and diversify them so that they are neither too conservative nor too aggressive. For example, if the trustee of a $500,000 special needs trust invested all of the funds in a certificate of deposit, receiving 1 percent return, while a properly balanced portfolio would make a 7 percent return, the trustee could be liable to the trust for the difference. Contrarily, if the trustee invested in risky growth funds and lost value in the trust, the trustee would be responsible for the difference between the loss and expected rate of return, had the funds been properly invested.

Another requirement of the trustee is to provide for the personal needs of the beneficiary. These needs include factoring how distributions will affect eligibility for public benefits, adhering to the ultimate intent of the trust document, and, in many cases, advocating for the care and safety of the beneficiary.

It is imperative that parents think beyond maintaining eligibility for government benefits and think more broadly when creating an estate plan to provide for their child. Especially when the beneficiary may need assistance in advocating for his or her own needs. Advocacy duties may be the most important task of the trustee. The ideal trustee must continue advocacy upon a parent's incapacity or death.

Accountability and Keeping the Trust on Track:

Accountability involves reviewing the activities of the trustee and other advisors. If, for instance, the beneficiary of the special needs trust is a 12-year-old boy with autism, it is very possible that he could live for another 75 years or longer. How likely is it that you can select a person or entity that can guarantee to meet his needs for the next 75 years? In fact, what is the likelihood that the public benefits system and government programs that provide for his needs today will resemble the system 30 years from now?

If we establish a checks-and-balance system, then someone should independently review the performance of the trust and have the power to replace any party that is not able or willing to meet the trust objectives. This person or entity can also amend the trust to conform to changes in the system and the law as time goes on. In some cases, the person or entity might be an advisory committee or family, friends, and professional care managers. This could also be what is called a "trust protector"—a person or entity that has specific powers to amend or revise the trust as well as replace trustees.

There is always an inclination to appoint family members as trustees of special needs trusts. Many trusts fail because of ill-equipped trustees, no matter how well intentioned. While appointing a family member may be convenient and seem like the best thing to do, private professional trustees often outperform family members in the same role. In addition, the need for attorney advisement and the risk of a benefits battle is greatly reduced when a trust is directed by an experienced professional trustee. With the exception of smaller trusts, professionals are better equipped to handle the job.

Generally speaking, most corporate trustees or banks in the [Geographic Area] require a minimum [$ amount] in trust to be cost effective. This does not mean that family should not be included. This means only that they play more of a supervisory role.

There Are a Variety of Special Needs Trust Jobs That Need Filling:

- **Trustee.** Who should be trustee with complete discretion to make distributions that do not jeopardize means-tested government benefits, while improving the beneficiary's quality of life? Should the trustee be a financial institution like a bank or trust company, an attorney or accountant, a parent, sibling, or other individual, or a nonprofit pooled trust? Should there be co-trustees? If individuals are named, who will serve as successor or substitute trustee if the original trustee is unable to serve?
- **Trust protector.** Special needs trusts sometimes name a "trust protector" to monitor the chosen trustee's performance, appoint a new trustee if necessary, and have the authority to ask a court to modify the trust to comply with changes in the law. If a trust protector will be used, who should be named? Should it be the attorney, the family accountant, a parent, or sibling of the beneficiary? If that person can no longer act, who should serve as successor trust protector?
- **Trust advisor or advisory committee.** Special needs trusts may also name a "trust advisor" or an "advisory committee" to advise the trustee about the disabled beneficiary's special needs. This position could be filled by the beneficiary's parents, other family members, longtime caregivers, the manager of a group home where the beneficiary resides, a member of the local Arc or National Alliance on Mental Illness (NAMI) chapter, a case manager, or the beneficiary's guardian. Who should serve 50 years down the line when the child is a senior citizen? There are many factors to consider.

Factors to Weigh When Making Choices:

The beneficiary's age, circumstances, and prognosis. This is information that family members know best. What is the nature of the beneficiary's disability? What is the beneficiary's current living arrangement and what may be the child's future living plans? Does the beneficiary have the mental capacity to monitor trust accountings in the long run or must others be assigned to that role? What is the beneficiary's estimated life expectancy? What government benefits is the beneficiary currently receiving? What benefits might the beneficiary be eligible for in the future and what is the relative importance of those programs to the child's well-being?

These factors can influence the choice of trustee, trust protector, or trust advisor. For example, if a child requires 24/7 care and lives at home, the caregiver parents may simply not have the time or energy to effectively serve as lead trustee. The parents could also have a conflict of interest regarding trust distributions—for instance, it can sometimes be difficult to distinguish between those home improvements and services that are solely for the benefit of the beneficiary with disabilities and those that also benefit the parents or the beneficiary's siblings. By contrast, if an adult child with a disability is firmly situated in a group home and the parent's main role is supervisory, the parent may well be the best person to serve as initial trustee, perhaps with younger family members as successor trustees, so long as all individual trustees are clearly authorized to pay for any needed professional assistance regarding trust taxes, government benefits, or investment matters.

The Amount, Source, and Timing of Funding for the Special Needs Trust:
The investment expertise needed to handle a $5,000,000 personal injury settlement is clearly different from the expertise needed to handle a $50,000 inheritance from a child's grandmother. In the first case, a professional trustee may be advisable with the parent serving as co-trustee or advisory committee member or trust protector. In the second case, a parent or other family member who will not charge a commission could be a better choice of trustee. For such smaller trusts, a professional trustee may not even be an option because they often will not agree to serve as trustee of trusts below a certain amount.

Trusts funded at a parent's death by bequests in a will, life insurance proceeds, or other death benefits raise more difficult trustee team issues because the parent is not available to serve in any capacity. It is in these circumstances that the existence of a detailed care plan prepared by parents is extremely important to assist the family members or professionals the parents have chosen to look after their child's special needs.

The Skills, Availability, and Possible Conflicts of Interest of a Trustee:
A special needs trust must be a discretionary, spendthrift trust where the beneficiary has no control whatever over distributions. For this reason, the trustee must have absolutely no conflict regarding serving the beneficiary's interests above all others. Parents often think that they or other family members are best suited to serve as trustee because they love the beneficiary and best understand his or her needs, especially when the family trustee is authorized to seek professional assistance with tax, investment, and government benefits issues. A serious problem arises, however, if parents also want

to name the same family member as the residuary beneficiary of the special needs trust to receive any funds left at the beneficiary's death. This is an obvious conflict of interest because it creates a situation where the trustee will benefit personally from minimizing what is paid out of the trust. If leaving the remainder of the trust to family members is important, parents should consider an independent trustee, perhaps with family members in advisory roles. However, if it is more important for a family member to serve as trustee, the parents might consider naming a charity as the residuary beneficiary.

Many families may prefer that a sibling or other family member serve as trustee, but fear that the person does not have the required expertise to serve in this role. In these cases, family members may be named as co-trustees with a professional trustee. The professional could be a bank or an attorney experienced in serving as trustee of a special needs trust. If a bank is selected, it should be a bank with a trust department that has a good track record for managing money. If an attorney is selected, he or she should have either a good track record for investing money or agree to employ a professional money manager to manage the investments. If the investments do well, the beneficiary's lifestyle will be enriched. If the investments do poorly, the individual's standard of living will be adversely affected.

One factor that can cause hesitation at appointing a professional trustee is the fees involved. Trustee's fees typically run 1–1.5 percent of trust assets on an annual basis. However, the difference between money management by a professional and money management by a family member is usually far greater than the trustee's fee. In most cases, the trustee's fee should be considered an investment rather than a cost. The trustee should be someone who (1) is responsible for managing finances, (2) understands the beneficiary's special needs, (3) understands the rules governing the beneficiary's public benefits programs, and (4) will be an ardent advocate for the beneficiary's best interests.

The Availability and Cost of Backup Support for Trustees:

Professional trustees like banks, or perhaps the family certified public accountant or regular estate planning attorney, may know how to invest trust funds and do the trust taxes, but may not know much about government benefits rules or the particular needs of a beneficiary over time. These professionals will often need advice from other experts—special needs attorneys, care managers, family caregivers—and the trust instrument should authorize paying for that advice. Similarly, the family member who is closely attuned to the beneficiary's needs, and who may be an excellent advocate for the beneficiary regarding government benefit programs, is probably not an investment or tax expert.

However, the backup help needed to support family member trustees is becoming more widely available as some brokerage firms and trust companies are responding to families' needs for financial and other support services for special needs trusts.

In other words, help is available, but that help may cost money. Parents should attempt a careful analysis of expected investment advice charges, money management charges, tax preparation charges, and attorney fees when considering naming a family member as trustee of a special needs trust. They should compare these charges to the commissions and extra charges that a bank or trust company might charge to serve as trustee, as well as the usually lower commissions charged by nonprofit pooled trusts.

After you have considered all of these factors, please call our office to schedule a follow-up conference to discuss your thoughts about what might be the appropriate structure of the special needs trust we are creating and who you believe might be the best fit for each role. Thank you—we look forward to working with you on this matter.

Sincerely,
[Firm Name]

[Attorney Name]

APPENDIX L

Special Needs Alliance Trustees Handbook

Administering a Special Needs Trust

A Handbook For Trustees
(2022 Edition)

SNA
SPECIAL NEEDS ALLIANCE
Attorneys for special needs planning.

Administering a Special Needs Trust
TABLE OF CONTENTS

Administering a Special Needs Trust: A Handbook for Trustees

Introduction and Definition of Terms

"Special Needs" trusts are complicated and can be hard to understand and administer. They are like other trusts in many respects—the general rules of trust accounting, law and taxation apply—but unlike more familiar trusts in other respects. The very notion of "more familiar" types of trusts will, for many, be amusing—most people have no particular experience dealing with formal trust arrangements, and special needs trusts are often established for the benefit of individuals who would not otherwise expect to have experience with trust concepts.

The essential purpose of a special needs trust is usually to improve the quality of an individual's life without disqualifying him or her from eligibility for public benefits. Therefore, one of the central duties of the trustee of a special needs trust is to understand what public benefits programs might be available to the beneficiary and how receipt of income, or provision of food or shelter, might affect eligibility. Because there are numerous programs, competing (and sometimes even conflicting) eligibility rules, and at least two different types of special needs trusts to contend with, the entire area is fraught with opportunities to make mistakes. Because the stakes are often so high—the public benefits programs may well be providing all the necessities of life to the beneficiary—a good understanding of the rules and programs is critically important.

> The essential purpose of a special needs trust is usually to improve the quality of an individual's life without disqualifying him or her from eligibility to receive public benefits.

Before delving into a detailed discussion of special needs trust principles, it might be useful to define a few terms:

GRANTOR (sometimes "Settlor" or "Trustor")—the person who establishes the trust and generally the person whose assets fund the trust. There might be more than one grantor for a given trust. The tax agency may define the term differently than the public benefits agency. Special needs trusts can make this term more confusing than other types of trusts, since the true grantor for some purposes may not be the same as the person signing the trust instrument. If, for example, a parent creates a trust for the benefit of a child with a disability, and the parent's own money funds the trust, the parent is the grantor. In another case, where a parent has established a special needs trust to handle settlement proceeds from a personal injury lawsuit or improperly directed inheritance, the minor child (through a guardian) or an adult child will be the grantor, even though he or she did not decide to establish the trust or sign any trust documents.

TRUSTEE—the person who manages trust assets and administers the trust provisions. Once again, there may be two (or more) trustees acting at the same time. The grantor(s) may also be the trustee(s) in some cases. The trustee may be a professional trustee (such as a bank trust department or a lawyer), or may be a family member or trusted adviser—though it may be difficult to qualify a non-professional to serve as trustee.

BENEFICIARY—the person for whose benefit the trust is established. The beneficiary of a special needs trust will usually (but not always) be disabled. While a beneficiary may also act as trustee in some types of trusts, a special needs trust beneficiary will almost never be able to act as trustee.

DISABILITY—for most purposes involving special needs trusts, "disability" refers to the standard used to determine eligibility for Social Security Disability Insurance or Supplemental Security Income benefits: the inability to perform any substantial gainful employment.

INCAPACITY (sometimes Incompetence)—although "incapacity" and "incompetence" are not interchangeable, for our purposes they may both refer to the inability of a trustee to manage the trust, usually because of mental limitations. Incapacity is usually important when applied to the trustee (rather than the beneficiary), since the trust will ordinarily provide a mechanism for transition of power to a successor trustee if the original trustee becomes unable to manage the trust. Incapacity of a beneficiary may sometimes be important as well. Not every disability will result in a finding of incapacity; it is possible for a special needs trust beneficiary to be disabled, but not mentally incapacitated. Minors are considered to be incapacitated as a matter of law. The age of majority differs slightly from state to state, though it is 18 in all but a handful of states.

REVOCABLE TRUST—refers to any trust which is, by its own terms, revocable and/or amendable, meaning able to be undone, or changed. Many trusts in common use today are revocable, but special needs trusts are usually irrevocable, meaning permanent or irreversible.

IRREVOCABLE TRUST—means any trust which was established as irrevocable (that is, no one reserved the power to revoke the trust) or which has become irrevocable (for example, because of the death of the original grantor).

SOCIAL SECURITY DISABILITY INSURANCE—sometimes referred to as SSDI or SSD, this benefit program is available to individuals with a disability who either have sufficient work history prior to becoming disabled or are entitled to receive benefits by virtue of being a dependent or survivor of a disabled, retired, or deceased insured worker. There is no "means" test for SSDI eligibility, and so special needs trusts may not be necessary for some beneficiaries—they can qualify for entitlements like SSD and Medicare even though they receive income or have available resources. SSDI beneficiaries may also, however, qualify for SSI (see below) and/or Medicaid benefits, requiring protection of their assets and income to maintain eligibility. Of course, just because a beneficiary's benefits are not means-tested, it does not follow that the beneficiary will not benefit from the protection of a trust for other reasons.

SUPPLEMENTAL SECURITY INCOME—better known by the initials "SSI," this benefit program is available to low-income individuals who are disabled, blind or elderly and have limited income and few assets. SSI eligibility rules form the basis for most other government program rules, and so they become the central focus for much special needs trust planning and administration.

MEDICARE—one of the two principal health care programs operated and funded by government—in this case, the federal government. Medicare benefits are available to all those age 65 and over (provided only that they would be entitled to receive Social Security benefits if they chose to retire, whether or not they actually are retired) and those under 65 who have been receiving SSDI for at least two years. Medicare eligibility may forestall the need for or usefulness of a special needs trust. Medicare recipients without substantial assets or income may find that they have a difficult time paying for medications (which historically have not been covered by Medicare but began to be partially covered in 2004) or long-term care (which remains largely outside Medicare's list of benefits).

MEDICAID—the second major government-run health care program. Medicaid differs from Medicare in three important ways: it is run by state governments (though partially funded by federal payments), it is available to those who meet financial eligibility requirements rather than being based on the age of the recipient, and it covers all necessary medical care (though it is easy to argue that Medicaid's definition of "necessary" care is too narrow). Because it is a "means-tested" health care program, its continued availability is often the central focus of special needs trust administration. Because Medicare covers such a small portion of long-term care costs, Medicaid eligibility becomes centrally important for many persons with disabilities.

The Most Important Distinction

Two entirely different types of trusts are usually lumped together as "special needs" trusts. The two trust types will be treated differently for tax purposes, for benefit determinations, and for court involvement. For most of the discussion that follows, it will be necessary to first distinguish between the two types of trusts. The distinction is further complicated by the fact that the grantor (the person establishing the trust, and the easiest way to distinguish between the two trust types) is not always the person who actually signs the trust document.

"Self-Settled" Special Needs Trusts

Some trusts are established by the beneficiary (or by someone acting on his or her behalf) with the beneficiary's funds for the purpose of retaining or obtaining eligibility for public benefits—such a trust is usually referred to as a "self-settled" special needs trust. The beneficiary might, for example, have received an outright inheritance, or won a lottery. By far the most common source of funds for "self-settled" special needs trusts, however, is proceeds from a lawsuit—often (but not always) a lawsuit over the injury that resulted in the disability. Another common scenario requiring a person with a disability to establish a self-settled trust is when they receive a direct inheritance from a well-intentioned, but ill-advised relative.

A given trust may be treated as having been "established" by the beneficiary even if the beneficiary is completely unable to execute documents, and even if a court, family member, or lawyer representing the beneficiary actually signed the trust documents. The key test in determining whether a trust is self-settled is to determine whether the beneficiary had the right to outright possession of the proceeds prior to the act establishing the trust. If so, public benefits eligibility rules will treat the beneficiary as having set up the trust even though the actual implementation may have been undertaken by someone else acting on their behalf. Virtually all special needs trusts established with funds recovered in litigation or through a direct inheritance will be "self-settled" trusts.

Self-settled special needs trusts are different from third-party trusts in two important ways. First, self-settled trusts must include a provision directing the trustee, if the trust contains any funds upon the death of the beneficiary, to pay back anything the state Medicaid program has paid for the beneficiary. Second, in many states, the rules governing permissible distributions for self-settled special needs trusts

continued on page 6

continued from page 5

are significantly more restrictive than those controlling third-party special needs trusts.

Because Social Security law specifically describes self-settled special needs trusts, these instruments are sometimes referred to by the statutory section authorizing transfers to such trusts and directing that trust assets will not be treated as available and countable for SSI purposes. That statutory section is 42 U.S.C. §1396p(d)(4)(A), and so self-settled special needs trusts are sometimes called, simply, "d4A" trusts.

"Third-party" Special Needs Trusts

The second type of special needs trust is one established by someone other than the person with disabilities (usually, but not always, a parent) with assets that never belonged to the beneficiary. It is often used, when proper planning is done for a disabled person's family, to hold an inheritance or gift. Without planning, a well-meaning family member might simply leave an inheritance to an individual with a disability. Even though it may be possible to set up a trust after the fact, the funds will have been legally available to the beneficiary. That means that any trust will probably be a "self-settled" special needs trust, even though the funds came from a third party.

> Some trusts are established by the beneficiary for the purpose of retaining or obtaining eligibility for public benefits with the beneficiary's funds. By far the most common source of funds for "self-settled" special needs trusts is proceeds from a lawsuit—often (but not always) a lawsuit over the injury that resulted in the disability.

Parents, grandparents and others with the foresight to leave funds in a third party special needs trust will provide significantly better benefits to the beneficiary who has a disability. This type of trust will not need to include a "payback" provision for Medicaid benefits upon the beneficiary's death. During the beneficiary's life, the kinds of payments the trust can make will usually be more generous and flexible.

The "Sole Benefit" Trust

Although there are two primary types of special needs trusts, there is actually a third type that might be appropriate under certain unusual circumstances. Because Medicaid rules permit applicants to make unlimited gifts to or "for the sole benefit of" disabled children or spouses, some individuals with assets may choose to establish a special needs trust for a child or grandchild with disabilities in hopes of securing eligibility for Medicaid for both themselves as grantor and for the disabled beneficiary. A number of states are very restrictive in their interpretation of the "sole benefit" requirement, so that such trusts are rarely seen. In many ways they look like a hybrid of the two other trust types; they may be taxed and treated as third-party trusts, but require a payback provision like a self-settled trust (at least in some states).

The Second Most Important Distinction

Once the type of trust is determined, the next important issue is discerning the type of government program providing benefits. Some programs (like SSDI and Medicare) do not impose financial eligibility requirements; a beneficiary receiving income and all his or her medical care from those two programs might not need a special needs trust at all, or might benefit from more flexibility given to the trustee. A recipient of SSI and/or Medicaid, however, may need more restrictive language in the trust document and closer attention on the part of the trustee.

SSDI/Medicare Recipients

Neither Social Security Disability Insurance benefits nor Medicare are "means–tested." Consequently, it may be unnecessary to create a special needs trust for someone who receives benefits only from those two programs. After 24 months of SSDI eligibility, the beneficiary will qualify for Medicare benefits as well, so it may be appropriate to provide special needs provisions to get the SSDI recipient through that two-year period, during which he or she may rely on Medicaid for medical care. Restrictive special needs trust language may actually work against an SSDI beneficiary if it prevents distribution of cash to the beneficiary in all circumstances; an SSDI recipient will almost always benefit from broad language giving more discretion to the trustee.

Some SSDI/Medicare recipients may also receive SSI and/or Medicaid benefits. It may be critically important for those individuals to have strict special needs language controlling use of any assets or income that would otherwise be available. As the Medicare prescription drug benefit evolves over the next few years, this concern may be somewhat lessened—but for the moment, it remains true that availability of the drug coverage provided by Medicaid is critically important to many Medicare recipients.

Even an SSDI/Medicare beneficiary who does not receive any SSI or Medicaid benefits may be a good candidate for special needs trust planning. Future developments in public benefits programs, including housing, are uncertain, but constant budget pressure may well make benefits now taken for granted completely or partially indexed to income and/or assets in the future. Medical conditions also change, of course, and some persons with disabilities living in the community who presently receive adequate support from

Medicare may one day become dependent on Medicaid for services not available under Medicare–like long term care.

SSI/Medicaid Recipients

Most special needs trust beneficiaries are eligible for (or seeking eligibility for) Supplemental Security Income payments. In many states, receipt of SSI payments automatically qualifies one for Medicaid eligibility. Many other government programs explicitly rely on SSI eligibility rules as well, so that SSI eligibility rules become the central concern for those charged with administering special needs trusts.

Veterans' Benefits

"Veterans' benefits" is the term used to describe the benefits available to veterans, the surviving spouses, children or parents of a deceased veteran, dependents of disabled veterans, active duty military service members, and members of the Reserves or National Guard. These benefits are administered by the U.S. Department of Veterans Affairs ("VA").

Parents, grandparents and others with the foresight to leave funds in a third-party special needs trust will provide significantly better benefits to a beneficiary with disabilities.

The benefits available to veterans include monetary compensation (based on individual unemployability or at least ten-percent disability from a service-connected condition), pension (if permanently and totally disabled or over the age of 65 and have limited income and net worth), health care, vocational rehabilitation and employment, education and training, home loans and life insurance. Although the pension is available to low-income veterans, it is important to note that some income, such as child's SSI or wages earned by dependent children, is excluded when determining the veteran's annual income. Also keep in mind that a service-connected disability payment will not offset SSDI, but any VA disability payment will offset SSI.

The benefits available to dependents and survivors of the veteran include Dependency and Indemnity Compensation ("DIC") and, in certain circumstances, home loans.

Transferring a VA recipient's assets into a special needs trust may not be fully effective. According to VA interpretation, the assets of such a trust will be counted as part of the claimant's net worth when calculating an improved pension. It is important to remember that the VA may place a "freeze" on new enrollees in order to manage the rapid influx of new veterans or older veterans who did not previously enroll for services. Therefore, it is important to evaluate current and future need for VA services in order to anticipate and plan for a situation where a person is otherwise eligible for VA benefits but, due to a freeze, cannot receive services. Under a new law, attorneys must become accredited with the VA to advise clients in this area.

Subsidized Housing

FEDERAL SUBSIDIZED HOUSING

The U.S. Department of Housing and Urban Development ("HUD") provides opportunities to low-income individuals and families to rent property at a cost that is lower than the open market. This is especially important to those people who are expected to pay for their shelter costs (rent or mortgage, plus utilities) with their insufficient SSI income. There are two issues to consider when evaluating the role of special needs trusts and subsidized housing: the initial eligibility for subsidized housing and the rent determination.

Eligibility for subsidized housing depends on the family's annual income. Annual income includes earned income, SSI, SSDI, pension, unemployment compensation, alimony, and child support, among other items. Annual income also includes unearned income, which is comprised, in part, of interest generated by assets. If the family has net family assets in excess of $5,000, the annual income includes the greater of the actual income derived from all net family assets or a percentage of the value of such assets based on the current passbook savings rate, as determined by HUD.

Assets that are not included as income upon receipt are lump sums, such as inheritances and insurance settlements for losses (although the income they generate will be countable), reimbursement for medical expenses, PASS set-asides, work training programs funded by HUD and the income of a live-in aide.

In general, to qualify for federal subsidized housing, an individual's countable income may not exceed eighty percent of the median income in the area to be considered "low income", and the individual's income may not exceed fifty percent of the median income to be considered "very low income". The result is a disparity in eligibility depending on where the person resides within the county, state, and region of the country.

There is no asset limit to be eligible for federal subsidized housing, although as described above, if countable assets are greater than $5,000, the interest income generated will be counted towards eligibility. If a person transfers an asset for less than its fair market value, then HUD will treat the asset as if it were still owned by the individual for two years after the transfer. HUD will assume that the asset generates income at the passbook rate and will include that income in calculating the individual's rent. Therefore, it is very likely that HUD will treat transfers to a special needs trust as a transfer for less than fair market value and, for the next two years, will include

continued on page 8

continued from page 7

the interest generated by the special needs trust as income to the individual, either at the passbook rate or the actual earnings, whichever is greater.

Special Needs Trusts are excluded from family assets and the income generated by the trust assets is not included once the two-year penalty period has expired. It is important to note that, similar to other programs such as Medicaid and SSI, "regular" distributions from a special needs trust, even if made to a third-party provider, will be treated as countable income, even if used for non-food and shelter items.

> In many states, receipt of SSI payments automatically qualifies one for Medicaid eligibility. Many other government programs explicitly rely on SSI eligibility rules as well, so that SSI eligibility rules become the central concern for those charged with administering special needs trusts.

The second issue relating to subsidized housing and a special needs trust is determining the monthly rent. Generally, an individual/family's rent will be thirty percent of their adjusted gross income. Similar to treatment under the threshold eligibility rules, the special needs trust and the income generated by trust assets are excluded, but "regular" distributions made directly to the beneficiary (as opposed to a third-party provider of goods or services) will be considered as income.

SECTION 8

Section 8 is a voucher program that is administered by HUD but managed by local public housing authorities ("PHA") or metropolitan housing authorities ("MHA"). The tenant pays their rent, typically thirty percent of their net adjusted income, to the landlord. The PHA pays the remaining balance due, which is called the voucher, to the landlord. The rent is based on the market value for the area and established by the PHA according to payment standards issued by HUD.

While a family member generally cannot serve as a Section 8 landlord, it is possible for a special needs trust to do so, even if the trustee is a family member. Although there are special rules applicable to a Section 8 landlord, it can be a beneficial relationship. The trust beneficiary would pay rent to the trustee (using the thirty percent of income rule) and the PHA would pay the remainder to the trustee.

It is important to investigate how your local housing authority's rules differ from the general rules listed above.

Temporary Assistance for Needy Families ("TANF")

TANF provides assistance and work opportunities to needy families. TANF is administered locally by the states, but is overseen by The Office of Family Assistance ("OFA"), which is located in the United States Department of Health and Human Services, Administration for Children and Families. TANF is a result of combining two other programs: Aid to Families with Dependent Children ("AFDC") and Job Opportunities and Basic Skills Training ("JOBS"). Because TANF is administered on a local level, the program and eligibility rules vary greatly from state to state. However, it is safe to assume that distributions directly made to the beneficiary of a special needs trust, or to the beneficiary's family if a minor, may be considered income and will impact eligibility for TANF.

Other Means-Tested Benefits Programs

State supplements to SSI and other government benefit programs, like vocational rehabilitation services, also play important roles in the lives of many individuals with disabilities. Because the welter of eligibility programs is confusing and the reach of most other programs is not as broad as those described in detail here, those other programs are not described in any depth. In analyzing the proper approach to establishment or administration of a special needs trust, however, care should be taken to consider all the available program resources and restrictions on use of trust funds mandated by those programs.

Eligibility Rules for Means- Tested Programs

As previously noted, the primary program with financial eligibility restrictions is SSI, the Supplemental Security Income program. Because the concepts are central to an understanding of other eligibility rules, and because many other programs explicitly utilize SSI standards, the SSI rules become the most important ones to grasp. They are described here in a general way, with a few notations where other programs (particularly long-term care Medicaid) differ from the SSI rules.

Income

SSI eligibility requires limited income and assets. SSI rules have a simple way of distinguishing between income and assets: Money received in a given month is income in that month, and any portion of that income remaining on the first day of the next month becomes an asset. SSI rules also distinguish between what is "countable" or "excluded," "regular" or "irregular," and "unearned" or "earned" income. "Countable" income means that it is used to compute eligibility and benefit amount. "Excluded" means that it is not counted. "Regular" means that it is received on a periodic basis, at least two or more times per quarter or in consecutive months, and "irregular" or "infrequent" means that it is not periodic or predictable. "Unearned" means that it is passively received, such as SSDI benefits or bank account interest. "Earned" means that work is performed in exchange for the income. An SSI recipient is permitted to receive a small amount of any kind of income ($20 per month) without reducing benefits. That amount is sometimes referred to as the SSI "disregard" amount.

Each classification or grouping has a somewhat different rule, and it is an understatement to call these income rules "confusing." Any unearned income reduces the SSI benefit by the amount of the income, so investment income or gifted money simply reduces the benefit dollar for dollar, less the disregard. Earned income is treated more favorably, only reducing benefits by about half of the earnings. This is designed to encourage SSI recipients to return to the workforce. Keeping in mind that disability is defined as "unable to perform any substantial gainful activity," it is easy to see that any significant amount of earned income will eventually imperil SSI eligibility and, since trust administration does not usually involve earned income in any event, we will not attempt to deal with those issues here.

SSI also has a concept of "in-kind support and maintenance" (ISM) that is central to much understanding of special needs trust administration. Any payment from a third party (including a trust) for necessities of life—food or shelter (note that the federal government deleted "clothing" from the list of necessities in March 2005) to a third party provider of goods or services—will be treated as countable income, albeit subject to special rules for calculating its effect.

The effect of receiving ISM on SSI benefits is different from the receipt of cash distributions. Where as cash payments reduce the SSI payment dollar for dollar, ISM reduces the benefit by the lesser of the presumed maximum value of the items provided or an amount calculated by dividing the maximum SSI benefit by three and adding the $20 disregard amount.

For 2022 the maximum federal SSI benefit for a single person is $841. One-third of that amount is $283.33, and so the maximum reduction in benefits caused by ISM (no matter how high the value) is $303.33 per month. The meaning of that confusing collection of information is best illustrated using an example (CAUTION: some states provide SSI supplemental payments that affect this calculation).

Consider John, who is disabled as a result of his serious mental illness. He has no work history, and he does not qualify for SSDI. He is an adult, living on his own. He qualifies for the maximum federal SSI benefit of $841; he lives in a state which does not provide an SSI supplement.

If John's mother gives him $100 cash per month (for food and cigarettes), he is required to report that as countable unearned income each month. Although SSI may take two or three months to accomplish the adjustment, the program will eventually withhold $80 ($100 minus the $20 disregard) from his benefit for each month in which his mother makes a cash gift to him. The same result will obtain if John's mother is trustee of a special needs trust for John and the cash comes from that trust.

If, however, John's mother does not give him the $100 directly, but instead purchases $70 worth of food and $30 worth of cigarettes each month, only the food will affect his SSI payment—reducing it by $50 ($70 minus the $20 disregard). If she purchases $20 worth of food and $80 worth of cigarettes, there will be no effect at all—the food purchase is within the $20 monthly disregard amount. Similarly, if she purchases $20 worth of cigarettes and $30 worth of movie tickets, there will be no effect—provided that the movie tickets cannot be turned in for cash (because if the movie tickets can be converted to cash, John could—even if he does not—convert the movie tickets into payment for food or shelter).

In other words, the effect of John's mother's payments to him or for his benefit changes with the nature of her payments. Any cash she provides to him (over the $20 monthly amount ignored by SSI) reduces his SSI payment directly. Direct purchase of items other than food or shelter does not affect his SSI, so long as the purchased items cannot be converted to food or shelter. Finally, any payment she makes for food or shelter reduces his SSI check as well, but not as harshly as cash payments directly to John.

Now suppose that John's mother decides to give up on trying to work around the strictures of SSI rules, and she simply pays his rent at an adult care facility that provides his meals. Assume that the facility costs her $1500 per month, which she pays from her own pocket. Because of the ISM rules, John's SSI benefit will be reduced by only $303.33 per month, and so his SSI check will be $540.67. Critically important, however, John will still qualify for Medicaid benefits in most states because he receives some amount of SSI. If the adult care home payment comes from a special needs trust for John's benefit, the same result will occur, assuming that the room and board portion of the payment exceeds $303.33. Incidentally, the same result will also obtain if John's mother simply takes him in and allows him to live and eat with her without charging him rent.

Now assume that John does have a work history before becoming disabled, and that he qualifies to receive $600 per month from SSDI. Because he has been receiving SSDI for more than two years, he also qualifies for Medicare. Because his countable income is less than $841, he continues to receive $261 in SSI benefits ($20 of the SSD is disregarded), and qualifies for Medicaid as well (we will ignore the effect

continued on page 10

continued from page 9

of the QMB and SLMB programs for qualified, special low-income Medicare beneficiaries, and the Medicare Part B premium which would ordinarily be withheld from his SSDI check). Now if John's mother pays his rent at the adult care home, or takes him into her own home, he will lose his SSI altogether—since he is receiving less than $303.33 per month from SSI, the effect of the ISM rules will be to knock him off the program. Unless he separately qualifies for Medicaid, he will also lose his coverage under that program. The income strictures are the same or similar for other programs, with one important exception. In some states, but not all, eligibility for community or long-term care Medicaid is also dependent on countable income. The income tests vary. In some, you can "spend down" excess income over the limit to become eligible. In others, if countable income exceeds the benefit "cap" (like SSI), you cannot become eligible at all.

Some states also attempt to limit expenditures from self-settled (and even third-party) special needs trusts, and can require amendments to the language of those trusts in order to allow eligibility. While a good argument can be made that the Medicaid program does not have that ability, as a practical matter, the trustee of the special needs trust will have to either litigate that issue or acquiesce in the Medicaid agency's demands.

Assets

The limitation on assets for SSI eligibility may be somewhat easier to master, or at least to describe. A single person must have no more than $2,000 in available resources in order to qualify for SSI. Some types of assets are not counted as available (called "non-countable"), including the beneficiary's home, one automobile, household furnishings, prepaid burial amounts plus up to $1500 set aside for funeral expenses (or life insurance in that amount), tools of the beneficiary's trade, and a handful of other, less important items. Each of these categories of assets is subject to special rules and exceptions, so it is easy to become tangled in the asset eligibility structure.

Deeming

The SSI program considers portions of the income and assets of non-disabled, ineligible parents of minor disabled children and of an ineligible spouse living with the SSI recipient as available, and countable for eligibility purposes. This is called "deeming". A certain portion of the ineligible person's income and assets is considered as necessary for his or her own living expenses, and therefore is excluded.

As soon as a child reaches age 18, parental deeming no longer occurs, even if the child continues to live in the household. If spouses voluntarily separate and live in different households, then deeming from the separate spouse or parent also ends. However, in both instances, if the separate person continues to provide support or maintenance to the SSI eligible individual, it will still count as income as described above unless a Court orders it to be deposited directly into the trust. There is also a limited exception to all parental deeming for a severely disabled minor child returning home from an institution or whose condition would otherwise qualify them for institutionalization, which is called a waiver.

"I Want to Buy a..." or "I Want to Pay for..."

What do these complicated rules mean for expenditures from a special needs trust? In-kind purchases, meaning purchase of goods or services for the benefit of the beneficiary, only potentially affect the SSI benefit amount, and not Medicaid benefits, although the Medicaid agency may restrict expenditures for approved things. There are a number of specific purchases that frequently recur:

Home, Upkeep and Utilities

Keep in mind that SSI's in-kind support and maintenance (ISM) rules deal specifically with payments for "food and shelter." The Social Security Administration includes only these items as food and shelter:

1. Food
2. Mortgage (including property insurance required by the mortgage holder)
3. Real property taxes (less any tax rebate/credit)
4. Rent
5. Heating fuel
6. Gas
7. Electricity
8. Water
9. Sewer
10. Garbage removal

The rules make special note of the fact that condominium assessments may in some cases be at least partial payments for water, sewer, garbage removal and the like.

In other words, a payment for rent will implicate the ISM rules, as will monthly mortgage payments. The outright purchase of a home, whether in the name of the beneficiary or the trust, will not cause loss of SSI (although it may reduce the beneficiary's SSI benefit for the single month in which the home is purchased). This brings up another consideration. Purchase of a home in the trust's name will subject it to a Medicaid "payback" requirement on the death of the beneficiary, whereas purchase in the name of the beneficiary may allow other planning that will avoid the home becoming part of the payback. This complicated interplay of trust rules, ISM definition, estate-recovery rules, and home ownership makes this area of special needs trust administration particularly fraught with difficulty.

However, the Medicaid state agency's treatment of distributions from special needs trusts may differ from the Social Security interpretation—especially when the beneficiary of a self-settled trust is eligible for Medicaid benefits. For example, contrary to putting the house in the individual's name, a state may require that any purchase of a home by such a trust would result in title being held in the trust's name, thereby ensuring that the state will at least receive the proceeds from the sale of the residence upon the death of the beneficiary.

Clothing

Until March 7, 2005, purchase of clothing by a trust was considered as ISM for SSI, similar to shelter and food. Since then, a clothing purchase for the beneficiary will not affect the benefit amount or eligibility, whether the clothing in question is special garments related to the disability or just ordinary street clothes and shoes. Not all state Medicaid regulations reflect this change.

> As soon as a child reaches age 18, parental deeming no longer occurs even if the child continues to live in the household.

Phone, Cable, and Internet Services

Other than those utilities listed above, there is no federal limitation on utility payments. In other words, the trust can pay for cable, telephone, high-speed internet connection, newspaper, and other "utilities" not on the list.

Vehicle, Insurance, Maintenance, Gas

Purchase of a vehicle and maintenance (including gas and insurance) is permitted under federal law. Note that there is a mechanical difficulty in providing gasoline without providing cash that could be converted to food or shelter. One technique which has worked well has been to arrange for the beneficiary to have a gas-company credit card. Because eligibility for such cards is easier to meet, and because the cards cannot be used to purchase groceries, administration of the credit account is easier to set up and monitor, and the card can then be billed directly to the trust.

Some state Medicaid agencies put limitations on the value, type, and title ownership of vehicles, such as only allowing a vehicle valued at up to $5,000, handicapped-equipped, or requiring a lien in favor of the payback trust on the title. The SSI program does not specifically require or monitor such limitations.

Pre-paid Burial/Funeral Arrangements

Nothing in federal law prohibits or restricts use of special needs trust funds for purchase of burial and funeral arrangements during the beneficiary's lifetime— except to the extent that the beneficiary has access to the funds used to pay for the arrangements, and thereby subject to the asset limitations affecting SSI recipients. State Medicaid agencies may limit the value of the burial contract. It is important to ask for an "irrevocable, pre-paid" funeral plan.

Tuition, Books, Tutoring

No limit under either federal or state law. This is an excellent use of special needs trust funds.

Travel and Entertainment

Once again, no limit except that there may be some concern about payment for hotels. When the beneficiary still maintains a residence at home, the hotel stay and restaurant may be considered "shelter" and "food" expenses. Some states may impose limitations on companion travel not found in federal law. These might include not allowing recipients to have the special needs trust pay for more than one traveling companion, the companion must be necessary to provide care, and the companion may not be a person obligated to support the beneficiary such as a minor beneficiary's parent. Note that foreign travel can have two other adverse effects: (1) airline tickets to foreign destinations, if refundable, will be treated as being convertible into food and shelter, and (2) if an SSI recipient is out of the country for more than a month, he or she may lose eligibility until return. For those reasons, foreign travel, unlike domestic travel, usually must be limited in time.

Household Furnishings and Furniture

The trust can be used to purchase appliances, furniture, fixtures and the like. Before March 2005, there was a theoretical concern in the SSI program that the value of household furnishings might exceed an arbitrary limit and affect the beneficiary's eligibility; that value limit has now been removed.

Television, Computers and Electronics

There is no specific limitation on purchase of household televisions or other electronic devices, although under SSI rules the individual is only allowed to own "ordinary household goods" that are not kept for collectible value and are used on a regular basis. The trust can also provide a computer for the beneficiary, plus software and upgrades.

Durable Medical Equipment

There is no federal limitation on any medical related equipment, but individual states may limit purchase of some equipment as not being "necessary." Problem areas could be if the equipment could also be considered as recreational, such as a heated swimming pool needed for arthritic or other joint conditions.

continued on page 12

continued from page 11

Care Management

No federal limitation, but many states attempt to limit payments for care or management if made to a family member or other relative, especially if there is an obligation of support (e.g., parents of minor children).

Therapy, Medications, Alternative Treatments

Same principle as durable medical equipment, above, so long as the state does not regulate the treatment, there is no federal limitation.

Taxes

No federal limitation, but states may attempt to direct trust language on what taxes can be paid for, such as taxes incurred as a result of trust assets or at the death of the beneficiary. Since it is difficult to imagine an SSI or Medicaid beneficiary having significant non-trust income, it is hard to see how this limitation is so much troublesome as it is quarrelsome.

Legal, Guardianship and Trustee Fees

At least some states allow legal, guardianship, and trustee fees to be paid from the trust, although some federal law indicates that payment of guardian's fees or guardian's attorney fees may really benefit the guardian and not the beneficiary. Payments for trust administration expenses, including the trust's attorney's fees, are clearly permissible under both federal and state law, and are rarely limited beyond reasonableness standards.

> It is generally beneficial for a self-settled special needs trust to be a grantor trust. This is true because the tax rates for non-grantor trusts are tightly compressed, and the highest marginal tax rate on income is reached very quickly for trusts.

Loans, Credit, Debit and Gift Cards

Receipt of a "loan" will not count as income for the SSI or Medicaid programs, which means that a trust can make a loan of cash directly to a beneficiary. There are rules that must be followed for loans to be valid and non-countable. There must be an enforceable agreement at the time that the loan is made that the loan will be paid back at some point, which usually means that it should be in writing. The agreement to pay back cannot be based on a future contingency such as, "I only have to pay it back if I win the lottery..." Finally, the loan must be considered as "feasible," meaning that there is a reasonable expectation that the beneficiary will have the means at some point to pay back the loan.

If a loan is forgiven, then it would count as income at that time. Also, if the beneficiary still has the loaned amount in the following month, it will then count as a resource. However, school loans are not countable as income or as a resource so long as the funds are spent for tuition, room and board, and other education-related expenses within nine months of receipt.

Since goods or services purchased with a credit card are actually a "loan" that must be paid back to the credit card company, they are also not considered as income to the beneficiary at time of purchase. As long as the beneficiary doesn't sell the goods for cash, there is also the added advantage that the trust can pay back the credit card company without the payment counting as income, except for purchases that are considered as food or shelter. Food and shelter related purchases use the same ISM countable income rules (and particularly the countable income limits) described above.

Use of a debit card by a beneficiary when purchases are made for payment through a trust-funded bank account is income to the beneficiary for the amount accessed. The total amount in the account available to be accessed could possibly be a countable resource. Is a gift card purchased by a trust and provided to a beneficiary considered to be a distribution of income, a line of credit to a vendor (similar to a credit card), or just access for in-kind purchase of goods or services on behalf of a beneficiary by the trust? SSI rules are not yet clear on this point, and it is probable that different Social Security and Medicaid offices will treat the use of debit and gift cards differently until precise guidelines are provided by the agencies. The safe approach is to use them in a very limited way; if they are to be used at all, keep receipts for all special needs items, and be prepared for adverse treatment.

Trust Administration and Accounting

Actual administration of a special needs trust is in most respects similar to administration of any other trust. A trustee has a general obligation to account to beneficiaries and other interested parties. Tax returns may need to be filed (though not always), and tax filing requirements will be based on the tax rules, not special needs trust rules. Some special needs trusts, but by no means all, will be subject to court supervision and control.

Trustee's Duties

As with general trust law requirements, the trustee of a special needs trust has an obligation not to self-deal, not to delegate the trustee's duties impermissibly, not to favor either income or remainder beneficiaries over one another, and to invest trust assets prudently. The obligations of a trustee are well-discussed in several centuries of legal precedent, and cannot be taken lightly. Legal counsel (and professional investment, tax and accounting assistance) will be required in administration of almost every special needs trust.

A few cardinal trust rules bear special mention:

NO SELF-DEALING

As with other trusts, the trustee of a special needs trust is prohibited from self-dealing. That means no investment of trust assets in the trustee's business or assets, no mingling of trust and personal assets, no borrowing from the trust, no purchase of goods or services (by the trust) from the trustee (other than, of course, trust administration services), and no sale of trust assets to the trustee. The same strictures also apply to the trustee's immediate family members, and the existence of an appraisal, or the favorable terms of a transaction, do not change these rules.

IMPARTIALITY

Because the trust has both an "income" beneficiary (the person with disabilities) and a "remainder" beneficiary (the state, in the case of a Medicaid payback trust, or the individuals who will receive assets when the income beneficiary dies), the trustee has a necessarily divided loyalty. It is important to remain impartial as between the trust's beneficiaries. Thus, investment in assets exclusively designed to maximize income at the expense of growth, or vice versa, may violate the trustee's duty to the negatively affected class of beneficiaries. Note that a trust may, by its terms, make clear that the interests of one or the other class of beneficiaries should be paramount—though such language will probably earn the disapproval of the Medicaid agency in any self-settled trust which must be submitted to Medicaid for approval.

> A trustee has a general obligation to account to beneficiaries and other interested parties. Tax returns may need to be filed (though not always), and tax filing requirements will be based on the tax rules, not special needs trust rules.

DELEGATION

Generally speaking, a trustee may delegate functions but may not avoid liability by doing so. In other words, while the trustee may hire investment advisers, tax preparers and the like, he or she will remain liable for any failures by such professionals.

Some states do limit the trustee's liability. For example, in states which have adopted the Uniform Prudent Investor Act, delegating investment authority pursuant to the Act will limit the trustee's liability so that he or she will only be required to carefully select and monitor the investment adviser.

INVESTMENT

Any trustee should be familiar with the principles of Modern Portfolio Theory, with its emphasis on risk tolerance and asset diversification. A trustee who holds himself, herself, or itself out as having special expertise in investments or asset management will be held to a higher standard, but any trustee will be required to understand and implement prudent investment practices. Some courts will institute an investment policy that requires a percentage of assets to be held in fixed income investments and the remainder in securities (e.g., a 60/40 split is common).

Bond

A trustee, especially one who administers a special needs trust supervised by a probate court, may need to be bonded. Bond is a type of insurance arrangement whereby the trustee pays a premium in order to guarantee that the trustee manages the trust and carries out his or her fiduciary duties correctly. The bond premium is an acceptable expense of the trust, and need not come out of the trustee's own pocket. If the trustee fails to exercise his or her fiduciary duty and the trust loses money as a result, the insurance company that issued the bond will compensate the trust and take action to collect from the trustee.

The bond premium depends on multiple factors, including the credit history of the trustee and the value of the trust. Most corporate trustees are exempt from posting bond. Individual trustees must "post bond"; that is, provide written documentation to the probate court that the individual is bonded. The bond is typically issued for a set period of time, for example one year, and at the expiration of the time period, the trustee must pay an additional premium or show the bond issuer that bond is no longer required by the probate court.

It is possible in most states, at least when the trust is supervised by a court, to ask the court for permission to deposit the assets in a restricted or "blocked" account with a financial institution rather than posting bond. While this circumvents the issue of being bonded, the financial institution should require a certified copy of the court's order authorizing the expenditure of funds prior to making a distribution from the special needs trust. This can result in frequent in-person trips to the bank by the trustee, although it avoids the sometimes costly bond premium.

Titling Assets

The trust assets should not be titled in the beneficiary's name except in limited circumstances, such as when it is advantageous to title the home in the individual's name. Typically, the trust assets should be titled in the name of the trustee. For example, if James Jones is the trustee of the Lisa Martin Special Needs Trust, and that trust was signed

continued on page 14

continued from page 13

on March 15, 2007, then the trust assets should be titled as follows: "James Jones, Trustee of the Lisa Martin Special Needs Trust u/a/d March 15, 2007" ("u/a/d" means "under agreement dated").

It is important that most assets not be held in James Jones's or Lisa Martin's name individually. If the assets are not titled properly, then the assets may be counted as a resource, or the interest earned counted as income, by the agencies that administer means-tested government benefits, which will frustrate the purpose of the special needs trust, as well as contribute to confusion during tax preparation. Additionally, as discussed in further detail below, it may also be important to request a separate Tax ID number for the trust as well as properly title the assets.

Accounting Requirements

A trustee is required to provide adequate accounting information to beneficiaries of the trust. That requirement generally means annual accountings. While there is no specific form required for accountings if the trust is not under court supervision, it is important to provide enough information that a reader could determine the nature and amount of any payment or investment. For some trusts, a simple "check register" accounting may be sufficient, showing interest income and the names of payees, with dates and amounts. Any trust with significant assets or diverse investments, however, should provide a thorough accounting.

> The trustee of a special needs trust is prohibited from self-dealing. That means no investment of trust assets in the trustee's business or assets, no mingling of trust and personal assets, no borrowing from the trust, no purchase of goods or services (by the trust) from the trustee (other than, of course, trust administration services), and no sale of trust assets to the trustee.

Regular, complete accountings are critical. A beneficiary is generally foreclosed from later raising objections to investments or expenditures if he or she received adequate disclosure in the annual accounting at the time. In other words, thorough accounting can limit the trustee's later exposure to claims by beneficiaries, and therefore benefits the trustee.

In addition to the accounting requirements to the beneficiary, the trustee may be required to provide an annual or biennial accounting to the probate court. The trustee should use the county-specific forms available upon request from the court, and may also be required to provide the court with copies of bank statements and cancelled checks or receipts as evidence of trust distributions and deposits. This requires the trustee to be organized or be prepared to pay potentially substantial bank fees for duplicate account statements or cancelled checks.

Reporting to Social Security

The simple term "income" has different meanings in trust accounting, tax preparation, and public benefits eligibility determinations. Trustees sometimes raise concerns that thorough trust accountings (to SSI, especially) may result in suspension of benefits, or that tax return information may be used to terminate SSI or other benefits. While such things undoubtedly do occur, Social Security workers are increasingly likely to be relatively sophisticated about such distinctions, and willing to work through any problems. In a general way, then, it is better to disclose more fully to Social Security rather than withhold any information. Annual accountings of any self-settled trust naming an SSI recipient as beneficiary should be provided to Social Security. Any third-party trust which makes significant distributions for the benefit of an SSI recipient should probably be provided to Social Security, just to prevent later problems that could have been headed off. If distributions disrupt eligibility, the problem is with the distribution, not with the accounting.

If the beneficiary receives only SSDI and not any concurrent SSI, there is no point in providing accounting information to Social Security, because SSDI benefits are not means-tested. If the trust is a third-party trust, the trustee may not have any obligation to provide accounting information, though the beneficiary may (if the beneficiary receives SSI and trust distributions invoke the ISM rules) be required to do so.

Although it no longer occurs as regularly, some Social Security eligibility workers may misunderstand the effect of special needs trust expenditures or terms and reduce or eliminate benefits improperly. When this does occur, it should be possible to remedy the error, but the beneficiary may suffer for months (or years) while the system works out the problem. Far better to head off problems in advance, rather than have to spend substantial resources and time resolving them after the fact. Be aware that fees for a trustee's time spent directly dealing with Social Security on the beneficiary's behalf may be subject to approval by SSA.

Reporting to Medicaid

If the beneficiary resides in a state where the receipt of SSI results in the beneficiary also being automatically enrolled in Medicaid, then no separate accounting requirement need be made to the Medicaid agency. However, if the individual is in a state where SSI and Medicaid are not interrelated, then it may be necessary to account to both agencies. The Medicaid consumer (or their guardian) is required to notify Medicaid of a change in resources or income within a set period of time, usually as short as ten days. This includes situations where the Medicaid consumer receives an inheritance or settlement and immediately transfers the funds to a special needs trust.

The trustee of a third-party special needs trust may not have the same duty to account, but may choose to provide accounting information to Medicaid rather than risk later disqualification of the beneficiary, even though Medicaid's power to consider trust expenditures may be subject to challenge.

Reporting to the Court

Many self-settled special needs trusts will be treated in essentially the same fashion as a conservatorship or guardianship of the estate. This is so because, typically, the court was initially asked to authorize establishment of the trust. Most courts expect any trust established by the court to remain under court supervision, including bonding, seeking authority to expend funds, and filing periodic accountings.

Even if the trust does not require court accounting, some consideration should be given to seeking court involvement. One great advantage of court supervision of the trust is that each year's accounting is then final as to all items described in that accounting (provided, of course, that the appropriate notice has been given to beneficiaries who might otherwise complain about the trust's administration and other court procedural requirements are followed).

The Court may also have a set fee schedule that governs the amount the trustee can be compensated for providing trust administration services.

Modification of Trust

As explained above, a special needs trust must be irrevocable in order for the trust to be considered an exempt resource. However, that does not preclude the trust itself from permitting the trustee to amend or modify the trust in limited ways, particularly as it relates to program eligibility for the beneficiary. This is particularly important since we cannot predict future changes to the laws governing means-tested benefits. The courts may also be willing to modify or terminate a trust whose purpose has been frustrated by law changes or other factors, such as the trust assets being valued at a nominal amount.

Wrapping up the Trust

If the special needs trust is a self-settled trust with a provision requiring repayment of Medicaid expenses, it will obviously be necessary to determine the "payback" amount upon the death of the beneficiary or termination of the trust. Because Medicaid's historical experience with these trusts is still slight, state agencies may have difficulty providing a reliable and final figure. The prudent trustee will request a written statement of the amount due, including evidence showing how it was calculated and a statement of authority to make the final determination. Once any payback issues have been addressed (and remember that most third-party special needs trusts will have no requirement of repayment to the state), then termination of the trust will follow the usual requirements of tax preparation and filing, final accounting and distribution according to the trust instrument. Remember, because Social Security requires that Medicaid reimbursement and certain tax liabilities must be squared away before the trustee may even pay for the beneficiary's funeral, purchase during the beneficiary's lifetime of an irrevocable pre-paid funeral is critical.

Income Taxation of Special Needs Trusts

Special needs trusts, like other types of trusts, can complicate income tax preparation. The first question to be addressed is whether—for income tax purposes–the trust is a "grantor" trust or not. Tax rules defining "grantor" trusts are neither simple nor intuitive, but fortunately there are some easy rules of thumb to apply, and they will work for most special needs trusts.

"Grantor" Trusts

A "grantor" trust is treated for tax purposes as a transparent entity. In other words, the grantor of a "grantor" trust is treated as having received the income directly, even though the accounts are titled to the trust and all income shows up in the name of the trust.

Generally speaking, a self-settled special needs trust will be a grantor trust if a family member is the trustee. If the trust names an independent trustee it may still be a grantor trust if one of several specific provisions exists in the trust. A qualified accountant or lawyer should be able to tell whether a given trust is a grantor trust at a glance. If it is, it remains a grantor trust for its entire life—or at least until the death of the grantor (when the trust may either terminate or convert into a non-grantor trust as to its new beneficiaries). Until the trust has been reviewed by an expert, assume that it is probably a grantor trust.

It is generally beneficial for a self-settled special needs trust to be a grantor trust. This is true because the tax rates for non-grantor trusts are tightly compressed, and the highest marginal tax rate on income is reached very quickly for trusts. The practical difference will be small if the trust actually makes distributions for the benefit of the beneficiary in excess of its annual taxable income, but the proper tax reporting approach should still be followed.

TAX ID NUMBERS

A grantor trust may, but need not, obtain an Employer Identification Number (an EIN). Some attorneys and

continued on page 16

continued from page 15

accountants choose to secure an EIN in each case, while others resist doing so—either approach is defensible. Although banks, brokerage houses and other financial institutions may insist that the trust requires its own EIN, they are simply wrong. There is widespread confusion about the necessity for an EIN for irrevocable trusts, but a confident and well-informed trustee, attorney or accountant should be able to convince the financial institution that no separate EIN is required. Instead, the trustee can simply provide the financial institution with the grantor's Social Security number.

FILING TAX RETURNS

A grantor trust ordinarily will not file a separate tax return. If a grantor trust has been assigned an EIN, it may file an "informational" return. The return can include a paragraph indicating that the trust is a grantor trust, that all income is being reported on the beneficiary's individual return, and that no substantive information will be included in the fiduciary income tax return. Actually, completing the fiduciary income tax return is not an option for a grantor trust, although again there is much confusion on this point, even among some professionals.

Non-Grantor Trusts

Virtually all third-party, and some self-settled, special needs trusts will be non-grantor trusts. Because income will not be treated as having been earned by the beneficiary, a fiduciary income tax return (IRS form 1041) will be required.

TAX ID NUMBERS

A non-grantor trust will need to obtain its own EIN by filing a federal form SS-4. Nearly all third-party special needs trusts will be "complex" trusts—this designation simply means that the trust is not required to distribute all its income to the income beneficiary each year. Although the trust will be listed as "complex" on the SS-4, it may in fact alternate between "complex" and "simple" on each year's 1041.

FILING TAX RETURNS

The non-grantor trust must file a 1041 each year. All distributions for the benefit of the beneficiary are conclusively presumed to be of income first, so any trust expenditures in excess of deductions will result in a Form K-1 showing income imputed to the beneficiary. This should not cause particular concern, since Social Security (and even Medicaid) eligibility workers are increasingly likely to understand that "income" for tax purposes is different from "income" for public benefits eligibility purposes. Any tax liability incurred by the individual beneficiary as a result of this imputation can be paid by the trust, though the trustee may not have the authority to prepare and sign the individual's tax return.

Administrative and other deductible expenses on an individual tax return must reach 2% of the taxpayer's income before being deducted at all. The same is not true of a trust tax return, leading to a modest benefit to treatment as a non-grantor trust in some cases. This benefit may not offset the compressed income tax rates levied against non-grantor trusts, but each case will be different. The difficulty in determining the proper—and the best—income tax treatment is made worse when one adds the confusing option of treatment as a "Qualified Disability Trust."

Qualified Disability Trust

Beginning in 2002, Congress allowed some non-grantor special needs trusts to receive a modest income tax benefit. Trusts qualifying under Internal Revenue Code Section 642(b)(2)(C) receive a special benefit—they are granted a larger and special deduction on their federal income taxes. In tax year 2022 (that is, the taxes that will be paid in April, 2023) for example, a Qualified Disability Trust can deduct $4,400 before any tax payment is due. That figure is slated to increase each year. Once the trust deducts that amount from its income, any remaining income might then be passed through to the beneficiary's tax return; the beneficiary may well pay no tax, or a very low rate of tax.

Coupled with the greater flexibility available to non-grantor trusts in deducting administrative expenses, Qualified Disability Trust treatment may be advantageous in some cases. Typically, the Qualified Disability Trust election will be attractive when there is a fair amount of income on trust assets, and relatively few medical or other expenses incurred on behalf of the beneficiary. Careful review with a qualified income tax professional is usually necessary to determine whether to pursue Qualified Disability Trust treatment.

Seeking Professional Tax Advice

It should be apparent from this brief discussion of taxation of special needs trusts that professional tax preparation and advice are essential. Although most accountants are qualified to prepare fiduciary (trust) income tax returns, most do not have much experience in the field. A first question to ask a prospective accountant might be "How many 1041s do you typically prepare in a year?" Follow that with "Could you please explain the concept of Qualified Disability Trusts to me?" and you will quickly locate any truly proficient practitioner. You probably will not want to automatically reject an accountant who cannot tell you about Qualified Disability Trusts immediately, unless you are prepared to deal with an accountant in another city—there are simply not very many accountants or tax preparers who have ever had occasion to claim that status on any fiduciary income tax return.
As always, you can get some assistance in complicated special needs trust issues from the attorney who prepared the document, or the attorney who advises you as trustee. Members of the Special Needs Alliance® are usually among the very few who are familiar with these concepts, and your attorney may have worked with an accountant in your area who is familiar with the special tax treatment of these trusts.

For Further Reading

There are a handful of books and articles, and a growing number of websites, available to aid trustees of special needs trusts. Among our favorites:

Special Needs Trust Administration Manual: A Guide for Trustees, by Jackins, Blank, Macy and Shulman—this guide is among the best available. It was written by four Massachusetts lawyers, and is frankly focused on Massachusetts law and practice. Much of what the authors have to say, however, is applicable to special needs trusts in every state.

Special People, Special Planning: Creating a Safe Legal Haven for Families with Special Needs, by Hoyt and Pollock—provides some general advice and direction, but is more conversational than detailed. This volume also tends to focus on the "why" more than the "how", which is an important message but not as useful to someone who is already administering a special needs trust.

Special Needs Trusts: Protect Your Child's Financial Future, by Elias—this recent addition to the literature comes from Nolo Press, an organization that many lawyers find annoying at best. We disagree. This is a plain-language, straightforward explanation of special needs trusts from a lawyer who doesn't even practice in the area (his previous books for Nolo Press include explanations of bankruptcy, trademark and other areas of law).

APPENDIX M

Trust Distribution Standards (a Sampler)

1. Mandatory income, discretionary principal
Trustee shall distribute all of the income to the beneficiary, at least quarterly. In addition, trustee may from time to time distribute so much of the principal to or for the benefit of the beneficiary as the trustee shall determine, in his or her absolute discretion, to be necessary or appropriate to provide for the health, education, maintenance, or support of the beneficiary.

2. Support with ascertainable standard
Trustee shall distribute so much of the income or principal of the trust estate to or for the benefit of the beneficiary as may be required for the health, education, maintenance, or support of the beneficiary. Any income not so distributed shall be added to and become a part of the principal of the trust estate.

3. Discretionary support
Trustee may distribute so much of the income or principal to or for the benefit of the beneficiary as the trustee shall determine, in his or her absolute discretion, to be necessary for the support in reasonable comfort of the beneficiary. Any income not so distributed shall be added to and become a part of the principal of the trust estate.

4. Full discretion
Trustee may distribute so much of the income or principal of the trust estate to or for the beneficiary as the trustee may determine, in his or her sole and absolute discretion, that might improve the beneficiary's comfort or happiness. Any income not so distributed shall be added to and become a part of the principal of the trust estate.

5. Special needs discretion
Trustee shall distribute so much of the net income and principal to or for the benefit of the beneficiary as the trustee may determine, in his or her sole and absolute discretion, that might be appropriate to provide for the extra and supplemental needs of the beneficiary. In making this determination, the trustee should consider what effect any proposed distribution might have on the beneficiary's eligibility to receive public benefits, and/or the level of benefits he or she might receive after distribution, if any. [Trustee shall have the power to make any distributions he or she might deem appropriate for the beneficiary's extra and supplemental needs, even though such distribution(s) might temporarily or permanently reduce or eliminate any particular benefit, if the trustee determines that such reduction or elimination will be offset by the positive benefits to the beneficiary flowing from the considered distribution.]

APPENDIX N

ABLE Account, Special Needs, and Pooled Trust Comparison Chart[1]

1. © ABLE National Resource Center & Special Needs Alliance, reprinted with permission. Be sure to check the website for the most current version of the document at https://www.ablenrc.org/wp-content/uploads/2022/11/2022_SNT_ABLE_comparison.pdf.

The age for ABLE accounts is being raised to 46 in 2026, so be sure to check the website regularly for this and other changes.

ABLE NATIONAL RESOURCE CENTER
ACHIEVING A BETTER LIFE EXPERIENCE ACT

SNA
SPECIAL NEEDS ALLIANCE
Attorneys for special needs planning.

ABLE Account, Special Needs and Pooled Trust Comparison Chart

Individuals who work and receive Medicaid, Supplemental Security Income (SSI) or other public benefits may find it difficult to save money and still maintain their benefits. This is especially important for "means-tested" benefits, i.e., benefits in which income and countable resources of more than $2,000 are considered when determining eligibility.

Protected savings accounts make it possible for individuals to have savings / resource limits greater than $2,000 and still maintain eligibility for benefits such as Medicaid, Free Application for Federal Student Aid (FAFSA), Housing and Urban Development (HUD), Social Security Income (SSI) and the Supplemental Nutrition Assistance Program (SNAP). This fact sheet provides basic information on three options for establishing protected savings accounts: ABLE, Pooled Trust and Special Needs Trust (first and third party).

ABLE National Resource Center partnered with the Special Needs Alliance to prepare this comparison chart. The chart that follows contains a comparison tool to help determine which option(s) best meet the needs of an individual.

Achieving a Better Life Experience (ABLE)

ABLE accounts are tax-advantaged savings accounts for individuals with disabilities who had an onset of disability prior to age 26. The beneficiary of the account is the account owner. The individual and their family, friends and employers, may make direct contributions into the account using post-tax dollars up to annual limits. Some states allow for state income tax deductions for contributions made to an ABLE account.

ABLE funds can be spent on Qualified Disability Expenses (QDE) such as costs for maintaining or improving health, independence or quality of life. These include expenses for education, food, housing, transportation, employment training and support, assistive technology, personal support services, health, prevention and wellness, financial management, administrative services, legal fees, expenses for oversight and monitoring and funeral and burial expenses.

Pooled Trust

Pooled trusts are managed by nonprofit organizations that pool the assets of multiple individuals into separate sub-accounts. The agency administrator makes decisions on how to invest and disburse the funds and is responsible for meeting reporting requirements to government agencies including the Social Security Administration (SSA). In consideration of a beneficiary's public benefits, Pooled Trust funds may be authorized directly to purchase a home and to cover expenses that enhance a beneficiary's life such as cable and recreation; pre-paid funeral expenses are allowable.

Special Needs Trusts (SNT)

A Special Needs Trust also may be used to cover supplemental needs, some of which public benefits may not cover. The trust may be funded by a person with a disability or by a third party.

A First Party account, funded from the person with a disability, comes from sources such as earnings, divorce settlement, inheritance, life insurance, a personal injury award or retirement.

A Third Party account, funded by someone other than the person with a disability (e.g., a parent or grandparent or someone else), comes from sources such as income, life insurance, trust or will.

Protected Savings Option Comparison Chart

Comparison Criteria	ABLE	Pooled Trust (First or Third Party)	Special Needs Trust (First Party)	Special Needs Trust (Third Party)
Eligibility	Onset of a disability prior to age 26.	Disability or moderate impairment. First Party Account: established before age 65. Third Party Account: no age limitation.	Disability: established before age 65.	No limitations.
Allowed Accounts	One (1)	May have multiple first and third party accounts.	May have multiple first party accounts.	May have multiple third party accounts.
Account Opened By	Account may be opened at any age by person with a disability or others in this order: individual selected by person with a disability; individual's agent under power of attorney, conservator, or legal guardian; a spouse, parent, sibling or grandparent; or representative payee (ind. or org.). An ABLE account set up by the rep. payee must comply with SSA rep. payee rules and regulations.	First Party: Account set up by the beneficiary, a parent, grandparent, court or legal guardian or by someone with authority to act for the beneficiary (e.g., an agent under a power of attorney).Third Party: Account set up by anyone other than the beneficiary.	Account set up by the beneficiary, a parent, grandparent, court or legal guardian or by someone with authority to act for the beneficiary (e.g., an agent under a power of attorney).	Account set up by grantor (anyone but the beneficiary).

Comparison Criteria	ABLE	**Pooled Trust** (First or Third Party)	**Special Needs Trust** (First Party)	**Special Needs Trust** (Third Party)
Allowable Use	Qualified disability expenses including food, housing, education, transportation, emergency needs, employment training and support, assistive technology, personal support services, health care expenses, financial management, administrative services, funeral and burial and other expenses determined by ABLE account owner; assistance by legal guardian or power of attorney allowable.	As determined by trust administrator; food or housing expenses may generate special issues. Administrator provides oversight and manages funds.	As determined by trustee; food or housing expenses may generate special issues, as may any direct distributions to the beneficiary.	As determined by trustee; no required limitation on food or housing expenses, but may cause reduction in some benefits. Direct distributions to the beneficiary may reduce or eliminate eligibility.
Startup Cost	Initial minimum deposit between $0 to $50.	Typically $200–$1,000.	Attorney fees vary, and may include court costs; $1,000s.	Attorney fees vary $100s–$1,000s.
Minimum Contribution	Average $0–$50.	Typically $2,000–$10,000.	No limitation, but costs make it inefficient for smaller trusts.	No limitation.

Comparison Criteria	ABLE	Pooled Trust (First or Third Party)	Special Needs Trust (First Party)	Special Needs Trust (Third Party)
Annual Contribution Limit	$16,000 total from owner, family, friends, 529 College Savings Account, or a Pooled Trust or Special Needs Trust.	No limit.	No limit.	No limit.
Additional Contributions Allowed	Additional contributions by ABLE owners are permitted from unearned income or from earnings when the beneficiary or their employer do not contribute into an employer-sponsored retirement account in the calendar year. In those cases, additional amounts may be as much as $12,880. The increase for residents of Alaska may be up to $16,090, and residents of Hawaii up to $14,820 (2022).	Some pooled accounts allow for beneficiary to contribute earnings.	Third party funds should not be added to a first party Special Needs Trust.	Other family members may contribute additional amounts to a third party Special Needs Trust, but no funds of the beneficiary may be added.

Comparison Criteria	ABLE	Pooled Trust (First or Third Party)	Special Needs Trust (First Party)	Special Needs Trust (Third Party)
Maximum Holdings	Varies by ABLE plan $235,000–$550,000.	NA	NA	NA
Ongoing Management Fees	Fees vary with each ABLE plan. Costs are nominal and average $0–$60 per calendar year.	Average $200+. Enrollment and administration fees are almost always higher than those associated with ABLE accounts, but lower than for-profit businesses that offer trust services. Management fees for a pooled SNT can be less than 1% on an annual basis. A fee schedule should be available.	Often 1%–2%. Enrollment and administration fees are likely higher than those associated with ABLE accounts, but are often lower than for-profit businesses that offer trust services. Many first party trusts require court oversight, which may add expenses.	Often 1%–2%. Trustee's fees and associated costs are almost certainly higher than those associated with ABLE accounts, but may be lower than for-profit businesses that offer trust services.
Debit Card or Checks	Availability of prepaid debit cards, checking options and contribution gift cards; fees vary by ABLE plan.	Yes – often arranged through TrueLink or similar card.	Yes – often arranged through TrueLink or similar card.	Yes – often arranged through TrueLink or similar card.

Comparison Criteria	**ABLE**	**Pooled Trust** (First or Third Party)	**Special Needs Trust** (First Party)	**Special Needs Trust** (Third Party)
Investment Options	Yes, 3 – 14; options vary with each ABLE plan.	Yes. Trust funds are pooled for investment purposes and an account is maintained in each beneficiary's sub-account. Pooled Trust administrator decides, often in consultation with beneficiary and/or family.	Yes. The investment options are within the discretion of the trustee / administrator.	Yes. The investment options are within the discretion of the trustee / administrator.
Investment Option Fees	Yes, vary by actual investment product.	Yes, vary by actual investment product.	Yes, vary by actual investment product.	Yes, vary by actual investment product.
Medicaid Cost Payback Upon Death	Yes, Medicaid payback is subject to federal and state probate laws applicable to Medicaid expenses paid since opening an ABLE account. ABLE funds first pay for outstanding qualified disability expenses, including funeral and burial expenses, prior to Medicaid payback.	First party: Yes, though nonprofit trustee may be permitted to retain some or all of the balance rather than repaying Medicaid. (trustee arrangements vary). Third party: No payback requirement. Funds may be used for funeral or other last expenses.	Yes, if applicable; funds may not be used for funeral expenses prior to payback.	No. Remaining funds may be used for funeral or other final expenses, and remaining funds are then distributed to named beneficiaries.

Comparison Criteria	ABLE	Pooled Trust (First or Third Party)	Special Needs Trust (First Party)	Special Needs Trust (Third Party)
	The remaining account is reduced by all premiums paid to a Medicaid Buy-In program, prior to Medicaid payback.			
SSI Resource	If ABLE account balance exceeds $100,000, either alone or with other resources, which cause the SSI resource limit to be exceeded, the SSI benefit is suspended until balance falls under threshold. Otherwise, an ABLE account is not counted as a resource for SSI purposes. Any amount of ABLE savings does not impact Medicaid eligibility.	Depends on date of establishment guidelines and source of trust funds. Third party Pooled Trust: see SNT – third party.	Trust principal is counted as a resource if: (1) a trust beneficiary has legal authority to revoke or terminate the trust and use the funds to meet food or shelter needs; (2) if the trust beneficiary can direct the use of the trust principal for his or her support and maintenance under the terms of the trust; or (3) if the trust beneficiary can sell his or her beneficiary interest in the trust, that interest is a resource.	Trust principal is counted as a resource if: (1) a trust beneficiary has legal authority to revoke or terminate the trust and use the funds to meet food or shelter needs; (2) if the trust beneficiary can direct the use of the trust principal for his or her support and maintenance under the terms of the trust; or (3) if the trust beneficiary can sell his or her beneficiary interest in the trust, that interest is a resource.

Comparison Criteria	ABLE	**Pooled Trust** (First or Third Party)	**Special Needs Trust** (First Party)	**Special Needs Trust** (Third Party)
SSI Income	Disbursements may be made for qualified expenses such as shelter expenses, rent, mortgage payments, insurance, taxes, utilities and food without resulting in a one-third loss of SSI due to unearned income. However, money taken out for rent, housing expenses, or housing-related expenses must be paid in the same month as the distribution or it is counted as a resource.	Cash, including gift cards or certificates paid directly from the trust to the SSI recipient, is unearned income and will reduce SSI. Food or shelter or shelter costs such as rent, mortgage payments, taxes and utilities received as a disbursement by a trustee / administrator to a third party is considered in-kind support for SSI and can reduce SSI benefits, but not necessarily by the amount of the distribution. Some disbursements from the trust that are not cash to the individual, or third party payments that are not in-kind	Cash, including gift cards or certificates paid directly from the trust to the individual, is unearned income. Food or shelter or shelter costs such as rent, mortgage payments, taxes and utilities received as a disbursement by a trustee / administrator to a third party is in-kind support and maintenance under the presumed maximum value rule. Some disbursements from the trust that are not cash to the individual or third party payments that are not in-kind support and maintenance are not countable income. Examples are educational	When trust principal is not a resource, disbursements from the trust may or may not be income depending on the nature of the disbursement. Cash, including gift cards or certificates paid directly from the trust to the individual, is unearned income. Food or shelter or shelter costs such as rent, mortgage payments, taxes and utilities received as a disbursement by a trustee / administrator to a third party is considered in-kind support for SSI and can reduce SSI benefits unless it is contributed to an ABLE account and paid from that account

Comparison Criteria	ABLE	Pooled Trust (First or Third Party)	Special Needs Trust (First Party)	Special Needs Trust (Third Party)
		support and maintenance, are not countable income. Examples are educational expenses, therapy, medical services, phone bills, recreation and entertainment.	expenses, therapy, medical services, phone bills, recreation and entertainment.	Some disbursements from the trust that are not cash to the individual or third party payments that are not in-kind support and maintenance are not countable income. Examples are educational expenses, therapy, medical services, phone bills, recreation and entertainment.
State Tax Qualified Contributions	Maybe: depends on the ABLE plan and/or state law.	No	No	No

Comparison Criteria	ABLE	Pooled Trust (First or Third Party)	Special Needs Trust (First Party)	Special Needs Trust (Third Party)
Federal Tax Deductible Contributions?	Not for federal tax purposes; state deduction or credit may apply. Employed ABLE owners may qualify for Saver's Credit.	No	No	No
Revocable	Yes, revocable. ABLE funds can be transferred to another qualifying individual (sibling, half-sibling or adopted sibling with some restrictions).	No, a first party Pooled Trust is irrevocable. A third party Pooled Trust can be revocable or irrevocable. If the beneficiary has the power to revoke, public benefits may be jeopardized.	No, the trust is irrevocable.	The trust can be revocable or irrevocable. If the beneficiary has the power to revoke, public benefits may be jeopardized.

Comparison Criteria	ABLE	Pooled Trust (First or Third Party)	Special Needs Trust (First Party)	Special Needs Trust (Third Party)
Death of Owner/Trustee	Balance paid in following priority: Qualified disability expenses including funeral and burial expenses, Medicaid payback subject to state and federal law, for expenses accrued since opening ABLE account. This is subject to a reduction for any Medicaid Buy-in program premium payments made by or on behalf of the ABLE account owner to a Medicaid Buy-In program under that State's Medicaid program. Remaining funds are payable to the ABLE beneficiary's estate or, if the plan permits, to a named beneficiary.	Balance paid in following priority: 1. Trust retention, if any; 2. Medicaid payback (for First party only); 3. Final distribution as required by trust agreement and joinder. Third party: the trust's terms will control distributions upon death Agency may retain a portion of account balance at the time of beneficiary's death (Trustee arrangements vary).	Balance paid in following priority: 1. Medicaid payback for lifetime of beneficiary; 2. Final distribution as required by trust agreement and/ or laws of decedent's jurisdiction.	The trust's terms will control distributions on death of the beneficiary.

Comparison Criteria	ABLE	**Pooled Trust** (First or Third Party)	**Special Needs Trust** (First Party)	**Special Needs Trust** (Third Party)
Heirs upon Death of ABLE account owner (ABLE account) or Beneficiary (Trusts) of Owner/Trustee after Medicaid Recovery	ABLE plans may allow for a designated beneficiary or the beneficiary is defined in the ABLE account owner's Last Will and Testament.	Specific beneficiaries can be designated in the document.	State laws may vary, but generally remaining balances are payable to the beneficiary's heirs or estate.	Specific beneficiaries can be designated in the document.

*Some states recognize special types of trusts designed to reduce countable income to qualify for Medicaid. These trusts are called Qualifying Income Trusts, commonly known as "Miller Trusts." In some states they may have other names such as Income Only Trusts, Income Diversion Trusts, Medicaid Income-Only Trusts, Income Assignment Trusts, Income Cap Trusts and (d)(4)(B) trusts. This document is meant to compare trusts commonly used to exclude resources to maintain eligibility for federally funded, means-tested benefits.

Please remember that individuals may want to make use of more than one, or all, of these protected savings options. For example, funds from Pooled and Special Needs Trusts can often be deposited directly into an ABLE account. This strategy expands options for people, empowering them to spend the funds as they choose, within the range of qualified disability expenses. In addition, and equally important, the ABLE account owner can be in charge of the timing and payment of ordinary living expenses.

Funds spent on items not within allowable guidelines of ABLE, Pooled and Special Needs Trusts may cause a beneficiary to lose eligibility for SSI and Medicaid during the time the funds were determined as countable income or resources. Unapproved payments from an ABLE account may result in very modest income tax liability for the ABLE account owner.

Please note: ABLE information provided by ABLE NRC; Pooled and Special Needs Trust information prepared by Special Needs Alliance.

For More Information:

ABLE National Resource Center: ABLE National Resource Center website

Special Needs Alliance: Special Needs Alliance website

Updated 3/2022

APPENDIX O

Transmittal 64

3257. TRANSFERS OF ASSETS AND TREATMENT OF TRUSTS

A. General.—Section 13611 of the Omnibus Budget Reconciliation Act of 1993 (OBRA 1993) amended § 1917 of the Act by incorporating in §§ 1917(c) and (d) new requirements for treatment of transfers of assets for less than fair market value and for treatment of trusts. The following instructions apply only to transfers made and trusts established after the effective date explained in § 3258.2. For transfers made and trusts established before that effective date, the old policies regarding treatment of trusts and transfers apply. See §§ 3215 and 3250 for instructions on the treatment of trusts established and transfers made before August 11, 1993.

B. Definitions.—The following definitions apply, as appropriate, to both transfers of assets and trusts:

1. Individual.—As used in this instruction, the term "individual" includes the individual himself or herself, as well as:

o The individual's spouse, where the spouse is acting in the place of or on behalf of the individual;

o A person, including a court or administrative body, with legal authority to act in place of or on behalf of the individual or the individual's spouse; and

o Any person, including a court or administrative body, acting at the direction or upon the request of the individual or the individual's spouse.

2. Spouse.—This is a person who is considered legally married to an individual under the laws of the State in which the individual is applying for or receiving Medicaid.

3. Assets.—For purposes of this section, assets include all income and resources of the individual and of the individual[']s spouse. This includes income or resources which the individual or the individual[']s spouse is entitled to but does not receive because of any action by:

o The individual or the individual's spouse;

o A person, including a court or administrative body, with legal authority to act in place of or on behalf of the individual or the individual's spouse; or

o Any person, including a court or administrative body, acting at the direction or upon the request of the individual or the individual's spouse.

For purposes of this section, the term "assets an individual or spouse is entitled to" includes assets to which the individual is entitled or would be entitled if action had not been taken to avoid receiving the assets.

The following are examples of actions which would cause income or resources not to be received:

o Irrevocably waiving pension income;

o Waiving the right to receive an inheritance;

o Not accepting or accessing injury settlements;

o Tort settlements which are diverted by the defendant into a trust or similar device to be held for the benefit of an individual who is a plaintiff; and

o Refusal to take legal action to obtain a court ordered payment that is not being paid, such as child support or alimony.

However, failure to cause assets to be received does not entail a transfer of assets for less than fair market value in all instances. For example, the individual may not be able to afford to take the necessary action to obtain the assets. Or, the cost of obtaining the assets may be greater than the assets are worth, thus effectively rendering the assets worthless to the individual. Examine the specific circumstances of each case before making a decision whether an uncompensated asset transfer occurred.

4. Resources.—For purposes of this section, the definition of resources is the same definition used by the Supplemental Security Income (SSI) program, except that the home is not excluded for institutionalized individuals. In determining whether a transfer of assets or a trust involves an SSI-countable resource, use those resource exclusions and disregards used by the SSI program, except for the exclusion of the home for institutionalized individuals.

In determining whether resources have been transferred for less than fair market value, you may not apply more liberal definitions of resources which you may be using under § 1902(r)(2) of the Act. For transfer of assets purposes, if you are a 209(b) State, you cannot use more restrictive definitions of resources that you may have in your State plan.

However, in determining whether and how a trust is counted in determining eligibility, you may apply more liberal methodologies for resources which you may be using under § 1902(r)(2) of the Act. For trust purposes, if you are a 209(b) State, you may use more restrictive definitions of resources that you may have in your State plan.

For noninstitutionalized individuals, the home remains an exempt resource.

5. Income.—For purposes of this section, the definition of income is the same definition used by the SSI program. In determining whether a transfer of assets involves SSI-countable income, take into account those income exclusions and disregards used by the SSI program.

You may not, for transfer of assets purposes, apply more liberal definitions of income that you may be using under § 1902(r)(2) of the Act. If you are a 209(b) State, you cannot use more restrictive definitions of income that you may have in your State plan.

However, in determining whether and how a trust is counted in determining eligibility, you may apply more liberal methodologies for income which you may be using under § 1902(r)(2) of the Act. Also, for trust purposes, if you are a 209(b) State, you may use more restrictive definitions of income that you may have in your State plan.

6. For the Sole Benefit of.—A transfer is considered to be for the sole benefit of a spouse, blind or disabled child, or a disabled individual if the transfer is arranged in such a way that no individual or entity except the spouse, blind or disabled child, or disabled individual can benefit from the assets transferred in any way, whether at the time of the transfer or at any time in the future.

Similarly, a trust is considered to be established for the sole benefit of a spouse, blind or disabled child, or disabled individual if the trust benefits no one but that individual, whether at the time the trust is established or any time in the future. However, the trust may provide for reasonable compensation, as defined by the State, for a trustee or trustees to manage the trust, as well as for reasonable costs associated with investing or otherwise managing the funds or property in the trust. In defining what is reasonable compensation, consider the amount of time and effort involved in managing a trust of the size involved, as well as the prevailing rate of compensation, if any, for managing a trust of similar size and complexity.

A transfer, transfer instrument, or trust that provides for funds or property to pass to a beneficiary who is not the spouse, blind or disabled child, or disabled individual is not considered to be established for the sole benefit of one of these individuals. In order for a transfer or trust to be considered to be for the sole benefit of one of these individuals, the instrument or document must provide for the spending of the funds involved for the benefit of the individual on a basis that is actuarially sound based on the life expectancy of the individual involved. When the instrument or document does not so provide, any potential exemption from penalty or consideration for eligibility purposes is void.

An exception to this requirement exists for trusts discussed in § 3259.7. Under these exceptions, the trust instrument must provide that any funds remaining in the trust upon the death of the individual must go to the State, up to the amount of Medicaid benefits paid on the individual's behalf. When these exceptions require that the trust be for the sole benefit of an individual, the restriction discussed in the previous paragraph does not apply when the trust instrument designates the State as the recipient of funds from the trust. Also, the trust may provide for disbursal of funds to other beneficiaries, provided the trust does not permit such disbursals until the State's claim is satisfied. Finally, "pooled" trusts may provide that the trust can retain a certain percentage of the funds in the trust account upon the death of the beneficiary.

3258. TRANSFERS OF ASSETS FOR LESS THAN FAIR MARKET VALUE

3258.1 General.—Under the transfer of assets provisions in § 1917(c) of the Act, as amended by OBRA 1993, you must deny coverage of certain Medicaid services to otherwise eligible institutionalized individuals who transfer (or whose spouses transfer) assets for less than fair market value. You may also choose to deny coverage for certain other services for noninstitutionalized individuals who transfer (or whose spouses transfer) assets for less than fair market value. The following instructions explain the specific circumstances and rules under which you must deny Medicaid services.

The provisions explained in these instructions apply to all States, including those using more restrictive eligibility criteria than are used by the SSI program, under § 1902(f) of the Act. Thus, 209(b) States cannot apply periods of ineligibility due to a transfer of resources for less than fair market value except in accordance with these instructions.

A. Definitions.—The following definitions apply to transfers of assets.

1. Fair Market Value.—Fair market value is an estimate of the value of an asset, if sold at the prevailing price at the time it was actually transferred. Value is based on criteria you use in appraising the value of assets for the purpose of determining Medicaid eligibility.

NOTE: For an asset to be considered transferred for fair market value or to be considered to be transferred for valuable consideration, the compensation received for the asset must be in a tangible form with intrinsic value. A transfer for love and consideration, for example, is not considered a transfer for fair market value. Also, while relatives and family members legitimately can be paid for care they provide to the individual, HCFA presumes that services provided for free at the time were intended to be provided without compensation. Thus, a transfer to a relative for care provided for free in the past is a transfer of assets for less than fair market value. However, an individual can rebut this presumption with tangible evidence that is acceptable to the State. For example, you may require that a payback arrangement had been agreed to in writing at the time services were provided.

2. Valuable Consideration.—Valuable consideration means that an individual receives in exchange for his or her right or interest in an asset some act, object, service, or other benefit which has a tangible and/or intrinsic value to the individual that is roughly equivalent to or greater than the value of the transferred asset.

3. Uncompensated Value.—The uncompensated value is the difference between the fair market value at the time of transfer (less any outstanding loans, mortgages, or other encumbrances on the asset) and the amount received for the asset.

4. Institutionalized Individual.—An institutionalized individual is an individual who is:

o An inpatient in a nursing facility;

o An inpatient in a medical institution for whom payment is based on a level of care provided in a nursing facility; or

o A home and community-based services recipient described in § 1902(a)(10)(A)(ii)(VI) of the Act. For purposes of this section, a medical institution includes an intermediate care facility for the mentally retarded (ICF/MR). (See 42 CFR 435.1009.)

5. Noninstitutionalized Individual.—A noninstitutionalized individual is an individual receiving any of the services described in § 3258.8.

6. Nursing Facility Services.—Nursing facility services are services as described in the State Medicaid Plan as nursing facility services.

3258.2 Effective Date.—This section applies to all transfers which are made on or after August 11, 1993. Transfers made before August 11, 1993, are treated under the rules in § 3250. While this section applies to transfers made on or after August 11, 1993, penalties for transfers for less than fair market value, as described in § 3258.8, cannot be applied to services provided before October 1, 1993. Instead, for the period prior to October 1, 1993, apply pre-OBRA 1993 rules regarding transfers of assets to transfers made on or after August 11, 1993, and before October 1, 1993.

EXAMPLE: An individual who applies for Medicaid transfers an asset on September 1, 1993. The transfer is found to have been made for less than fair market value. As such, a penalty, as described in § 3258.8, is assessed. Because the transfer occurred after August 11, 1993, the transfer is assessed under the new rules set forth in this section. However, because a penalty under OBRA 1993 rules cannot apply before October 1, 1993, the penalty assessed under OBRA 1993 in this case begins on October 1, 1993. Pre-OBRA 1993 rules are used to determine whether a penalty is assessed for the period between September 1 and October 1. On October 1, begin using the OBRA 1993 rules for the transfer described in this example.

3258.3 Individuals To Whom Transfer of Assets Provisions Apply.—You must apply these provisions when an institutionalized individual or the individual's spouse disposes of assets for less than fair market value on or after the look-back date explained in § 3258.4. You also have the option of applying this provision to noninstitutionalized individuals when those individuals or their spouses dispose of assets for less than fair market value.

See § 3258 for definitions of institutionalized and noninstitutionalized individuals.

For purposes of this section, assets transferred by a parent, guardian, court or administrative body, or anyone acting in place of or on behalf of or at the request or direction of the individual or spouse, are considered to be transferred by the individual or spouse.

For noninstitutionalized individuals, you have the option of applying these provisions. If you wish to apply these provisions to noninstitutionalized individuals, you have the further option of choosing the groups to which the provisions apply. You may apply them to all noninstitutionalized individuals, or to specific categorical groups. However, if you choose to apply these provisions only to some groups, the groups you choose must be recognized groups as listed in § 1905(a) of the Act.

3258.4 Look-Back Date and Look-Back Period.—The look-back date is the earliest date on which a penalty for transferring assets for less than fair market value can be assessed. Penalties can be assessed for transfers which take place on or after the look-back date. Penalties cannot be assessed for transfers which take place prior to the look-back date. The look-back date varies for individuals transferring assets, depending on whether they are institutionalized, and there are special rules for some trusts, as described in subsection E.

A. Institutionalized Individual.—For an individual in an institution, the look-back date is 36 months prior to the baseline date. The baseline date is the first date as of which the individual was:

- o Institutionalized; and
- o Applied for medical assistance under the State plan.

When an individual is already a Medicaid recipient and becomes institutionalized, the baseline date is the date upon which both of the above conditions are met, that is, the first day of institutionalization.

B. Noninstitutionalized Individual.—For a noninstitutionalized individual, the look-back date is 36 months prior to the baseline date, which is the date the individual:

- o Applies for medical assistance under the State plan; or, if later,
- o The date on which the individual disposes of assets for less than fair market value.

C. Multiple Periods of Institutionalization and Multiple Applications.—When an individual has multiple periods of institutionalization or has made multiple applications for Medicaid (whether or not they are successful), the look-back date is based on a baseline date that is the first date upon which the individual has both applied for Medicaid and is institutionalized. Similarly, if a noninstitutionalized individual has applied for Medicaid more than once and has made more than one transfer of assets, the baseline date is that date on which the individual has first applied for Medicaid or, if later, made the first transfer of assets for less than fair market value after applying. Thus, each individual has only one look-back date, regardless of the number of periods of institutionalization, applications for Medicaid, periods of eligibility, or transfers of assets.

D. Look-Back Period.—The look-back period is the period that begins with the look-back date and ends with the baseline date. This can be 36 or 60 months, depending on whether certain kinds of trusts are involved. (See subsection E for look-back periods involving trusts.) The look-back period is the period of time prior to the baseline date during which a previous transfer of assets for less than fair market value can be penalized. However, it is important to note that transfers which occur after the baseline date are also subject to penalty if they are made for less than fair market value.

NOTE: The 36 month look-back periods described above do not become fully effective until August 11, 1996. Prior to that date, a 36 month look-back period actually begins at some time before the date transfers are covered by these rules. While the 36 month look-back period is effective for transfers made on or after August 11, 1993, any transfers actually made before that date are treated under the rules described in § 3250. Thus, the look-back period is phased in over the 36-month period ending August 11, 1996.

EXAMPLE 1: Institutionalized Individual

An individual is institutionalized on February 13, 1997. He/she applies for Medicaid on April 7, 1997. The look-back date is the date 36 months prior to the baseline date, when both initiating requirements are met, i.e., institutionalization and application for Medicaid. That date is April 7, 1997. Thus, the look-back date is April 7, 1994. The look-back period is from April 7, 1994, through April 7, 1997.

EXAMPLE 2: Institutionalized Individual

An individual is institutionalized on February 13, 1995. He/she applies for Medicaid on April 7, 1995. The look-back date is 36 months prior to April 7, 1995, or April 7, 1992. However, because the transfer provisions of OBRA 1993 apply only to transfers made on or after August 11, 1993, any transfers made prior to August 11, 1993, are treated under the rules in § 3250.

EXAMPLE 3: Noninstitutionalized Individual

An individual applies for Medicaid on February 13, 1997. On April 7, 1997, he/she transfers an asset for less than fair market value. The look-back date in this case is April 7, 1994, 36 months prior to the baseline date on which he/she transferred the asset. If the asset had been transferred before February 13, 1997 (the date of application for Medicaid), the baseline date would have been February 13, 1997 (the date of application). The look-back period would begin February 13, 1994, and extend to February 13, 1997.

E. Look-Back Period for Transfers of Assets Involving Trusts.—When an individual establishes a revocable trust a portion of which is disbursed to someone other than the grantor or for the benefit of the grantor, that portion is treated as a transfer of assets for less than fair market value. When an individual establishes an irrevocable trust in which all or a portion of the trust cannot be disbursed to or on behalf of the individual, that portion is treated as a transfer of assets for less than fair market value. When a portion of a trust is treated as a transfer, the look-back period discussed in subsection D is extended to 60 months from:

- o The date the individual applied for Medicaid and was institutionalized; or,

- o For a noninstitutionalized individual, the date the individual applied for Medicaid or, if later, the date the transfer was made.

When a trust is irrevocable but some or all of the trust can be disbursed to or for the benefit of the individual, the look-back period applying to disbursements which could be made to or for the individual but are made to another person or persons is 36 months.

When the trust is revocable, the transfer is considered to take place on the date upon which the payment to someone other than the grantor was made. If the trust is irrevocable, the transfer is considered to have been made as of the date the trust was established or, if later, the date upon which payment to the grantor was foreclosed.

When an individual places assets into an irrevocable trust and can still benefit from those assets, the amount transferred is any of those assets which have been paid out for a purpose other than to or for the benefit of the individual. When an individual places assets in an irrevocable trust and can no longer benefit from some or all of those assets, that unavailable portion of the trust is considered as transferred for less than fair market value. The value of these assets is not reduced by any payments from the trust which may be made from these unavailable assets at a later date.

See §§ 3259ff. for a discussion of treatment of trusts in determining eligibility for Medicaid.

See § 3259.6 for rules which apply when assets which may involve a transfer of assets for less than fair market value are placed in a trust.

3258.5 Penalty Periods.—When an individual (or spouse) makes a transfer of assets for less than fair market value, payment for certain services received by the individual is denied for a specified period of time. However, the individual remains eligible for Medicaid and can have payment made for services not subject to penalty. (See § 3258.8.) For example, an institutionalized individual who transfers assets for less than fair market value must be denied reimbursement for nursing facility services. However, he or she may still be eligible for reimbursement for physician's services, provided such services are not provided as part of the individual's nursing home care.

A. Penalty Date.—The penalty date is the beginning date of each penalty period that is imposed for an uncompensated transfer. The penalty date for all individuals who transfer assets for less than fair market value is the first day of the month in which the asset was transferred (or, at State option, the first day of the month following the month of transfer), provided that date does not occur during an existing penalty period. If an asset was transferred prior to the look-back date discussed in § 3258.4, no penalty can be imposed for that transfer.

B. Penalty Period - General.—The penalty period is the period of time during which payment for specified services is denied. Unlike the penalty period under the rules discussed in § 3250, which was limited to 30 months, the penalty period under the OBRA 1993 rules has no statutory limit. Rather, the length of the penalty period is based solely on the value of the assets transferred and the cost of nursing facility care.

C. Transfer of Assets Takes Place During Existing Penalty Period.—When a transfer for less than fair market value takes place during an existing penalty period, whether imposed under the pre-OBRA 1993 or post-OBRA 1993 rules, a new penalty period cannot begin until the existing penalty period has expired.

EXAMPLE: An individual transferred an asset in May 1993 for which a penalty of 12 months was imposed. The individual transfers another asset in October 1993 to which another 12 month penalty applies. Because the second transfer took place within the first 12 month penalty period, the second penalty period cannot begin until the first expires, on April 30, 1994. Thus, the first penalty period runs from May 1, 1993, through April 30, 1994, and the second runs from May 1, 1994, through April 30, 1995.

D. Restricted Coverage - Institutionalized Individual.—The penalty for an institutionalized individual consists of ineligibility for certain services for a period or periods of ineligibility that equal the number of months calculated by taking the total, cumulative uncompensated value of all assets transferred by the individual or spouse on or after the look-back date discussed in § 3258.4, divided by the average monthly cost to a private patient of nursing facility services in the State at the time of application. As an alternative, the State may use the average monthly cost in the community in which the individual is institutionalized.

When the amount of the transfer is less than the monthly cost of nursing facility care, you have the option of not imposing a penalty or imposing a penalty for less than a full month. Under the latter option, the actual length of the penalty is based on the proportion of the State[']s private nursing facility rate that was transferred. If you choose to impose penalties for less than a full month, you must impose such penalties in all cases where a partial month penalty applies.

When an individual makes a series of transfers, each of which is less than the private nursing facility rate for a month, you have the option of imposing no penalty or imposing a series of penalties, each for less than a full month.

E. Restricted Coverage - Noninstitutionalized Individual.—The penalty period for a noninstitutionalized individual is calculated using the same method that is used for an institutionalized individual, including use of the average monthly cost of nursing facility services. The penalty for a noninstitutionalized individual cannot exceed the number of months calculated using this method. However, you may impose shorter penalty periods if you wish to do so. Obtain HCFA approval for any shorter penalty period you choose to impose, including approval of the methodology you use to calculate the shorter penalty period. See subsection D for transfers which are less than the private monthly rate for nursing facility care.

F. Individual Has Penalty Period Both As Institutionalized And Noninstitutionalized Individual.—When an individual incurs separate penalty periods as both institutionalized and noninstitutionalized for the same transfer, the total penalty period cannot exceed the penalty period that is applicable under only one category. In other words, a penalty imposed during a period of institutionalization reduces a penalty imposed for the same transfer or transfers made during the period of noninstitutionalization and vice versa.

EXAMPLE: An institutionalized individual transfers assets for less than fair market value, thereby incurring a transfer penalty of 24 months. After 12 months have elapsed, the individual leaves the institution and returns home. Because the State imposes penalties on noninstitutionalized individuals for transfers for less than fair market value, the same 24 month penalty applies to the individual, even though he/she left the institution. However, because of the limits on total penalty described above, the individual incurs only the 12 month penalty remaining from the transfer which occurred while he/she was institutionalized.

G. Multiple Transfers - General.—OBRA 1993 provides that the number of months of restricted coverage discussed in subsections C and D is based on the total, cumulative uncompensated value of the assets transferred. When a single asset is transferred or a number of assets are transferred during the same month, the penalty period is calculated using the total value of the asset(s) divided by the average monthly cost of nursing facility care. When assets are transferred at different times, use the following methods for calculating the penalty periods.

H. Transfers Made So That Penalty Periods Overlap.—When assets have been transferred in amounts and/or frequency that make the calculated penalty periods overlap, add together the value of all assets transferred, and divide by the cost of nursing facility care. This produces a single penalty period which begins on the first day of the month in which the first transfer was made.

EXAMPLE: An individual transfers $10,000 in January, $10,000 in February, and $10,000 in March, all of which are uncompensated. Calculated individually, based on a nursing facility cost of $2,500 a month, the penalty for the first transfer is from January through April, the second is from February through May, and the third is from March through June. Because these periods overlap, calculate the penalty period by adding the transfers together (a total of $30,000) and dividing by the nursing home cost ($2,500). This yields a penalty period of 12 months, which runs from January 1 through December 31 of that year.

As an alternative, calculate the individual penalty periods, as above, and impose them sequentially. Thus, the penalty for the first transfer extends from January through April, the second extends from May through August, and the third extends from September through December. In this example, the result is the same regardless of the method used.

I. Transfers Made So That Penalty Periods Do Not Overlap.—When multiple transfers are made in such a way that the penalty periods for each do not overlap, treat each transfer as a separate event with its own penalty period.

EXAMPLE: An individual transfers $5,000 in January, $5,000 in May, and $5,000 in October, all of which are uncompensated. Assuming a State private nursing facility cost of $2,500 a month, the penalty periods for transfers are, respectively, January through February, May through June, and October through November.

If you wish to use other methodologies for determining penalty periods, you may do so, provided you obtain HCFA approval for those methods. However, any alternative method must adhere to the basic principles that:

- o The total, cumulative uncompensated value of the asset or assets transferred is used to determine the length of the penalty period or periods;
- o Penalty periods do not overlap, nor in any way run concurrently; and
- o No penalty period can begin while a previous penalty period is in effect.

J. Transfer By a Spouse That Results in Penalty Period for the Individual.—When a spouse transfers an asset that results in a penalty for the individual, the penalty period must, in certain instances, be apportioned between the spouses. You must apportion the penalty when:

o The spouse is eligible for Medicaid;

o A penalty could, under normal circumstances, be assessed against the spouse, i.e., the spouse is institutionalized, or the State has elected to impose penalties on noninstitutionalized individuals; and

o Some portion of the penalty against the individual remains at the time the above conditions are met.

When these conditions are met, you must apportion any existing penalty period between the spouses. You may use any reasonable methodology you wish to determine how the penalty is apportioned. However, the methodology you use must provide that the total penalty imposed on both spouses does not exceed the length of the penalty originally imposed on the individual.

EXAMPLE: Mr. Able enters a nursing facility and applies for Medicaid. Mrs. Able transfers an asset that results in a 36 month penalty against Mr. Able. Twelve months into the penalty period, Mrs. Able enters a nursing facility and becomes eligible for Medicaid. The penalty period against Mr. Able still has 24 months to run. Because Mrs. Able is now in a nursing facility, and a portion of the original penalty period remains, you must apportion the remaining 24 months of penalty between Mr. and Mrs. Able. You may apportion the remaining penalty period in any way you wish, provided that the total remaining penalty period assessed against both spouses does not exceed 24 months.

When, for some reason, one spouse is no longer subject to a penalty (e.g., the spouse no longer receives nursing facility services, or the spouse dies), the remaining penalty period applicable to both spouses must be served by the remaining spouse.

In the above example, assume the 24 month penalty period was apportioned equally between Mr. and Mrs. Able. After six months, Mr. Able leaves the nursing facility, but Mrs. Able remains. Because Mr. Able is no longer subject to the penalty, the remaining total penalty (12 months) must be imposed on Mrs. Able. If Mr. Able returns to the nursing facility before the end of the 12 month period, the remaining penalty is again apportioned between the two spouses.

K. Penalty Period When Individual Leaves Institution.—A penalty period imposed for a transfer of assets runs continuously from the first date of the penalty period (the penalty date), regardless of whether the individual remains in or leaves the institution (or waiver program). Thus, if the individual leaves the nursing facility, the penalty period nevertheless continues until the end of the calculated period.

3258.6 Treatment Of Income As Asset.—Under OBRA 1993, income, in addition to resources, is considered to be an asset for transfer (and trust) purposes. Thus, when an individual[']s income is given or assigned in some manner to another person, such a gift or assignment can be considered a transfer of assets for less than fair market value.

In determining whether income has been transferred, do not attempt to ascertain in detail the individual's spending habits during the 36 or 60 month look-back period. Absent some reason to believe otherwise, assume that ordinary household income was legitimately spent on the normal costs of daily living.

However, you should attempt to determine whether the individual has transferred lump sum payments actually received in a month. Such payments, while counted as income in the month received for eligibility purposes, are counted as resources in the following month if they were retained. Disposal of such lump sum payments before they can be counted as resources could constitute an uncompensated transfer of assets. Also attempt to determine whether amounts of regularly scheduled income or lump sum payments, which the individual would otherwise have received, have been transferred. Normally, such a transfer takes the form of a transfer of the right to receive income. For example, a private pension may be diverted to a trust and no longer be paid to the individual. You may raise questions on whether lump sums of income or the right to income have been transferred based on information given on the Medicaid application or through active questioning of the individual concerning sources of income, income levels in the past versus the present, direct questions about giving income to others, etc.

When you find that income or the right to income has been transferred, a penalty for that transfer must be imposed for institutionalized individuals (if no exceptions apply). In determining the length of the penalty period, you may use several methods of treating the income involved.

When a single lump sum is transferred (e.g., a stock dividend check is given to another person in the month in which it is received by the individual), the penalty period is calculated on the basis of the value of the lump sum payment. When the amount of the payment is small enough that a full month's penalty does not result, you have the option of not imposing a penalty or, if you choose, applying the penalty for only part of the month.

EXAMPLE: A lump sum amount of $1,000 is transferred, but the State's private nursing facility rate is $2,000. You can either impose no penalty or apply a penalty for half of the month.

When a stream of income, (i.e., income received in a regular basis, such as a pension) or the right to a stream of income is transferred, you can calculate the penalty period as you would for a single lump sum. Using this method, a penalty period is imposed for each income payment. When the transfer involves a right to income (as opposed to periodic transfers of income the individual owns) you can, as an alternative, make a determination of the total amount of income expected to be transferred during the individual's life, based on an actuarial projection of the individual's life expectancy, and calculate the penalty on the basis of the projected total income.

You may choose to use alternative methods for determining the length of the penalty period where income is transferred. However, you must obtain approval from HCFA for use of alternative methods.

3258.7 Treatment Of Jointly Owned Assets.—When an asset is held by an individual in common with another person or persons via joint tenancy, tenancy in common, joint ownership, or a similar arrangement, the asset (or affected portion of the asset) is considered to be transferred by the individual when any action is taken, either by the individual or any other person, that reduces or eliminates the individual's ownership or control of the asset.

Under this provision, merely placing another person's name on an account or asset as a joint owner might not constitute a transfer of assets subject, of course, to the specific circumstances of the situation. In such a situation, the individual may still possess ownership rights to the account or asset and thus have the right to withdraw all of the funds in the account or possess the asset at any time. Thus, the account or asset is still considered to belong to the individual. However, actual withdrawal of funds from the account or removal of the asset by the other person removes the funds or property from the control of the individual and so constitutes a transfer of assets. Also, if placing another person's name on the account or asset actually limits the individual's right to sell or otherwise dispose of the asset (e.g., the addition of another person's name requires that the person agree to the sale or disposal of the asset where no such agreement was necessary before), such placement constitutes a transfer of assets.

Use regular Medicaid rules to determine what portion of a jointly held asset is presumed to belong to an applicant or recipient. This portion is subject to a transfer penalty if it is withdrawn by a joint owner. However, you must also provide an opportunity for the owners to rebut the presumption of ownership. If either the applicant/recipient or the other person can establish to your satisfaction that the funds withdrawn were, in fact, the sole property of and contributed to the account by the other person, and thus did not belong to the applicant/recipient, withdrawal of those funds should not result in the imposition of a penalty.

3258.8 Penalties for Transfers of Assets for Less Than Fair Market Value.—When you find that assets have been transferred for less than fair market value, OBRA 1993 provides for specific penalties. These penalties involve the denial of reimbursement for certain services received by the individual. The specific services for which reimbursement must be withheld depend on the individual's situation.

A. Penalties For Institutionalized Individuals.—For institutionalized individuals, the services for which payment must be withheld are:

- o Nursing facility services, as defined in the State Medicaid Plan;
- o A level of care in any institution equivalent to that of nursing facility services; and
- o Home and community-based services provided under a waiver for individuals eligible for such services under § 1915(c) or (d) of the Act.

B. Penalties for Noninstitutionalized Individuals.—For a noninstitutionalized individual, the services for which payment must be withheld are the following, not including those services described above:

- o Home health services, as described in § 1905(a)(7) of the Act;
- o Home and community care (to the extent allowed and as defined in § 1929 of the Act) for functionally disabled elderly adults (see § 1905(a)(22) of the Act); and
- o Personal care services furnished to individuals who are not inpatients in certain medical institutions. (See § 1905(a)(24) of the Act.)

At the option of the State, you may also withhold reimbursement for services provided to noninstitutionalized individuals for other long term care services for which medical assistance is otherwise available under the State plan to individuals requiring long term care. Such services might include, for example, private duty nursing. However, the specific services involved depend on your own State plan.

3258.9 Treatment of Certain Kinds of Transfers for Less Than Fair Market Value.—Certain financial transactions or purchases may constitute a transfer of assets for less than fair market value. Treat the following as described.

A. Life Estates.—Under a life estate, an individual who owns property transfers ownership of that property to another individual while retaining, for the rest of his or her life (or the life of another person), certain rights to that property. Generally, a life estate entitles the owner of the life estate (the grantor) to possess, use, and obtain profits from the property as long as he or she lives. However, actual ownership of the property has passed to another individual.

In a transaction involving a life estate, a transfer of assets is involved. This transfer is for less than fair market value whenever the value of the transferred asset is greater than the value of the rights conferred by the life estate.

In determining whether a penalty is assessed because of a life estate and how long that penalty should be, compute the value of the asset transferred and the value of the life estate, and calculate the difference between the two.

The value of the asset transferred is computed by using the regular Medicaid rules for determining the value of assets. To calculate the value of the life estate, use the life estate table below (from POMS SI 01140.120). Determine the value of the life estate by multiplying the current market value of the property by the life estate factor that corresponds to the grantor's age. The value of the life estate is then subtracted from the value of the asset transferred to determine the portion of the asset that was transferred for less than fair market value. Or, if only the value of the transferred portion is needed, multiply the current market value of the asset by the remainder factor.

EXAMPLE: Mrs. Able, age 65, owns a house with a small farm attached to it, worth $100,000 in total. She deeds the house and farm to her son but retains a life estate in the property. Under the terms of the life estate, Mrs. Able is entitled to live in the house for the rest of her life and to any produce, income, etc. generated by the farm. To determine the value of Mrs. Able's life estate, the current market value of the property ($100,000) is multiplied by a life estate factor corresponding to Mrs. Able[']s age in the table (.67970), resulting in a life estate worth $67,970. The penalty is assessed for the difference between the value of the asset transferred ($100,000) and the value of the life estate ($67,790), or a penalty based on $32,030 of assets transferred for less than fair market value.

Some States allow life estates with powers, wherein the owner of the property creates a life estate for himself or herself, retaining the power to sell the property, with a remainder interest to someone else, e.g., a child. Since the life estate holder retains the power to sell the property, its value as a resource is its full equity value. In this situation, the individual has not transferred anything of value, because he or she can terminate the life estate at any time and restore full ownership to himself or herself. Instead, the full value of the asset in question is treated as a countable resource to the individual (assuming, of course, that it is not an otherwise excluded resource).

LIFE ESTATE AND REMAINDER INTEREST TABLE

(See 26 CFR 20.2031-7 and 49 FR Vol. 49 No. 93/5-11-84.)

AGE	LIFE ESTATE	REMAINDER	AGE	LIFE ESTATE	REMAINDER
0	.97188	.02812	35	.93868	.06132
1	.98988	.01012	36	.93460	.06540
2	.99017	.00983	37	.93026	.06974
3	.99008	.00992	38	.92567	.07433
4	.98981	.01019	39	.92083	.07917
5	.98938	.01062	40	.91571	.08429
6	.98884	.01116	41	.91030	.08970
7	.98822	.01178	42	.90457	.09543
8	.98748	.01252	43	.89855	.10145
9	.98663	.01337	44	.89221	.10779
10	.98565	.01435	45	.88558	.11442
11	.98453	.01547	46	.87863	.12137
12	.98329	.01671	47	.87137	.12863
13	.98198	.01802	48	.86374	.13626
14	.98066	.01934	49	.85578	.14422
15	.97937	.02063	50	.84743	.15257
16	.97815	.02185	51	.83674	.16126
17	.97700	.02300	52	.82969	.17031
18	.97590	.02410	53	.82028	.17972
19	.97480	.02520	54	.81054	.18946
20	.97365	.02635	55	.80046	.19954
21	.97245	.02755	56	.79006	.20994
22	.97120	.02880	57	.77931	.22069
23	.96986	.03014	58	.76822	.23178
24	.96841	.03159	59	.75675	.24325
25	.96678	.03322	60	.74491	.25509
26	.96495	.03505	61	.73267	.26733
27	.96290	.03710	62	.72002	.27998
28	.96062	.03938	63	.70696	.29304
29	.95813	.04187	64	.69352	.30648
30	.95543	.04457	65	.67970	.32030
31	.95254	.04746	66	.66551	.33449
32	.94942	.05058	67	.65098	.34902
33	.94608	.05392	68	.63610	.36390
34	.94250	.05750	69	.62086	.37914

LIFE ESTATE AND REMAINDER INTEREST TABLE (Cont.)

AGE	LIFE ESTATE	REMAINDER	AGE	LIFE ESTATE	REMAINDER
70	.60522	.39478	90	.28221	.71779
71	.58914	.41086	91	.26955	.73045
72	.57261	.42739	92	.25771	.74229
73	.55571	.44429	93	.24692	.75308
74	.53862	.46138	94	.23728	.76272
75	.52149	.47851	95	.22887	.77113
76	.50441	.49559	96	.22181	.77819
77	.48742	.51258	97	.21550	.78450
78	.47049	.52951	98	.21000	.79000
79	.45357	.54643	99	.20486	.79514
80	.43659	.56341	100	.19975	.80025
81	.41967	.58033	101	.19532	.80468
82	.40295	.59705	102	.19054	.80946
83	.38642	.61358	103	.18437	.81563
84	.36998	.63002	104	.17856	.82144
85	.35359	.64641	105	.16962	.83038
86	.33764	.66236	106	.15488	.84512
87	.32262	.67738	107	.13409	.86591
88	.30859	.69141	108	.10068	.89932
89	.29526	.70474	109	.04545	.95455

B. Annuities.—Section 1917(d)(6) of the Act provides that the term "trust" includes an annuity to the extent and in such manner as the Secretary specifies. This subsection describes how annuities are treated under the trust/transfer provisions.

When an individual purchases an annuity, he or she generally pays to the entity issuing the annuity (e.g., a bank or insurance company) a lump sum of money, in return for which he or she is promised regular payments of income in certain amounts. These payments may continue for a fixed period of time (for example, 10 years) or for as long as the individual (or another designated beneficiary) lives, thus creating an ongoing income stream. The annuity may or may not include a remainder clause under which, if the annuitant dies, the contracting entity converts whatever is remaining in the annuity into a lump sum and pays it to a designated beneficiary.

Annuities, although usually purchased in order to provide a source of income for retirement, are occasionally used to shelter assets so that individuals purchasing them can become eligible for Medicaid. In order to avoid penalizing annuities validly purchased as part of a retirement plan but to capture those annuities which abusively shelter assets, a determination must be made with regard to the ultimate purpose of the annuity (i.e., whether the purchase of the annuity constitutes a transfer of assets for less than fair market value). If the expected return on the annuity is commensurate with a reasonable estimate of the life expectancy of the beneficiary, the annuity can be deemed actuarially sound.

To make this determination, use the following life expectancy tables, compiled from information published by the Office of the Actuary of the Social Security Administration. The average number of years of expected life remaining for the individual must coincide with the life of the annuity. If the individual is not reasonably expected to live longer than the guarantee period of the annuity, the individual will not receive fair market value for the annuity based on the projected return. In this case, the annuity is not actuarially sound and a transfer of assets for less than fair market value has taken place, subjecting the individual to a penalty. The penalty is assessed based on a transfer of assets for less than fair market value that is considered to have occurred at the time the annuity was purchased.

For example, if a male at age 65 purchases a $10,000 annuity to be paid over the course of 10 years, his life expectancy according to the table is 14.96 years. Thus, the annuity is actuarially sound. However, if a male at age 80 purchases the same annuity for $10,000 to be paid over the course of 10 years, his life expectancy is only 6.98 years. Thus, a payout of the annuity for approximately 3 years is considered a transfer of assets for less than fair market value and that amount is subject to penalty.

LIFE EXPECTANCY TABLE - MALES

Age	Life Expectancy	Age	Life Expectancy	Age	Life Expectancy
0	71.80	40	35.05	80	6.98
1	71.53	41	34.15	81	6.59
2	70.58	42	33.26	82	6.21
3	69.62	43	32.37	83	5.85
4	68.65	44	31.49	84	5.51
5	67.67	45	30.61	85	5.19
6	66.69	46	29.74	86	4.89
7	65.71	47	28.88	87	4.61
8	64.73	48	28.02	88	4.34
9	63.74	49	27.17	89	4.09
10	62.75	50	26.32	90	3.86
11	61.76	51	25.48	91	3.64
12	60.78	52	24.65	92	3.43
13	59.79	53	23.82	93	3.24
14	58.82	54	23.01	94	3.06
15	57.85	55	22.21	95	2.90
16	56.91	56	21.43	96	2.74
17	55.97	57	20.66	97	2.60
18	55.05	58	19.90	98	2.47
19	54.13	59	19.15	99	2.34
20	53.21	60	18.42	100	2.22
21	52.29	61	17.70	101	2.11
22	51.38	62	16.99	102	1.99
23	50.46	63	16.30	103	1.89
24	49.55	64	15.62	104	1.78
25	48.63	65	14.96	105	1.68
26	47.72	66	14.32	106	1.59
27	46.80	67	13.70	107	1.50
28	45.88	68	13.09	108	1.41
29	44.97	69	12.50	109	1.33
30	44.06	70	11.92	110	1.25
31	43.15	71	11.35	111	1.17
32	42.24	72	10.80	112	1.10
33	41.33	73	10.27	113	1.02
34	40.23	74	9.27	114	0.96
35	39.52	75	9.24	115	0.89
36	38.62	76	8.76	116	0.83
37	37.73	77	8.29	117	0.77
38	36.83	78	7.83	118	0.71
39	35.94	79	7.40	119	0.66

LIFE EXPECTANCY TABLE - FEMALES

Age	Life Expectancy	Age	Life Expectancy	Age	Life Expectancy
0	78.79	40	40.61	80	9.11
1	78.42	41	39.66	81	8.58
2	77.48	42	38.72	82	8.06
3	76.51	43	37.78	83	7.56
4	75.54	44	36.85	84	7.08
5	74.56	45	35.92	85	6.63
6	73.57	46	35.00	86	6.20
7	72.59	47	34.08	87	5.79
8	71.60	48	33.17	88	5.41
9	70.61	49	32.27	89	5.05
10	69.62	50	31.37	90	4.71
11	68.63	51	30.48	91	4.40
12	67.64	52	29.60	92	4.11
13	66.65	53	28.72	93	3.84
14	65.67	54	27.86	94	3.59
15	64.68	55	27.00	95	3.36
16	63.71	56	26.15	96	3.16
17	62.74	57	25.31	97	2.97
18	61.77	58	24.48	98	2.80
19	60.80	59	23.67	99	2.64
20	59.83	60	22.86	100	2.48
21	58.86	61	22.06	101	2.34
22	57.89	62	21.27	102	2.20
23	56.92	63	20.49	103	2.06
24	55.95	64	19.72	104	1.93
25	54.98	65	18.96	105	1.81
26	54.02	66	18.21	106	1.69
27	53.05	67	17.48	107	1.58
28	52.08	68	16.76	108	1.48
29	51.12	69	16.04	109	1.38
30	50.15	70	15.35	110	1.28
31	49.19	71	14.66	111	1.19
32	48.23	72	13.99	112	1.10
33	47.27	73	13.33	113	1.02
34	46.31	74	12.68	114	0.96
35	45.35	75	12.05	115	0.89
36	44.40	76	11.43	116	0.83
37	43.45	77	10.83	117	0.77
38	42.50	78	10.24	118	0.71
39	41.55	79	9.67	119	0.66

3258.10 Exceptions to Application of Transfer of Assets Penalties.—There are a number of instances where, even if an asset is transferred for less than fair market value, the penalties discussed above do not apply. These exceptions are:

A. The asset transferred is the individual[']s home, and title to the home is transferred to:

- o The spouse of the individual;
- o A child of the individual who is under age 21;
- o A child who is blind or permanently and totally disabled as defined by a State program established under title XVI in States eligible to participate in such programs or blind or disabled as defined by the SSI program in all other States;
- o The sibling of the individual who has an equity interest in the home and who has been residing in the home for a period of at least one year immediately before the date the individual becomes institutionalized; or
- o A son or daughter of the individual (other than a child as described above) who was residing in the home for at least two years immediately before the date the individual becomes institutionalized, and who (as determined by the State) provided care to the individual which permitted the individual to reside at home, rather than in an institution or facility.

B. The assets were:

- o Transferred to the individual[']s spouse or to another for the sole benefit of the individual's spouse;
- o Transferred from the individual[']s spouse to another for the sole benefit of the individual's spouse;
- o Transferred to the individual[']s child, or to a trust (including a trust described in § 3259.7) established solely for the benefit of the individual's child (The child must be blind or permanently and totally disabled, as defined by a State program established under title XVI, in States eligible to participate in such programs or blind or disabled as defined under SSI in all other States); or
- o Transferred to a trust (including a trust as discussed in [§] 3259.7) established for the sole benefit of an individual under 65 years of age who is disabled as defined under SSI.

1. For the Sole Benefit of.—See § 3257 for a definition of the term "for the sole benefit of."

In determining whether an asset was transferred for the sole benefit of a spouse, child, or disabled individual, ensure that the transfer was accomplished via a written instrument of transfer (e.g., a trust document) which legally binds the parties to a specified course of action and which clearly sets out the conditions under which the transfer was made, as well as who can benefit from the transfer. A transfer without such a document cannot be said to have been made for the sole benefit of the spouse, child, or disabled individual, since there is no way to establish, without a document, that only the specified individuals will benefit from the transfer.

2. Blind or Disabled as Defined Under SSI Program.—When it is alleged that an asset was transferred to or for the benefit of an individual who is blind or totally and permanently disabled, you must determine that the individual in fact meets the definitions of blindness or disability used by the SSI program (which are currently the same definitions as under the title II program) or under the State plan programs established under title XVI or under the title II program. If the individual is receiving SSI benefits or is eligible for Medicaid as a result of blindness or disability, you can accept the determination of blindness or disability as valid evidence. However, if the individual is not receiving SSI and/or Medicaid, you must make a separate determination of blindness or disability. When such a determination is necessary, follow the procedures usually used in your State when an individual applies for Medicaid on the basis of blindness or disability. However, if you use more restrictive criteria under § 1902(f) of the Act, you may not use a more restrictive definition of blindness or disability. Instead, you must use the definitions used by the SSI program.

C. In addition to the above, a penalty for transferring an asset for less than fair market value is not assessed if a satisfactory showing is made to the State that:

o The individual intended to dispose of the assets either at fair market value or for other valuable consideration;

o The assets were transferred exclusively for a purpose other than to qualify for Medicaid;

o All of the assets transferred for less than fair market value have been returned to the individual; or

o Imposition of a penalty would work an undue hardship.

Pending publication of regulations on transfers of assets that will provide guidelines on what is meant by the term "satisfactory showing," you must determine what constitutes a satisfactory showing in your State.

1. Intent to Dispose of Assets for Fair Market Value or for Other Valuable Consideration.—See § 3258.1 for a definition of the term "valuable consideration." In determining whether an individual intended to dispose of an asset for fair market value or for other valuable consideration you should require that the individual establish, to your satisfaction, the circumstances which caused him or her to transfer the asset for less than fair market value. Verbal statements alone generally are not sufficient. Instead, require the individual to provide written evidence of attempts to dispose of the asset for fair market value, as well as evidence to support the value (if any) at which the asset was disposed.

2. Transfers Exclusively for a Purpose Other Than to Qualify for Medicaid.—Require the individual to establish, to your satisfaction, that the asset was transferred for a purpose other than to qualify for Medicaid. Verbal assurances that the individual was not considering Medicaid when the asset was disposed of are not sufficient. Rather, convincing evidence must be presented as to the specific purpose for which the asset was transferred.

In some instances, the individual may argue that the asset was not transferred to obtain Medicaid because the individual is already eligible for Medicaid. This may, in fact, be a valid argument. However, the validity of the argument must be determined on a case-by-case basis, based on the individual's specific circumstances. For example, while the individual may now be eligible for Medicaid, the asset in question (e.g., a home) might be counted as a resource in the future, thus compromising the individual's future eligibility. In such a situation, the argument that the individual was already eligible for Medicaid does not suffice.

3. <u>All Assets Transferred for Less Than Fair Market Value Are Returned to the Individual</u>.—When all assets transferred are returned to the individual, no penalty for transferring assets can be assessed. In this situation, you must ensure that any benefits due on behalf of the individual are, in fact, paid. When a penalty has been assessed and payment for services denied, a return of the assets requires a retroactive adjustment, including erasure of the penalty, back to the beginning of the penalty period.

However, such an adjustment does not necessarily mean that benefits must be paid on behalf of the individual. Return of the assets in question to the individual leaves the individual with assets which must be counted in determining eligibility during the retroactive period. Counting those assets as available may result in the individual being ineligible for Medicaid for some or all of the retroactive period, (because of excess income/resources) as well as for a period of time after the assets are returned.

It is important to note that, to void imposition of a penalty, <u>all</u> of the assets in question or their fair market equivalent must be returned. If, for example, the asset was sold by the individual who received it, the full market value of the asset must be returned to the transferor, either in cash or another form acceptable to the State.

When only part of an asset or its equivalent value is returned, a penalty period can be modified but not eliminated. For example, if only half the value of the asset is returned, the penalty period can be reduced by one-half.

4. <u>Imposition of Penalty Would Work Undue Hardship</u>.—When application of the transfer of assets provisions discussed in these sections would work an undue hardship, those provisions do not apply. Unlike the policies applying to transfers made on or before August 10, 1993, which only required that you acknowledge that the statute included an undue hardship provision, under OBRA 1993 you must implement an undue hardship procedure for transfers of assets. Further, that procedure must be described in your Medicaid State Plan. You have considerable flexibility in implementing an undue hardship provision. However, your undue hardship procedure must meet the requirements discussed in subsection 5.

5. <u>Undue Hardship Defined</u>.—Undue hardship exists when application of the transfer of assets provisions would deprive the individual of medical care such that his/her health or his/her life would be endangered. Undue hardship also exists when application of the transfer of assets provisions would deprive the individual of food, clothing, shelter, or other necessities of life.

Undue hardship does not exist when application of the transfer of assets provisions merely causes the individual inconvenience or when such application might restrict his or her lifestyle but would not put him/her at risk of serious deprivation.

You have considerable flexibility in deciding the circumstances under which you will not impose penalties under the transfer of assets provisions because of undue hardship. For example, you can specify the criteria to be used in determining whether the individual's life or health would be endangered and whether application of a penalty would deprive the individual of food, clothing, or shelter. You can also specify the extent to which an individual must make an effort to recover assets transferred for less than fair market value. As a general rule, you have the flexibility to establish whatever criteria you believe are appropriate, as long as you adhere to the basic definition of undue hardship described above.

However, your undue hardship procedure must, at a minimum, provide for and discuss the following administrative requirements:

- o Notice to recipients that an undue hardship exception exists;
- o A timely process for determining whether an undue hardship waiver will be granted; and
- o A process under which an adverse determination can be appealed.

3258.11 <u>Transfers of Assets and Spousal Impoverishment Provisions</u>.—Under § 1917(c)(2)(B) of the Act, certain transfers of assets for less than fair market value are exempt from penalty. (See § 3258.10 for a complete discussion of those exemptions.) Among those exemptions are transfers from an individual to a spouse, transfers from an individual to a third party for the sole benefit of a spouse, and transfers from a spouse to a third party for the sole benefit of the spouse.

Section 1924 of the Act sets forth the requirements for treatment of income and resources where there is an individual in a medical institution with a spouse still living in the community. This section of the Act provides for apportioning income and resources between the institutional spouse and the community spouse so that the community spouse does not become impoverished because the individual is in a medical institution. (See § 3260 for a complete discussion of the spousal impoverishment provisions.)

The exceptions to the transfer of assets penalties regarding interspousal transfers and transfers to a third party for the sole benefit of a spouse apply even under the spousal impoverishment provisions. Thus, the institutional spouse can transfer unlimited assets to the community spouse or to a third party for the sole benefit of the community spouse.

When transfers between spouses are involved, the unlimited transfer exception should have little effect on the eligibility determination, primarily because resources belonging to both spouses are combined in determining eligibility for the institutionalized spouse. Thus, resources transferred to a community spouse are still be considered available to the institutionalized spouse for eligibility purposes.

The exception for transfers to a third party for the sole benefit of the spouse may have greater impact on eligibility because resources may potentially be placed beyond the reach of either spouse and thus not be counted for eligibility purposes. However, for the exception to be applicable, the definition of what is for the sole benefit of the spouse (see § 3257) must be fully met. This definition is fairly restrictive, in that it requires that any funds transferred be spent for the benefit of the spouse within a time-frame actuarially commensurate with the spouse[']s life expectancy. If this requirement is not met, the exemption is void, and a transfer to a third party may then be subject to a transfer penalty.

3259. TREATMENT OF TRUSTS

3259.1 General.—Under the trust provisions in § 1917(d) of the Act, you must consider whether and to what extent a trust is counted in determining eligibility for Medicaid. The following instructions explain the rules under which trusts are considered. These instructions apply to eligibility determinations for all individuals, including cash assistance recipients and others who are otherwise automatically eligible and whose income and resources are not ordinarily measured against an independent Medicaid eligibility standard. Also, these instructions apply to post-eligibility determinations as well as eligibility determinations.

A. Definitions.—The following definitions apply to trusts.

1. Trust.—For purposes of this section, a trust is any arrangement in which a grantor transfers property to a trustee or trustees with the intention that it be held, managed, or administered by the trustee(s) for the benefit of the grantor or certain designated individuals (beneficiaries). The trust must be valid under State law and manifested by a valid trust instrument or agreement. A trustee holds a fiduciary responsibility to hold or manage the trust[']s corpus and income for the benefit of the beneficiaries. The term "trust" also includes any legal instrument or device that is similar to a trust. It does not cover trusts established by will. Such trusts must be dealt with using applicable cash assistance program policies.

2. Legal Instrument or Device Similar to Trust.—This is any legal instrument, device, or arrangement which may not be called a trust under State law but which is similar to a trust. That is, it involves a grantor who transfers property to an individual or entity with fiduciary obligations (considered a trustee for purposes of this section). The grantor makes the transfer with the intention that it be held, managed, or administered by the individual or entity for the benefit of the grantor or others. This can include (but is not limited to) escrow accounts, investment accounts, pension funds, and other similar devices managed by an individual or entity with fiduciary obligations.

3. Trustee.—A trustee is any individual, individuals, or entity (such as an insurance company or bank) that manages a trust or similar device and has fiduciary responsibilities.

4. Grantor.—A grantor is any individual who creates a trust. For purposes of this section, the term "grantor" includes:

- o The individual;
- o The individual's spouse;
- o A person, including a court or administrative body, with legal authority to act in place of or on behalf of the individual or the individual's spouse; and
- o A person, including a court or administrative body, acting at the direction or upon the request of the individual, or the individual's spouse.

5. Revocable Trust.—A revocable trust is a trust which can under State law be revoked by the grantor. A trust which provides that the trust can only be modified or terminated by a court is considered to be a revocable trust,

since the grantor (or his/her representative) can petition the court to terminate the trust. Also, a trust which is called irrevocable but which terminates if some action is taken by the grantor is a revocable trust for purposes of this instruction. For example, a trust may require a trustee to terminate a trust and disburse the funds to the grantor if the grantor leaves a nursing facility and returns home. Such a trust is considered to be revocable.

6. Irrevocable Trust.—An irrevocable trust is a trust which cannot, in any way, be revoked by the grantor.

7. Beneficiary.—A beneficiary is any individual or individuals designated in the trust instrument as benefiting in some way from the trust, excluding the trustee or any other individual whose benefit consists only of reasonable fees or payments for managing or administering the trust. The beneficiary can be the grantor himself, another individual or individuals, or a combination of any of these parties.

8. Payment.—For purposes of this section a payment from a trust is any disbursal from the corpus of the trust or from income generated by the trust which benefits the party receiving it. A payment may include actual cash, as well as noncash or property disbursements, such as the right to use and occupy real property.

9. Annuity.—An annuity is a right to receive fixed, periodic payments, either for life or a term of years. See § 3258.9.B for a discussion of how to treat annuities.

3259.2 Effective Date.—This section applies to all trusts established on or after August 11, 1993. However, the provisions in this instruction are effective December 13, 1994. For the period prior to this date, you may use any reasonable interpretations of the statute in dealing with trusts. Trusts established before August 11, 1993, are treated under the rules in § 3215. Also, trusts established before August 11, 1993, but added to or otherwise augmented on or after that date are treated under the rules in § 3215. (However, additions to an established trust on or after August 11, 1993, may be considered transfers of assets for less than fair market value under §§ 3258ff.) While this section applies to trusts established on or after August 11, 1993, you cannot deny eligibility for Medicaid or apply the rules under this section based on an individual creating a trust until October 1, 1993. For a trust established on or after August 11, 1993, but prior to October 1, 1993, apply pre-OBRA 1993 rules until October 1. On October 1, begin using the OBRA 1993 rules for treating trusts.

When the Secretary determines that your State requires enabling legislation (other than legislation to appropriate funds) to implement the trust provisions in §§ 3259ff, you may delay complying with the effective date of the statute (October 1, 1993). The compliance date can be delayed until after the close of the first regular legislative session that begins after August 10, 1993. It can be delayed until the first day of the first calendar quarter beginning after this session closes. In the case of a 2-year legislative session, each year is considered a separate regular session.

The statutory effective date of October 1, 1993, remains in effect even if a State is granted a delayed compliance date. However, no compliance action will be taken against a State which requires legislation to enact the trust provisions. Once enabling legislation is enacted, a State can choose whether to enforce the trust provisions retroactively.

To obtain a delayed compliance date, submit a written request to your HCFA regional office with an opinion from the State's Attorney General concerning the necessity of passing enabling legislation.

3259.3 Individuals to Whom Trust Provisions Apply.—This section applies to any individual who establishes a trust and who is an applicant for or recipient of Medicaid. An individual is considered to have established a trust if his or her assets (regardless of how little) were used to form part or all of the corpus of the trust and if any of the parties described as a grantor in § 3259.1 established the trust, other than by will. (See also § 3257 for a definition of individual as it is used in this section.)

3259.4 Individual's Assets Form Only Part of Trust.—When a trust corpus includes assets of another person or persons as well as assets of the individual, the rules in §§ 3259ff apply only to the portion of the trust attributable to the assets of the individual. Thus, in determining countable income and resources in the trust for eligibility and post-eligibility purposes, you must prorate any amounts of income and resources, based on the proportion of the individual[']s assets in the trust to those of other persons.

3259.5 Application of Trust Provisions.—The rules set forth in this section apply to trusts without regard to:

- o The purpose for which the trust is established;
- o Whether the trustee(s), has or exercises any discretion under the trust;
- o Any restrictions on when or whether distributions can be made from the trust; or
- o Any restrictions on the use of distributions from the trust.

This means that any trust which meets the basic definition of a trust can be counted in determining eligibility for Medicaid. No clause or requirement in the trust, no matter how specifically it applies to Medicaid or other Federal or State programs (i.e., an exculpatory clause), precludes a trust from being considered under the rules in §§ 3259ff.

NOTE: While exculpatory clauses, use clauses, trustee discretion, and restrictions on distributions, etc., do not affect a trust's countability, they do have an impact on how the various components of specific trusts are treated. (See § 3259.6 for a detailed discussion of how various types of trusts are treated.)

3259.6 Treatment of Trusts.—How a specific trust is counted for eligibility purposes depends on the characteristics of the trust. The following are the rules for counting various kinds of trusts.

A. Revocable Trust.—In the case of a revocable trust:

- o The entire corpus of the trust is counted as an available resource to the individual;

- o Any payments from the trust made to or for the benefit of the individual are counted as income to the individual (see § 3257 for the definition of income);

- o Any payments from the trust which are not made to or for the benefit of the individual are considered assets disposed of for less than fair market value. (See §§ 3258ff. for the treatment of transfers of assets for less than fair market value.)

When a portion of a revocable trust is treated as a transfer of assets for less than fair market value, the look-back period described in § 3258.4 is extended from the usual 36 months to 60 months. (See § 3258.4 for how to determine the look-back period for transfers of assets for less than fair market value.)

EXAMPLE: Mr. Baker establishes a revocable trust with a corpus of $100,000 on March 1, 1994, enters a nursing facility on November 15, 1997, and applies for Medicaid on February 15, 1998. Under the terms of the trust, the trustee has complete discretion in disbursing funds from the trust. Each month, the trustee disburses $100 as an allowance to Mr. Baker and $500 to a property management firm for the upkeep of Mr. Baker's home. On June 15, 1994, the trustee gives $50,000 from the corpus to Mr. Baker's brother.

In this example, the $100 personal allowance and the $500 for upkeep of the house counts as income each month to Mr. Baker. Because the trust is revocable, the entire value of the corpus is considered a resource to Mr. Baker. Originally, this was $100,000. However, in June 1994, the trustee gave away $50,000. Thus, only the remaining $50,000 is countable as a resource to Mr. Baker.

However, the giveaway is treated as a transfer of assets for less than fair market value. When a trust is revocable, the look-back period for such transfers is 60 months rather than the usual 36 months. The look-back period in this case starts on February 15, 1993, (60 months prior to February 15, 1998, the date Mr. Baker was both in an institution and applied for Medicaid). Because the transfer occurred in June 1994, it falls within the look-back period. Thus, a penalty under the transfer of assets provisions is imposed, beginning June 1, 1994, (the beginning of the month in which the transfer occurred). This penalty, which is denial of payment for Mr. Baker's nursing home care, is based on the amount of the transfer ($50,000), divided by the State's average monthly cost of private nursing facility care. (See § 3258ff. for the transfer of assets rules.)

B. Irrevocable Trust - Payment Can Be Made to Individual Under Terms of Trust.—In the case of an irrevocable trust, where there are any circumstances under which payment can be made to or for the benefit of the individual from all or a portion of the trust, the following rules apply to that portion:

- Payments from income or from the corpus made to or for the benefit of the individual are treated as income to the individual;

- Income on the corpus of the trust which could be paid to or for the benefit of the individual is treated as a resource available to the individual;

- The portion of the corpus that could be paid to or for the benefit of the individual is treated as a resource available to the individual; and

- Payments from income or from the corpus that are made but not to or for the benefit of the individual are treated as a transfer of assets for less than fair market value. (See §§ 3258ff. for treatment of transfers for less than fair market value.)

EXAMPLE: Use the same facts that were used in the previous example, but treat the trust as an irrevocable trust. The trustee has discretion to disburse the entire corpus of the trust and all income from the trust to anyone, including the grantor. The $100 personal allowance and $500 for home upkeep are income to Mr. Baker. The $50,000 left after the gift to Mr. Baker's brother is a countable resource to Mr. Baker, since there are circumstances under which payment of this amount could be made to Mr. Baker. The $50,000 gift to Mr. Baker's brother is treated as a transfer of assets for less than fair market value. However, the look-back period for this type of trust is only 36 months. (See § 3258.4 for transfer look-back periods as they apply to trusts.) The transfer occurred outside of the look-back period. Thus, no penalty for transferring an asset for less than fair market value can be imposed.

C. Irrevocable Trust - Payments From All or Portion of Trust Cannot, Under Any Circumstances, Be Made to or for the Benefit of the Individual.—When all or a portion of the corpus or income on the corpus of a trust cannot be paid to the individual, treat all or any such portion or income as a transfer of assets for less than fair market value, per instructions in §§ 3258ff.

In treating these portions as a transfer of assets, the date of the transfer is considered to be:

- The date the trust was established; or,

- If later, the date on which payment to the individual was foreclosed.

In determining for transfer of assets purposes the value of the portion of the trust which cannot be paid to the individual, do not subtract from the value of the trust any payments made, for whatever purpose, after the date the trust was established or, if later, the date payment to the individual was foreclosed. If the trustee or the grantor adds funds to that portion of the trust after these dates, the addition of those funds is considered to be a new transfer of assets, effective on the date the funds are added to that portion of the trust.

Thus, in treating portions of a trust which cannot be paid to an individual, the value of the transferred amount is no less than its value on the date the trust is established or payment is foreclosed. When additional funds are added to this portion of the trust, those funds are treated as a new transfer of assets for less than fair market value.

When that portion of a trust which cannot be paid to an individual is treated as a transfer of assets for less than fair market value, the usual 36 month look-back period is extended to 60 months. (See § 3258.4 for the look-back period for transfers of assets for less than fair market value.)

EXAMPLE: Use the same facts that are used in the examples in subsections A and B, except that the trustee is precluded by the trust from disbursing any of the corpus of the trust to or for the benefit of Mr. Baker. Again, the $100 and $500 (which come from income to the trust) count as income to Mr. Baker. Because none of the corpus can be disbursed to Mr. Baker, the entire value of the corpus at the time the trust was created ($100,000 in March 1994) is treated as a transfer of assets for less than fair market value.

As with the revocable trust discussed in subsection A, the date of transfer is within the 60 month look-back period that applies to portions of trusts that cannot be disbursed to or for the individual. Thus, a transfer of assets is considered to have occurred as of March 1, 1994. The fact that $50,000 was actually transferred out of the trust to Mr. Baker's brother does not alter the amount of the transfer upon which the penalty is based. That amount remains $100,000, even after the gift to Mr. Baker's brother.

If, at some point after establishing the trust, Mr. Baker places an additional $50,000 in the trust, none of which can be disbursed to him, that $50,000 is treated as an additional transfer of assets. The penalty period that applies to that $50,000 starts when those funds are placed in the trust, provided no penalty period from the previous transfer of $100,000 is still running. If a previous penalty period is still in effect, the new penalty period cannot begin until the previous penalty period has expired. (See §§ 3258ff. for transfers of assets for less than fair market value.)

Amounts are considered transferred as of the time the trust is first established or, if later, payment to the individual is foreclosed. Each time the individual places a new amount into the trust, payment to the individual from this new portion is foreclosed. It is this later date that determines when a transfer has occurred.

D. Payments Made From Revocable Or Irrevocable Trusts to or on Behalf of Individual.—Payments are considered to be made to the individual when any amount from the trust, including an amount from the corpus or income produced by the corpus, is paid directly to the individual or to someone acting on his/her behalf, e.g., a guardian or legal representative.

Payments made for the benefit of the individual are payments of any sort, including an amount from the corpus or income produced by the corpus, paid to another person or entity such that the individual derives some benefit from the payment. For example, such payments could include purchase of clothing or other items, such as a radio or television, for the individual. Also, such payments could include payment for services the individual may require, or care, whether medical or personal, that the individual may need. Payments to maintain a home are also payments for the benefit of the individual.

NOTE: A payment to or for the benefit of the individual is counted under this provision only if such a payment is ordinarily counted as income under the SSI program. For example, payments made on behalf of an individual for medical care are not counted in determining income eligibility under the SSI program. Thus, such payments are not counted as income under the trust provision.

E. Circumstances Under Which Payments Can or Cannot Be Made.—In determining whether payments can or cannot be made from a trust to or for an individual, take into account any restrictions on payments, such as use restrictions, exculpatory clauses, or limits on trustee discretion that may be included in the trust.

For example, if an irrevocable trust provides that the trustee can disburse only $1,000 to or for the individual out of a $20,000 trust, only the $1,000 is treated as a payment that could be made under the rules in subsection B. The remaining $19,000 is treated as an amount which cannot, under any circumstances, be paid to or for the benefit of the individual. On the other hand, if a trust contains $50,000 that the trustee can pay to the grantor only in the event that the grantor needs, for example, a heart transplant, this full amount is considered as payment that could be made under some circumstances, even though the likelihood of payment is remote. Similarly, if a payment cannot be made until some point in the distant future, it is still payment that can be made under some circumstances.

F. Placement of Excluded Assets in Trust.—Section 1917(e) of the Act provides that, for trust and transfer purposes, assets include both income and resources. Section 1917(e) of the Act further provides that income has the meaning given the term in § 1612 of the Act and resources has the meaning given that term in § 1613 of the Act. The only exception is that for institutionalized individuals, the home is not an excluded resource.

Thus, transferring an excluded asset (either income or a resource, with the exception of the home of an institutionalized individual) for less than fair market value does not result in a penalty under the transfer provisions because the excluded asset is not an asset for transfer purposes. Similarly, placement of an excluded asset in a trust does not change the excluded nature of that asset; it remains excluded. As noted in the previous paragraph, the only exception is the home of an institutionalized individual. Because § 1917(e) of the Act provides that the home is not an excluded resource for institutionalized individuals, placement of the home of an institutionalized individual in a trust results in the home becoming a countable resource.

G. Use of Trust vs. Transfer Rules for Assets Placed in Trust.—When a nonexcluded asset is placed in a trust, a transfer of assets for less than fair market value generally takes place. An individual placing an asset in a trust generally gives up ownership of the asset to the trust. If the individual does not receive fair compensation in return, you can impose a penalty under the transfer of assets provisions.

However, the trust provisions contain specific requirements for treatment of assets placed in trusts. As discussed in subsections A through C, these requirements deal with counting assets placed in trusts as available income, available resources, and/or a transfer of assets for less than fair market value, depending on the circumstances of the particular trust. Application of the trust provisions, along with imposition of a penalty for the transfer of the assets into the trust, could result in the individual being penalized twice for actions involving the same asset.

To avoid such a double penalty, application of one provision must take precedence over application of the other provision. Because the trust provisions are more specific and detailed in their requirements for dealing with funds placed in a trust, the trust provisions are given precedence in dealing with assets placed in trusts. Deal with assets placed in trusts exclusively under the trust provisions (which, in some instances, require that trust assets be treated as a transfer of assets for less than fair market value).

3259.7 Exceptions to Treatment of Trusts Under Trust Provisions.—The rules concerning treatment of trusts set forth in § 3259.6 do not apply to any of the following trusts, i.e., the trusts discussed below are treated differently in determining eligibility for Medicaid. Funds entering and leaving these trusts are generally treated according to the rules of the cash assistance programs, the State's more restrictive rules under § 1902(f) of the Act, or more liberal rules under § 1902(r)(2) of the Act, as appropriate.

As is noted in each exception below, one common feature of all of the excepted trusts is a requirement that the trust provide that upon the death of the individual, any funds remaining in the trust go to the State agency, up to the amount paid in Medicaid benefits on the individual's behalf. When an individual has resided in more than one State, the trust must provide that the funds remaining in the trust are distributed to each State in which the individual received Medicaid, based on the State's proportionate share of the total amount of Medicaid benefits paid by all of the States on the individual's behalf. For example, if an individual received $20,000 in Medicaid benefits in one State and $10,000 in benefits in another State, the first State receives two-thirds of the amount remaining in the trust, and the second State receives one-third, up to the amount each State actually paid in Medicaid benefits.

A. Special Needs Trusts.—A trust containing the assets of an individual under age 65 who is disabled (as defined by the SSI program in § 1614(a)(3) of the Act) and which is established for the sole benefit of the individual by a parent, grandparent, legal guardian of the individual, or a court is often referred to as a special needs trust. To qualify for an exception to the rules in this section, the trust must contain a provision stating that, upon the death of the individual, the State receives all amounts remaining in the trust, up to an amount equal to the total amount of medical assistance paid on behalf of the individual under your State Medicaid plan. In addition to the assets of the individual, the trust may also contain the assets of individuals other than the disabled individual.

When a trust is established for a disabled individual under age 65, the exception for the trust discussed above continues even after the individual becomes age 65. However, such a trust cannot be added to or otherwise augmented after the individual reaches age 65. Any such addition or augmentation after age 65 involves assets that were not the assets of an individual under age 65. Thus, those assets are not be subject to the exemption discussed in this section.

To qualify for this exception, the trust must be established for a disabled individual, as defined in § 1614(a)(3) of the Act. When the individual in question is receiving either title II or SSI benefits as a disabled individual, accept the disability determination made for those programs. If the individual is not receiving those benefits, you must make a determination concerning the individual's disability. In making this determination, follow the normal procedures used in your State to make disability determinations for Medicaid purposes. If you are a 209(b) State, you must use the disability criteria of the SSI program, rather than any more restrictive criteria you may use under your State plan. The only exception to this requirement is if you had a more restrictive trust policy in general in 1972 than the policy described in §§ 3259ff. If so, you may use any more restrictive definition of disability which applied to that 1972 policy. If not, you must use the disability criteria of the SSI program.

NOTE: Establishment of a trust as described above does not constitute a transfer of assets for less than fair market value if the transfer is made into a trust established solely for the benefit of a disabled individual under age 65. However, if the trust is not solely for the benefit of the disabled person or if the disabled person is over age 65 transfer penalties may apply. (See § 3258.10 for the exceptions to imposing penalties for certain transfers of assets.)

B. Pooled Trusts.—A pooled trust is a trust containing the assets of a disabled individual as defined by the SSI program in § 1614(a)(3) of the Act, that meets the following conditions:

- o The trust is established and managed by a non-profit association;
- o A separate account is maintained for each beneficiary of the trust but for purposes of investment and management of funds the trust pools the funds in these accounts;
- o Accounts in the trust are established solely for the benefit of disabled individuals by the individual, by the parent, grandparent, legal guardian of the individual, or by a court (see § 3257 for a definition of the term "solely for the benefit of"); and
- o To the extent that any amounts remaining in the beneficiary's account upon the death of the beneficiary are not retained by the trust, the trust pays to the State the amount remaining in the account up to an amount equal to the total amount of medical assistance paid on behalf of the beneficiary under your State Medicaid plan. To meet this requirement, the trust must include a provision specifically providing for such payment.

To qualify as an excepted trust, the trust account must be established for a disabled individual, as defined in § 1614(a)(3) of the Act. When the individual in question is receiving either title II or SSI benefits as a disabled individual, accept the disability determination made for those programs. If the individual is not receiving those benefits, you must make a determination concerning the individual's disability. In making this determination, follow the normal procedures used in your State to make disability determinations for Medicaid purposes. If you are a 209(b) State, you must use the disability criteria of the SSI program. The only exception to this requirement is if you had a more restrictive trust policy in general in 1972 than the policy described in this instruction. If so, you may use any more restrictive definition of disability which applied to that 1972 policy. If not, you must use the disability criteria of the SSI program.

NOTE: Establishing an account in the kind of trust described above may or may not constitute a transfer of assets for less than fair market value. For example, the transfer provisions exempt from a penalty trusts established solely for disabled individuals who are under age 65 or for an individual's disabled child. As a result, a special needs trust established for a disabled individual who is age 66 could be subject to a transfer penalty. (See § 3258.10 for the exceptions to imposing penalties for certain transfers of assets.)

While trusts for the disabled (as well as Miller trusts described in subsection C) are exempt from treatment under the trust rules described in § 3259.6, funds entering and leaving them are not necessarily exempt from treatment under the rules of the appropriate cash assistance program. The following are rules applicable to funds entering and leaving both kinds of exempt trusts for the disabled.

1. Trusts Established with Income.—While most trusts for the disabled are created using the individual's resources, some may be created using the individual's income, either solely or in conjunction with resources. When an exempt trust for a disabled individual is established using the individual's income (i.e., income considered to be received by the individual under the rules of the SSI program), the policies set forth in subsection C for treatment of income used to create Miller trusts apply.

NOTE: The following policies assume that the income placed in the trust is the individual's own income, placed in the trust after he or she receives it. When the right to income placed in the trust actually belongs to the trust and not the individual the income does not count under SSI rules as income received by the individual.

The policies pertaining to treatment of income belonging to the individual include:

- Not counting for eligibility purposes income before it is placed in the trust;

- Application of transfer of assets rules (where a transfer into trust for a disabled individual is not exempt from penalty under the exceptions to the transfer of assets rules explained in § 3258.10);

- Application of post-eligibility treatment of income rules to income placed in the trust;

- Counting as income, per cash assistance rules, funds paid out of the trust to or for the benefit of the individual (This rule applies to any payment from an exempt trust, regardless of whether the trust is established using income, resources, or both.); and

- Spousal impoverishment provisions as they apply to exempt trusts.

For a detailed discussion of how these policies apply to income placed in an exempt trust for a disabled individual, see subsection C.

2. Trusts Established with Resources.—When an exempt trust is established for a disabled individual using resources either in whole or in part, those resources are treated as follows.

Resources placed in an exempt irrevocable trust for a disabled individual may or may not count as resources to the individual in determining eligibility, depending on the circumstances. Resources are counted as resources only during those months in which they are in the possession of the individual, up to but not including the month in which the resources are placed in the trust. Beginning with the month the resources are placed in the trust, they are exempt from being counted as resources to the individual.

Resources placed in an exempt trust for a disabled individual are subject to imposition of a penalty under the transfer of assets provisions unless the transfer is specifically exempt from penalty as explained in § 3258.10 or unless the resources placed in the trust are used to benefit the individual, and the trust purchases items and services for the individual at fair market value. See subsection C for the rules concerning application of the transfer of assets provisions to assets placed in an exempt trust. These rules apply to both income and resources placed in the exempt trusts discussed in this section.

C. Miller-Type or Qualifying Income Trusts (QIT).—This type of trust, established for the benefit of an individual, meets the following requirements:

o The trust is composed only of pension, Social Security, and other income to the individual, including accumulated interest in the trust; and

o Upon the death of the individual, the State receives all amounts remaining in the trust, up to an amount equal to the total medical assistance paid on behalf of the individual under your State Medicaid plan. To qualify for this exception, the trust must include a provision to this effect.

NOTE: HCFA has interpreted § 1917(d)(4)(B) of the Act as explained below to avoid reading it as a nullity. This interpretation applies to those situations in which an individual first receives income and then places it into a Miller trust. It does not apply to situations in which an individual has irrevocably transferred his or her right to receive income to the trust. Under SSI rules, this income is no longer considered to be the individual's income. As a result, a trust established with income the right to which has been transferred to the trust does not meet the requirements for exemption under this section, since the statute requires that a Miller trust be established using the income of the individual.

This type of trust is applicable in your State only if your State Medicaid plan provides Medicaid to individuals eligible under a special income level, as described in § 1902(a)(10)(A)(ii)(V) of the Act but does not provide Medicaid for nursing facility services to the medically needy, who are described in § 1902(a)(10)(C) of the Act.

To qualify for this exception, the trust must be composed only of income to the individual, from whatever source. The trust may contain accumulated income, i.e., income that has not been paid out of the trust. However, no resources, as defined by SSI, may be used to establish or augment the trust. Inclusion of resources voids this exception.

While Miller trusts (as well as the trusts for the disabled described in subsections A and B) are exempt from treatment under the trust rules described in § 3259.6, funds entering and leaving them are not necessarily exempt from treatment under the rules of the appropriate cash assistance program. The following are rules applicable to funds entering and leaving Miller trusts.

1. Miller Trust Meets All Requirements for Exemption Under § 1917(d)(4)(B) of the Act.—When a trust meets all requirements for exemption, and is irrevocable, the corpus of the trust is exempt from being counted as available to the individual. A revocable trust is exempt under the Miller trust provisions. However, a revocable trust is counted under SSI rules as an available resource to the individual.

2. Income Placed In Miller Trust.—Income placed in a trust that meets all of the requirements for exemption as a Miller trust meets the SSI definition of income but is not counted in determining the individual's eligibility for Medicaid. Thus, any income, including Social Security benefits, VA pensions, private pensions, etc., can be placed directly into a Miller trust by the recipient of those funds, without those funds adversely affecting the individual[']s eligibility for Medicaid. Also, income generated by the trust which remains in the trust is not income to the individual.

3. Application of Transfer of Assets Provisions of OBRA 1993.—The transfer of assets provisions described in §§ 3258ff. apply to funds placed in a Miller trust. Under the transfer of assets provisions, income is considered to be an asset. In placing income in an irrevocable trust, including a Miller trust, an individual gives up direct access to and control over that income. Thus, placement of funds, including income, in a trust can be a transfer of assets for less than fair market value. As such, placing funds in a Miller trust normally subjects the individual to the penalties provided for under the transfer of assets provisions.

However, transfer of assets penalties do not apply to income placed in a Miller trust to the extent that the trust instrument provides that the income placed in the trust will, in turn, be paid out of the trust for medical care provided to the individual, including nursing home care and care under a home and community-based waiver. When such payments are made, the individual is considered to have received fair market value for the income placed in the trust, up to the amount actually paid for medical care provided to the individual and to the extent that the payments purchased care at fair market value.

Because of certain exemptions from the transfer of assets penalties, funds placed in a Miller trust can be transferred for the sole benefit of a spouse without incurring such penalties. This can include, among other things, payments by the trust for medical care for the community spouse. Section 1917(c)(2)(B) of the Act provides that transfer penalties do not apply to assets transferred to a spouse or to a third party for the sole benefit of the spouse. A trust could be considered a third party for purposes of this transfer exemption. For an individual to avoid the transfer penalty that results from a transfer of property to a trust, the trust must be drafted to require that this particular property can be used only for the benefit of the individual's spouse while the trust exists and that the trust cannot be terminated and distributed to any other individuals or entities for any other purpose.

When payments are made for the individual's medical care you must require that the payments be made at intervals specified by your State (e.g., every month or by the end of the month following the month the funds were placed in the trust). An individual cannot be considered to have received fair market value for funds placed in a trust until payments for some item or service are actually made. Thus, funds cannot be allowed to accumulate indefinitely in a Miller trust and still avoid transfer of assets penalties.

The individual is considered to have received fair market value for funds placed in a Miller trust for any other payments made from the trust which are for the benefit of the individual and which reflect fair payments for any items or services which were purchased. For example, funds placed in the trust can be used to pay the administrative fees of the trust, income tax owed by the trust, attorney's fees which the trust is obligated to pay (in proportion to whatever part of the trust benefits the individual), food or clothing for the individual, or mortgage payments for the individual's home.

When income placed in the trust exceeds the amount paid out of the trust for medical services or other items or services which benefit the individual, the excess income is subject to penalties under the transfer of assets provisions.

It is important to note that, although an individual may not be subject to a transfer penalty if funds he or she transferred to a trust are used by the trustee to make payments that provide fair market value to the individual, these payments from the trust may still count as income to the individual, as explained in subsection 4.

4. Treatment of Payments Made from Trust.—While Miller trusts are exempt from treatment under the trust provisions described in § 3259.6, payments made from these trusts are still subject to the usual rules under the State Medicaid plan. In most States, these are the SSI rules. Any payments made from a Miller trust directly to the individual are counted as income to the individual, provided the individual could use the payments for food, clothing, or shelter for himself or herself. This rule applies whether or not the payments actually are used for these purposes, as long as there are no legal impediments which prevent the individual from using the payments this way.

Any payments made by the trustee to purchase something in kind for the individual also can count as income to the individual. In kind income includes actual food, clothing, or shelter, or something the individual can use to obtain one of these. For example, if the trustee makes a mortgage payment for the individual, that payment is a shelter expense and counts as income.

However, as another example, assume that the trust provides that $500 is paid each month toward the cost of the individual's nursing facility care. Under SSI policy, medical expenses paid on behalf of an individual are not counted as income to the individual. Thus, the $500 in this instance is not considered income.

5. Post-eligibility Treatment of Income.—All of the post-eligibility treatment of income rules in 42 CFR 435.725, 733, 735, and 832, as well as § 1924 of the Act, apply in cases involving Miller trusts, as follows.

a. Income Not Placed in a Miller Trust.—Income retained by the individual (i.e., not placed in a Miller trust) is income to the individual, according to SSI policy. Thus, such income is subject to the post-eligibility rules.

b. Income Placed in a Miller Trust.—Income placed in a Miller trust is income for SSI purposes although it is not counted as available in determining Medicaid eligibility. Thus, such income is also subject to the post-eligibility rules.

Because income placed in a Miller trust is income as defined by SSI (although it is not counted for Medicaid eligibility purposes), all income placed in a Miller trust is combined with countable income not placed in the trust for post-eligibility purposes. For example, an individual with $2,000 a month in income retains $1,338 (the maximum currently permitted for eligibility under a special income level) and places the remaining $662 in a Miller trust. The entire $2,000 is income as defined by SSI, although only the $1,338 is counted as income for eligibility purposes. Thus, the $2,000 forms the basis for the post-eligibility computation.

Using the $2,000 as the individual's total income for post-eligibility purposes, the State deducts, as applicable:

- o A personal needs allowance;

- o Family maintenance allowances, including the spousal and family allowances provided for in § 1924 of the Act;

- o An allowance for maintenance of a home, if such allowance is included in the State plan; and

- o Medical expenses not subject to third party payment.

The remainder is the amount by which the State reduces its payment to the medical institution or for home and community-based waiver services.

c. Payments Made From Miller Trust.—Payments made from a Miller trust to the individual may count for eligibility purposes as income to the individual under SSI rules. However, such payments are not subject to treatment under the post-eligibility rules. Post-eligibility has already been applied to all income entering the trust. Thus, there is no need to consider, for purposes of post-eligibility, payments made from the trust.

6. Miller Trust and Spousal Impoverishment.—As explained in subsection 5, funds placed in a Miller trust are subject to the post-eligibility treatment of income rules, including those applicable to spousal impoverishment in § 1924 of the Act.

3259.8 Application of Trust Provisions Would Work Undue Hardship.—When application of the trust provisions discussed in §§ 3259ff would work an undue hardship those provisions do not apply. Unlike the policies applying to trusts established on or before August 10, 1993, which only required that you acknowledge that the statute included an undue hardship provision, under OBRA 1993 you must implement an undue hardship provision for trusts. Further, that policy must be described in your Medicaid State Plan. You have considerable flexibility in implementing an undue hardship provision. However, your undue hardship provision must meet the requirements discussed below.

A. Undue Hardship Defined.—Undue hardship exists when application of the trust provisions would deprive the individual of medical care such that his/her health or his/her life would be endangered. Undue hardship also exists when application of the trust provisions would deprive the individual of food, clothing, shelter, or other necessities of life.

Undue hardship does not exist when application of the trust provisions merely causes the individual inconvenience or when such application might restrict his or her lifestyle but would not put him or her at risk of serious deprivation.

B. Burial Trusts And Undue Hardship.—A burial trust is a trust established by an individual for the purpose of paying, at some point in the future, for the various expenses associated with the individual's funeral and burial. At your option, you may exempt a burial trust from treatment as a trust under the State's undue hardship policies provided the total value of the trust does not exceed an amount specified by the State. For example, you may choose to exempt from being counted as a trust under your undue hardship policies any burial trust that does not exceed $5,000 in value.

C. State Flexibility.—You have considerable flexibility in deciding the circumstances under which you will not count funds in trusts under the trust provisions because of undue hardship. For example, you may specify the criteria to be used in determining whether the individual's life or health would be endangered, and whether application of a penalty would deprive the individual of food, clothing, or shelter. You may also specify the extent to which an individual must make an effort to recover assets placed in a trust. As a general rule, you have the flexibility to establish whatever criteria you believe are appropriate, as long as you adhere to the basic definition of undue hardship described above.

However, your undue hardship provision must, at a minimum, provide for:

o Notice to recipients that an undue hardship exception exists;

o A timely process for determining whether an undue hardship waiver will be granted;

o A process under which an adverse determination can be appealed.

Your undue hardship provision must discuss how you will meet these requirements.

INDEX